The Wordsworth A to Z
of English Literature

'Oliver amazed at the Dodger's mode of "going to work"'
by George Cruickshank, from Charles Dickens's *Oliver Twist*

THE WORDSWORTH A TO Z OF
ENGLISH LITERATURE

DAVID ROTHWELL

*for
the Academically Anxious,
the Bemused Buffer and
the Confused Cleric*

Wordsworth Reference

In loving memory of
MICHAEL TRAYLER
the founder of Wordsworth Editions

I

Readers who are interested in other titles from
Wordsworth Editions are invited to visit our website at
www.wordsworth-editions.com

For our latest list and a full mail-order service, contact
Bibliophile Books, 5 Datapoint, South Crescent, London E16 4TL
TEL: +44 (0)20 7474 2474 FAX: +44 (0)20 7474 8589
ORDERS: orders@bibliophilebooks.com
WEBSITE: www.bibliophilebooks.com

First published in 2010 by
Wordsworth Editions Limited
8B East Street, Ware, Hertfordshire SG12 9HJ

ISBN 978 1 84022 650 8

Typeset in Great Britain by Antony Gray
Printed and bound by Clays Ltd, St Ives plc

Preface

This entirely indispensable book will be invaluable to the following types of people:

1 To anyone who has at least a vague interest in English literature but who does not want to plunge into solemn academic books.

2 To anyone, child or adult, who is studying English literature at GCSE, A level or even degree level and who wants a painless guide to the major writers and topics of English literature.

3 To the expert in soil chemistry, Burgundian tapestries or Peruvian geology who wants to understand what all these literary types get so excited about.

Clearly the above three categories embrace many thousands of people in Rutland alone, let alone the myriads in Blackburn, so what distinguishes this book from all the other worthy tomes that clamour for your attention?

I suppose the most significant element about his book is that it is idiosyncratic and light-hearted. I've taken care to get the facts right, but I see no reason why I should be solemn about it.

Secondly, I have made no pretence at objectivity. Most reference books seem to pretend that their opinions are part of revealed truth. When *The Oxford Companion to English Literature* states that *The Monk*, a novel by M. G. Lewis, is 'extravagant in its mixture of the supernatural, the terrible, and the indecent', it is not stating a fact, it is expressing an opinion. However, *The Oxford Companion* and volumes like it choose to express these opinions as if they were divine certainties. They aren't.

Thirdly, this book is based on the premise that reading literature is one of life's most enjoyable activities. Its only rivals are listening to music, having sex and watching England win at cricket.

Fourthly, this book is massively shorter than such worthy tomes as *The Oxford Companion to English Literature* and kindred volumes. There are three reasons for this. *The Oxford Companion* and its peers are directed at people who already *know* that they are interested in literature. As a result, such readers are going to want a much broader and deeper coverage than the humble beginners at whom this volume is directed. Secondly, the scholarly volumes to which I refer employ scores of specialists for their compilation. This volume only has me. Despite my vast learning and incredible sagacity, I cannot pretend to rival the capability of those scores of PhDs.

Fifthly, the objective of this book is different from that of the Oxford and Cambridge guides. They are invaluable reference books. Clearly, to some extent, this volume is another reference book, but it is also an introduction to literature. When I write about Browning or Bunyan, I quote examples of their work. The Oxford and Cambridge guides don't do this. They provide mini-biographies, which I don't, but don't provide examples of Browning's verse or Bunyan's prose, which I do. I must confess that this has always puzzled me. These volumes call themselves companions or guides to English literature, but they never give any examples of literature.

So this volume, despite its relative brevity, gives you a much bigger sample of literature so that you can decide whether or not a particular writer appeals to you. Look up Wordsworth, and you can see some of his poetry. Look up Jane Austen, and you can read some of her prose. I'm not concerned where George Eliot had her dresses made, or what Shakespeare had to eat at the Globe Theatre. I am concerned about what these people wrote.

What, then, does this book contain? Basically, everything that anyone needs to know about English literature. Every significant writer is illuminated by a sage entry, every literary form is explained and every literary technique is demonstrated. If a person or item does not appear in this book, then that is because the person or item is not significant. You will, of course, be aghast at such an arrogant avowal, but all reference books operate under such terms. For instance, at the time of writing (2009), the most intelligent and enjoyable detective novelist in English is Reginald Hill, but there is no mention of him in the 1993 edition of *The Cambridge Guide to Literature in English* or in the 2000 edition of *The Oxford Companion to English Literature*. Why not? Because the respective editors of those volumes did not consider Hill significant enough to be included, though they both regarded Sherlock Holmes, the detective invented by Conan Doyle, as worthy of an entry. It follows, therefore, that this book is more honest than these esteemed reference books. I admit that everything in this book is there because I chose to put it there. That explains too why the personal pronoun 'I' is so frequent. I apologise if this irritates you, but it seemed my only honest course. The university presses of Cambridge and Oxford prefer to pretend that their books have been dictated by the Almighty.

In conclusion, I do need to mention another reference book. Wordsworth, the publishers of this invaluable volume, did, in 1994, produce a reference book entitled *The Wordsworth Companion to Literature in English*. In fact, this was a reprint of Cambridge University's 1988 *Companion to Literature in English*. Edited by Ian Ousby and contributed to by over a hundred people, it contains invaluable entries on J. Hector St John de Crèvecoeur, *The Mabinogion* and the Stoner Letters. At over a thousand pages, it is a stupendous achievement, but it is not a guide to literature. This book is.

So, now you know. Hurry off now to the counter and purchase this vital volume. I hope you find it useful, and I hope it enhances your reading of English literature.

Acknowledgements

I would like to acknowledge how much I owe to the teachers who gave me a love of English literature. Most of them are dead now, but I owe a lot to Steve Huntley at my secondary school, to John Harvey, John Killham and Gabriel Pearson from my undergraduate days, and to Andor Gomme from my M Litt course. It was a matter of deep regret that Andor died while I was writing this book. Obviously I owe a lot to sundry reference tools. These I list as follows: Chris Baldick, *Concise Dictionary of Literary Terms*, Oxford University Press, 1991; *Cambridge Guide to Literature in English*, edited by Ian Ousby, Cambridge University Press, 2nd edition, 1993; *Companion to Literature in English*, Wordsworth Editions, 1994, though this is more or less a reprint of the book immediately above; *The Literature Lover's Companion*, Diagram Visual Information, 2004; *The Oxford Companion to English Literature*, edited by Margaret Drabble, Oxford University Press, 2000; *The Penguin Dictionary of Literary Terms and Literary Theory*, 4th edition, J. A. Cuddon & C. E. Preston, Penguin, 1998. And most valuable of all was the Internet.

I also owe a lot to Scilla Edwards, who proof-read my typescript. As a graduate in Chemistry and Maths, she was ideally qualified to spot places where I had made invalid assumptions. After all, not everybody knows that Christopher Marlowe was a contemporary of Shakespeare's or that Ted Hughes was married to Sylvia Plath. Scilla was invaluable in pointing out occasions when I had assumed too much, and I thank her. Finally, while I was writing this book, my much loved daughter gave birth to her first child, and you will not be surprised to learn that no more beautiful or delightful grandchild has ever been born in the history of the world. To her, Jennifer Elizabeth, I dedicate this book in the hope that she will come to gain as much pleasure from literature as I have.

'They always looked another way'
by Hugh Thomson, from Jane Austen's *Northanger Abbey*

A

A

Apart from being the first letter of the alphabet, A is also used as a piece of shorthand for excellence. Thus, if you are awarded an A for an essay or for an exam, you have achieved the highest grade. Writers too are often placed in the A category, and people argue in pubs about such matters:

'You can't honestly class Buchan as an A writer.'
'Oh I don't know. For me *The Thirty-Nine Steps* is markedly better than *The Pickwick Papers*, and no one would deny an A category to **Dickens**.'

It is arguments like this, many feel, that have led to an increase in knife crime in Britain. The result has been an inflation. In order to get into Oxford or Cambridge University now, you need at least one A level grade at A*.

Absalom and Achitophel

This alliterative title (and see **alliteration** if you don't know what 'alliterative' means) is the title of a poem (and see **poetry** if you don't know what a poem is) by **John Dryden** (1631–1700). You can look Dryden up too, of course, but you are probably puzzled as to why on earth a scholarly and serious guide to English literature should virtually begin with the title of a poem that is clearly about two people of whom you've never heard. There are a number of reasons:

1 *Absalom and Achitophel* is an allegory, so that forces you to look up **allegory** in this unrivalled textbook.
2 *Absalom and Achitophel* is a satire, so that forces you to look up **satire** in this unrivalled textbook.
3 *Absalom and Achitophel* is generally regarded as the greatest political poem in the English language, and so beginning this book with a political masterpiece provides a welcome contrast with the political ineptitude of today.
4 *Absalom and Achitophel* takes as its basis a biblical story, and **the Bible** is an indispensable source for understanding English

literature. (Incidentally, Ian Ousby's *Cambridge Guide to Literature in English* [1993] says that the Bible story can be found in the second book of Kings. It can't, so the lesson is clear: trust no reference books other than this one.)

By beginning with *Absalom and Achitophel*, four or five essential aspects or themes in English literature are revealed.

Lets begin with the allegory. If you've read the entry on this topic, you will know that an allegory is a work in which the characters are meant to signify a person in real life. Thus, in *Absalom and Achitophel* the Israelite king David is meant to represent King Charles II, Absalom is Charles's oldest and illegitimate son, the Duke of Monmouth, Architophel is the Earl of Shaftesbury, and so on. In this way, Dryden can poke fun at contemporary figures without running the risk of libel. You see the same tactic in television comedy. A pretend prime minister is revealed to be avaricious, vain, devious and unprincipled. Everyone knows that it is meant to be Tony Blair (or, frankly, almost any other prime minister), but part of the fun lies in disguising this. Hence, when Dryden writes:

> Michal, of Royal Blood, the Crown did wear,
> A soil ungrateful to the Tiller's care;

everybody knew that he was referring to Queen Catherine, whom King Charles married in 1662, but who failed to produce an heir to the throne. Of course, this does mean that when we read *Absalom and Achitophel* today, we miss out on most of the political satire. After all, we are not bound to know that Saul in the poem is meant to represent Oliver Cromwell, and we are very unlikely to know that the poem is representing to some extent the Exclusion Crisis and the Popish Plot. Indeed it is not very likely that we have any idea at all as to what the Exclusion Crisis and Popish Plot actually were. So, if we don't understand the allegory, fail to pick up on most of the political satire, and, in addition, know nothing about the story of David and Absalom told in the second book of Samuel (Chapters 13 to 15) in the Old Testament, there seems no point whatsoever in actually reading *Absalom and Achitophel*. This, however, would be a false conclusion. Clearly it would help if you did some homework – a degree in seventeenth-century English history and a doctorate in theology should be sufficient – but even when burdened with complete ignorance, *Absalom and Achitophel* is well worth reading. The poem begins like this:

> In pious times, e'r Priest-craft did begin,
> Before *Polygamy* was made a sin;
> When man, on many, multiply'd his kind,
> E'r one to one was, cursedly, confin'd:
> When Nature prompted, and no law deny'd
> Promiscuous use of Concubine and Bride;
> Then, *Israel's* monarch, after Heaven's own heart,
> His vigorous warmth did, variously, impart
> To Wives and Slaves; And, wide as his Command,
> Scatter'd his Maker's Image through the Land.

Few, surely, can resist this plea for polygamy. More relevantly, few surely can resist Dryden's dry wit. This is why you should read *Absalom and Achitophel*: it is very funny. A second part was produced in 1682. This, though, was written mostly by Nahum Tate, though Dryden did revise it and contribute 200 lines of savage satire against two of his rivals, Thomas Shadwell and Elkanah Settle.

abstract poem

This term is used to describe poems that rely for their effect upon their sound rather than on their meaning. Now of course all poems ought to rely to some extent upon their sound. The poetry of **Milton** *sounds* very different from the poetry of **Tennyson**. But both those poets linked sound and meaning so that the two created a unified and coherent whole. In 1922, however, Edith Sitwell produced *Façade*, a series of poems that relied almost entirely on their sound. Here is the hornpipe from the collection:

> Sailor come
> To the drum
> Out of Babylon;
>   Hobby-horses
> Foam, the dumb
> Sky rhinoceros glum
> Watched the courses of the breakers' rocking-horses and with Glaucis,
> Lady Venus on the settee of the horsehair sea!
> Where Lord Tennyson in laurels wore a gloria free,
> In a borealic iceberg came Victoria; she
> Knew Prince Albert's tall memorial took the colours of the floreal
> And the borealic iceberg; floating on they see

abstract poem

New-arisen Madam Venus for whose sake from far
Came the fat and zebra'd emperor from Zanzibar
Where like golden bouquets lay far Asia, Africa, Cathay,
All laid before that shady lady by the fibroid Shah.
Captain Fracasse stout as any water-butt came, stood
With Sir Bacchus both a-drinking the black tarr'd grapes' blood
Plucked among the tartan leafage
By the furry wind whose grief age
Could not wither – like a squirrel with a gold star-nut.
Queen Victoria sitting shocked upon the rocking horse
Of a wave said to the Laureate, 'This minx of course
Is as sharp as any lynx and blacker-deeper than the drinks
and quite as
Hot as any hottentot, without remose!
    For the minx',
      Said she,
   'And the drinks,
     You can see
Are hot as any hottentot and not the goods for me!'

Now I am an antediluvian reactionary, and find no sense at all in 'poetry' dependent only on its sound. As always, you are entirely free to ignore my subterranean mutterings.

accent

When words are spoken, some words or syllables have a greater stress that other words or syllables. That stress is called an accent, and poetry, of course, often depends for its success upon its handling of accents. After all, the regularity or otherwise of those accents are what constitutes the poem's **metre**.

act

A play is frequently divided into major sections, and each of those sections is called an act. Each of **Shakespeare**'s plays, for instance, is divided into five acts. Yet Shakespeare did not do this. The division into acts was done many years after his death, and so one suspects that division into acts has little point. Indeed many twentieth-century playwrights like **Shaw**, Brecht, Pirandello and **Becket** did without them entirely.

14

Adam

You doubtless do know that Adam, according to the book of Genesis in **the Bible**, was the first man. Created by God, together with a wife, Eve, he was placed in the idyllic Garden of Eden. The fact that Adam and Eve disobeyed God's command by eating the fruit of a particular tree accounts for the whole sorry story of man's sojourn on Earth. You need to know this in order to understand English literature at all, simply because the references to Adam are so dauntingly plentiful. **Milton**'s massive poem *Paradise Lost* is all about Adam and Eve in the Garden of Eden, and from **Chaucer**'s *Canterbury Tales* in the fourteenth century to **T. S. Eliot** in the twentieth, the myth of Adam seems to be omnipresent. Indeed, 'Adam' has also entered the language in numerous slang expressions: 'to adam and eve' means to have sexual intercourse, 'adam's ale' is water, 'adam's whip' is a penis, and so on. In rhyming slang, 'to Adam and Eve it' is to believe it. A number of fictional characters have also been named after the biblical character, though Adam in Shakespeare's *As You Like It* and Adam Bede in **George Eliot**'s novel of the same name are the only ones I can remember. Don't bother sending me lists of others; it would be a complete waste of time.

Adam Bede

This is **George Eliot**'s first novel. Published in 1859, it had its origin in a story told by George Eliot's aunt of a night she had spent in Nottingham jail comforting a girl who was about to be executed for the murder of her own child. Don't, therefore, expect *Adam Bede* to be a rollicking comedy. It is a tragic and an intensely moral novel. The combination – **tragedy** and morality – does not appear wildly appealing, but just read the opening pages:

> With a single drop of ink for a mirror, the Egyptian sorcerer undertakes to reveal to any chance comer far-reaching visions of the past. This is what I undertake to do for you, reader. With this drop of ink at the end of my pen, I will show you the roomy workshop of Mr Jonathan Burge, carpenter and builder, in the village of Hayslope, as it appeared on the eighteenth of June, in the year of our Lord 1799.
>
> The afternoon sun was warm on the five workmen there, busy upon doors and window-frames and wainscoting. A scent of pine-wood from a tent-like pile of planks outside the open door mingled itself with the scent of the elder-bushes which were spreading their summer snow close to the open window opposite; the slanting sunbeams shone

through the transparent shavings that flew before the steady plane, and lit up the fine grain of the oak panelling which stood propped against the wall. On a heap of those soft shavings, a rough grey shepherd-dog had made himself a pleasant bed, and was lying with his nose between his forepaws, occasionally wrinkling his brows to cast a glance at the tallest of the five workmen, who was carving a shield in the centre of a wooden mantelpiece. It was to this workman that the strong baritone belonged which was heard above the sound of plane and hammer singing –

> 'Awake, my soul, and with the sun
> Thy daily stage of duty run;
> Shake off dull sloth . . . '

Here some measurement was to be taken which required more concentrated attention, and the sonorous voice subsided into a low whistle; but it presently broke out again with renewed vigour –

> 'Let all thy converse be sincere,
> Thy conscience as the noonday clear.'

Such a voice could only come from a broad chest, and the broad chest belonged to a large-boned muscular man nearly six feet high, with a back so flat and a head so well poised that when he drew himself up to take a more distant survey of his work, he had the air of a soldier standing at ease. The sleeve rolled up above the elbow showed an arm that was likely to win the prize for feats of strength; yet the long supple hand, with its broad fingertips, looked ready for works of skill. In his tall stalwartness Adam Bede was a Saxon, and justified his name; but the jet-black hair, made the more noticeable by its contrast with the light paper cap, and the keen glance of the dark eyes that shone from under strongly marked, prominent and mobile eyebrows, indicated a mixture of Celtic blood. The face was large and roughly hewn, and when in repose had no other beauty than such as belongs to an expression of good-humoured honest intelligence.

It is clear at a glance that the next workman is Adam's brother. He is nearly as tall; he has the same type of features, the same hue of hair and complexion; but the strength of the family likeness seems only to render more conspicuous the remarkable difference of expression both in form and face. Seth's broad shoulders have a slight stoop; his eyes are grey; his eyebrows have less prominence and more repose than his brother's; and his glance, instead of being keen, is confiding and benignant. He has thrown off his paper cap, and you see that his hair is not thick and straight, like Adam's, but thin and wavy, allowing you to discern the exact contour of a coronal arch that predominates very decidedly over the brow.

The idle tramps always felt sure they could get a copper from Seth; they scarcely ever spoke to Adam.

The concert of the tools and Adam's voice was at last broken by Seth, who, lifting the door at which he had been working intently, placed it against the wall, and said – 'There! I've finished my door today, anyhow.'

The workmen all looked up; Jim Salt, a burly red-haired man, known as Sandy Jim, paused from his planing, and Adam said to Seth, with a sharp glance of surprise – 'What! dost think thee'st finished the door?'

'Ay, sure,' said Seth, with answering surprise; 'what's a-wanting to't?'

A loud roar of laughter from the other three workmen made Seth look round confusedly. Adam did not join in the laughter, but there was a slight smile on his face as he said, in a gentler tone than before – 'Why, thee'st forgot the panels.'

The laughter burst out afresh as Seth clapped his hands to his head, and coloured over brow and crown.

'Hoorray!' shouted a small lithe fellow, called Wiry Ben, running forward and seizing the door. 'We'll hang up th' door at fur end o' th' shop an' write on't "Seth Bede, the Methody, his work". Here, Jim, lend's hould o' th' red-pot.'

'Nonsense!' said Adam. 'Let it alone, Ben Cranage. You'll mayhap be making such a slip yourself someday; you'll laugh o' th' other side o' your mouth then.'

'Catch me at it, Adam. It'll be a good while afore my head's full o' th' Methodies,' said Ben.

'Nay, but it's often full o' drink, and that's worse.'

Ben, however, had now got the 'red-pot', in his hand, and was about to begin writing his inscription, making, by way of preliminary, an imaginary S in the air.

'Let it alone, will you?' Adam called out, laying down his tools, striding up to Ben, and seizing his right shoulder. 'Let it alone, or I'll shake the soul out o' your body.'

Ben shook in Adam's iron grasp, but, like a plucky small man as he was, he didn't mean to give in. With his left hand he snatched the brush from his powerless right, and made a movement as if he would perform the feat of writing with his left. In a moment Adam turned him round, seized his other shoulder, and, pushing him along, pinned him against the wall. But now Seth spoke.

'Let be, Addy, let be. Ben will be joking. Why, he's i' the right to laugh at me – I canna help laughing at myself.'

'I shan't loose him, till he promises to let the door alone,' said Adam.

'Come, Ben, lad,' said Seth, in a persuasive tone, 'don't let's have a quarrel about it. You know Adam will have his way. You may's well try to turn a waggon in a narrow lane. Say you'll leave the door alone, and make an end on't.'

'I binna frighted at Adam,' said Ben, 'but I donna mind sayin' as I'll let 't alone at your askin', Seth.'

Don't you find that already you are sucked into this earnest and rural context? This is the first attempt by one of Britain's greatest novelists, but already she has mastered the art of creating characters with whom you become involved.

Adams, Douglas (1952–2001)

Adams became famous when, at the age of twenty-seven, he turned his radio series *The Hitchhiker's Guide to the Galaxy* into a novel. It was followed by four others, *The Restaurant at the End of the Universe* in 1980, *Life, the Universe and Everything* in 1982, *So Long, and Thanks for All the Fish* in 1984 and *Mostly Harmless* in 1992. As their titles would indicate, these novels are examples of **science fiction**, but it is extremely amusing science fiction, full of profound truths that you wish you'd thought of:

In the beginning the Universe was created. This has made a lot of people very angry and has been widely regarded as a bad move.

It is a mistake to think you can solve any major problems just with potatoes.

The ships hung in the sky in much the same way that bricks don't.

Adams also wrote three novels featuring Dirk Gently's holistic detective agency, at least one work of philosophy, a number of short stories, a large number of radio programmes, and was activity engaged with Richard Dawkins in promoting atheism. It is a major sadness that Adams died at the early age of forty-nine, and it is no surprise that something of a cult has grown up around him and his work. His remark

I love deadlines. I like the whooshing sound they make as they fly by!

seems to typify the man. He must have been great company, and his books are a genial delight.

Addison, Joseph (1672–1719)

Addison was an influential writer. His first major work was a book about the lives of the English poets, published in 1694, but he is most remembered for his work as an essayist in periodicals like *The Tatler* and *The Spectator*, a journal which he founded in 1711. In 1713 he wrote a play entitled *Cato* which was received with much praise, but today he is remembered, if at all, for the words of wisdom which frequently appeared in his essays:

> He who would pass his declining years with honour and comfort, should, when young, consider that he may one day become old, and remember when he is old, that he has once been young.

> It is only imperfection that complains of what is imperfect. The more perfect we are the more gentle and quiet we become towards the defects of others.

> Men may change their climate, but they cannot change their nature. A man that goes out a fool cannot ride or sail himself into common sense.

> One should take good care not to grow too wise for so great a pleasure of life as laughter

Since Addison contributed more than 250 essays to *The Spectator*, the above examples could be quintupled with no difficulty. His writings were much esteemed by the eighteenth-century middle class, and it is almost dispiriting that today Addison is virtually forgotten.

Adonais

This is a marvellous elegy by P. B. Shelley. Written to commemorate John Keats, it gives you the opportunity to look up **elegy**, **Shelley** and **Keats**. When you've done that, you might like to come back and learn that *Adonais* is written in 55 Spenserian stanzas and was published in 1821. On the other hand, since you now have to look up **Spenser** and **stanza**, you may prefer not to come back. That would be a pity because I'm about to tell you that Adonais was the beautiful Greek youth loved by Aphrodite, and that, in personifying Keats in this way, Shelley was paying him the greatest of compliments. An even bigger compliment lies in the fact that *Adonais* is a marvellous poem. Just look how it begins:

> I weep for Adonais – he is dead!
> O, weep for Adonais! though our tears
> Thaw not the frost which binds so dear a head!
> And thou, sad Hour, selected from all years
> To mourn our loss, rouse thy obscure compeers,
> And teach them thine own sorrow, say: 'With me
> Died Adonais; till the Future dares
> Forget the Past, his fate and fame shall be
> An echo and a light unto eternity!'

Now grab your collected Shelley and read the succeeding 54 stanzas. Your soul will benefit.

Aesop (c. 620–560 BC)

Since there is doubt that anyone called Aesop ever existed, and since, if he did, he thrived in ancient Greece, his appearance here might be surprising. However, a large number of moral tales attributed to Aesop were passed down by word of mouth until, at about 300 BC, they were written out. These fables remained popular, and hence, in 1484, were printed in English by William Caxton. They have remained popular ever since, and have become part of the British literary heritage. Here is an example:

> At a country fair there was a Buffoon who made all the people laugh by imitating the cries of various animals. He finished off by squeaking so like a pig that the spectators thought that he had a porker concealed about him. But a Countryman who stood by said: 'Call that a pig's squeak! Nothing like it. You give me till tomorrow and I will show you what it's like.'
>
> The audience laughed, but next day, sure enough, the Countryman appeared on the stage, and putting his head down squealed so hideously that the spectators hissed and threw stones at him to make him stop. 'You fools!' he cried, 'see what you have been hissing,' and held up a little pig whose ear he had been pinching to make him utter the squeals.

The moral of this particular fable is that men often applaud an imitation and hiss the real thing. Thus the moral fabric of Britain owes much to an obscure Greek slave.

aesthetics

Aesthetics is the philosophical exploration of beauty and the appreciation of beauty. It consequently has never reached any firm conclusions or arrived at any consensus. Nor is it in any way relevant. If you believe that Ian Fleming is the world's greatest novelist, rational argument is not going to do anything to alter your view. Taste is entirely personal. You have good taste; everyone else has prejudices.

affective fallacy

> I don't like despots and dictators.
> Marlowe's *Tamburlaine the Great* is about a despot.
> Therefore Marlowe's play is a bad one.

This is an example of the affective fallacy whereby a work of art is praised or blamed, not for its inherent qualities, but because of the effect that it produces in the reader or audience. In fact, of course, if it turns out that you are very dubious indeed about the status of Tamburlaine, then that is a tribute to **Marlowe**'s skill.

air

Originally an air was a song or a tune. However, one can write a gentle poem that is itself musical, and that poem can be called an air.

Alastor, or The Spirit of Solitude

This is a poem of 720 lines by **Shelley**. It is too long to quote here, but have a look at its opening lines:

> Earth, Ocean, Air, belovèd brotherhood!
> If our great Mother has imbued my soul
> With aught of natural piety to feel
> Your love, and recompense the boon with mine;
> If dewy morn, and odorous noon, and even,
> With sunset and its gorgeous ministers,
> And solemn midnight's tingling silentness;
> If Autumn's hollow sighs in the sere wood,
> And Winter robing with pure snow and crowns
> Of starry ice the grey grass and bare boughs;
> If Spring's voluptuous pantings when she breathes
> Her first sweet kisses, – have been dear to me;

If no bright bird, insect, or gentle beast
I consciously have injured, but still loved
And cherished these my kindred; then forgive
This boast, belovèd brethren, and withdraw
No portion of your wonted favour now!

One could hardly have a more romantic example of romanticism. The whole poem explores the condition of a contemplative idealist in a way that seventeenth-century and eighteenth-poets like **Dryden** and **Pope** would have found inconceivable. Indeed, in one sense the poem is schizophrenic, condemning the contemplative idealist as being self-centred and yet finding the condition of the real world so unpleasant as to leave idealism as one's only recourse.

Alchemist, The

This is the title of a play by **Ben Jonson**. Jonson had a keen eye for the follies of his contemporaries, and in this play he particularly satirises human gullibility. He displays considerable understanding of alchemy and makes many jokes based on its symbolism. In case you don't know, alchemy was a 'science' devoted to finding a way in which base metals like iron could be transfigured into gold. It was, of course, a delusion, but not everyone understood that, and alchemy had been a mirage for centuries. The action takes place in Lovewit's house in London, while he is away in the country. A crafty servant, Face, left behind by Lovewit, asks his friends, a con artist named Subtle and a prostitute named Dol Common, to help him with his plan. Together, they will convince their hapless 'clients' that Subtle is an alchemist who can turn any substance into gold. A listing of the characters who appear in the play gives some indication of the chaos that Jonson creates:

SUBTLE: *the alchemist*

FACE: *the housekeeper*

DOL COMMON: *The conspirator of Subtle and Face*

LOVEWIT: *the owner of the house in which Subtle sets up his work*

DAPPER: *a lawyer's clerk, who wants Subtle to help him in gambling*

ABEL DRUGGER: *a tobacco merchant, who wants Subtle to assist him, through magic, in setting up an apothecary's shop*

SIR EPICURE MAMMON: *a knight, who wants Subtle's help in making him wealthy*

TRIBULATION WHOLESOME: *a pastor of Amsterdam*
ANANIAS: *a deacon, colleague of Tribulation. These religious brothers want Subtle's help in minting money with which to establish Puritanism in Britain.*
KASTRIL: *the angry boy, recently come into an inheritance. He wants Subtle's help in aiding him to win fights.*
DAME PLIANT: *a widow, sister of Kastril, wants to know her fortune in marriage*
PERTINAX SURLY: *a gamester, who sees through the deceptions*

The play is regarded by some as one of the great comedies in English.

Alcott, Louisa May (1832–1888)

I do not know whether it happens today, but when I was a child, most literate children read L. M. Alcott's **Little Women** (1868) and *Good Wives* (1869). Based on Alcott's own home life in Massachusetts, these are delightful children's novels. Notice how, from the beginning of *Little Women*, one is sucked into the context:

'Christmas won't be Christmas without any presents,' grumbled Jo, lying on the rug.

'It's so dreadful to be poor!' sighed Meg, looking down at her old dress.

'I don't think it's fair for some girls to have plenty of pretty things, and other girls nothing at all,' added little Amy, with an injured sniff.

'We've got Father and Mother, and each other,' said Beth contentedly from her corner.

The four young faces on which the firelight shone brightened at the cheerful words, but darkened again as Jo said sadly, 'We haven't got Father, and shall not have him for a long time.' She didn't say 'perhaps never', but each silently added it, thinking of Father far away, where the fighting was.

Straightaway one is concerned and involved. And one certainly wants to carry on reading. Yet Alcott produced nearly 300 titles, so most of her work, rightly or wrongly, is completely disregarded today. So there is an easy way to make your name: produce a definitive volume on the writings of L. M. Alcott.

alexandrine

Most iambic lines in English poetry are of five feet. (Now look up **iambic** and **foot**.) An alexandrine is an iambic line of six feet. It is so called in memory of Alexander the Great, and one is tempted to assume that he was six feet tall. Alas, the real reason that the line is called an alexandrine is simply because some French poems about Alexander the Great were written in this metre. It is not very common in English poetry, though you do find it as the final line of a Spenserian stanza. Here is an example from **Keats**'s *The Eve of Saint Agnes*:

> She knelt, so pure a thing, so free from mortal taint.

alienation effect

The German dramatist Bertolt Brecht (1898–1956) was always anxious that drama should have an alienation effect. By this he meant that both actors and audience should preserve an attitude of critical detachment. Hence, when Polonius is killed in *Hamlet*, we should not experience shock. Instead we should ask ourselves, 'Is **Shakespeare** making a point here about the role of fathers in society?' or something equally asinine. Now Brecht, of course, did have a point. If you immerse yourself totally within the play, you are not going to have the necessary objectivity to form a reasoned judgement. On the other hand, if you don't grieve over the death of Cordelia in *King Lear*, you might as well be dead.

allegory

An allegory is a piece of deceit. You are reading a story about Tim and Margery Pearson when it slowly becomes apparent to you that in fact you are reading the sordid details of the life of Al Capone and his wife. We have already met an allegory of this nature in *Absalom and Achitophel*. More often, though, allegories are less specific. While Napoleon in **Orwell**'s *Animal Farm* might represent Stalin, Una in **Spenser**'s *The Fairie Queene* is just representative of the Christian soul, as, indeed, is Christian in **Bunyan**'s *Pilgrim's Progress*. The English poet William Blake wrote a number of allegories, but since they are entirely incomprehensible, you may ignore them. **Herman Melville**'s novel *Moby Dick* is also said to be an allegory, but since it is largely a tedious textbook on whale catching, you may ignore that too.

Allingham, Margery (1904–66)

Margery Allingham is one of the great detective-story writers. Her tec, called Albert Campion, is in the same tradition as Sherlock Holmes and Lord Peter Wimsey, a talented amateur, and the novels featuring him are pleasing and intelligent escapist literature.

alliteration

Many of us were entertained by alliteration as schoolchildren and we used to recite 'Peter Piper picked a peck of pickled pepper'. As you can see, it is the repetition of a sound, and, as a literary technique, can rapidly become juvenile and tiresome. **Gerard Manley Hopkins** uses it in his poem *The Windhover*:

I caught this morning morning's minion, king-
dom of daylight's dauphin, dapple-dawn-drawn Falcon, in his riding
Of the rolling level underneath him steady air . . .

This is widely admired, but Hopkins does attract acolytes like a candle flame attracts moths. Personally I find it juvenile and tiresome, but it is unwise to say so; the massed ranks of Hopkins admirers believe strongly in vengeance. In fact, Old English (**Anglo-Saxon**) and Middle English writers wrote verse that was wholly alliterative. To me the prospect is very unappealing, but I cannot condemn something of which I have no personal experience.

allusion

If you allude to something, you just mention it in passing. Hence if you were talking about boxing, you might, in passing, allude to stupidity, insensitivity, cruelty and barbarism. In literature, however, an allusion can be a very significant element. In **Milton**'s *Lycidas*, for instance, it is written:

Were it not better done, as others use,
To sport with Amaryllis in the shade,
Or with the tangles of Neaera's hair?

The allusion to Amaryllis is meant to recall for us the sullen rages of Amaryllis as depicted in Virgil's eclogues. Neaera has a number of mentions in a variety of classical authors, and her tangled hair was well known. Milton mentions them both in order to accentuate the pointlessness of a proposed action. Thus the allusions act as symbols of futility, and give me the opportunity of appearing much more scholarly than I really am. Again, in *The Love Song of J. Alfred Prufrock*, **T. S .Eliot** tells us:

> In the room the women come and go
> Talking of Michelangelo.

Here Michelangelo, one of finest creators in history, is used as an ironic contrast to the triviality of the context. Thus an allusion can expand the significance of the moment, can add an extra layer of meaning. It can also be pretentious and arrogant, crimes normally associated with politicians.

alternative literature

This is an entirely irrelevant piece of jargon. Alternative literature is supposed to be literature that does not fit into the main stream of literary development. For instance, I write poems using only words that I can find in **Samuel Johnson**'s *Dictionary of the English Language*. Instead of describing this as half-witted pretention, I describe it as alternative literature.

Alton Locke

This is a novel by **Charles Kingsley**, published in 1850. It only appears in this volume because I think that it is the worst novel that I have ever read. Avoid it. When I get to Y, I probably won't have the energy to mention *Yeast*, another dreadful novel by Kingsley. Avoid that too.

ambiguity

Ambiguity is what happens when a word, sentence, paragraph or whatever can be understood in more than one way. Ever since William Empson published *Seven Types of Ambiguity* (1930), this word has had a talismanic force. Ambiguity is supposed to add richness to a work. By and large, this is piffle. If the meaning of a sentence is ambiguous, this is because the writer has been incompetent. If, for instance, I do not know whether the phrase 'hunting dogs' in a sentence means that a group are hunting dogs that have gone astray or are using hunting dogs to track down the bison, then that sentence is badly written. Its ambiguity is a fault. If, however, I find a character in a play ambiguous, that may well be because the character is ambiguous. Most of us are mixtures of incompatible traits, and spend life trying to reconcile them. Hamlet, of course, is the perennial example. He is full of determination and racked by indecision. That is why he is such a rich character. So ambiguity can be the product of careless writing, or the richness of a complex character or situation.

Amis, Kingsley (1922–95)

For reasons that have always struck me as obscure, Kingsley Amis is considered to have belonged to a group of 1950s writers known as Angry Young Men. Writers are too idiosyncratic to be lumped into groups, and Kingsley Amis, who wrote poetry, a ghost story, a detective novel, a biography of Kipling, newspaper columns on wine, and amusing satirical novels is impossible to categorise with a label. Amis, though, was perhaps unfortunate. His first novel, *Lucky Jim* (1954), was so successful and possesses such brio, that nothing he did afterwards quite matched it. To console him for this, Amis was knighted in 1990.

Amis, Martin (1949–)

Martin Amis is the son of **Kingsley Amis** and also a novelist. Personally I find his writing mannered and pretentious, but I've never been fond of scatology.

Amoretti

Everybody in the sixteenth century wrote sonnets, and this sequence of 89 of them is by **Edmund Spenser**. Here is the second in the sequence:

> Unquiet thought, whom at the first I bred,
> Of th' inward bale of my love pined heart:
> and sithence have with sighs and sorrows fed,
> till greater than my womb thou woxen art.
> Break forth at length out of the inner part,
> in which thou lurkest like to viper's brood:
> and seek some succour both to ease my smart
> and also to sustain thy self with food.
> But if in presence of that fairest proud
> thou chance to come, fall lowly at her feet:
> and with meek humbless and afflicted mood,
> pardon for thee, and grace for me intreat.
> Which if she grant, then live and my love cherish,
> if not, die soon, and I with thee will perish.

This, like most of the others, strikes me as a highly competent piece of work. Note, however, its rhyme scheme: abab bcbc cdcd ee. So far as I know, this scheme is confined to Spenser; no one else uses it.

Amours de Voyage

This is a verse novel in five cantos written by **A. H. Clough**. Nothing very much happens within it – it is more a series of philosophical reflections – but Clough is an underrated poet, and *Amours de Voyage* is well worth reading.

analogy

An analogy is when you try to explain x by comparing it with y. For instance, you discover little Brian playing with a rattlesnake. Immediately you say, 'Don't play with that, love. Remember what happened to Cleopatra.' Thus you try to dissuade five-year-old Brian from playing with the snake by reminding him of what happened when Cleopatra played with an asp. The trouble is, human circumstances are rarely identical, and so arguing by analogy is often imprecise. Little Brian, for instance, is likely to look up and say, 'But, mum, Cleopatra was playing with an asp, whereas I've got a rattlesnake, and anyway Cleopatra wanted to commit suicide, whereas I don't, so your analogy falls down on at least two counts.' At this point, one hopes the snake bites Brian.

analysis

In the ideal world, analysis is what a critic does to a work of literature. He or she illuminates the author's meaning, dissects the structure of the work in question, analyses the imagery, discusses the style of writing, and compares the work with any other appropriate works. As a result, the reader ends up with a fuller and rounder understanding of the work in question.

anapaest

If I tell you that an anapaest is a reversed **dactyl**, are you likely to swear? But it is. A dactyl is a metrical foot comprising a stressed syllable followed by two unstressed ones. Hence an anapaest is a foot consisting of two unstressed syllables followed by one stressed one. Sometimes people use the word 'long' as a synonym for 'stressed' and 'short' as a substitute for 'unstressed', though I am totally incapable of seeing any reason for this. Anyway, you can find anapaests in a poem that most of us encounter at some time or other, **Robert Browning**'s *How They Brought the Good News from Ghent to Aix*:

> Not a word to each other; we kept the great pace
> Neck by neck, stride by stride, never changing our place.

Mind you, I can also see no point in knowing what an anapaest is. I bet Browning never said to himself, 'Let's have a couple of lines of anapaests here.' He just wrote what seemed appropriate to him, and it turned out to be anapaests. So be careful; it could happen to you.

Anderson, Hans Christian (1805–75)

This Danish writer is a nineteenth century **Aesop**. Between 1835 and 1872, he wrote 165 fairy tales, and those tales have entered the nurseries and primary schools of most nations since. *The Ugly Duckling* and *The Emperor's New Clothes* are more widely known than *King Lear* or *Paradise Lost* ever will be.

Andrea del Sarto

This is a dramatic monologue by **Robert Browning** which appeared in the 1855 volume *Men and Women*. Of all the great poems in *Men and Women*, this one is my favourite. It follows, therefore, that it is the best.

Anglo-Saxon

This is a language that preceded English. Apparently we are now supposed to say 'Old English', but does this look like English?

> hwæt we gar-dena in geardagum,
> peodcyninga prym gefrunon,
> hu da æpelingas ellen fremedon.
> oft scyld scefing sceapena preatum,
> monegum mægpum meodosetla ofteah,
> egsode eorlas, syddan ærest weard
> feasceaft funden; he pæs frofre gebad,
> weox under wolcnum, weordmyndum pah,
> odpæt him æghwylc pær ymbsittendra
> ofer hronrade hyran scolde,
> gomban gyldan. pæt wæs god cyning!

Of course it doesn't.

Animal Farm

This is a novel by **George Orwell** (1903–50) in which the animals oust the human owners of a farm and take it over themselves. Published in 1945, it was supposed to be a satire on Stalin's Russia, but many people these days take it as a fantasy for children.

Antony and Cleopatra

Every play by **William Shakespeare** is worthy of study, but *Antony and Cleopatra* demands worship. It is totally marvellous. I shall tell you nothing about it, but just read this:

> Nay, but this dotage of our general's
> O'erflows the measure: those his goodly eyes,
> That o'er the files and musters of the war
> Have glow'd like plated Mars, now bend, now turn,
> The office and devotion of their view
> Upon a tawny front: his captain's heart,
> Which in the scuffles of great fights hath burst
> The buckles on his breast, reneges all temper,
> And is become the bellows and the fan
> To cool a gypsy's lust.

These are the opening lines of the play. They are spoken by Philo, a character who never appears again in the play and who, quite frankly, is of the utmost insignificance. Yet just read again that verse. Has contempt ever been better expressed? Can derision be more perfectly spoken? And this is from a character who is so minor that most people never remember his name. There is verse of equal quality from almost everyone who appears in the play, and the story is of a complexity, magnificence and human fallibility as to exalt the soul and tear the heart.

aphorism

An aphorism is a general statement expressing some general principle. Of course, one could say that the poetry of **Wilfred Owen** tends to depress the reader. That is a general statement expressing a general principle, but it is not really an aphorism because aphorisms have to be witty, or wise, or concisely memorable. Hence **William Blake**'s 'The road of excess leads to the palace of wisdom' is an aphorism, though wrong, while the statement 'Watching darts on television is intensely boring' is not an aphorism, though self-evidently correct. For what it's worth, my favourite aphorism is

> Any time things appear to be going better, you have overlooked something.

Wikipedia provides some entertaining examples from which I extract six:

- *Mediocrity is forgiven more easily than talent.* EMIL KROTKY

- *Nothing great was ever achieved without enthusiasm.*
  RALPH WALDO EMERSON

- *Death with dignity is better than life with humiliation.*
  HUSAYN IBN ALI

- *That which does not destroy us makes us stronger.*
  FRIEDRICH NIETZSCHE

- *If you see the teeth of the lion, do not think that the lion is smiling at you.*
  AL-MUTANABBI

- *When your legs get weaker time starts running faster.*
  MIKHAIL TUROVSKY

Hundreds more can be found on the Internet if you really want a surfeit.

Apocrypha

This is Greek for 'things hidden', and the word is used to describe writings that are somewhat dubious – in some way not fully valid. Thus there are a number of books that never quite made it into the Bible, but which are still felt to be of spiritual worth. The play *Edward III* is apocryphal **Shakespeare**.

archetype

In the Middle Ages when I was an undergraduate, archetypes seemed to be the flavour of the month. What on earth are they? Wikipedia defines them as follows:

An **archetype** is an original model of a person, object, or concept from which similar instances are derived, copied, patterned, or emulated. In psychology, an archetype is a model of a person, personality, or behavior. This article is about personality as described in literature analysis and the study of the psyche.

In the analysis of personality, the term *archetype* is often broadly used to refer to

1 a stereotype – personality type observed multiple times, especially an oversimplification of such a type; or
2 an epitome – personality type exemplified, especially the 'greatest' such example;
3 a literary term to express details.

Archetype refers to a generic version of a personality. In this sense 'mother figure' may be considered an archetype and may be identified in various characters with otherwise distinct (non-generic) personalities.

Archetypes are likewise supposed to have been present in folklore and literature for thousands of years, including prehistoric artwork. The use of archetypes to analyze personality and literature was advanced by Carl Jung early in the twentieth century, who suggested the existence of a kind of heritable racial memory comprised of collective human experiences reaching back into prehistory. Thus, in fictional narratives, it is assumed characters with strong archetypal features will automatically and unconsciously resonate with a large audience.

Archetypes are cited as important to both ancient mythology and modern narratives, as argued by Joseph Campbell in works such as *The Hero With a Thousand Faces*. A number of cinematic and dramatic formulae have been devised based on these notions, including books like Carol S. Pearson's *The Hero Within: Six Archetypes We Live By*. Such formulae typically describe fixed categories into which a work may fall, or narrative stages guided by archetypal figures.

I'm sorry to have burdened you with so long a quotation, but one needed a reasonable length to savour the pretention of it all. As far as literature is concerned, an archetype is simply an example of a human quality. Hence Othello is an archetype of jealousy, Hamlet an archetype of indecision, Macbeth an archetype of ambition, George Bush an archetype of sub-normality, and so on. And that is all there is to it. People talk about Jungian analysis, but there is absolutely no need. When you read **Dickens**'s ***Little Dorrit*** and you notice that Little Dorrit herself is an emblem of self-sacrifice, then you can, if you like, call her an archetype of consideration. It doesn't illuminate anything for you to do so, but it doesn't do any harm either.

Areopagitica

This is the title of a pamphlet by **John Milton** arguing for the abolition of censorship. As such, it holds an honourable position in the story of freedom of expression. The title is derived from the Areopagus, the hill in Athens where the judicial tribunal of the city used to meet. The pamphlet should be required reading for every MP.

Arnold, Matthew (1822–88)

Arnold spent thirty-five years of his life as a school inspector, so one could hardly expect major achievements from him, yet much of his poetry is very pleasing. 'Dover Beach', for instance, is a short poem, but is near perfect:

> The sea is calm tonight.
> The tide is full, the moon lies fair
> Upon the straits; on the French coast the light
> Gleams and is gone; the cliffs of England stand;
> Glimmering and vast, out in the tranquil bay.
> Come to the window, sweet is the night-air!
> Only, from the long line of spray
> Where the sea meets the moon-blanched land,
> Listen! you hear the grating roar
> Of pebbles which the waves draw back, and fling,
> At their return, up the high strand,
> Begin, and cease, and then again begin,
> With tremulous cadence slow, and bring
> The eternal note of sadness in.
>
> Sophocles long ago
> Heard it on the Aegean, and it brought
> Into his mind the turbid ebb and flow
> Of human misery; we
> Find also in the sound a thought,
> Hearing it by this distant northern sea.
>
> The Sea of Faith
> Was once, too, at the full, and round earth's shore
> Lay like the folds of a bright girdle furled.
> But now I only hear
> Its melancholy, long, withdrawing roar,

>Retreating, to the breath
>Of the night-wind, down the vast edges drear
>And naked shingles of the world.
>
>Ah, love, let us be true
>To one another! for the world, which seems
>To lie before us like a land of dreams,
>So various, so beautiful, so new,
>Hath really neither joy, nor love, nor light,
>Nor certitude, nor peace, nor help for pain;
>And we are here as on a darkling plain
>Swept with confused alarms of struggle and flight,
>Where ignorant armies clash by night.

Some of Arnold's long poems like *The Scholar Gipsy* and *Sohrab and Rustum* are also quite impressive. Arnold also wrote considerable criticism, but this can be safely ignored. One needs to make up one's own mind about literature, not crib someone else's opinion.

art for art's sake

This phrase is meant to denote the idea that a literary work should be valued for itself, and not for the didactic, moral, emotional or intellectual effect that it has on you. I hope that you can see that this is about as sensible as valuing your wife's cooking for itself and not for its taste.

Asimov, Isaac (1920–92)

Asimov was one of the twentieth century's most successful science-fiction writers, but since he had a PhD and taught biochemistry at Columbia University, one feels that he had an unfair advantage.

assonance

Assonance is the repetition of vowel sounds within a short passage of verse or prose. It is not a technique much used by writers since it can easily sound trite and mannered:

>The rain in Spain falls mainly on the plain.

>We love to spoon 'neath the moon in June.

Tennyson gets away with it (just) in *The Lady of Shalott*:

>On either side the river lie
>Long fields of barley and of rye

Milton, with assonance on u and o, certainly gets away with it in this example from *Paradise Lost*:

> . . . the broad circumference
> Hung on his shoulders like the Moon, whose Orb
> Through Optic Glass the Tuscan Artist views
> At ev'ning from the top of Fesole . . .

On the whole though, don't try assonance yourself until you have been made Poet Laureate.

Astrophil and Stella

This is the title of a sonnet sequence by **Sir Philip Sidney** that was published in 1591. Like **Spenser**'s *Amoretti*, it is of a remarkably high standard. Of its 108 sonnets, this is the seventh:

> When Nature made her chief worke, *Stellas* eyes,
> In colour blacke why wrapt she beames so bright?
> Would she in beamy blacke, like Painter wise,
> Frame daintiest lustre, mixt of shades and light?
> Or did she else that sober hue devise,
> In obiect best to knit and strength our sight;
> Least, if no vaile these brave gleames did disguise,
> They, sunlike, should more dazzle than delight?
> Or would she her miraculous power show,
> That, whereas black seems Beauties contrary,
> She even in black doth make all beauties flow?
> Both so, and thus, she, minding Love should be
> Plac'd ever there, gave him this mourning weede
> To honour all their deaths who for her bleed.

Auden, W. H. (1907–73)

We divide things by centuries, even though there is nothing remotely significant about one year being in the sixteenth century and the next year being in the seventeenth. However, that is what we do, and in any one century, there are a certain number of people who turn out to be great poets. Normally there are few of these, and the twentieth century was particularly impoverished. I sometimes doubt if there were more than two, and W. H. Auden was one of those two.

Why is Auden a great poet? Clearly it needs a book to answer that question properly, which provides me with an extremely convenient excuse for not doing so here. Yet it is interesting that neither *The Oxford Companion to English Literature* nor *The Cambridge Guide to Literature in English* makes the slightest attempt either to analyse Auden's mastery. They both hail him as a major poet, but provide no clue as to why he is one. I suspect that this reticence might even be because Auden is just so English that it is almost embarrassing to atomise his merits. It begins to sound like nationalist self-praise.

Take, for instance, his well-known poem *Musée des Beaux Arts*:

> About suffering they were never wrong,
> The Old Masters; how well, they understood
> Its human position; how it takes place
> While someone else is eating or opening a window or just
> walking dully along;
> How, when the aged are reverently, passionately waiting
> For the miraculous birth, there always must be
> Children who did not specially want it to happen, skating
> On a pond at the edge of the wood:
> They never forgot
> That even the dreadful martyrdom must run its course
> Anyhow in a corner, some untidy spot
> Where the dogs go on with their doggy life and the torturer's horse
> Scratches its innocent behind on a tree.
> In Breughel's *Icarus*, for instance: how everything turns away
> Quite leisurely from the disaster; the ploughman may
> Have heard the splash, the forsaken cry,
> But for him it was not an important failure; the sun shone
> As it had to on the white legs disappearing into the green
> Water; and the expensive delicate ship that must have seen
> Something amazing, a boy falling out of the sky,
> had somewhere to get to and sailed calmly on.

Is there not a tone of typically British understatement here? The outlandish sight of a boy falling into the sea from the sky merits a casual glance, but we all have our own lives to lead and so cannot be distracted by this personal disaster. Yet, because Auden is a great poet, his apparently disinterested tone helps to heighten the basic message of the poem. *Musée des Beaux Arts* is about perspective, and the poem brilliantly makes us all aware that we self-centred humans can disregard anything, no matter how shameful or astounding, if it is not relevant to our own lives. There is no hectoring tone here, no evangelical passion, yet, ironically, Auden's calm, placid tone makes the point more powerfully than any rhetoric. Control of tone is not the only element within a poem, but it is the most crucial, and it was something at which Auden excelled.

Augustan Age

I include this label, not because it serves any useful purpose, but because it is occasionally used, and it is useful if you know what it is meant to mean. The Augustan Age was the period in England from about 1660 to about 1820. It is the time when people like **John Dryden**, **Alexander Pope** and **Samuel Johnson** were writing. Their writing was formal, ordered, disciplined and correct, and the label 'Augustan Age' is supposed to refer to a period in English literature when poetry and prose were uniformly elegant. It refers back, of course, to the reign of the Roman emperor Augustus (27BC–AD14) when distinguished writers like Horace, Ovid, Tibullus and Virgil all flourished.

Austen, Jane (1775–1817)

There are only four major English novelists, and Jane Austen is one of them. It hardly seems worth saying any more, but I shall be berated by the Janeites if I don't contribute some worshipping words. If you want to know what 'irony' is, don't look it up in this book, just go and read some Jane Austen. She is England's greatest ironic writer, and consequently is very funny and very wise. For goodness sake, don't watch a BBC adaptation of *Emma*, *Pride and Prejudice* or anything else. Jane Austen wrote to be read, and at her best (*Emma*, *Pride and Prejudice*), there is not a finer writer to be found.

Let me give one or two examples. *Pride and Prejudice* opens with the following sentence:

> It is a truth universally acknowledged, that a single man in possession of a good fortune, must be in want of a wife.

This sentence is so urbane and polished that one reads it and almost automatically accepts it. Then one stops and thinks for a moment. The sentence, of course, is total nonsense. But lots of mothers of eligible daughters tended to think that any single man in the area was a prospective catch for their offspring. So Jane Austen has taken the pious hope of doting mothers, and exalted it to a universal truth. She does it so elegantly and so matter-of-factly that one is almost duped by her into believing it oneself. Also from *Pride and Prejudice* are these comments on marriage:

Happiness in marriage is entirely a matter of chance. If the dispositions of the parties are ever so well known to each other or ever so similar beforehand, it does not advance their felicity in the least. They always continue to grow sufficiently unlike afterwards to have their share of vexation; and it is better to know as little as possible of the defects of the person with whom you are to pass your life.

Jane Austen writes with such assurance that she could persuade you that arson was a benefit to mankind. Yet it is in her dissection of human relations that Miss Austen is so astute. She begins *Persuasion* by depicting the Elliot family:

Sir Walter Elliot, of Kellynch-hall, in Somersetshire, was a man who, for his own amusement, never took up any book but the Baronetage;

'Anne was obliged to touch him before she could catch his notice'
by Hugh Thomson, from Jane Austen's *Persuasion*

there he found occupation for an idle hour, and consolation in a distressed one . . .

There, in half a sentence, we know all that we ever need to know about Sir Walter: the man is an arrogant, bovine clod. As Jane Austen adds a couple of paragraphs later, 'Vanity was the beginning and the end of Sir Walter Elliot's character.' She then moves on to his three daughters:

Elizabeth had succeeded at sixteen to all that was possible of her mother's rights and consequence; and being very handsome, and very like himself, her influence had always been great, and they had gone on together most happily. His other two children were of very inferior value. Mary had acquired a little artificial importance by becoming Mrs Charles Musgrove; but Anne, with an elegance of mind and sweetness of character, which must have placed her high with any people of real understanding, was nobody with either father or sister; her word had no weight, her convenience was always to give way – she was only Anne.

And so the chief characters are outlined, and they are outlined with such precision, such economy and such irony that we are already ensnared into Jane Austen's world. That is what great writers do: they ensnare one, and one can become their prisoners for life.

Authorised Version

This is the term applied to the version of **the Bible** that was supposedly authorised by King James I, and which appeared in 1611. It is itself a great work of literature, and because, in the seventeenth, eighteenth and nineteenth centuries, Britain was largely speaking a Christian country, the authorised version has probably had more influence on English literature than any other work.

autobiography

A series of self-justifications and lies about oneself. No more reliable than a biography.

avant-garde

In any artistic realm, the avant-garde are those pioneers who are breaking new ground, setting new standards, and inducing shock and horror among the traditionalists. **Wordsworth**, **Coleridge**, **Shelley** and **Byron** were once the avant-garde, breaking away from the eighteenth-century conventions that they inherited.

B

ballad

This word conjures up a relaxed and jolly ditty, which is doubtless why a great many ballads are concerned with sexual infidelity, accidents at sea, robbery on horseback and death in childbirth. In other words, most ballads tell a story, and although that story may be tragic, ballad tunes and ballad metres often do sound remarkably benign. However, it is difficult to offer any generalisations about ballads because one can always find an exception. The most common author of ballads is a chap called anonymous, and such ballads are often sung to folk tunes that have no discernable origin. Traditional ballads derive from a pre-literate rural community, and tend to be heroic, romantic and/or tragic. Street ballads stem from an urban community, and tend to be more comic in tone. Both types perforce lend themselves to being sung, and both types have influenced literary ballads.

If we confine ourselves to literary ballads, we have a wide range to choose from. **Keats** wrote a famous ballad called *La Belle Dame Sans Merci*:

> 'O what can ail thee, knight-at-arms,
>   Alone and palely loitering?
> The sedge has wither'd from the lake,
>   And no bird sings.
>
> O what can ail thee, knight-at-arms!
>   So haggard and so woe-begone?
> The squirrel's granary is full,
>   And the harvest's done.
>
> I see a lily on thy brow
>   With anguish moist and fever dew,
> And on thy cheeks a fading rose
>   Fast withereth too.'
>
> 'I met a lady in the meads,
>   Full beautiful – a faery's child,
> Her hair was long, her foot was light,
>   And her eyes were wild.

I made a garland for her head,
  And bracelets too, and fragrant zone;
She look'd at me as she did love,
  And made sweet moan.

I set her on my pacing steed,
  And nothing else saw all day long,
For sideways would she bend, and sing
  A faery's song.

She found me roots of relish sweet,
  And honey wild, and manna dew,
And sure in language strange she said –
  "I love thee true."

She took me to her elfin grot,
  And there she wept, and sigh'd fill sore,
And there I shut her wild wild eyes
  With kisses four.

And there she lulled me asleep,
  And there I dream'd – Ah! woe betide!
The latest dream I ever dream'd
  On the cold hill's side.

I saw pale kings and princes too,
  Pale warriors, death-pale were they all;
They cried – "La belle dame sans merci
  Hath thee in thrall!"

I saw their starved lips in the gloam,
  With horrid warning gaped wide,
And I awoke and found me here,
  On the cold hill's side.

And this is why I sojourn here,
  Alone and palely loitering,
Though the sedge is wither'd from the lake,
  And no birds sing.'

I have quoted the whole of that because I like it, and I'd now like to
quote the whole of **Coleridge**'s *The Rime of the Ancient Mariner*,

Alfred Noyes' *The Highwayman* and **Oscar Wilde**'s *The Ballad of Reading Gaol*. I shan't, however, because that would make life too easy for you. Go and search each one out and read it. It will teach you no more about the ballad form, but it will improve your soul.

Ballantyne, Robert Michael (1825–94)

Of the large number of adventure stories that I read as a child, I think that it is Ballantyne's *The Coral Island* (1858) that I remember most fondly. It was voted one of the top twenty Scottish novels in the 2006 15th International World Wide Web Conference, and although such a ranking is somewhat risible, it is an excellent story. The plot is notable in that all the schoolboys in the novel, schoolboys who find themselves wrecked on a desert island, none the less continue to uphold the finest traditions of Great Britain. This moral improbability so enraged **William Golding** that he wrote *Lord of the Flies* as a response. In the Golding novel, the boys become savages. This is doubtless psychologically more plausible, but as a ten-year-old, I greatly enjoyed the make-believe of Ballantyne. What, however, I did not know as a ten-year-old was that Ballantyne had written dozens of books:

1 *The Hudson Bay Company*, 1848
2 *The Young Fur Traders; or Snowflakes and Sunbeams*, 1856
3 *Mister Fox*. A children's book of nursery rhymes, songs, music, pictures and stories by 'Comus' (RMB's pseudonym for his nursery work), 1856
4 *The Coral Island*, 1857
5 *Ungava*, 1858
6 *Martin Rattler: The Adventures of a Boy in the Forests of Brazil*, 1858
7 *Handbook to the new Gold-Fields: A full account of the richness and extent of the Fraser and Thompson River gold-mines; with a geographical and physical account of the country, its inhabitants, routes, etc.*, 1858
8 *The Dog Crusoe and his Master: A Story of the Western Prairies*, 1860
9 *The World of Ice*, 1860
10 *The Gorilla Hunters*, 1861
11 *The Golden Dream: A Tale of the Diggings*, 1861
12 *The Red Eric; or, The Whaler's Last Cruise*, 1861
13 *Away in the Wilderness: Red Indians and Fur Traders of North America*, 1863
14 *Fighting the Whales: Doings and Dangers on a Fishing Cruise*, 1863
15 *The Wild Man of the West: A Tale of the Rocky Mountains*, 1863
16 *Man on the Ocean*, 1863
17 *Fast in the Ice*, 1863

18 *Gascoyne: The Sandalwood Trader*, 1864

19 *The Lifeboat: A Tale of our Coast Heroes*, 1864

20 *Chasing the Sun; or, Rambles in Norway*, 1864

21 *Freaks on the Fells; and, Why I did not Become a Sailor; also, Papers from Norway*, 1864

22 *The Lighthouse: The Bell Rock*, 1865

23 *Fighting the Flames: The London Fire Brigade, and How it Works*, 1867

24 *Silver Lake*, 1867

25 *Deep Down: A Tale of the Cornish Mines*, 1868

26 *Shifting Winds: A Tough Yarn*, 1868

27 *Hunting the Lions: The Land of the Negro*, 1869

28 *Over the Rocky Mountains: Wandering Will in the Land of the Red Skins*, 1869

29 *Saved by the Lifeboat*, 1869

30 *Erling the Bold: A Tale of the Norse Sea Kings*, 1869

31 *The Battle and the Breeze: Fights & Fancies of a British Tar*, 1869

32 *Up in the Clouds; or, Balloon Voyages*, 1869

33 *The Cannibal Islands: Captain Cook's Adventures in the South Seas*, 1869

34 *Lost in the Forest*, 1869

35 *Digging for Gold: Adventures in California*, 1869

36 *Sunk at Sea: Adventures of Wandering Will in the Pacific*, 1869

37 *The Floating Light off the Goodwin Sands*, 1870

38 *The Iron Horse; or Life on the Line – a Railway Tale*, 1871

39 *The Norsemen in the West; or America Before Columbus*, 1872

40 *The Pioneers: A Tale of the Western Wilderness*, 1872

41 *Black Ivory: Adventures Among the Slavers of East Africa*, 1873

42 *Life in the Red Brigade.* A short novel about the life and times of some more of the London Firemen, about 1870. See also *Fighting the Flames* of 1867. 1873

43 *Fort Desolation.* A short novel about a fur trading station in Labrador. 1873

44 *The Ocean and its Wonders*, 1874

45 *The Pirate City: An Algerine Tale*, 1874

46 *The Butterfly's Ball and the Grasshopper's Feast*, 1874

47 *The Story of the Rock: The Eddystone Lighthouse*, 1875

48 *Rivers of Ice: Alpine Adventure and Glacier Action*, 1875

49 *Under the Waves; or, Diving in Deep Waters*, 1876

50 *The Settler and the Savage: Peace & War in South Africa*, 1877

51 *In the Track of the Troops: A Tale of Modern War*, 1878

52 *Jarwin and Cuffy*, 1878

53 *Philosopher Jack: A Tale of the Southern Seas*, 1879

54 *Six Months at the Cape: Letters to Periwinkle from South Africa*, 1879

55 *Post Haste: A Tale of Her Majesty's Mails*, 1880

The only other one that I discovered was *Martin Rattler*, which I also enjoyed. I am, of course, aware that in research for this book I ought to have read the remaining eighty-eight. But I didn't. And how anyone, in a pre-word-processor era, managed to write ninety books staggers my imagination, particularly when it took him less than twenty years.

Bard, The

The Bard is a title that is often and irritatingly given to **Shakespeare**. It is supposed to mark him out as poetically supreme, but since he is incandescently poetically supreme, there seems no need for the title.

I believe the Welsh also use the term in quaint festivals called eisteddfods, but since the head of the Gorsedd of Bards is the Archdruid, I think that we can ignore such Celtic make-believe.

The real reason that *The Bard* appears in this book is because it is the title of a poem by Thomas Gray. Few people read Gray today, and when they do, they tend to drowse over *Elegy Written in a Country Churchyard*. You are, however, unlikely to drowse over *The Bard* which begins in the liveliest of fashions:

> 'Ruin seize thee, ruthless King!
> Confusion on thy banners wait!
> Tho' fanned by Conquest's crimson wing,
> They mock the air with idle state.
> Helm, nor hauberk's twisted mail,
> Nor e'en thy virtues, Tyrant, shall avail
> To save thy secret soul from nightly fears,
> From Cambria's curse, from Cambria's tears!'
> Such were the sounds that o'er the crested pride
> Of the first Edward scattered wild dismay,
> As down the steep of Snowdon's shaggy side
> He wound with toilsome march his long array.
> Stout Glo'ster stood aghast in speechless trance:
> 'To arms!' cried Mortimer, and couched his quiv'ring lance.

I'm not claiming that *The Bard* is a great poem, but it is an enjoyable one, ought to be better known than it is, and will probably give you pleasure if you now read the rest of it.

bardolatry

This word is used to describe excessive praise for the works of William Shakespeare. Since it is impossible to praise the works of Shakespeare excessively, the word has no utility.

bathos

Bathos is most people's favourite literary technique because it is always funny and always accidental. Bathos occurs when something important and significant is linked with something else that is trivial. The result is a disjunction that is comic. 'The ballerina rose gracefully *en pointe* and extended one slender leg behind her, like a dog at a fire hydrant.'

Bawden, Nina (1925–)

Nina Bawden has written both adult and children's fiction; she appears here because her 1973 novel, *Carrie's War*, is a genuinely moving creation.

Beckett, Samuel (1906–89)

Beckett was an Irish-born playwright and novelist, but in the popular mind is associated with just one play, *Waiting for Godot*, first produced in French in 1953 and in English in 1955. This play attracted considerable attention because nothing whatsoever happens in it. At the beginning of the play, two tramps, Vladimir and Estragon, are waiting for Godot. Estragon is trying to pull off his boot. He gives up, and then Estragon enters. Once again, Estragon tries to remove his footwear:

ESTRAGON: (*giving up again*) Nothing to be done.

VLADIMIR: (*advancing with short, stiff strides, legs wide apart*) I'm beginning to come round to that opinion. All my life I've tried to put it from me, saying Vladimir, be reasonable, you haven't yet tried everything. And I resumed the struggle. (*He broods, musing on the struggle. Turning to Estragon*) So there you are again.

ESTRAGON: Am I?

VLADIMIR: I'm glad to see you back. I thought you were gone for ever.

ESTRAGON: Me too.

VLADIMIR: Together again at last! We'll have to celebrate this. But how? (*He reflects.*) Get up till I embrace you.

ESTRAGON: (*irritably*) Not now, not now.

VLADIMIR: (*hurt, coldly*) May one enquire where His Highness spent the night?

ESTRAGON: In a ditch.

VLADIMIR: (*admiringly*) A ditch! Where?

ESTRAGON: (*without gesture*) Over there.

VLADIMIR: And they didn't beat you?

ESTRAGON: Beat me? Certainly they beat me.

VLADIMIR: The same lot as usual?

ESTRAGON: The same? I don't know.

VLADIMIR: When I think of it . . . all these years . . . but for me . . . where would you be . . . (*Decisively*) You'd be nothing more than a little heap of bones at the present minute, no doubt about it.

ESTRAGON: And what of it?

VLADIMIR: (*gloomily*) It's too much for one man. (*Pause. Cheerfully*) On the other hand what's the good of losing heart now, that's what I say. We should have thought of it a million years ago, in the nineties.

ESTRAGON: Ah stop blathering and help me off with this bloody thing.

And so it goes on. At the end of the play, they are still waiting for Godot. Yet Beckett did produce much, much more, including five novels, seven novellas, three volumes of poetry, five volumes of short stories, about twenty other plays, and sundry translations and works of non-fiction. He also valiantly aided the French Resistance during the Second World War. In almost every way, Beckett is a fascinating character and prodigious producer. Yet he has always remained the preserve of the academic intellectual. For the general public, Beckett's works are about as well known as the poetry of Coventry Patmore.

Bellow, Saul (1915–2005)

This American novelist was awarded the Nobel Prize for Literature in 1976. Novels like *Henderson the Rain King* (1959) and *Herzog* (1964) suggest that it might have been justified. But it was Bellow's third novel, *The Adventures of Augie March* (1953) that first attracted attention. This rich picaresque novel recounts the seemingly unconnected experiences of its hero in his quest for self-understanding. Augie March, the protagonist, is born into an immigrant Jewish family in Chicago before the Depression. Bellow's own parents were immigrants, having moved from Russia to Canada, and so, unsurprisingly, the novel deals with some of Bellow's own perceptions of the role of immigrants. Augie also, particularly in his love of women, reflects Bellow himself. In addition, Augie March has many similarities with Moses E. Herzog, the protagonist of the 1964 novel. Then in 1975 the novel *Humboldt's Gift* was awarded the Pulitzer Prize. Indeed, at Bellow's death in 2005, Philip Roth claimed that, 'The backbone of twentieth-century American literature has been provided by two novelists – **William Faulkner** and Saul Bellow. Together they are the **Melville**, Hawthorne, and **Twain** of the twentieth century.' Personally I think that this is an overstatement, particularly in view of the fact that Bellow never learnt from experience: he got married five times. As he himself said, 'All a writer has to do to get a woman is to say he's a writer. It's an aphrodisiac.' Obviously Bellow proclaimed himself to be a writer a fraction too often. But it was true. Bellow was a writer – and a very good one.

Bennett, Arnold (1867–1931)

Arnold Bennett is an enjoyable novelist who accomplished something that at first glance would appear to be impossible: he made the Potteries area of north Staffordshire appear to be interesting. It was in 1902 that Bennett wrote *Anna of the Five Towns*, the first of his novels centred round the five towns that together make up Stoke-on-Trent. (Actually there are six towns, but Bennett missed out Fenton, a very understandable omission.) After *Anna*, Bennett seemed to write non-stop, both fiction and non-fiction, and his best novels, *The Old Wives' Tale* and *Clayhanger*, are very good. Bennett, though, wrote for money and not posterity. As a result, some of his work is distinctly uninspired. Don't, therefore, feel ashamed if you don't read all of his novels. After all, it was Bennett himself who said, 'Does there, I wonder, exist a being who has read all, or approximately all, that the person of average culture is supposed to have read, and that not to have read is a social sin? If such a being does exist, surely he is an old, a very old man.'

Betjeman, Sir John (1906–84)

Before I say anything else, just read this poem. It is called *Death in Leamington*:

> She died in the upstairs bedroom
>   By the light of the ev'ning star
> That shone through the plate glass window
>   From over Leamington Spa
>
> Beside her the lonely crochet
>   Lay patiently and unstirred,
> But the fingers that would have work'd it
>   Were dead as the spoken word.
>
> And Nurse came in with the tea-things
>   Breast high 'mid the stands and chairs –
> But Nurse was alone with her own little soul,
>   And the things were alone with theirs.
>
> She bolted the big round window,
>   She let the blinds unroll,
> She set a match to the mantle,
>   She covered the fire with coal.

And 'Tea!' she said in a tiny voice,
   'Wake up! It's nearly *five*.'
Oh! Chintzy, chintzy cheeriness,
   Half dead and half alive!

Do you know that the stucco is peeling?
   Do you know that the heart will stop?
From those yellow Italianate arches
   Do you hear the plaster drop?

Nurse looked at the silent bedstead,
   At the grey, decaying face,
As the calm of a Leamington ev'ning
   Drifted into the place.

She moved the table of bottles
   Away from the bed to the wall;
And tiptoeing gently over the stairs
   Turned down the gas in the hall.

It will be no surprise to you to learn that John Betjeman wrote that poem, but what did you think about it? Clearly it had a number of extremely serious faults. To start with, it was relatively easy to understand, while we all know that poetry is supposed to be difficult. Secondly it was written in four-line verses that rhymed, and everybody knows that twentieth-century poetry doesn't rhyme. Thirdly, it has a very unsettling ambivalence about it. It is all so relaxed and comfortable, yet, by the end, one is left with an almost incongruous grief. Consequently, in the 1950s and 1960s, Betjeman was not a very highly regarded poet. After all, the general public tended to like him, and poetry can only be properly appreciated by Oxford intellectuals. Yet even when Betjeman was still alive, there were significant figures who were not ashamed to say that they enjoyed his poetry. **W. H. Auden** and **Philip Larkin** were among them. Now that Betjeman is safely dead, many more are saying that he wasn't bad. Hugo Williams, in an article in the *Guardian* in 2006, argued that, 'John Betjeman makes most modern poets look either desperately amateurish or desperately professional.' And this, of course, is part of the trouble. Betjeman has such a sure touch, and it all seems so easy, that most poets look incompetent beside him. But because it does look so easy, and because Betjeman never seems solemn, he can't really be a serious poet. For instance, you can't write a hymn like this:

> The Church's Restoration
> In eighteen-eighty-three
> Has left for contemplation
> Not what there used to be.
> How well the ancient woodwork
> Looks round the Rect'ry hall,
> Memorial of the good work
> Of him who plann'd it all.
>
> He who took down the pew-ends
> And sold them anywhere
> But kindly spared a few ends
> Work'd up into a chair.
> O worthy persecution
> Of dust! O hue divine!
> O cheerful substitution,
> Thou varnishéd pitch-pine!
>
> Church furnishing! Church furnishing!
> Sing art and crafty praise!
> He gave the brass for burnishing
> He gave the thick red baize,
> He gave the new addition,
> Pull'd down the dull old aisle,
> – To pave the sweet transition
> He gave th' encaustic tile.
>
> Of marble brown and veinéd
> He did the pulpit make;
> He order'd windows stainéd
> Light red and crimson lake.
> Sing on, with hymns uproarious,
> Ye humble and aloof,
> Look up! and oh how glorious
> He has restored the roof!

There are not many poems that make me laugh out loud, but that one does. But Betjeman is certainly more than just a jester. Try reading him, and make up your own mind.

Bible, the

For two reasons, the Bible is an indispensable source for anyone interested in English literature. For many centuries, Britain was a Christian country. As a result, much of her literature is imbued with the characters and stories contained within the Bible. Secondly, in 1611 there was produced what was known as the **Authorised Version** of the Bible. This happens to be a major work of literature itself. Just look at how the Gospel of St John opens:

1 In the beginning was the Word, and the Word was with God, and the Word was God.
2 The same was in the beginning with God.
3 All things were made by him; and without him was not any thing made that was made.
4 In him was life; and the life was the light of men.
5 And the light shineth in darkness; and the darkness comprehended it not.
6 There was a man sent from God, whose name was John.
7 The same came for a witness, to bear witness of the Light, that all men through him might believe.
8 He was not that Light, but was sent to bear witness of that Light.
9 That was the true Light, which lighteth every man that cometh into the world.
10 He was in the world, and the world was made by him, and the world knew him not.
11 He came unto his own, and his own received him not.
12 But as many as received him, to them gave he power to become the sons of God, even to them that believe on his name:
13 Which were born, not of blood, nor of the will of the flesh, nor of the will of man, but of God.
14 And the Word was made flesh, and dwelt among us, (and we beheld his glory, the glory as of the only begotten of the Father,) full of grace and truth.

Writing as good as this almost secures conversion by itself. Certainly the Devil doesn't have anything as good.

bibliography

This is a list of books. You can have a bibliography of all the books written by **Anthony Trollope**, a bibliography of all the books in print on the topic of mermaids or a bibliography of all the books in your study.

Big Brother

In **Orwell**'s novel *Nineteen Eighty-Four*, there is a presiding presence who never actually appears, but who permeates the novel. He is Big Brother. He has become a symbol of modern times, and in an age of ID cards and surveillance cameras, most citizens these days think that Big Brother is watching them. He appears in this dictionary because he has become an **allusion** that one cannot do without.

'Billy Budd'

This is the title of a magical short story by **Herman Melville**. I mention it here because the entry on Melville is somewhat grudging, but this melodramatic but totally absorbing story deserves celebration. I also note that the Wordsworth *Companion to Literature in English* calls it a short novel. I leave it to you to decide whether it is a long short story or a short novel.

biography

A biography is the story of someone's life. Most biographies recount the story of someone who is dead. There are a number of problems with this:

a) the person concerned is dead, and consequently the biographer cannot consult the person who is the best informed;

b) most of the written evidence has been lost, burnt or hidden;

c) most or all of the subject's friends have also died, and so cannot be consulted;

d) the biographer either wants to praise or to defame the person whose biography they are writing. The biographer is therefore not objective enough to do an adequate job.

Occasionally a biography is written about someone who is still alive. It is consequently impossible to gain a true perspective, and equally impossible to escape from bias. We may therefore confidently assume that 'biography' is a synonym for 'fiction'. There has also been a tendency in the late twentieth century for biographies to be produced of men and women who still have most of their lives to live. Archibald Carter, aged twenty-one, scored the winning goal for Tranmere Rovers against Bristol City in the 2nd round of the FA Cup. He accordingly produces a biography entitled *Shooting Scores*, despite the fact that Archibald writes English as well as my fifteen-stone grandmother dances *Swan Lake*. And people buy this nonsense. Biographies have become the literary heroin of the twenty-first century.

Bishop Blougram's Apology

This is the title of one of **Browning**'s most successful **dramatic monologues**. It is of particular interest because after listening to the bishop's reflections one still doesn't know the extent of his faith. The poem is a masterpiece of theological ambiguity.

> No more wine? then we'll push back chairs and talk.
> A final glass for me, though: cool, i' faith!
> We ought to have our Abbey back, you see.
> It's different, preaching in basilicas,
> And doing duty in some masterpiece
> Like this of brother Pugin's, bless his heart!
> I doubt if they're half baked, those chalk rosettes,
> Ciphers and stucco-twiddlings everywhere;
> It's just like breathing in a lime-kiln: eh?
> These hot long ceremonies of our church
> Cost us a little – oh, they pay the price,
> You take me – amply pay it! Now, we'll talk.
>
> So, you despise me, Mr Gigadibs?
> No deprecation – nay, I beg you, sir!
> Beside 'tis our engagement: don't you know,
> I promised, if you'd watch a dinner out,
> We'd see truth dawn together? – truth that peeps
> Over the glasses' edge when dinner's done . . .

Black Beauty

This is a children's novel of 1877 written by **Anna Sewell**. As a child, I loved it, and it is certainly one of the best animal stories ever written.

black comedy

In a sense, this is an oxymoron because, by definition, a comedy is amusing and light-hearted, the opposite of black. The term has been employed, however, to describe a comedy that has, at its core, something far from comic. The novel *Catch-22* by Joseph Heller is very funny, but it hinges on the fact that, in order to stopping flying, you have to prove that you are insane, but if you submit being insane as your reason, that in itself proves that you are sane, and consequently you will not be grounded.

Blake, William (1757–1827)

The trouble with dictionaries and encyclopaedias is that one never has the space to do one's subjects justice. Of few is this more true than of William Blake. He was a Christian, a mystic, an artist, a poet and a political radical. The man was complex, contradictory and impossible, but he could produce lyrics as simple as this:

The Lamb

Little lamb, who made thee?
Dost thou know who made thee,
Gave thee life, and bid thee feed
By the stream and o'er the mead;
Gave thee clothing of delight,
Softest clothing, woolly, bright;
Gave thee such a tender voice,
Making all the vales rejoice?
Little lamb, who made thee?
Dost thou know who made thee?

Little lamb, I'll tell thee;
Little lamb, I'll tell thee:
He is called by thy name,
For He calls Himself a Lamb.
He is meek, and He is mild,
He became a little child.
I a child, and thou a lamb,
We are called by His name.
Little lamb, God bless thee!
Little lamb, God bless thee!

Yet in another lyric, *The Clod and the Pebble*, things are not quite so simple:

> 'Love seeketh not itself to please,
> Nor for itself hath any care,
> But for another gives its ease,
> And builds a heaven in hell's despair.'
>
> So sung a little clod of clay,
> Trodden with the cattle's feet,
> But a pebble of the brook
> Warbled out these metres meet:
>
> 'Love seeketh only Self to please,
> To bind another to its delight,
> Joys in another's loss of ease,
> And builds a hell in heaven's despite.'

Yet in both those poems, Blake manages, by the simplest of means, to create something that is moving and rich. It all looks so easy, yet it takes no more than the fingers of one hand to count the English poets who have been able to do it. Try it yourself.

But, master of English lyrics though Blake was, much of his other poetic work is formidably obscure. The so-called prophetic books – *The Song of Los, The First Book of Urizen, Vala, or the Four Zoas*, etc. – appear to defy explication. Here is the opening of *Vala*:

> Four Mighty Ones are in every Man; a Perfect Unity
> Cannot Exist. but from the Universal Brotherhood of Eden
> The Universal Man. To Whom be Glory Evermore Amen
> What are the Natures of those Living Creatures the Heavenly
>   Father only
> Knoweth no Individual Knoweth nor Can know in all Eternity
> Los was the fourth immortal starry one, & in the Earth
> Of a bright Universe Empery attended day & night
> Days & nights of revolving joy, Urthona was his name
> In Eden; in the Auricular Nerves of Human life
> Which is the Earth of Eden, he his Emanations propagated
> Fairies of Albion afterwards Gods of the Heathen, Daughter of
>   Beulah Sing
> His fall into Division & his Resurrection to Unity
> His fall into the Generation of Decay & Death & his Regeneration
>   by the Resurrection from the dead

Begin with Tharmas Parent power. darkning in the West
Lost! Lost! Lost! are my Emanations Enion O Enion
We are become a Victim to the Living We hide in secret
I have hidden Jerusalem in Silent Contrition O Pity Me
I will build thee a Labyrinth also O pity me O Enion
Why hast thou taken sweet Jerusalem from my inmost Soul
Let her Lay secret in the Soft recess of darkness & silence
It is not Love I bear to Enitharmon It is Pity
She hath taken refuge in my bosom & I cannot cast her out.

In my edition of Blake, there are about another 170 pages of this, not to mention another 600 or so devoted to the other prophetic books. Blake is not easy, so it might be wise, after you have read his marvellous *Songs of Innocence* and *Songs of Experience*, from which my first two examples came, gently to bypass Blake.

blank verse

This sounds like a contradiction in terms: if it is verse, it self-evidently cannot be blank. In fact, of course, it simply means verse, normally in iambic pentameters, that does not rhyme. There are, after all, disadvantages to poetry that rhymes. There is an inevitable artificiality about a rhyme, and that artificiality can militate against realism. In **Shakespeare**'s play *The Merchant of Venice*, Shylock has just been asked to lend some money to Antonio. This is what Shylock has to say:

Signior Antonio, many a time and oft
In the Rialto you have rated me
About my moneys and my usances:
Still have I borne it with a patient shrug,
For sufferance is the badge of all our tribe.
You call me misbeliever, cut-throat dog,
And spit upon my Jewish gaberdine,
And all for use of that which is mine own.
Well then, it now appears you need my help:
Go to, then; you come to me, and you say
'Shylock, we would have moneys' – you say so;
You, that did void your rheum upon my beard
And foot me as you spurn a stranger cur
Over your threshold: moneys is your suit.
What should I say to you? Should I not say

> 'Hath a dog money? is it possible
> A cur can lend three thousand ducats?' Or
> Shall I bend low and in a bondman's key,
> With bated breath, and whispering humbleness,
> Say this: 'Fair sir, you spit on me on Wednesday last;
> You spurn'd me such a day; another time
> You call'd me dog; and for these courtesies
> I'll lend you thus much moneys'?

That is blank verse. Now imagine that this speech was in rhyming verse. It might go something like this:

> Signior Antonio, many a time and oft
> Have you brandished loudly aloft
> Your dislike of my practice of lending
> To men who approach with knees bending.
> These insults I've borne with a patient shrug,
> Though it's never made me give you a hug
> When you have called me a cut-throat dog
> Or spat on me 'cause you thought me a frog.

I won't continue, but I'm sure that you get the point.

Bleak House

This is a novel by **Charles Dickens**, a novel that is well worth reading. Its heroine, Esther Summerson, is tediously wet, and the plot of the novel makes a Gilbert and Sullivan operetta look like social realism, yet for all that, *Bleak House* is a powerful work. It is a savage and justified attack on the legal system, has in Mr Chadband, Jo, Miss Flite, Krook, the Dedlocks and others some memorable characters, and is touched throughout by the unmistakable genius of Dickens. It opens with one of Dickens's most evocative pictures:

> London. Michaelmas Term lately over, and the Lord Chancellor sitting in Lincoln's Inn Hall. Implacable November weather. As much mud in the streets as if the waters had but newly retired from the face of the earth, and it would not be wonderful to meet a Megalosaurus, forty feet long or so, waddling like an elephantine lizard up Holborn Hill. Smoke lowering down from chimney-pots, making a soft black drizzle, with flakes of soot in it as big as full-grown snow-flakes – gone into mourning, one might imagine, for

the death of the sun. Dogs, undistinguishable in mire. Horses, scarcely better; splashed to their very blinkers. Foot passengers, jostling one another's umbrellas in a general infection of ill-temper, and losing their foot-hold at street-corners, where tens of thousands of other foot passengers have been slipping and sliding since the day broke (if the day ever broke), adding new deposits to the crust upon crust of mud, sticking at those points tenaciously to the pavement, and accumulating at compound interest.

Fog everywhere. Fog up the river, where it flows among green aits and meadows; fog down the river, where it rolls defiled among the tiers of shipping and the waterside pollutions of a great (and dirty) city. Fog on the Essex marshes, fog on the Kentish heights. Fog creeping into the cabooses of collier-brigs; fog lying out on the yards, and hovering in the rigging of great ships; fog drooping on the gunwales of barges and small boats. Fog in the eyes and throats of ancient Greenwich pensioners, wheezing by the firesides of their wards; fog in the stem and bowl of the afternoon pipe of the wrathful skipper, down in his close cabin; fog cruelly pinching the toes and fingers of his shivering little 'prentice boy on deck. Chance people on the bridges peeping over the parapets into a nether sky of fog, with fog all round them, as if they were up in a balloon, and hanging in the misty clouds.

Gas looming through the fog in divers places in the streets, much as the sun may, from the spongey fields, be seen to loom by husband-man and ploughboy. Most of the shops lighted two hours before their time – as the gas seems to know, for it has a haggard and unwilling look.

That opening is so powerful that it has seduced many critics into thinking that the fog is a structural image in the novel. It isn't, but confronted by writing like that, who cares?

bluestocking

This is a label for a literary woman. If you are female and given to studying almost any branch of scholarship, you are likely to be called a bluestocking. The term does have a slight tinge of contempt associated with it, as if the woman concerned ought to be doing something more profitable like nursing children or preparing meals.

Blyton, Enid (1897–1968)

When I was at school, there was a slight disapproval attached to the children's fiction of Enid Blyton. Her vocabulary was too limited, her attitudes were too snobbish, and so on. The trouble was that children kept reading her books. They still do so, and I gather that it is now sensibly taken that it is better that children should get into the habit of reading, even if not everything they read measures up to the standards of the liberal *Guardian*-reading adults. And with Enid Blyton, there is plenty to read. She produced books at such a rate that some people during her lifetime believed that she employed a team of fellow writers. She didn't.

bowdlerise

If you bowdlerise something, you remove from it anything that might offend a maiden aunt. This operation was undertaken for the works of **Shakespeare** by a Dr Thomas Bowdler in 1818. Since Shakespeare is just about the most sexually overt writer in the English language, his plays are much shorter in the Bowdler version. In addition, Shakespeare and his characters were made to conform to Christian standards. Thus oaths were sanitised, and Bowdler had Ophelia, for example, drowned by accident rather than committing suicide. Most intelligent and educated people thought, even in 1818, that the idea was idiotic, but by 1850, eleven editions of Bowdler's Shakespeare had none the less been printed and the poet **Algernon Swinburne** said: 'More nauseous and foolish cant was never chattered than that which would deride the memory or depreciate the merits of Bowdler. No man ever did better service to Shakespeare than the man who made it possible to put him into the hands of intelligent and imaginative children.'

This saddens me. Swinburne was not a stupid man, but this is a stupid remark.

Boz

This was an early pseudonym of **Charles Dickens**, apparently derived from his own infant mispronunciation of Moses.

Bradbury, Malcolm (1932–)

Bradbury began as an amusing novelist, who, in his first two novels, *Eating People is Wrong* (1959) and *Stepping Westward* (1965), drew on the inexhaustible comic potentials of academic life. However, as Professor of American Studies at the University of East Anglia, he has, since the 1970s, presided over a university course in creative writing. This has produced some excellent writers, though it is, of course, impossible to say whether or not the UEA course had anything to do with their success.

Braine, John (1922–86)

Braine is another unfortunate who is only remembered for one novel, *Room at the Top* (1957) though he did write five others.

Brewer's Dictionary of Phrase and Fable

No home should be without this invaluable book. Yet it is surprisingly difficult to say precisely what *Brewer's Dictionary of Phrase and Fable* actually is. It claims to catalogue words that have a tale to tell, but that definition is so amorphous as to tell us nothing. Others have said that it is reference book that you turn to when you've failed to find data anywhere else! Let me just list twenty consecutive entries from the letter A:

Abecedarian	Abo
Abelard and Héloise	Abolitionists
Abelites	Abominable Snowman
Abenezra	Abomination of Desolation
Abhidhamma	Abou-Bekr
Abhorrers	Abou Hassan
Abif	About the size of it
Abigail	Above-board
Abingdon Law	Ab ovo
Abiogenesis	Abracadabra

Now you have to admit that such a reference book is irresistible. Carol Rumens in a review of the book in the *Independent* newspaper for 12 September 2008 describes it as the book of a lifetime, and particularises the letter M:

Dip in, and swim around the letter M. What kaleidoscopic scenery extends from Maat to Mount Zion, from Mugwump to Myton. The explanation of Mugwump alerts us to another reason why this Dictionary is a Johnsonian delight. 'A word borrowed from the Algonquin, meaning one who thinks and acts independently,' Brewer begins. This sounds approving, we mugwumps note. But then comes a sharp and timeless caution: 'turncoats are mugwumps, and all political Pharisees whose party vote cannot be relied on'.

Surely, if you don't already possess a *Brewer*, you cannot resist getting one now. In addition, the original compiler was called Ebenezer Cobham Brewer. No wonder the book is essential.

Bridges, Robert (1844–1930)

If being set to music were a criterion of quality, then Robert Bridges would be a major English poet, having been harmonised by Hubert Parry, Gustav Holst and Gerald Finzi. Yet, despite being made Poet Laureate in 1913, Bridges has never been massively popular. Eric Ormsby attempts an explanation of this fact, though it is difficult to be sure how serious he is being:

> Robert Bridges is perhaps the most conspicuous example of that faintly alarming figure, the happy poet. His strenuously archaic diction, his eccentric devotion to syllabic and quantitative measures, his bizarre attempts to simplify English spelling, as well as his unvaryingly placid manner, all obstruct the appreciation of his genius; but it is his happiness, a matter of conviction as well as temperament, that most repels contemporary readers. We prefer our poets to be wracked with anguish or, at least, chronically depressed and raving on Paxil. We want dark nights of the soul from our bards, not breezy afternoons. Happiness looks suspect; it appears obtuse, oblivious, smug. Of all states of mind, happiness is the most fleeting; it ignores past and future to celebrate the ephemeral moment; it obviates memory as well as prophecy. In this sense, Bridges's poetry seems not simply dated but dateless.

Consequently it seems better to let you make the judgement. Here is a poem by Bridges entitled 'Absence':

> When my love was away,
> Full three days were not sped,
> I caught my fancy astray
> Thinking if she were dead,
>
> And I alone, alone:
> It seem'd in my misery
> In all the world was none
> Ever so lone as I.

I wept; but it did not shame
Nor comfort my heart: away
I rode as I might, and came
To my love at close of day.

The sight of her still'd my fears,
My fairest-hearted love:
And yet in her eyes were tears:
Which when I question'd of,

'O now thou art come,' she cried,
' 'Tis fled: but I thought today
I never could here abide,
If thou wert longer away.'

Who knows, you might be tempted to try some more, though the major service to English literature performed by Robert Bridges lies in the fact that, in 1918, he published the collected poetry of **Gerard Manley Hopkins**. It is interesting that the 4th edition of the Sir Paul Harvey version of *The Oxford Companion to English Literature* (1967) doesn't mention this fact at all, while the Margaret Drabble version of 2000 does. We can deduce that in the thirty-three years between 1967 and 2000, the reputation of Bridges went down, while that of Hopkins went up. I wonder what will be the state of play by the time this book is published.

Bridges is also known for his theory of elision, a theory that he developed while working on a prosodic analysis of **Milton**'s poems. I only mention this because it would make a superb question in your local pub quiz; no one could answer it, and you would possibly be lynched.

Brighton Rock

This is a novel by **Graham Greene**, published in 1938. I suspect that it is just about the most depressing novel that I have ever read. N.B. That is not at all the same as saying it is a bad novel.

Brontës, the

The Brontës are a west Yorkshire industry. In a hilly village called Haworth, there lived a collection of strange eccentrics. Three of them, Anne, Charlotte and Emily, wrote novels, and, ever since, those novels have been plumbed for Freudian obsessions, Jungian archetypes, York-shire folk perversions and secret-service ciphers. However, at least two of the novels, *Villette* (1853) by Charlotte and *Wuthering Heights* (1847) by Emily, show evidence of quality, and you are likely to enjoy them. Do not, however, join the Brontë industry without first gaining a degree in psychology. **Elizabeth Gaskell** wrote a biography of Charlotte and it was published in 1857. It helped create the myth of a doomed family living in romantic solitude. Anne and Emily died of tuberculosis, and Charlotte, desperate and married to a man she despised, starved herself to death while pregnant.

Browning, Elizabeth Barrett (1806–61)

The story of Elizabeth Barrett Browning, her tyrannical father and her marriage to **Robert Browning** are well known, having been subjected to the Hollywood treatment. Yet most people are almost unaware of her poetry. In her day, however, Elizabeth Barrett was much esteemed, and, in 1850, when **Wordsworth** died, she was seriously in the running to replace him as Poet Laureate. In that year, Elizabeth published her Petrarchan **sonnets**, *Sonnets from the Portuguese*, poems written during her courtship by Robert. They were very popular, and one can see why:

> How do I love thee? Let me count the ways.
> I love thee to the depth and breadth and height
> My soul can reach, when feeling out of sight
> For the ends of Being and ideal Grace.
> I love thee to the level of everyday's
> Most quiet need, by sun and candlelight.
> I love thee freely, as men strive for Right;
> I love thee purely, as they turn from Praise.
> I love thee with the passion put to use
> In my old griefs, and with my childhood's faith.
> I love thee with a love I seemed to lose
> With my lost saints – I love thee with the breath,
> Smiles, tears, of all my life! – and, if God choose,
> I shall but love thee better after death.

It is surely impossible not to be touched by this. There are many other impressive pieces of work too.

At about the same time, E. B.Browning wrote *Casa Guidi Windows*, a beautifully poised and passionate piece of writing, 1,999 lines in length.

In 1847, Florence had its civil liberties restored by Grand Duke Leopold II, and E.B.B., in delight, wrote Part One of the poem. She describes Florence memorably:

> I can but muse upon the shore
> Of golden Arno as it shoots away
> Straight through the heart of Florence, 'neath the four
> Bent bridges, seeming to strain off like bows,
> And tremble, while the arrowy undertide
> Shoots on and cleaves the marble as it goes,
> And strikes up palace-walls on either side
> And froths the cornice out . . .

The liberties of Florence, however, were not maintained, and in 1850 Elizabeth mourned this fact by writing Part Two. Both parts were published in 1851.

Much the longest of Elizabeth's poems is *Aurora Leigh*. Published in 1857, it comprises 11,000 lines of blank verse tracing the life and growth of a female poet. It has frequently been singled out for praise as an early example of **feminism**, but this, of course, says nothing about its poetic qualities. On that, there is much division of opinion. Clearly I cannot quote all 11,000 lines, but here are the opening 28.

> Of writing many books there is no end;
> And I who have written much in prose and verse
> For others' uses, will write now for mine –
> Will write my story for my better self,
> As when you paint your portrait for a friend,
> Who keeps it in a drawer and looks at it
> Long after he has ceased to love you, just
> To hold together what he was and is.
> I, writing thus, am still what men call young;
> I have not so far left the coasts of life
> To travel inland, that I cannot hear
> That murmur of the outer Infinite
> Which unweaned babies smile at in their sleep
> When wondered at for smiling; not so far,
> But still I catch my mother at her post
> Beside the nursery-door, with finger up,
> 'Hush, hush – here's too much noise!' while her sweet eyes

Leap forward, taking part against her word
In the child's riot. Still I sit and feel
My father's slow hand, when she had left us both,
Stroke out my childish curls across his knee;
And hear Assunta's daily jest (she knew
He liked it better than a better jest)
Inquire how many golden scudi went
To make such ringlets. O my father's hand,
Stroke the poor hair down, stroke it heavily –
Draw, press the child's head closer to thy knee!
I'm still too young, too young to sit alone.

Does that tempt you to go on and read the rest? Personally, I am not convinced that it is a poetic masterpiece, but it is far from dull and is of very considerable psychological interest.

Browning, Robert (1812–89)

Robert Browning was a poet, and at his best, an extremely good one. He is also famous for having married another poet, **Elizabeth Barrett**, who lived as a semi-invalid and virtual prisoner in her father's house in Wimpole Street. Gradually a significant romance developed between them, leading to their secret marriage and flight in 1846.

Browning's poetry was known to the cognoscenti from fairly early on in his life, but he remained relatively obscure as a poet till his middle age. In 1855, when Browning published *Men and Women*, now regarded as containing most of his greatest work, not much notice was taken. It was not until 1868 when Browning published *The Ring and the Book* that he really gained significant recognition. This is odd because *The Ring and the Book* is massively long (over 20,000 lines), is in **blank verse**, comprises twelve books, and tells the same story ten times. It is actually quite impressive, but it requires considerable stamina.

Today Browning is probably most famous for his **dramatic monologues**, a form at which he excelled. In these poems, someone tells a story or recounts a situation. Clearly much of the interest lies in the story being told, but Browning cleverly adds another layer of interest. As the story is being told, we slowly begin to piece together some understanding of the person telling the story, and that slowly begins to be even more absorbing than the actual narration. Try reading 'My Last Duchess' and see what you make of it:

That's my last Duchess painted on the wall,
Looking as if she were alive. I call
That piece a wonder, now: Frà Pandolf's hands
Worked busily a day, and there she stands.
Will 't please you sit and look at her? I said
'Frà Pandolf' by design, for never read
Strangers like you that pictured countenance,
The depth and passion of its earnest glance,
But to myself they turned (since none puts by
The curtain I have drawn for you, but I)
And seemed as they would ask me, if they durst,
How such a glance came there; so, not the first
Are you to turn and ask thus. Sir, 'twas not
Her husband's presence only, called that spot
Of joy into the Duchess' cheek: perhaps
Frà Pandolf chanced to say, 'Her mantle laps
Over my lady's wrist too much,' or, 'Paint
Must never hope to reproduce the faint
Half-flush that dies along her throat:' such stuff
Was courtesy, she thought, and cause enough
For calling up that spot of joy. She had
A heart – how shall I say? – too soon made glad,
Too easily impressed; she liked whate'er
She looked on, and her looks went everywhere.
Sir, 'twas all one! My favour at her breast,
The dropping of the daylight in the West,
The bough of cherries some officious fool
Broke in the orchard for her, the white mule
She rode with round the terrace – all and each
Would draw from her alike the approving speech,
Or blush, at least. She thanked men – good! but thanked
Somehow – I know not how – as if she ranked
My gift of a nine-hundred-years-old name
With anybody's gift. Who'd stoop to blame
This sort of trifling? Even had you skill
In speech – (which I have not) – to make your will
Quite clear to such an one, and say, 'Just this
Or that in you disgusts me; here you miss,
Or there exceed the mark' – and if she let

Herself be lessoned so, nor plainly set
Her wits to yours, forsooth, and made excuse,
– E'en then would be some stooping; and I choose
Never to stoop. Oh, sir, she smiled, no doubt,
Whene'er I passed her; but who passed without
Much the same smile? This grew; I gave commands;
Then all smiles stopped together. There she stands
As if alive. Will't please you rise? We'll meet
The company below then. I repeat,
The Count your master's known munificence
Is ample warrant that no just pretence
Of mine for dowry will be disallowed;
Though his fair daughter's self, as I avowed
At starting, is my object. Nay, we'll go
Together down, sir. Notice Neptune, though,
Taming a sea-horse, thought a rarity,
Which Claus of Innsbruck cast in bronze for me!

It is a chilling thought that the Duke is now negotiating for another wife as we slowly realise what happened to the last duchess. Perhaps the dramatic monologues are so esteemed because they appeal to the amateur detective in us.

Bunyan, John (1628–88)

Somewhat unfairly, Bunyan is known only for one book, *The Pilgrim's Progress*, and even there, many more have heard of it than have read it. As a positively devout non-Christian, the 'message' of the book is distinctly alien to me, yet Bunyan's style impels one to read on:

As I walked through the wilderness of this world, I lighted on a certain place where was a den [the gaol], and I laid me down in that place to sleep: and as I slept, I dreamed a dream. I dreamed, and behold I saw a man clothed with rags standing in a certain place, with his face from his own house, a book in his hand, and a great burden upon his back. [Isaiah 64:6; Luke 14:33; Psalm 38:4] I looked, and saw him open the book, and read therein; and as he read, he wept and trembled; and, not being able longer to contain, he brake out with a lamentable cry, saying, 'What shall I do?' [Acts 2:37; 16:30–31; Hebrews 2:2–3]

In this plight, therefore, he went home, and restrained himself as long as he could, that his wife and children should not perceive his distress; but he could not be silent long, because that his trouble increased: wherefore at length he brake his mind to his wife and children; and thus he began to talk to them: 'O my dear wife,' said he, 'and you the children of my bowels, I, your dear friend, am in myself undone, by reason of a burden that lies hard upon me; moreover, I am for certain informed that this our city will be burned with fire from heaven, in which fearful overthrow, both myself, with thee, my wife, and you, my sweet babes, shall miserably come to ruin; except (the which yet I see not) some way of escape can be found, whereby we may be delivered.'

At this his relations were sore amazed; not for that they believed that what he had said to them was true, but because they thought that some frenzy distemper had got into his head; therefore, it drawing towards night, and they hoping that sleep might settle his brains, with all haste they got him to bed; but the night was as troublesome to him as the day: wherefore, instead of sleeping, he spent it in sighs and tears. So, when the morning was come, they would know how he did: he told them, 'Worse and worse.' He also set to talking to them again; but they began to be hardened. They also thought to drive away his distemper by harsh and surly conduct to him: sometimes they would deride; sometimes they would chide; and sometimes they would quite neglect him. Wherefore he began to retire himself to his chamber, to pray for and pity them, and also to condole his own misery. He would also walk solitarily in the fields, sometimes reading and sometimes praying; and thus for some days he spent his time.

Don't you now want to know what happens next? It has been claimed that *The Pilgrim's Progress* is one of the most fundamental works of English literature, so you can't claim to be an expert in English literature until you have read it.

Burney, Fanny (1752–1840)

Fanny Burney holds an honoured place in all literary histories because her diaries and letters give, among other things, first-hand accounts of Garrick and Johnson, but she makes an appearance in this volume because of the three novels she wrote, *Evelina* (1778), *Cecilia* (1782) and *Camilla* (1796). These are not great novels, but they are agreeable, and almost certainly influenced the writing of **Jane Austen**.

Burns, Robert (1759–96)

As you doubtless know, Robert Burns is a Scottish icon. How many Scots read his poetry, I have no idea, but every year there is Burns Night, providing yet another excuse for the inhabitants of Scotland to get drunk. The man whom they celebrate is so esteemed because he wrote much of his poetry in the Scots dialect, thereby rendering it incomprehensible to readers of English. Here is a typical example:

Address to a Haggis

Fair fa' your honest, sonsie face,
Great chieftain o' the puddin'-race!
Aboon them a' ye tak your place,
        Painch, tripe, or thairm:
Weel are ye wordy o' a grace
        As lang's my arm.

The groaning trencher there ye fill,
Your hurdies like a distant hill,
Your pin wad help to mend a mill
        In time o' need,
While thro your pores the dews distil
        Like amber bead.

His knife see rustic Labour dight,
An' cut you up wi' ready seight,
Trenching your gushing entrails bright,
        Like onie ditch;
And then, O what a glorious sight,
        Warm-reekin', rich!

Then, horn for horn, they stretch an' strive:
Deil tak the hindmost, on they drive,
Till a' their weel-swall'd kytes belyve
        Are bent like drums;
The auld guidman, maist like to rive,
        'Bethankit' hums.

Is there that owre his French ragout,
Or olio that wad staw a sow,
Or fricassee wad mak her spew

Wi' perfect sconner,
Looks down wi' sneering, scornfu' view
On sic a dinner?

Poor devil! see him owre his trash,
As feckless as a wither'd rash,
His spindle shank a guid whip-lash,
His nieve a nit:
Thro' bloody flood or field to dash,
O how unfit!

But mark the Rustic, haggis-fed,
The trembling earth resounds his tread!
Clap in his walie nieve a blade,
He'll make it whissle;
An' legs, an' arms, an' heads will sned,
Like taps o' thrissle.

Ye Pow'rs, wha mak mankind your care,
And dish them out their bill o' fare,
Auld Scotland wants nae skinking ware
That jaups in luggies:
But, if ye wish her gratefu' prayer,
Gie her a Haggis!

Butler, Samuel (1835–1902)

The son of a clergyman and grandson of a bishop, it seems almost inevitable that Samuel Butler should be violently anti-religious. His autobiographical novel, *The Way of All Flesh*, published posthumously in 1903, indicates the strains of such an upbringing, though his earlier novel, *Erewhon* (which you have instantly realised is an anagram of 'Nowhere'), is perhaps a more amusing satire on nineteenth-century England and its religious tone.

Byron, George Gordon (1788–1824)

Most societies need a whipping boy, and for the opening years of the nineteenth century, Lord Byron performed that function. He was irreligious, immoral, politically radical and very amusing. He was also a poet of genius, though his comments on poetry were suitable downbeat:

I can never get people to understand that poetry is the expression of excited passion, and that there is no such thing as a life of passion any more than a continuous earthquake, or an eternal fever. Besides, who would ever shave themselves in such a state?

Lord Byron, in a letter to Thomas Moore, 5 July 1821

His greatest poem is probably **Don Juan**, but that is massively long. The one that I'm going to quote is called *The Destruction of Sennacherib*:

> The Assyrian came down like the wolf on the fold,
> And his cohorts were gleaming in purple and gold;
> And the sheen of their spears was like stars on the sea,
> When the blue wave rolls nightly on deep Galilee.
>
> Like the leaves of the forest when summer is green,
> That host with their banners at sunset were seen:
> Like the leaves of the forest when autumn hath blown,
> That host on the morrow lay withered and strown.
>
> For the Angel of Death spread his wings on the blast,
> And breathed in the face of the foe as he passed;
> And the eyes of the sleepers waxed deadly and chill,
> And their hearts but once heaved, and for ever grew still.
>
> And there lay the steed with his nostril all wide,
> But through it there rolled not the breath of his pride:
> And the foam of his gasping lay white on the turf,
> And cold as the spray of the rock-beating surf.
>
> And there lay the rider, distorted and pale,
> With the dew on his brow and the rust on his mail;
> And the tents were all silent, the banners alone,
> The lances unlifted, the trumpet unblown.
>
> And the widows of Ashur are loud in their wail,
> And the idols are broke in the temple of Baal;
> And the might of the Gentile, unsmote by the sword,
> Hath melted like snow in the glance of the Lord!

If the sheer brio and energy of that poem doesn't excite you, that is probably because you are dead.

C

caesura

A caesura is simply a break or pause in a line of poetry. It may be marked by a comma or just occur naturally anyway. Here are two lines from a **Shakespeare sonnet**. I mark the caesura with a /, and as you can see, one caesura has a comma and the other doesn't:

> This thou perceiv'st, / which makes thy love more strong,
> To love that well / which thou must leave ere long.

Cambridge School

This term is applied to a group of critics of the 1920s and 1930s who were associated with the University of Cambridge. They included **F. R. Leavis**, William Empson, I. A. Richards and Q. D. Leavis, and their emphasis on close analysis had a profound effect on literary criticism.

canon

Strictly speaking the word 'canon' refers to works which are accepted as being definitely by a specific author. Thus, *Macbeth* is accepted as being part of the canon of **Shakespeare**, while *The Spanish Tragedy* isn't, largely because it was written by Thomas Kyd, not William Shakespeare. However, the word is also often used as an approval word by literary snobs: 'Oh I don't think that anyone seriously accepts **D. H. Lawrence** as belonging to the canon.' This whole book is permeated by this form of supercilious arrogance.

cant

The word 'cant' has more than one meaning (see my *Dictionary of Homonyms*), but the meaning that secures the word's entry in this book is when it appertains to a particular idiom or slang of speech. For instance, pop musicians have their own vocabulary, as do pickpockets, lawyers, geologists and so on. You may, for instance, be blagging hard to the castle, though it's a dead hard mark and you can hardly front the gaff. (You may be travelling quickly to the rich man's house, though its only approachable by the expert tramp and you can hardly call at the entrance.)

Canterbury Tales, The

In the fourteenth century a man called **Geoffrey Chaucer** wrote an enormously long work called *The Canterbury Tales*, mostly in rhyming couplets. You have to imagine a group of people leaving London on a pilgrimage to Canterbury. To amuse themselves, the pilgrims take it in turns to tell a story as they make their slow way to Canterbury. Since this book is designed mostly for the non-academic reader, I shall tell you virtually nothing about Chaucer or his *Canterbury Tales*. This is because the English of the fourteenth century makes difficult reading today. Just have a look at how the Prologue to *The Canterbury Tales* begins:

> Whan that Aprille with his shoures soote
> The droghte of March hath perced to the roote,
> And bathed every veyne in swich licour,
> Of which vertu engendred is the flour;
> Whan Zephirus eek with his swete breeth
> Inspired hath in every holt and heeth
> The tendre croppes, and the yonge sonne
> Hath in the Ram his halfe cours y-ronne,
> And smale fowles maken melodye,
> That slepen al the nyght with open ye
> (So priketh hem nature in hir corage):
> Than longen folk to goon on pilgrimages,
> And palmers for to seken straunge strondes,
> To ferne halwes couthe in sondry londes;
> And specially, from every shires ende
> Of Engelond, to Caunterbury they wende,
> The holy blisful martir for to seke,
> That hem hath holpen, whan that they were seke.

This is recognisably English, but not English that we can read with ease today. Hence, although Chaucer and his poems are vitally important in the story of English literature, they will only get the most passing of references in this book, and English literature earlier than Chaucer won't even get that. In some ways, this is an outrage. *The Canterbury Tales* is a massive work, and Chaucer is a towering genius. Alas, his poetry is now the preserve of the specialist.

canto

It is difficult to give a precise definition of the work 'canto'. It is the sub-division of a long poem, but more exactitude is impossible. **Spenser** in *The Faerie Queene*, for example, divides his poem into books, and each book into 12 cantos, each canto consisting of 45 to 65 nine-line **stanzas**. **Byron**, though, in *Don Juan*, has cantos that range from 14 eight-line verses to over 200. However, although precision is impossible, it is perfectly possible to get through life without ever mentioning the word 'canto' anyway.

Caretaker, The

This is a play by **Harold Pinter** that was first performed and published in 1960. The play has only three characters and they indulge in incomprehensible 'conversation' while engaged in a covert struggle to establish rights in the shabby room in which the 'action' takes place. Eventually one of the characters, Davies, is ejected, and the two brothers, Aston and Mick, resume their squalid tenure. Although nothing happens, and all three characters are neurotic losers, *The Caretaker* exudes a worrying atmosphere of menace and mystery.

carpe diem

This is a Latin phrase which means 'seize the day' or, more com-prehensibly, 'do something worthwhile with every second of the day instead of just lounging around'. As you will immediately realise, it is a very dubious imperative. If you lounge around, you hurt no one, but if you do something that you regard as worthwhile, you can end up with a Middle-Eastern war, the collapse of a bank, a writ for libel or a whole range of undesirable side effects.

Carroll, Lewis (1832–98)

Strictly speaking, of course, Lewis Carroll should have no dates following his name because he did not exist. It was the pen name of Charles Lutwidge Dodgson, a lecturer in mathematics at Oxford University. A shy, stammering man, not at all at ease in the world, Dodgson astonished everyone (including himself) by publishing in 1865 one of the most magical books ever written. A child's fantasy tale, *Alice in Wonderland* (as it is now called) captivated the world. It was followed in 1871 by *Alice Through the Looking Glass*, and it is difficult to think of a more enchanting pair of books. In 1876 Carroll published a long nonsense poem, *The Hunting of the Snark*, and that too is a delight. The poem is subtitled 'An Agony in Eight Fits', and here is Fit 1:

'Just the place for a Snark!' the Bellman cried,
  As he landed his crew with care;
Supporting each man on the top of the tide
  By a finger entwined in his hair.

'Just the place for a Snark! I have said it twice:
  That alone should encourage the crew.
Just the place for a Snark! I have said it thrice:
  What I tell you three times is true.'

The crew was complete: it included a Boots –
  A maker of Bonnets and Hoods –
A Barrister, brought to arrange their disputes –
  And a Broker, to value their goods.

A Billiard-marker, whose skill was immense,
  Might perhaps have won more than his share –
But a Banker, engaged at enormous expense,
  Had the whole of their cash in his care.

There was also a Beaver, that paced on the deck,
  Or would sit making lace in the bow:
And had often (the Bellman said) saved them from wreck,
  Though none of the sailors knew how.

There was one who was famed for the number of things
  He forgot when he entered the ship:
His umbrella, his watch, all his jewels and rings,
  And the clothes he had bought for the trip.

He had forty-two boxes, all carefully packed,
  With his name painted clearly on each:
But, since he omitted to mention the fact,
  They were all left behind on the beach.

The loss of his clothes hardly mattered, because
  He had seven coats on when he came,
With three pairs of boots – but the worst of it was,
  He had wholly forgotten his name.

He would answer to 'Hi!' or to any loud cry,
    Such as 'Fry me!' or 'Fritter my wig!'
To 'What-you-may-call-um!' or 'What-was-his-name!'
    But especially 'Thing-um-a-jig!'

While, for those who preferred a more forcible word,
    He had different names from these:
His intimate friends called him 'Candle-ends',
    And his enemies 'Toasted-cheese'.

'His form is ungainly – his intellect small – '
    (So the Bellman would often remark) –
'But his courage is perfect! And that, after all,
    Is the thing that one needs with a Snark.'

He would joke with hyenas, returning their stare
    With an impudent wag of the head:
And he once went a walk, paw-in-paw, with a bear,
    'Just to keep up its spirits,' he said.

He came as a Baker: but owned, when too late –
    And it drove the poor Bellman half-mad –
He could only bake Bridecake – for which, I may state,
    No materials were to be had.

The last of the crew needs especial remark,
    Though he looked an incredible dunce:
He had just one idea – but, that one being 'Snark,'
    The good Bellman engaged him at once.

He came as a Butcher: but gravely declared,
    When the ship had been sailing a week,
He could only kill Beavers. The Bellman looked scared,
    And was almost too frightened to speak:

But at length he explained, in a tremulous tone,
    There was only one Beaver on board;
And that was a tame one he had of his own,
    Whose death would be deeply deplored.

The Beaver, who happened to hear the remark,
    Protested, with tears in its eyes,

That not even the rapture of hunting the Snark
    Could atone for that dismal surprise!

It strongly advised that the Butcher should be
    Conveyed in a separate ship:
But the Bellman declared that would never agree
    With the plans he had made for the trip:

Navigation was always a difficult art,
    Though with only one ship and one bell:
And he feared he must really decline, for his part,
    Undertaking another as well.

The Beaver's best course was, no doubt, to procure
    A second-hand dagger-proof coat –
So the Baker advised it – and next, to insure
    Its life in some Office of note:

This the Banker suggested, and offered for hire
    (On moderate terms), or for sale,
Two excellent Policies, one Against Fire,
    And one Against Damage from Hail.

Yet still, ever after that sorrowful day,
    Whenever the Butcher was by,
The Beaver kept looking the opposite way,
    And appeared unaccountably shy.

Lewis Carroll was a child's writer of genius. Charles Dodgson seems to have been a shy misfit.

catharsis

Basically this is a word for the purging effect that you experience when you witness a major tragedy. If, for instance, you see a good production of *King Lear*, you stumble out of the theatre feeling as if you have been emptied of all feeling and consciousness.

Cavalier poets

This title is given to a group of poets active during the reign of Charles I (1625–49). None of them were major poets – Richard Lovelace, Thomas Carew, Sir John Suckling, Edmund Waller and **Robert Herrick** are not exactly household names – but none the less they wrote some most agreeable verse. Sir John Suckling, for instance, probably produced this (although it is also attributed to Owen Felltham):

> When, Dearest, I but think of thee,
> Methinks all things that lovely be
>   Are present, and my soul delighted:
> For beauties that from worth arise
> Are like the grace of deities,
>   Still present with us, tho' unsighted.
>
> Thus while I sit and sigh the day
> With all his borrow'd lights away,
>   Till night's black wings do overtake me,
> Thinking on thee, thy beauties then,
> As sudden lights do sleeping men,
>   So they by their bright rays awake me.
>
> Thus absence dies, and dying proves
> No absence can consist with loves
>   That do partake of fair perfection:
> Since in the darkest night they may
> By love's quick motion find a way
>   To see each other by reflection.
>
> The waving sea can with each flood
> Bathe some high promont that hath stood
>   Far from the main up in the river:
> O think not then but love can do
> As much! for that's an ocean too,
>   Which flows not every day, but ever!

This has the emotional wallop of a butterfly, but it's quite pretty. Turn to Carew's 'Eternity of Love Protested', and it's much the same:

> How ill doth he deserve a lover's name,
>   Whose pale weak flame
>   Cannot retain
> His heat, in spite of absence or disdain;
> But doth at once, like paper set on fire,
>   Burn and expire;

True love can never change his seat,
Nor did her ever love, that could retreat.

That noble flame, which my breast keeps alive,
    Shall still survive
    When my soul's fled;
Nor shall my love die, when my body's dead,
That shall wait on me to the lower shade,
    And never fade:
My very ashes in their urn
Shall, like a hallow'd lamp, for ever burn.

The Cavalier poets are also quite useful. Since most people have never heard of them, you can pinch one of their poems, transcribe it in a Christmas card for your partner, and pretend that you wrote it for her (or him). I am, though, only indulging in this flippant suggestion because, as the reader knows, the ruse would only deceive a nincompoop.

Cecil, Lord David (1902–86)

For just over twenty years, Cecil occupied the chair of English Literature at New College, Oxford, and occupied himself in part by writing studies of **Cowper**, Lord Melbourne, **Hardy**, **Gray**, **Jane Austen** and others. These books are excellently relaxed and urbane studies, but not, perhaps, very intellectually probing. As a result, Cecil attracted the scorn and contempt of **F. R. Leavis**, a lecturer in English at Cambridge. It is unfortunate that both men are now remembered more for their mutual animosity than for their writings.

Chandler, Raymond (1888–1959)

Chandler was an American writer of detective fiction, and his disillusioned gumshoe, Philip Marlowe, takes a distinguished place in the detectives' hall of fame, alongside Holmes, Campion, Poirot and Dalziel.

Chatterton, Thomas (1752–70)

Since Chatterton committed suicide at the age of seventeen, he left a limited amount of work for us to consider. He did, however, invent Thomas Rowley, an entirely imaginary figure who was supposed to be a fifteenth-century poet. Chatterton accordingly wrote some poems in archaic English as if they were by the mythical Rowley. After Chatterton's death, some of these poems were discovered, and, because they do show signs of talent, Chatterton became for a while a tragic genius that the world had lost too early. **Keats** dedicated his poem *Endymion* to his memory, and **Wordsworth** described him as 'the marvellous boy'.

Chaucer, Geoffrey (c. 1343–1400)

Chaucer is virtually the earliest writer whose language is recognisably English. Have a look at the brief extract that I give under **Canterbury Tales**. The **clerihew** that Chris Baldick quotes in his *Concise Dictionary of Literary Terms* (1990) is not at all fair:

> Geoffrey Chaucer
> Could hardly have been coarser.
> But this never harmed the sales
> Of his *Canterbury Tales*.

Generally regarded as the greatest poet of the Middle Ages, Chaucer handled humour, dialogue, realism, characterisation and poetic virtuosity with very impressive skill.

Chesterton, Gilbert Keith (1874–1936)

It seems demeaning to call someone with the talents of G. K. Chesterton a minor writer, but that, alas, is what he is. He wrote literary criticism (and his book on **Dickens** is still worth reading), detective stories featuring the amiable cleric Father Brown, one or two novels, numerous articles and some poetry. The last is little read these days, and one entitled 'A Christmas Carol' indicates why:

> The Christ-child lay on Mary's lap,
> His hair was like a light.
> (O weary, weary were the world,
> But here is all aright.)

> The Christ-child lay on Mary's breast,
> His hair was like a star.
> (O stern and cunning are the kings,
> But here the true hearts are.)

> The Christ-child lay on Mary's heart,
> His hair was like a fire.
> (O weary, weary is the world,
> But here the world's desire.)

The Christ-child stood at Mary's knee,
His hair was like a crown.
And all the flowers looked up at Him,
And all the stars looked down.

Actually, even for Chesterton, the above poem is fairly dire, but one needs some amusement in life.

Christmas Carol, A

This is a Christmas book of 1843 by **Charles Dickens**. It is sentimental, ludicrously fanciful, and contains two main characters, Scrooge and Bob Cratchit, who possess the emotional complexity of amoebae. It is also virtually the best known of all Dickens's writings, appears to be widely loved, and is frequently transformed into a pantomime at Christmas. For something to be that well known, there has to be some creative spark that gives the work life. Just look at how Scrooge is described in the first chapter of the book:

Oh! But he was a tight-fisted hand at the grindstone, Scrooge! a squeezing, wrenching, grasping, scraping, clutching, covetous, old sinner! Hard and sharp as flint, from which no steel had ever struck out generous fire; secret, and self-contained, and solitary as an oyster. The cold within him froze his old features, nipped his pointed nose, shrivelled his cheek, stiffened his gait; made his eyes red, his thin lips blue; and spoke out shrewdly in his grating voice. A frosty rime was on his head, and on his eyebrows, and his wiry chin. He carried his own low temperature always about with him; he iced his office in the dogdays; and didn't thaw it one degree at Christmas.

External heat and cold had little influence on Scrooge. No warmth could warm, no wintry weather chill him. No wind that blew was bitterer than he, no falling snow was more intent upon its purpose, no pelting rain less open to entreaty. Foul weather didn't know where to have him. The heaviest rain, and snow, and hail, and sleet could boast of the advantage over him in only one respect. They often 'came down' handsomely, and Scrooge never did.

This may not be the greatest writing, but it has a vitality, an energy, and a verve that is unmistakably Dickens. Needless to say, the story ends with a reformed Scrooge radiating goodness and light.

Cibber, Colley (1671–1757)

The son of an immigrant Danish sculptor, Cibber became an actor and, amazingly, Poet Laureate. He is largely remembered in English literature because he has been immortalised in **Pope**'s *Dunciad* as an emblem of dullness. *The Blind Boy*, which I reproduce below, is one of his better poems.

> O say what is that thing call'd Light,
> Which I must ne'er enjoy?
> What are the blessings of the sight,
> O tell your poor blind boy!
>
> You talk of wondrous things you see,
> You say the sun shines bright;
> I feel him warm, but how can he
> Or make it day or night?
>
> My day or night myself I make
> Whene'er I sleep or play;
> And could I ever keep awake
> With me 'twere always day.
>
> With heavy sighs I often hear
> You mourn my hapless woe;
> But sure with patience I can bear
> A loss I ne'er can know.
>
> Then let not what I cannot have
> My cheer of mind destroy:
> Whilst thus I sing, I am a king,
> Although a poor blind boy.

It does help one to understand Pope's impatience with Cibber.

Clare, John (1793–1864)

John Clare was the son of an agricultural labourer, and became one himself. In economic terms, he consequently came from the lowest stratum of society. Yet he became a poet, and by no means a bad one. His *Poems Descriptive of Rural Life* appeared in 1820, and the following year he produced *The Village Minstrel* which begins as follows:

While learned poets rush to bold extremes,
And sunbeams snatch to light the muse's fires,
An humble rustic hums his lowly dreams,
Far in the shade where poverty retires,
And sings what nature and what truth inspires;
The charms that rise from rural scenery,
Which he in pastures and in woods admires;
The sports, the feelings of his infancy,
And such like artless things how mean soe'er they be.

Clare did not handle celebrity terribly well, and his life was disordered and chaotic until eventually he was committed to an asylum. He still continued to write, and produced one of his most famous works. 'I am':

I am! yet what I am none cares or knows,
    My friends forsake me like a memory lost;
I am the self-consumer of my woes,
    They rise and vanish, an oblivious host,
Like shades in love and death's oblivion lost;
And yet I am! and live with shadows tost

Into the nothingness of scorn and noise,
    Into the living sea of waking dreams,
Where there is neither sense of life nor joys,
    But the vast shipwreck of my life's esteems;
And e'en the dearest – that I loved the best –
Are strange – nay, rather stranger than the rest.

I long for scenes where man has never trod;
    A place where woman never smil'd or wept;
There to abide with my creator, God,
    And sleep as I in childhood sweetly slept:
Untroubling and untroubled where I lie;
The grass below – above the vaulted sky.

How can anyone who wrote this be one of England's little known poets?

Clarissa

This is a novel of 1748 written by Samuel Richardson. As you can see from its date, it is one of the very earliest novels ever written in English.

However, you are unlikely ever to read it. To start with, it is enormously long, the longest novel in the English language. Secondly, the novel only contains four characters, and the 'story' is conveyed by our reading letters that these characters write to each other. Consequently the narrative proceeds at a pace that most snails would find sluggish. Thirdly, the story is simple in the extreme. Clarissa Harlowe is raped by Robert Lovelace, and naturally therefore buys herself a coffin and, for about 300 pages, gazes in remorse at the coffin until she dies. Clearly this is not a novel that any sane person would willingly read. I, however, have read it twice, and certainly hope to read it again before I die. It is a masterpiece of psychology. It is moving in the extreme. It is even tense. So change your mind: take a week's holiday in somewhere boring like Weston-super-Mare or Skegness and read *Clarissa*.

clerihew

I provide an example of a clerihew in the entry on **Chaucer**. It is simply a comic verse form comprising two rhyming couplets supposedly summing up a person's life or encapsulating an object of study:

> The art of biography
> Is different from geography.
> Geography is about maps,
> Biography is about chaps.

The form has gained its name simply because it was invented by Edmund Clerihew Bentley. One can't claim that it is a particularly elegant form, but there have been some quite witty examples produced:

George the Third	Cecil B. de Mille
Ought never to have occurred.	Rather against his will
One can only wonder	Was persuaded to leave Moses
At so grotesque a blunder.	Out of the Wars of the Roses.

cliché

A cliché is a figurative expression that, through repetition, has now lost whatever force it once possessed. Fortunately, at the end of the day, it is as easy as ABC to count one's chickens before they are hatched, but one then loses the cut and thrust and matters become as slippery as a bar of soap.

Even more fortunately, clichés are only ever used by other people.

Clough, Arthur Hugh (1819–61)

Even non-literary types tend to know that **Wordsworth** and **Tennyson** are poets even though they never read them, yet the majority of those who do read Wordsworth and/or Tennyson certainly never read any Clough. Indeed, most people have never heard of him. This is a shame. When he died, **Matthew Arnold** wrote a longish poem, *Thyrsis*, to commemorate him, and Clough himself, despite his extremely short life, wrote almost as much poetry as Arnold. I am not about to claim that these poems are masterpieces, but his three long poems, *The Bothie of Tober-na-Vuolich*, *Amours de Voyage* and particularly *Dipsychus*, seem to me to be better than anything Arnold ever wrote. We can't sample these here, but try this short one entitled 'The Latest Decalogue':

> Thou shalt have one God only; who
> Would tax himself to worship two?
> God's image nowhere shalt thou see,
> Save haply in the currency;
> Swear not at all, since for thy curse
> Thine enemy is not the worse;
> At church on Sunday to attend
> Will help to keep the world thy friend;
> Honour thy parents: that is, all
> From whom promotion may befall;
> Thou shalt not kill, but needst not strive
> Officiously to keep alive;
> Adultery it is not fit
> Or safe, for women, to commit;
> Thou shalt not steal: an empty feat,
> When 'tis so lucrative to cheat;
> False witness not to bear be strict;
> And cautious, ere you contradict.
> Thou shalt not covet: but tradition
> Sanctions the keenest competition.

>> The sum of all is, thou shalt love,
>> If anybody, God above:
>> At any rate shall never labour
>> *More* than thyself to love thy neighbour.

As that poem abundantly proclaims, Clough had a sharp, ironic wit and was not over-shackled by convention. He is great fun to read.

Coleridge, Samuel Taylor (1772–1834)

Coleridge is a problem. He inspired intense friendship which he then destroyed through quarrels, a process he accomplished with both Southey and **Wordsworth**. He had a brilliant mind which he tarnished through drug addiction. He was an inspired poet, yet only left three poems, *Christabel*, *Kubla Khan* and *The Ancient Mariner*, of real genius. He was a philosopher who befuddled things with mysticism. When I was a teenager, people were often categorised as being 'crazy, mixed-up kids'. It is a label that seems tailor-made for Coleridge. Yet let us just have a look at the miracle that is *Kubla Khan*:

> In Xanadu did Kubla Khan
>   A stately pleasure-dome decree:
> Where Alph, the sacred river, ran
> Through caverns measureless to man
>   Down to a sunless sea.
> So twice five miles of fertile ground
> With walls and towers were girdled round:
> And there were gardens bright with sinuous rills,
> Where blossomed many an incense-bearing tree;
> And here were forests ancient as the hills,
> Enfolding sunny spots of greenery.
>
> But oh! that deep romantic chasm which slanted
> Down the green hill athwart a cedarn cover!
> A savage place! as holy and enchanted
> As e'er beneath a waning moon was haunted
> By woman wailing for her demon-lover!
> And from this chasm, with ceaseless turmoil seething,
> As if this earth in fast thick pants were breathing,
> A mighty fountain momently was forced:
> Amid whose swift half-intermitted burst
> Huge fragments vaulted like rebounding hail,
> Or chaffy grain beneath the thresher's flail;
> And 'mid these dancing rocks at once and ever
> It flung up momently the sacred river.
> Five miles meandering with a mazy motion
> Through wood and dale the sacred river ran,
> Then reached the caverns measureless to man,

And sank in tumult to a lifeless ocean;
And 'mid this tumult Kubla heard from far
Ancestral voices prophesying war!

    The shadow of the dome of pleasure
        Floated midway on the waves;
    Where was heard the mingled measure
        From the fountain and the caves.
It was a miracle of rare device,
A sunny pleasure-dome with caves of ice!

    A damsel with a dulcimer
        In a vision once I saw:
    It was an Abyssinian maid,
        And on her dulcimer she played,
    Singing of Mount Abora.
    Could I revive within me
    Her symphony and song,
To such a deep delight 'twould win me,
That with music loud and long,
I would build that dome in air,
That sunny dome! those caves of ice!
And all who heard should see them there,
And all should cry, Beware! Beware!
His flashing eyes, his floating hair!
    Weave a circle round him thrice,
        And close your eyes with holy dread,
    For he on honey-dew hath fed,
        And drunk the milk of Paradise.

Clearly I cannot know your reaction to the above poem, but it seems to me that *Kubla Khan* is a triumphant demonstration of the fact that, at its best, poetry is magic. If you want to know what *Kubla Khan* actually means, then go to the Internet. There you will find learned articles that will explicate every syllable of the poem. They will even give you diagrams to explain the poem's structure

And the result will be confusion. Just read the poem. And then read it again. Go to the Internet if you must. You will even be given the opportunity to buy some essays of explication. But frankly, I wouldn't bother. For what it's worth, I think that the poem is actually about the act of creation. I think that Coleridge is trying to describe the process of poetic inspiration. But if you think that the poem is about the problems of breeding pigs, so be it. We each interpret a poem in our own way. If you do think that *Kubla Khan* is about breeding pigs, then I will confess to thinking that you are an idiot, but we are unlikely to meet, so it hardly matters.

Collins, Wilkie (1824–89)

Collins is most famous for having written the first ever detective novels, *The Woman in White* in 1860 and *The Moonstone* in 1868. They are both extremely enjoyable, and they both follows Collins's own admonition: 'Make 'em laugh, make 'em cry, make 'em wait.'

comedy

If you and a friend are talking about a comedy on television, you will be talking about a programme that raises laughter. In literary criticism, a comedy need do nothing of the kind. Its defining characteristic is that it has a happy ending.

Comedy of Errors, The

This play by **Shakespeare** was first acted at Gray's Inn in 1594. It has an entirely absurd plot, but is extremely enjoyable and even quite touching.

Comus

This is a masque, a poem, a pastoral drama written in 1634 by **John Milton** to celebrate the Earl of Bridgewater's being made President of Wales and the Marches. This poetical play is a drama designed to advocate chastity, though what the Earl of Bridgewater made of this admonition is not known. It was first put on in the courtyard of Ludlow Castle, and in something like 1959 I saw a re-enactment of this event. It was very effective. The poem opens with a spirit magically appearing within a wood. The spirit, however, has a mission:

> Before the starry threshold of Jove's court
> My mansion is, where those immortal shapes
> Of bright aerial spirits live insphered
> In regions mild of calm and serene air,
> Above the smoke and stir of this dim spot
> Which men call Earth, and, with low-thoughted care.

Confined and pestered in this pinfold here,
Strive to keep up a frail and feverish being,
Unmindful of the crown that Virtue gives,
After this mortal change, to her true servants
Amongst the enthron'd gods on sainted seats.
Yet some there be that by due steps aspire
To lay their just hands on that golden key
That opes the palace of eternity.
To such my errand is; and, but for such,
I would not soil these pure ambrosial weeds
With the rank vapours of this sin-worn mould.

    But to my task. Neptune, besides the sway
Of every salt flood and each ebbing stream,
Took in by lot 'twixt high and nether Jove
Imperial rule of all the sea-girt isles
That, like to rich and various gems, inlay
The unadorned bosom of the deep;
Which he, to grace his tributary gods,
By course commits to several government,
And gives them leave to wear their sapphire crowns
And wield their little tridents. But this Isle,
The greatest and the best of all the main,
He quarters to his blue-haired deities;
And all this tract that fronts the falling sun
A noble Peer of mickle trust and power
Has in his charge, with tempered awe to guide
An old and haughty nation, proud in arms:
Where his fair offspring, nursed in princely lore,
Are coming to attend their father's state,
And new-entrusted sceptre. But their way
Lies through the perplex'd paths of this drear wood,
The nodding horror of whose shady brows
Threats the forlorn and wand'ring passenger;
And here their tender age might suffer peril,
But that, by quick command from sovran Jove,
I was despatched for their defence and guard.
And listen why; for I will tell you now
What never yet was heard in tale or song,
From old or modern bard, in hall or bower.

As I have already indicated, much of that mission is to inculcate chastity. This is done in wondrous poetry, but, alas, this in itself is unlikely to be sufficient to guide your son or daughter down the path of purity.

conceit

Most of us think of 'conceit' as an unpleasant human quality exhibited by someone who makes it plain that he or she is superior to those around him or her. In literary criticism, however, a conceit is an elaborate metaphor or image. When **Donne** in his poem 'A Valediction: Forbidding Mourning' likens lovers to a pair of compasses, that is a conceit because the concept is surprising and the image is sustained for several lines:

> Our two souls therefore, which are one,
>   Though I must go, endure not yet
> A breach, but an expansion,
>   Like gold to airy thinness beat.
>
> If they be two, they are two so
>   As stiff twin compasses are two;
> Thy soul, the fix'd foot, makes no show
>   To move, but doth, if th' other do.
>
> And though it in the centre sit,
>   Yet, when the other far doth roam,
> It leans, and hearkens after it,
>   And grows erect, as it comes home.
>
> Such wilt thou be to me, who must,
>   Like th' other foot, obliquely run;
> Thy firmness makes my circle just,
>   And makes me end where I begun.

condition-of-England novel, the

In the 1840s a number of writers published novels that highlighted abuses and miseries that were then prevalent in England. The new Poor Law of 1834, the disgraces of factory work, appalling sanitary conditions, inadequate housing and the exclusion of most from political representation provided ample targets. Writers like **Dickens**, **Gaskell**, **Kingsley**, **Disraeli**, **the Brontës**, **George Eliot** and others all used their pens to express horror and alarm at the condition of England.

Congreve, William (1670–1729)

Congreve was a dramatist, one of England's wittiest. *The Way of the World* (1700) can still greatly amuse three hundred years later. It begins as follows:

ACT 1   SCENE 1   A Chocolate-house

MIRABELL and FAINALL rising from cards. BETTY waiting.

MIRABELL: You are a fortunate man, Mr Fainall.

FAINALL: Have we done?

MIRABELL: What you please. I'll play on to entertain you.

FAINALL: No, I'll give you your revenge another time, when you are not so indifferent; you are thinking of something else now, and play too negligently: the coldness of a losing gamester lessens the pleasure of the winner. I'd no more play with a man that slighted his ill fortune than I'd make love to a woman who undervalued the loss of her reputation.

MIRABELL: You have a taste extremely delicate, and are for refining on your pleasures.

FAINALL: Prithee, why so reserved? Something has put you out of humour.

MIRABELL: Not at all: I happen to be grave today, and you are gay; that's all.

FAINALL: Confess, Millamant and you quarrelled last night, after I left you; my fair cousin has some humours that would tempt the patience of a Stoic. What, some coxcomb came in, and was well received by her, while you were by?

MIRABELL: Witwoud and Petulant, and what was worse, her aunt, your wife's mother, my evil genius – or to sum up all in her own name, my old Lady Wishfort came in.

FAINALL: Oh, there it is then: she has a lasting passion for you, and with reason. – What, then my wife was there?

MIRABELL: Yes, and Mrs Marwood and three or four more, whom I never saw before; seeing me, they all put on their grave faces, whispered one another, then complained aloud of the vapours, and after fell into a profound silence.

FAINALL: They had a mind to be rid of you.

MIRABELL: For which reason I resolved not to stir. At last the good old lady broke through her painful taciturnity with an invective against long visits. I would not have understood her, but Millamant joining in the argument, I rose and with a constrained smile told her I thought nothing was so easy as to know when a visit began to be troublesome; she reddened and I withdrew, without expecting her reply.

FAINALL: You were to blame to resent what she spoke only in compliance with her aunt.

MIRABELL: She is more mistress of herself than to be under the necessity of such a resignation.

FAINALL: What? though half her fortune depends upon her marrying with my lady's approbation?

MIRABELL: I was then in such a humour, that I should have been better pleased if she had been less discreet.

FAINALL: Now I remember, I wonder not they were weary of you; last night was one of their cabal-nights: they have 'em three times a week and meet by turns at one another's apartments, where they come together like the coroner's inquest, to sit upon the murdered reputations of the week. You and I are excluded, and it was once proposed that all the male sex should be excepted; but somebody moved that to avoid scandal there might be one man of the community, upon which motion Witwoud and Petulant were enrolled members.

In fact, Mirabell, in order to marry Millamant, has to get the consent of Lady Wishfort. He also has to overcome the spite of Mrs Marwood. The result is two hours or so of entertaining intrigue.

Conrad, Joseph (1857–1924)

It is ironic that a Polish sailor wrote some of the greatest novels ever written in English, but such is the case with Józef Teodor Konrad Korzeniowski. In 1894, Conrad gave up his seafaring life, and devoted himself to writing, though the sea provides the setting for most of his works. Conrad expressed his object in writing in the Preface to *The Nigger of the 'Narcissus'* (1897): 'My task which I am trying to achieve is, by the power of the written word, to make you hear, to make you feel – it is, above all, to make you see. That – and no more, and it is everything.'

As you might intuit, Conrad had a strong moral impetus in his writing, and it was this that drew the approval of **F. R. Leavis**, who included

Conrad in his book *The Great Tradition*. Keiron O'Hara has argued that Conrad's themes – imperialism, terrorism, revolution, racism and guilt, as well as the multiple meanings of 'material interests' – ensure that a hundred years later he speaks to us in a way none of his contemporaries can. Take *Heart of Darkness* as an example. In that novel Conrad constantly utilises the images of light and dark to mold a vision which the reader is then able to use to decipher the literal and metaphorical meanings of the novel. Yet Conrad can be difficult. His language is often designed to obscure rather than reveal. **H. G. Wells**, reviewing *An Outcast of the Islands*, described Conrad's style as being 'like river-mist: for a space things are seen clearly, and then comes a great grey bank of printed matter, page upon page, creeping round the reader, swallowing him up'. To some extent, this is a consequence of Conrad's view that it was virtually impossible fully to know another human being. As his first great biographer Jocelyn Baines wrote: 'The essence of his art lies in the construction of a setting where a complex state of mind can be presented with the fullest emotional and dramatic effect.' Giles Foden, commenting on *Lord Jim* in a *Guardian* article of 1 December 2007, says that 'switches between sympathetic and negative responses to a character create depth by constant realignment and play of emotion. It is, to my mind, the nearest thing in fiction to the substance of one's real encounters with people.' One could hardly give a writer greater praise.

convention

In literature, a convention is an unspoken agreement between the reader and the author. For instance, you know and I know that people do not wander around speaking to each other in blank verse, but we allow **Shakespeare** and lots of others to do it all the time.

copyright

Anything that is produced by means of a creative act – writing, composing, painting, etc. – is subject to copyright. Basically this means that no one is allowed to reproduce the work in question without the permission of the author. Hence, if you reproduce, without acknowledgment, sections of this book in the Empingham parish magazine, you could be sued for millions of pounds. (Incidentally, Empingham is a village in Rutland, but, so far as I know, it doesn't have a parish magazine.)

Coriolanus

This is probably the last of Shakespeare's tragedies to be written. As one would expect, it contains some wonderful writing, but it has never been a popular play. This is almost certainly because Coriolanus, whose murder at the end of the play constitutes the tragedy, is such an arrogant creature that one is quite glad to see him go. In Act 4, Scene 5, Coriolanus has a monologue that provides quite a good self-portrait. Under his birth name Caius Marcius, Coriolanus has led the Roman army to attack the Volsces who are led by Tullus Aufidius. The defeat of the Volsces leads to Caius Marcius being granted the honorary name of Coriolanus, but a section of the Roman people decide that Coriolanus is too proud, and they decide to kill him. In outrage, Coriolanus flees, and goes to visit his old enemy, Tullus Aufidius. This is what he has to say:

> My name is Caius Marcius, who hath done
> To thee particularly and to all the Volsces
> Great hurt and mischief; thereto witness may
> My surname, Coriolanus. The painful service,
> The extreme dangers, and the drops of blood
> Shed for my thankless country are requited
> But with that surname – a good memory,
> And witness of the malice and displeasure
> Which thou shouldst bear me. Only that name remains.
> The cruelty and envy of the people,
> Permitted by our dastard nobles, who
> Have all forsook me, hath devoured the rest;
> And suffered me by th' voice of slaves to be
> Whooped out of Rome. Now this extremity
> Hath brought me to thy hearth, not out of hope –
> Mistake me not – to save my life; for if
> I had feared death, of all the men i' th' world
> I would have 'voided thee; but in mere spite,
> To be full quit of those my banishers,
> Stand I before thee here. Then if thou hast
> A heart of wreak in thee, that wilt revenge
> Thine own particular wrongs, and stop those maims
> Of shame seen through thy country, speed thee straight,
> And make my misery serve thy turn. So use it
> That my revengeful services may prove

As benefits to thee; for I will fight
Against my cank'red country with the spleen
Of all the under fiends. But if so be
Thou dar'st not this, and that to prove more fortunes
Th' art tired, then, in a word, I also am
Longer to live most weary; and present
My throat to thee and to thy ancient malice;
Which not to cut would show thee but a fool,
Since I have ever followed thee with hate,
Drawn tuns of blood out of thy country's breast,
And cannot live but to thy shame, unless
It be to do thee service.

Not, I am sure you will agree, the most engaging of characters. Yet despite this, *Coriolanus* is a fascinating play which you will now have to read because I am not going to tell you what happens next.

Country Wife, The

This is a play written in 1674 by **William Wycherley**. It is perhaps the finest example of a so-called **Restoration comedy**.

couplet

Strictly speaking a couplet is two lines of verse, but the word is almost invariably used to refer to a rhyming couplet:

The well-sung woes will sooth my pensive ghost;
He best can paint 'em, who shall feel 'em most.

It was used by **Chaucer** in the fourteenth century, is used today in the twenty-first, and has been used in every century in between. The most common form of couplet, that in iambic pentameters, is known as the **heroic couplet**.

Cowper, William (1731–1800)

William Cowper (pronounced 'Cooper') is not well known, even to English graduates, yet almost all of us know one or two of his works. Many of us have come across the hymns 'God moves in a mysterious way' and 'O for a closer walk with God', both by Cowper, and perhaps even more of us have delighted in the poem *John Gilpin*. This is so diverting that I shall not make a massive apology for reproducing it here, very long though it is:

John Gilpin was a citizen
   Of credit and renown,
A train-band captain eke was he,
   Of famous London town.

John Gilpin's spouse said to her dear,
   'Though wedded we have been
These twice ten tedious years, yet we
   No holiday have seen.

'Tomorrow is our wedding-day,
   And we will then repair
Unto the Bell at Edmonton,
   All in a chaise and pair.

'My sister, and my sister's child,
   Myself, and children three,
Will fill the chaise; so you must ride
   On horseback after we.'

He soon replied, 'I do admire
   Of womankind but one,
And you are she, my dearest dear,
   Therefore it shall be done.

'I am a linen-draper bold,
   As all the world doth know,
And my good friend the calender
   Will lend his horse to go.'

Quoth Mrs Gilpin, 'That's well said;
   And for that wine is dear,
We will be furnished with our own,
   Which is both bright and clear.'

John Gilpin kissed his loving wife;
   O'erjoyed was he to find
That though on pleasure she was bent,
   She had a frugal mind.

The morning came, the chaise was brought,
   But yet was not allowed
To drive up to the door, lest all
   Should say that she was proud.

So three doors off the chaise was stayed,
   Where they did all get in;

Six precious souls, and all agog
   To dash through thick and thin.

Smack went the whip, round went the wheels,
   Were never folks so glad!
The stones did rattle underneath
   As if Cheapside were mad.

John Gilpin at his horse's side
   Seized fast the flowing mane,
And up he got, in haste to ride,
   But soon came down again;

For saddle-tree scarce reached had he,
   His journey to begin,
When, turning round his head, he saw
   Three customers come in.

So down he came; for loss of time,
   Although it grieved him sore,
Yet loss of pence, full well he knew,
   Would trouble him much more.

'Twas long before the customers
   Were suited to their mind,
When Betty screaming came downstairs,
   'The wine is left behind!'

'Good lack!' quoth he, 'yet bring it me,
   My leathern belt likewise,
In which I bear my trusty sword
   When I do exercise.'

Now Mistress Gilpin (careful soul!)
   Had two stone bottles found,
To hold the liquor that she loved,
   And keep it safe and sound.

Each bottle had a curling ear,
   Through which the belt he drew,
And hung a bottle on each side,
   To make his balance true.

Then over all, that he might be
   Equipped from top to toe,

His long red cloak, well brushed and neat,
   He manfully did throw.

Now see him mounted once again
   Upon his nimble steed,
Full slowly pacing o'er the stones,
   With caution and good heed.

But finding soon a smoother road
   Beneath his well-shod feet,
The snorting beast began to trot,
   Which galled him in his seat.

'So, fair and softly!' John he cried,
   But John he cried in vain;
That trot became a gallop soon,
   In spite of curb and rein.

So stooping down, as needs he must
   Who cannot sit upright,
He grasped the mane with both his hands,
   And eke with all his might.

His horse, who never in that sort
   Had handled been before,
What thing upon his back had got,
   Did wonder more and more.

Away went Gilpin, neck or nought,
   Away went hat and wig;
He little dreamt, when he set out,
   Of running such a rig.

The wind did blow, the cloak did fly
   Like streamer long and gay,
Till, loop and button failing both.
   At last it flew away.

Then might all people well discern
   The bottles he had slung;
A bottle swinging at each side,
   As hath been said or sung.

The dogs did bark, the children screamed,
   Up flew the windows all;
And every soul cried out, 'Well done!'
   As loud as he could bawl.

Away went Gilpin – who but he?
　His fame soon spread around:
'He carries weight! he rides a race!
　'Tis for a thousand pound!'

And still as fast as he drew near,
　'Twas wonderful to view
How in a trice the turnpike-men
　Their gates wide open threw.

And now, as he went bowing down
　His reeking head full low,
The bottles twain behind his back
　Were shattered at a blow.

Down ran the wine into the road,
　Most piteous to be seen,
Which made the horse's flanks to smoke,
　As they had basted been.

But still he seemed to carry weight.
　With leathern girdle braced;
For all might see the bottle-necks
　Still dangling at his waist.

Thus all through merry Islington
　These gambols he did play,
Until he came unto the wash
　Of Edmonton so gay;

And there he threw the wash about
　On both sides of the way,
Just like unto a trundling mop,
　Or a wild goose at play.

At Edmonton his loving wife
　From the balcony spied
Her tender husband, wondering much
　To see how he did ride.

'Stop, stop, John Gilpin! – Here's the house!'
　They all at once did cry;
'The dinner waits, and we are tired.'
　Said Gilpin – 'So am I!'

But yet his horse was not a whit
   Inclined to tarry there;
For why? – his owner had a house
   Full ten miles off, at Ware.

So like an arrow swift he flew,
   Shot by an archer strong;
So did he fly – which brings me to
   The middle of my song.

Away went Gilpin, out of breath,
   And sore against his will,
Till at his friend the calender's
   His horse at last stood still.

The calender, amazed to see
   His neighbour in such trim,
Laid down his pipe, flew to the gate,
   And thus accosted him:

'What news? what news? your tidings tell;
   Tell me you must and shall –
Say why bareheaded you are come,
   Or why you come at all?'

Now Gilpin had a pleasant wit,
   And loved a timely joke;
And thus unto the calender
   In merry guise he spoke:

'I came because your horse would come;
   And, if I well forebode,
My hat and wig will soon be here,
   They are upon the road.'

The calender, right glad to find
   His friend in merry pin,
Returned him not a single word,
   But to the house went in;

Whence straight he came with hat and wig,
   A wig that flowed behind,
A hat not much the worse for wear,
   Each comely in its kind.

He held them up, and in his turn
      Thus showed his ready wit:
'My head is twice as big as yours,
      They therefore needs must fit.

'But let me scrape the dirt away,
      That hangs upon your face;
And stop and eat, for well you may
      Be in a hungry case.'

Said John, 'It is my wedding-day,
      And all the world would stare
If wife should dine at Edmonton,
      And I should dine at Ware.'

So turning to his horse, he said
      'I am in haste to dine;
'Twas for your pleasure you came here,
      You shall go back for mine.'

Ah! luckless speech, and bootless boast!
      For which he paid full dear;
For while he spake, a braying ass
      Did sing most loud and clear;

Whereat his horse did snort, as he
      Had heard a lion roar,
And galloped off with all his might,
      As he had done before.

Away went Gilpin, and away
      Went Gilpin's hat and wig;
He lost them sooner than at first,
      For why? – they were too big.

Now Mistress Gilpin, when she saw
      Her husband posting down
Into the country far away,
      She pulled out half-a-crown;

And thus unto the youth she said
      That drove them to the Bell,
'This shall be yours when you bring back
      My husband safe and well.'

The youth did ride, and soon did meet
   John coming back amain;
Whom in a trice he tried to stop,
   By catching at his rein.

But not performing what he meant,
   And gladly would have done,
The frighted steed he frighted more,
   And made him faster run.

Away went Gilpin, and away
   Went post-boy at his heels,
The post-boy's horse right glad to miss
   The lumbering of the wheels.

Six gentlemen upon the road,
   Thus seeing Gilpin fly,
With post-boy scampering in the rear.
   They raised the hue and cry.

'Stop thief! stop thief! a highwayman!'
Not one of them was mute;
   And all and each that passed that way
Did join in the pursuit.

And now the turnpike-gates again
   Flew open in short space,
The toll-men thinking, as before,
   That Gilpin rode a race.

And so he did, and won it too,
   For he got first to town;
Nor stopped till where he had got up,
   He did again get down.

Now let us sing, 'Long live the King,
   And Gilpin, long live he;'
And when he next doth ride abroad,
   May I be there to see!

His best-known long poem, *The Task*, is perhaps little read these days, but it is gently pleasant, and Cowper's letters are a delight. The man himself suffered badly from depression, and his last poem, *The Castaway*, reflects this all too well:

Obscurest night involv'd the sky,
    Th' Atlantic billows roar'd,
When such a destin'd wretch as I,
    Wash'd headlong from on board,
Of friends, of hope, of all bereft,
His floating home for ever left.

No braver chief could Albion boast
    Than he with whom he went,
Nor ever ship left Albion's coast,
    With warmer wishes sent.
He lov'd them both, but both in vain,
Nor him beheld, nor her again.

Not long beneath the whelming brine,
    Expert to swim, he lay;
Nor soon he felt his strength decline,
    Or courage die away;
But wag'd with death a lasting strife,
Supported by despair of life.

He shouted: nor his friends had fail'd
    To check the vessel's course,
But so the furious blast prevail'd,
    That, pitiless perforce,
They left their outcast mate behind,
And scudded still before the wind.

Some succour yet they could afford;
    And, such as storms allow,
The cask, the coop, the floated cord,
    Delay'd not to bestow.
But he (they knew) nor ship, nor shore,
Whate'er they gave, should visit more.

Nor, cruel as it seem'd, could he
    Their haste himself condemn,
Aware that flight, in such a sea,
    Alone could rescue them;
Yet bitter felt it still to die
Deserted, and his friends so nigh.

He long survives, who lives an hour
    In ocean, self-upheld;
And so long he, with unspent pow'r,
    His destiny repell'd;
And ever, as the minutes flew,
Entreated help, or cried – Adieu!

At length, his transient respite past,
    His comrades, who before
Had heard his voice in ev'ry blast,
    Could catch the sound no more.
For then, by toil subdued, he drank
The stifling wave, and then he sank.

No poet wept him: but the page
    Of narrative sincere,
That tells his name, his worth, his age,
    Is wet with Anson's tear.
And tears by bards or heroes shed
Alike immortalise the dead.

I therefore purpose not, or dream,
    Descanting on his fate,
To give the melancholy theme
    A more enduring date:
But misery still delights to trace
Its semblance in another's case.

No voice divine the storm allay'd,
    No light propitious shone;
When, snatch'd from all effectual aid,
    We perish'd, each alone:
But I beneath a rougher sea,
And whelm'd in deeper gulfs than he.

One feels saddened because Cowper, despite his depression, devoted much time to opposing slavery and fox hunting, and it seems unfair that so enlightened a being should not have had an easier lot.

Crabbe, George (1755–1832)

Crabbe did not lead a happy or an easy life, but **Byron** rated him
'Nature's sternest painter and the best'. In 1810, he wrote a long poem
entitled *The Borough*, and one of its sections is about Peter Grimes. As
you doubtless know, this was adapted by Benjamin Britten and turned
into one of his most popular operas. Crabbe's poem begins as follows:

> Old Peter Grimes made fishing his employ,
> His wife he cabin'd with him and his boy,
> And seem'd that life laborious to enjoy;
> To town came quiet Peter with his fish,
> And had of all a civil word and wish.
> He left his trade upon the sabbath-day,
> And took young Peter in his hand to pray;
> But soon the stubborn boy from care broke loose,
> At first refused, then added his abuse.
> His father's love he scorn'd, his power defied,
> But being drunk, wept sorely when he died.
>
> Yes! then he wept, and to his mind there came
> Much of his conduct, and he felt the shame –
> How he had oft the good old man reviled,
> And never paid the duty of a child;
> How, when the father in his Bible read,
> He in contempt and anger left the shed.
> 'It is the word of life,' the parent cried;
> 'This is the life itself,' the boy replied;
> And while old Peter in amazement stood,
> Gave the hot spirit to his boiling blood:
> How he, with oath and furious speech, began
> To prove his freedom and assert the man;
> And when the parent check'd his impious rage,
> How he had cursed the tyranny of age –
> Nay, once had dealt the sacrilegious blow
> On his bare head, and laid his parent low;
> The father groan'd – 'If thou art old,' said he,
> 'And hast a son – thou wilt remember me:
> Thy mother left me in a happy time,
> Thou kill'dst not her – Heav'n spares the double crime.'

As you can see, this is a tragic tale, and Crabbe was no stranger to life's vicissitudes.

criticism

According to Chris Baldick in his *Concise Dictionary of Literary Terms*, criticism is 'the reasoned discussion of literary works'. Sometimes it is, but there are at least two other motivations for criticism. First of all, a university lecturer wants to be promoted to senior lecturer or gain a chair at another university. For this to happen, he needs to publish, because it is a self-evident truth that the more articles and books that one has had published, the cleverer one is. As a result, the ambitious lecturer churns out seminal articles on the structural use of vegetable imagery in the poetry of Coventry Patmore and a magum opus entitled *Social Status in the Novels of Fanny Burney*. A second motivation springs from personal spite. Cyril Sycophant has just published an article arguing that **David Lodge** is the greatest novelist since **Lawrence**. Brian Balderdash can't stand Cyril and isn't that keen on David Lodge either. Consequently he writes an article for the *Sunday Times* pouring derision on the ideas of Cyril. The eventual result is guns at dawn in the courtyard of Trinity College.

Occasionally, however, Chris Baldock is right, and criticism attempts to show why **Marlowe**'s *The Jew of Malta* is a good play or why **Shakespeare**'s sonnets have been overpraised or why **Michael Drayton** is an unduly ignored poet. This is what criticism should be about: the attempt to demonstrate the virtues and/or defects of a work of art. Of course personal taste is an idiosyncratic interloper in this endeavour, and not even the most brilliantly argued paper is going to persuade everybody that **Edgar Allan Poe** is a great writer, but at its best, criticism is the disinterested evaluation of works of art in the hope of making that art more accessible to everyone.

Cymbeline

This is one of the last plays that **Shakespeare** ever wrote. Its plot is absurd and many of its characters ridiculous. The play includes decadent Romans wagering on a lady's honour, sturdy Romans invading Britain, magic potions, stolen babies, and a flying visit from Jupiter. Yet despite this, the play is moving in the extreme, and contains one of the most wondrous poems ever to have been written in English:

Dirge for Fidele

Fear no more the heat o' the sun,
   Nor the furious winter's rages;
Thou thy worldly task hast done,
   Home art gone, and ta'en thy wages;
Golden lads and girls all must,
As chimney-sweepers, come to dust.

Fear no more the frown o' the great,
   Thou art past the tyrant's stroke;
Care no more to clothe and eat,
   To thee the reed is as the oak.
The sceptre, learning, physic, must
All follow this, and come to dust.

Fear no more the lightning-flash,
   Nor the all-dreaded thunder-stone;
Fear not slander, censure rash;
   Thou hast finished joy and moan.
All lovers young, all lovers must
Consign to thee, and come to dust.

No exorciser harm thee!
   Nor no witchcraft charm thee!
Ghost unlaid forbear thee!
   Nothing ill come near thee!
Quiet consummation have,
And renownèd be thy grave!

D

dactyl

A metrical unit or foot consisting of one stressed syllable followed by two unstressed ones. This **metre** is not widely used in English, though **Tennyson** uses it in *The Charge of the Light Brigade*:

> Half a league, half a league,
> Half a league onward . . .

Browning employs it effectively in *The Lost Leader*:

> Just for a handful of silver he left us,
> Just for a riband to stick in his coat . . .

and if you gain satisfaction in scanning poetry, you'd set it out like this:

/ x x	/ x x	/ x x	/ x
Just for a	handful of	silver he	left us

As you can see, you have three feet of dactylic metre and the final foot is a trochee.

Dahl, Roald (1916–90)

Roald Dahl was a remarkably successful writer of children's fiction. In the 1970s and early 80s I read him on an almost daily basis to my children until I no longer needed the text in front of me. It goes without saying that Roald is extremely bad for children. He can be snobbish, he can be sexist, and he certainly depicts cruelty in a way that will deform and damage any child's mind. In addition, cruel adults in Dahl's stories often suffer revenge at the hands of triumphant children. This is morally dubious and inculcates entirely the wrong attitudes. The only difficulty is that children love him, and there have been no reports of Dahl inflicting lasting psychological damage on anyone's mind. Hence it seems safe to ignore the strictures of buttoned-up parents and apprehensive teachers.

Daniel, Samuel (c. 1562–1619)

In the sixteenth century and into the seventeenth, England was afflicted with a strange disease. Everybody wrote sonnets. On the whole, such sonnets were addressed, normally despairingly, to a woman, and quite often the poet concerned would write thirty, forty or fifty of such plaints, and then publish them as a **sonnet** sequence. Such was the case with Samuel Daniel, who wrote a sequence of fifty-five entitled *Delia*. Here is a typical example:

> Oft do I muse whether my *Delia*'s eyes
> Are eyes, or else two fair bright stars that shine;
> For how could nature ever thus devise
> Of earth on earth a substance so divine?
> Stars sure they are, whose motions rule desires,
> And calm and tempest follow their aspects;
> Their sweet appearing still such power inspires
> That makes the world admire so strange effects.
> Yet whether fixt or wand'ring stars are they,
> Whose influence rule the Orb of my poor heart,
> Fixt sure they are, but wand'ring make me stray,
> In endless errors whence I cannot part.
> Stars then, not eyes, move yet with milder view
> Your sweet aspect on him that honours you.

As you can see, a basic conceit is adopted – Delia's eyes are stars – and then developed through the 14 lines of the poem. It is a formula, and Daniel, like **Sidney**, **Shakespeare**, **Spenser** and all the others, executes it very competently. It is an exercise that you can carry out at home. Set a topic – keeping the bathroom tidy, for instance – and then all members of the family can write sonnets on this theme. The member adjudged to have written the finest sonnet can be given a new sponge as a prize.

Daniel Deronda

This is **George Eliot**'s last novel, and it is frequently damned with faint praise. None the less, the last time that I read this novel, I was greatly impressed both by its characters and by its theme. It is a big and ambitious work, and very, very few English novelists could have handled it so superbly. Her epigraph to Chapter 1 makes Eliot's seriousness of intent abundantly obvious:

Men can do nothing without the make-believe of a beginning. Even Science, the strict measurer, is obliged to start with a make-believe unit, and must fix on a point in the stars' unceasing journey when his sidereal clock shall pretend that time is at Nought. His less accurate grandmother Poetry has always been understood to start in the middle; but on reflection it appears that her proceeding is not very different from his; since Science, too, reckons backwards as well as forwards, divides his unit into billions, and with his clock-finger at Nought really sets off *in medias res*. No retrospect will take us to the true beginning; and whether our prologue be in heaven or on earth, it is but a fraction of that all-presupposing fact with which our story sets out.

When one adds that the novel deals with the nascent Zionist movement, and reflects the strong sympathies of a large sector of British society for restoration of the Jews, one can see that George Eliot is not planning on providing a relaxed and easy read. Yet Amazon provide some readers' reviews of the novel on an Internet site, and the responses are remarkable. One fifteen-year-old schoolgirl says, 'Within reading the first few chapters, *Daniel Deronda* became my most beloved and favourite of books.' Another reader comments, 'It is an intensely psychological novel, and Eliot's study of her emotionally self-centered heroine, Gwendolen Harleth, as she evolves, through experience, into an admirable woman, is really remarkable.' Yet another reader feels that *Daniel Deronda* deserves the title of Eliot's finest work rather than *Middlemarch*. I wouldn't agree with this – *Middlemarch* is stupendous – but *Daniel Deronda* is a great novel, and it is a shame that it is relatively little read.

Charles Darwin (1809–1882)

I am writing this entry in 2009 when the whole world is being swamped by books, exhibitions and lectures about Charles Darwin on the centenary of his birth. That, however, is not the reason for including Darwin in this book. He was, after all, a biologist, and, although he wrote books, they hardly fall into the category of imaginative fiction. But what Darwin did was to change the way that human beings look at the world. As a result, every writer after Darwin had had his or her mind affected by the concept of evolution. Hence what they wrote was inescapably influenced by that concept. Indeed, **George Eliot**, **Thomas Hardy** and **Joseph Conrad** all responded enthusiastically to Darwin's theory of evolution.

David Copperfield

As most people know, this is a novel by Charles Dickens. Often seen as partially autobiographical, Dickens claimed that it was his favourite novel, and certainly the public over the last 140 years have taken it to their hearts. It contains a plethora of Dickens's unforgettable caricatures, and perhaps the vitality and sheer invention of Miss Murdstone, Mr Dick, Traddles and Mr Micawber allow us to pass over the wearisome sentimentality. It is difficult too not to succumb to the engaging opening of the novel:

> Whether I shall turn out to be the hero of my own life, or whether that station will be held by anybody else, these pages must show. To begin my life with the beginning of my life, I record that I was born (as I have been informed and believe) on a Friday, at twelve o'clock at night. It was remarked that the clock began to strike, and I began to cry, simultaneously.
>
> In consideration of the day and hour of my birth, it was declared by the nurse, and by some sage women in the neighbourhood who had taken a lively interest in me several months before there was any possibility of our becoming personally acquainted, first, that I was destined to be unlucky in life; and secondly, that I was privileged to see ghosts and spirits; both these gifts inevitably attaching, as they believed, to all unlucky infants of either gender, born towards the small hours on a Friday night.
>
> I need say nothing here, on the first head, because nothing can show better than my history whether that prediction was verified or falsified by the result. On the second branch of the question, I will only remark, that unless I ran through that part of my inheritance while I was still a baby, I have not come into it yet. But I do not at all complain of having been kept out of this property; and if anybody else should be in the present enjoyment of it, he is heartily welcome to keep it.

For my money, *David Copperfield* is far from being Dickens's finest novel, but it is none the less a genuine delight.

dead metaphor

This is a metaphor that has been used so often that it has lost any vividness it once possessed. You might be green with envy at those who do not beat about the bush but who get to the heart of the matter in one fell swoop. On the other hand, you might cringe at so many dead metaphors that it is like a literary morgue. Try to avoid them. The trouble is, sentences like 'You might be purple with envy at those who do not pummel about the hedge but who get to the liver of the matter in one fell seizure' tend not to work at all.

decasyllable

A decasyllable is a line of verse of ten syllables. I have lived for over sixty years without ever needing to use this word. Indeed, I suspect that my gravestone will read,

> He never said 'decasyllable' in his life,
> Which is why he never had strife.

decorum

This is a strange and somewhat shifting term. Decorum refers to your writing with a sense of propriety. You would not, for instance, insert a joke about a sexually rampant mother-in-law in a funeral oration (or, I hope, anywhere else). Yet decorum is not simply about the subject matter of what you write. It is also about the way in which you write. For instance, in *A Midsummer Night's Dream* the workmen speak mostly in prose because that befits their lowly status:

FLUTE: Nay, faith, let me not play a woman; I have a beard coming.

QUINCE: That's all one: you shall play it in a mask, and you may speak as small as you will.

BOTTOM: An I may hide my face, let me play Thisby too. I'll speak in a monstrous little voice: 'Thisny? Thisny?' 'Ah, Pyramus, lover dear! thy Thisby dear, and lady dear!'

QUINCE: No, no; you must play Pyramus; and, Flute, you Thisby.

BOTTOM: Well, proceed.

QUINCE: Robin Starveling, the tailor?

STARVELING: Here, Peter Quince.

QUINCE: Robin Starveling, you must play Thisby's mother. Tom Snout, the tinker?

SNOUT: Here, Peter Quince.

QUINCE: You, Pyramus' father; myself, Thisby's father; Snug, the joiner, you, the lion's part; and, I hope, here is a play fitted.

SNUG: Have you the lion's part written? Pray you, if it be, give it me, for I am slow of study.

QUINCE: You may do it extempore, for it is nothing but roaring.

When, however, Helena and Demetrius are squabbling about love, the discourse is in verse:

DEMETRIUS: Do I entice you? do I speak you fair?
Or, rather, do I not in plainest truth
Tell you I do not, nor I cannot love you?
HELENA: And even for that do I love you the more.
I am your spaniel, and, Demetrius,
The more you beat me, I will fawn on you.
Use me but as your spaniel: spurn me, strike me,
Neglect me, lose me; only give me leave,
Unworthy as I am, to follow you.
What worser place can I beg in your love –
And yet a place of high respect with me –
Than to be used as you use your dog?
DEMETRIUS: Tempt not too much the hatred of my spirit;
For I am sick when I do look on thee.
HELENA: And I am sick when I look not on you.
DEMETRIUS: You do impeach your modesty too much,
To leave the city and commit yourself
Into the hands of one that loves you not;
To trust the opportunity of night
And the ill counsel of a desert place
With the rich worth of your virginity.

It is all a question of decorum.

Defoe, Daniel (1660–1731)

It is difficult not to warm to Daniel Defoe. The son of a butcher, he became a journalist and in 1701 attracted attention with a poem entitled *The True Born Englishman*. Just read its opening lines:

Wherever God erects a house of prayer,
The Devil always builds a chapel there:
And 'twill be found upon examination,
The latter has the larger congregation:
For ever since he first debauched the mind,
He made a perfect conquest of mankind.
With uniformity of service, he
Reigns with a general aristocracy.

No non-conforming sects disturb his reign,
For of his yoke there's very few complain.
He knows the genius and the inclination,
And matches proper sins for every nation.
He needs no standing-army government,
He always rules us by our own consent;
His laws are easy, and his gentle sway
Makes it exceeding pleasant to obey;
The list of his vicegerents and commanders
Outdoes your Cæsars or your Alexanders.

It is difficult not to be overcome by this civilised satire, and Defoe goes on to attack the widespread prejudice against the recently elected king, William of Orange, because he is Dutch. Defoe points out that the English are predominantly a mongrel race, and that consequently it behoves them ill to sneer at a Dutchman:

A Turkish horse can show more history,
To prove his well-descended family.
Conquest, as by the moderns it is expressed,
May give a title to the lands possessed;
But that the longest sword should be so civil
To make a Frenchman English, that's the devil.
   These are the heroes that despise the Dutch,
And rail at new-come foreigners so much,
Forgetting that themselves are all derived
From the most scoundrel race that ever lived . . .

The next year, however, Defoe overstepped the mark a little. He wrote a pamphlet entitled *The Shortest Way with Dissenters*, in which, by advocating the complete suppression of dissent, he hoped to illustrate the idiocy of any form of suppression. For his pains, he was fined, imprisoned and pilloried.

In the history of English literature, however, Defoe is best known as the inventor of the English novel. Virtually everybody has heard of **Robinson Crusoe** (1719), and *Moll Flanders* (1722) is quite well known too. *Captain Singleton* (1720) and *Colonel Jack* (1722) are relatively unknown, yet both are well worth reading. Given that Defoe had no models to guide him, it is an astounding achievement to have created such well-structured and accomplished novels. Crusoe and Flanders as characters have also become **archetypes** of the solitary man and the woman of easy virtue respectively. There are three or four other novels as well, including one based on an actual diary, *Journal of the Plague Year*. Between 1724 and 1726 Defoe produced a three-volume *Tour thro' the Whole Island of Great Britain*, a work that, like all his writings, is marked by clarity, common sense and candour. There are few in the story of English literature who can produce excellent satiric verse, novels that never bore and journalism of genius. Defoe could.

Dekker, Thomas (c. 1572–1632)

Most people have never heard of Thomas Dekker. The only reason that I have is that in 1957 I studied a play of his, *The Shoemaker's Holiday*, for A level. It is an excellent play, and Dekker is another figure in that unbelievable literary efflorescence that characterised sixteenth- and early seventeenth-century England. Have a look at the opening of *The Shoemaker's Holiday*. It has a vitality that is exciting:

LINCOLN: My lord mayor, you have sundry times
Feasted myself and many countries more:
Seldom or never can we be so kind
To make requital of your courtesy.
But leaving this, I hear my cousin Lacy
Is much affected to your daughter Rose.

LORD MAYOR: True, my good lord, and she loves him so well.

LINCOLN: Why, my lord mayor, think you it then a shame,
To join a Lacy with an Oteley's name?

LORD MAYOR: Too mean is my poor girl for his high birth;
Poor citizens must not with courtiers wed,
Who will in silks and gay apparel spend
More in one year than I am worth, by far:
Therefore your honour need not doubt my girl.

As you can see, we are at once plunged into a situation that is one of the stand-bys of English literature. Dekker, however, deals with it with an inventive verve that is captivating. However, *The Shoemaker's Holiday* does seem to have been the best of Dekker's fifty plays, and **Ben Jonson** criticised it at the time for structural weaknesses. Dekker's life, too, had structural weaknesses, and he lurched from catastrophe to catastrophe, even on occasion landing up in jail.

de la Mare, Walter

You will already be aware that this book practices total objectivity, and never allows personal bias to intervene. Thus you will accept without question that de la Mare was a writer of children's fiction and poetry who achieved great popularity in his lifetime largely because his quasi-romantic tweeness made an immediate appeal to the emotionally shallow. His best known poem is called *The Listeners*, and I must confess that its total spuriousness engenders within me a real rage:

> 'Is there anybody there?' said the Traveller,
>   Knocking on the moonlit door;
> And his horse in the silence champed the grasses
>   Of the forest's ferny floor:
> And a bird flew up out of the turret,
>   Above the Traveller's head:
>   And he smote upon the door again a second time,
>   'Is there anybody there?' he said.
> But no one descended to the Traveller;
>   No head from the leaf-fringed sill
> Leaned over and looked into his grey eyes,
>   Where he stood perplexed and still.
> But only a host of phantom listeners
>   That dwelt in the lone house then
> Stood listening in the quiet of the moonlight
>   To that voice from the world of men:
> Stood thronging the faint moonbeams on the dark stair,
>   That goes down to the empty hall,
> Hearkening in an air stirred and shaken
>   By the lonely Traveller's call.
> And he felt in his heart their strangeness,
>   Their stillness answering his cry,
> While his horse moved, cropping the dark turf,
>   'Neath the starred and leafy sky;
> For he suddenly smote on the door, even
>   Louder, and lifted his head:
> 'Tell them I came, and no one answered;
>   That I kept my word,' he said.
> Never the least stir made the listeners,
>   Though every word he spake

> Fell echoing through the shadowiness of the still house
> 　From the one man left awake:
> Ay, they heard his foot upon the stirrup,
> 　And the sound of iron on stone,
> And how the silence surged softly backward,
> 　When the plunging hoofs were gone.

Still, as they say, *chacun à son goût*, though de la Mare is certainly a long way from being my *goût*.

detective novel, the

It is a tribute to the enduring popularity of the detective novel that it makes an appearance at all in this excessively selective reference book. The truth is, detective fiction occupies a somewhat anomalous position. If you say to someone, 'I'm reading one of Conrad's novels at the moment,' you will gain street cred. To be reading **Conrad** is intellectually respectable. If, though, you say, 'I'm reading a Reginald Hill,' or, 'I'm reading a **Dorothy Sayers**,' you will gain no street cred whatsoever. Ever since **Wilkie Collins** wrote *The Moonstone* and **Conan Doyle** invented Sherlock Holmes, detective fiction has been the delight of millions of people, but it has never quite gained full respectability. Detective fiction is certainly much more worthy than romantic fiction, but it isn't as worthy as **Austen**, **Dickens** or even **Trollope**. Trying to account for this is difficult. It appears to be a fact that relatively intelligent people read detective fiction, while, on the whole, relatively stupid people read romantic fiction. Since it is intelligent people who read **Fielding**, **Thackeray**, *et al.*, why don't those people give as much credit to P. D. James or Michael Innes? Perhaps it is because a detective story has a tangible *raison d'être*. One needs to find out who killed Mary Randall or who stole the Picasso print. Once that is done, the story is over. A 'proper' novel, on the other hand, is more amorphous. It is concerned with spiritual resolution, with moral completion. Hence it exists on a higher plane than the detective novel.

You don't have to be very bright to realise that all this is pretentious guff, but I suspect that, consciously or unconsciously, it accounts for the down-grading of the detective novel.

deus ex machina

Translated as 'the god from the machine', this phrase refers to a device used in classical Greek plays, such as the lowering of a god or gods on to the stage to resolve the problems that the play has raised. As you can see, this is an easy dramatic option. King Clod has got himself into an impossible position by telling his wife that he was visiting Delphi last Thursday, persuading his son to dress up as a vestal virgin, convincing his mistress that his wife is dead, and instructing his daughter to train as a lyre player. Because of interactions between all five characters, King Clod now faces disgrace and the loss of his throne. Fortunately, Zeus now descends from the heavens, alters everybody's memory, and universal contentment ensues. As you will realise, this is not a wildly convincing or dramatically appropriate ending to the play. But for hundreds of years, dramatists have had recourse to a *deus ex machina*. It may not be a god descending from heaven, but instead the discovery of a long lost daughter, the finding of the buried treasure or the death of the villain in a mountaineering accident. A *deus ex machina* is when a situation is made resolvable by some exterior accident. It is artistically weak because the resolution does not come from inside the fabric of the play but is imposed upon it from outside.

Dickens, Charles (1812–70)

Charles Dickens is one of the greatest novelists that Britain has yet produced. This is surprising because he is so grossly sentimental as to become, at times, unreadable. This is surprising because he almost invariably creates caricatures, not characters. This is surprising because he can be so heavy-handed with his 'message' that he resembles a fundamentalist preacher. This is surprising because his plots are frequently contrived and often beggar belief. Why then, if Dickens is so flawed, is he accounted one of England's greatest writers?

The first reason is because Dickens created memorable characters in a way that had not been achieved since Shakespeare. Of course, having just said, 'he almost invariably creates caricatures, not characters', I appear to be contradicting myself. Not so. Take an example. You have known Sarah Jones for thirty years. You have worked together on the *Dereham Echo*. You and your husband have dinner with her and her spouse at least six times a year. You've babysat for each other. You even once went on holiday to the Pembrokeshire coast together. Yet did you know that she wrote about six letters a week for Amnesty International? Did you know that before she married Graham, she'd had an abortion? Did you know that Sarah had an almost encyclopaedic knowledge of Warwickshire Cricket Club? Of course you didn't. You only know the aspects of Sarah that she has chosen to reveal to you, or that have happened naturally to arise in the course of your mutual activities. I bet, for instance, that Sarah knows nothing about your passionate support for CND when you were an undergraduate. We none of us ever know a person fully. In most cases, even if we have known them for thirty years, we couldn't fill a quarto sheet about them. Hence, in reality, we really have contact with caricatures. Doris, another friend of Sarah's, knows a different Sarah from the one you know. We know that Mr Micawber in *David Copperfield* expects that something will turn up, but we know nothing about his interest in Devonian geology because, in the novel, it was not relevant to mention it. What Dickens does is create a character with some obsessive trait or quaint idiosyncrasy. We remember that, and then go on to accuse him of creating two dimensional characters, totally forgetting that although we've known Mrs Hollins for fifteen years, the only thing we really know about her is that she makes the Christmas cake for the Women's Institute. And notice too that when Dickens does give a character some besetting idiosyncrasy, that trait is a piece of shorthand for an important quality. When Mr Toots in *Dombey and Son* says that it is not a matter of any importance, we see the whole of his diffidence revealed. When we learn that Barkis is willin', we picture a whirlpool of passion hidden beneath his taciturnity. When Dickens selects one aspect of a character and reveals that vividly before us, it is not a fault. It is a virtue. **Shakespeare** does exactly the same. What do you know about Falstaff? He is a drunkard. You know nothing about his flower collection. What do you know about Iago? That he is a revengeful maniac, but not that he reads Dante. In other words, the characters of Shakespeare and Dickens are exactly like the characters of our everyday lives. How often do you hear, 'I'd never have thought Elsie would have done that.' Of course you wouldn't, because you don't know Elsie. When **Donne** said, 'No man is an island,' he got it entirely wrong. All men are islands.

Dickens can be rightly criticised for being over-moral, but we mustn't forget that, for most of us, some things are right and some things are wrong. It is a genuine strength in Dickens that, morally speaking, we know where we are. Aren't we, for instance, glad in *Great Expectations* that Biddy marries Joe who deserves her, rather than Pip who doesn't? Aren't we pleased in *A Tale of Two Cities* that Carton rescues Darnay from his undeserved execution? Of course we are.

Thirdly, Dickens tells a good story. Of course it is improbable in *Bleak*

House that Esther should turn out to be Lady Dedlock's daughter – but it's exciting. Fancy Monks being Oliver's half-brother in **Oliver Twist**. The convolutions of plot in *Our Mutual Friend* defy belief, but when we read it, it is like being caught up in the absurdities of a baroque opera, a sort of *Cosi fan tutte* squared.

So there we are: Dickens is a grievously flawed novelist, yet one who is so abundantly great that virtually all of us have to succumb to his power. And he can write. Just look at how *Great Expectations* opens; here we have atmosphere, action, excitement, humour and humanity:

My father's family name being Pirrip, and my Christian name Philip, my infant tongue could make of both names nothing longer or more explicit than Pip. So, I called myself Pip, and came to be called Pip.

I give Pirrip as my father's family name, on the authority of his tombstone and my sister – Mrs Joe Gargery, who married the black-smith. As I never saw my father or my mother, and never saw any likeness of either of them (for their days were long before the days of photographs), my first fancies regarding what they were like were unreasonably derived from their tombstones. The shape of the letters on my father's gave me an odd idea that he was a square, stout, dark man, with curly black hair. From the character and turn of the inscription, *Also Georgiana, Wife of the Above*, I drew a childish con-clusion that my mother was freckled and sickly. To five little stone lozenges, each about a foot and a half long, which were arranged in a neat row beside their grave, and were sacred to the memory of five little brothers of mine – who gave up trying to get a living exceedingly early in that universal struggle – I am indebted for a belief I religiously entertained that they had all been born on their backs with their hands in their trousers-pockets, and had never taken them out in this state of existence.

Ours was the marsh country, down by the river, within, as the river wound, twenty miles of the sea. My first most vivid and broad impression of the identity of things seems to me to have been gained on a memorable raw afternoon towards evening. At such a time I found out for certain that this bleak place overgrown with nettles was the churchyard; and that Philip Pirrip, late of this parish, and also Georgiana, wife of the above, were dead and buried; and that Alex-ander, Bartholomew, Abraham, Tobias and Roger, infant children of the aforesaid, were also dead and buried; and that the dark flat wilderness beyond the churchyard, intersected with dykes and mounds and gates, with scattered cattle feeding on it, was the marshes; and that the low leaden line beyond was the river; and that the distant savage lair, from which the wind was rushing, was the sea; and that the small bundle of shivers growing afraid of it all and beginning to cry was Pip.

'Hold your noise!' cried a terrible voice, as a man started up from among the graves at the side of the church porch. 'Keep still, you little devil, or I'll cut your throat!'

A fearful man, all in coarse grey, with a great iron on his leg. A man with no hat, and with broken shoes, and with an old rag tied round his head. A man who had been soaked in water, and smothered in mud, and lamed by stones, and cut by flints, and stung by nettles, and torn by briars; who limped, and shivered, and glared, and growled; and whose teeth chattered in his head as he seized me by the chin.

'Oh! Don't cut my throat, sir,' I pleaded in terror. 'Pray don't do it, sir.'

'Tell us your name!' said the man. 'Quick!'

'Pip, sir.'

'Once more,' said the man, staring at me. 'Give it mouth!'

'Pip. Pip, sir.'

How can anyone read that and not be forced to read on? Dickens had many flaws, but he had something else too: genius.

Dickinson, Emily (1830–86)

Emily Dickinson is an American poet – the phrase almost sounds like an **oxymoron**, doesn't it? – who published seven poems during her life, and left nearly two thousand to be discovered after her death. They were odd poems too. Let me just quote one selected at random from the 770 pages of the Faber edition of her collected poems:

> A little Road – not made of Man –
>   Enabled of the Eye –
> Accessible to Thill of Bee,
>   Or Cart of Butterfly;
>
> If Town it have – beyond itself,
>   'Tis that – I cannot say –
> I only know – no Curricle
>   That rumble there Bear me.

Clearly no one poem selected at random can adequately represent a poet's work, but the one above is entirely typical in several respects. It displays Dickinson's eccentric capitalisation, it shows her conviction that the dash is the only mode of punctuation that one ever needs, and it portrays that almost secret morbidity that so often afflicted Dickinson. SparkNotes summarise her work rather well in this paragraph:

> Of course, Dickinson's greatest achievement as a poet of inwardness is her brilliant, diamond-hard language. Dickinson often writes aphoristically, meaning that she compresses a great deal of meaning into a very small number of words. This can make her poems hard to understand on a first reading, but when their meaning does unveil itself, it often explodes in the mind all at once, and lines that seemed baffling can become intensely and unforgettably clear. Other poems – many of her most famous, in fact – are much less difficult to understand, and they exhibit her extraordinary powers of observation and description. Dickinson's imagination can lead her into very peculiar territory – some of her most famous poems are bizarre death-fantasies and astonishing metaphorical conceits – but she is equally deft in her navigation of the domestic, writing beautiful nature-lyrics alongside her wild flights of imagination and often combining the two with great facility.

It is also worth mentioning that Dickinson found it impossible to adhere to orthodox Christianity, and this produced a tension within her that often is reflected in her poetry. Yet that poetry was not published until 1955. I wonder if any other great poet has had to wait so long for recognition.

Dictionary of the English Language

The first really significant dictionary of the English language was produced by **Samuel Johnson**, and details of this incredible work will be found in the entry on the great man.

Dipsychus

This is the title of a poem by **A. H. Clough**. If you ever feel like an intellectual adrift in the world, this is the poem to read. *Dipsychus* was written in 1850 and is a hybrid between a poem and a play. It takes the form of scenes which, in various styles of verse, develop a dialogue between an idealist and a 'devil's advocate'. The word 'dipsychus' means 'divided mind' or 'two minds', and the work (which was never finished by Clough, nor published during his lifetime) depicts the ongoing squabble in the human soul between the starry-eyed do-gooder and the cynical hedonist. Being a starry-eyed do-gooder myself, it will not surprise you that I quote an entertaining section from the poem where the cynical hedonist holds sway:

> As I sat at the caf, I said to myself,
> They may talk as they please about what they call pelf,
> They may sneer as they like about eating and drinking
> But help it I cannot, I cannot help thinking,
>> How pleasant it is to have money, heigh ho!
>> How pleasant it is to have money.
>
> I sit at my table *en grand seigneur*,
> And when I have done, throw a crust to the poor;
> Not only the pleasure, one's self, of good living,
> But also the pleasure of now and then giving.
>> So pleasant it is to have money, heigh ho!
>> So pleasant it is to have money.
>
> It was but last winter I came up to town,
> But already I'm getting a little renown;
> I make new acquaintance where'er I appear;
> I am not too shy, and have nothing to fear.
>> So pleasant it is to have money, heigh ho!
>> So pleasant it is to have money.
>
> I drive through the streets, and I care not a d – n;
> The people they stare, and they ask who I am;
> And if I should chance to run over a cad,
> I can pay for the damage if ever so bad.
>> So pleasant it is to have money, heigh ho!
>> So pleasant it is to have money.
>
> We stroll to our box and look down on the pit,
> And if it weren't low should be tempted to spit;
> We loll and we talk until people look up,
> And when it's half over we go out to sup.
>> So pleasant it is to have money, heigh ho!
>> So pleasant it is to have money.

The best of the tables and the best of the fare –
And as for the others, the devil may care;
It isn't our fault if they dare not afford
To sup like a prince and be drunk as a lord.
    So pleasant it is to have money, heigh ho!
    So pleasant it is to have money.

We sit at our tables and tipple champagne;
Ere one bottle goes, comes another again;
The waiters they skip and they scuttle about,
And the landlord attends us so civilly out.
    So pleasant it is to have money, heigh ho!
    So pleasant it is to have money.

It was but last winter I came up to town,
But already I'm getting a little renown;
I get to good houses without much ado,
Am beginning to see the nobility too.
    So pleasant it is to have money, heigh ho!
    So pleasant it is to have money.

O dear! what a pity they ever should lose it!
For they are the gentry that know how to use it;
So grand and so graceful, such manners, such dinners,
But yet, after all, it is we are the winners.
    So pleasant it is to have money, heigh ho!
    So pleasant it is to have money.

Thus I sat at my table *en grand seigneur*,
And when I had done threw a crust to the poor;
Not only the pleasure, one's self, of good eating.
But also the pleasure of now and then treating,
    So pleasant it is to have money, heigh ho
    So pleasant it is to have money.

They may talk as they please about what they call pelf,
And how one ought never to think of one's self,
And how pleasures of thought surpass eating and drinking –
My pleasure of thought is the pleasure of thinking
    How pleasant it is to have money, heigh ho!
    How pleasant it is to have money.

But do not think that this rollicking ditty is typical of the poem. *Dipsychus* is so varied a work that no extract can be labelled as typical.

Disraeli, Benjamin (1804–81)

Disraeli was one of our more entertaining Prime Ministers who famously said, 'When I want to read a novel I write one.' Perhaps this was a pity, since as a novel writer Disraeli doesn't really rise much above a beta minus. *Sybil* and *Coningsby*, his two best known, do perhaps merit a B, and we should after all be grateful that British politics has given us at least one politician who was literate.

dissociation of sensibility

In 1921, **T. S. Eliot** wrote an essay entitled 'The Metaphysical Poets'. In this essay, Eliot argued that poets like Donne had been able to link intellectual endeavour and sensuous apprehension as a unified whole. However, since the mid-seventeenth century, he argued, there had been a dissociation of sensibility so that thought and feeling were now regarded as incompatible elements. This entirely unsubstantiated claim was taken up by a number of literary critics as evidence of the impoverishment of English literary history and/or evidence of the critic's insight.

dissonance

Just as our teeth grind together when we hear C and C sharp sounded together in a piece of music, so a writer can employ words or rhythms in such a way that they sound cacophonous. Here is an example from **Browning**'s poem *Childe Roland to the Dark Tower Came*:

> If there pushed any ragged thistle-stalk
> > Above its mates, the head was chopped; the bents
> > Were jealous else. What made those holes and rents
> In the dock's harsh swarth leaves, bruised as to baulk
> All hope of greenness? 'tis a brute must walk
> > Pashing their life out, with a brute's intents.

doggerel

> When in verse I want to share my feelings,
> The results are worse than potato peelings.
> So I've decided to give up verse;
> It only makes my writing worse.

The above four lines are an example of doggerel. Chris Baldick defines doggerel as being 'clumsy verse, usually monotonously rhymed, rhythmically awkward and often shallow in sentiment'. I'm not sure that doggerel needs all four elements to qualify as doggerel. I think an ability to make the reader wince is all that is required. **William McGonagall** never fails:

> 'Twas on the 26th of August, the sun was burning hot,
> In the year of 1346, which will never be forgot,
> Because the famous field of Cressy was slippery and gory,
> By the loss of innocent blood which I'll relate in story.

The doggerel that I wrote is just doggerel; that of McGonagall is the doggerel of genius!

Dombey and Son

This, in my opinion, is Dickens's first great novel. Published in 1848, it is grossly sentimental, has a plot that is laboured in the extreme, but has a power that transcends its defects superbly. It also possesses in Mr Toots one of the really great English characters. Mr Toots is not one of England's greatest intellects, but he has a heart and soul of infinite value. He falls in love with Florence Dombey, but this love is doomed to disappointment and he eventually marries Florence's nurse. No extract can be adequate because one needs to see it in context, but here is an extract from Chapter 62 where Mr Toots has some exciting news and where Dickens manages to create a scene that is funny, bizarre and deeply touching:

> But here is Mr Toots descending on the Midshipman with violent rapidity, and Mr Toots's face is very red as he bursts into the little parlour.
>
> 'Captain Gills,' says Mr Toots, 'and Mr Sols, I am happy to inform you that Mrs Toots has had an increase to her family.
>
> 'And it does her credit!' cries the Captain.
>
> 'I give you joy, Mr Toots!' says old Sol.
>
> 'Thank'ee,' chuckles Mr Toots, 'I'm very much obliged to you. I knew that you'd be glad to hear, and so I came down myself. We're positively getting on, you know. There's Florence, and Susan, and now here's another little stranger.'
>
> 'A female stranger?' enquires the Captain.

'Yes, Captain Gills,' says Mr Toots, 'and I'm glad of it. The oftener we can repeat that most extraordinary woman, my opinion is, the better!'

'Stand by!' says the Captain, turning to the old case-bottle with no throat – for it is evening, and the Midshipman's usual moderate provision of pipes and glasses is on the board. 'Here's to her, and may she have ever so many more!'

'Thank'ee, Captain Gills,' says the delighted Mr Toots. 'I echo the sentiment. If you'll allow me, as my so doing cannot be unpleasant to anybody, under the circumstances, I think I'll take a pipe.'

Mr Toots begins to smoke, accordingly, and in the openness of his heart is very loquacious.

'Of all the remarkable instances that that delightful woman has given of her excellent sense, Captain Gills and Mr Sols,' said Mr Toots, 'I think none is more remarkable than the perfection with which she has understood my devotion to Miss Dombey.'

Both his auditors assent.

'Because you know,' says Mr Toots, 'I have never changed my sentiments towards Miss Dombey. They are the same as ever. She is the same bright vision to me, at present, that she was before I made Walters's acquaintance. When Mrs Toots and myself first began to talk of – in short, of the tender passion, you know, Captain Gills – '

'Ay, ay, my lad,' says the Captain, 'as makes us all slue round – for which you'll overhaul the book – '

'I shall certainly do so, Captain Gills,' says Mr Toots, with great earnestness; 'when we first began to mention such subjects, I explained that I was what you may call a Blighted Flower, you know.'

The Captain approves of this figure greatly; and murmurs that no flower as blows is like the rose.

'But Lord bless me,' pursues Mr Toots, 'she was as entirely conscious of the state of my feelings as I was myself. There was nothing I could tell her. She was the only person who could have stood between me and the silent tomb, and she did it, in a manner to command my everlasting admiration. She knows that there's nobody in the world I look up to as I do to Miss Dombey. She knows that there's nothing on earth I wouldn't do for Miss Dombey. She knows that I consider Miss Dombey the most beautiful, the most amiable, the most angelic of her sex. What is her observation upon that? The perfection of sense. "My dear, you're right. *I* think so too." '

'And so do I!' says the Captain.

'So do I,' says Sol Gills.

'Then,' resumes Mr Toots, after some contemplative pulling at his pipe, during which his visage has expressed the most contented reflection, 'what an observant woman my wife is! What sagacity she possesses! What remarks she makes! It was only last night, when we were sitting in the enjoyment of connubial bliss – which, upon my word and honour, is a feeble term to express my feelings in the society of my wife – that she said how remarkable it was to consider the present position of our friend Walters. "Here," observes my wife, "he is, released from sea-going, after that first long voyage with his young bride" – as you know he was, Mr Sols.'

'Quite true,' says the old instrument-maker, rubbing his hands.

' "Here he is," says my wife, "released from that, immediately; appointed by the same establishment to a post of great trust and confidence at home; showing himself again worthy; mounting up the ladder with the greatest expedition; beloved by everybody; assisted by his uncle at the very best possible time of his fortunes" – which I think is the case, Mr Sols? My wife is always correct.'

'Why yes, yes – some of our lost ships, freighted with gold, have come home, truly,' returns old Sol, laughing. 'Small craft, Mr Toots, but serviceable to my boy!'

'Exactly so,' says Mr Toots. 'You'll never find my wife wrong. "Here he is," says that most remarkable woman, "so situated – and what follows? What follows?" observed Mrs Toots. Now pray remark, Captain Gills, and Mr Sols, the depth of my wife's penetration. "Why that, under the very eye of Mr Dombey, there is a foundation going on, upon which a – an Edifice;" that was Mrs Toots's word,' says Mr Toots exultingly, ' "is gradually rising, perhaps to equal, perhaps excel, that of which he was once the head, and the small beginnings of which" (a common fault, but a bad one, Mrs Toots said) "escaped his memory. Thus," said my wife, "from his daughter, after all, another Dombey and Son will ascend" – no "rise", that was Mrs Toots's word, "triumphant!" ' '

To appreciate that scene properly, you need to have read the preceding sixty-one chapters, so I suggest that as your task of the day.

Don Juan

This is **Byron**'s masterpiece. Published between 1819 and 1824 in 16 cantos, this poem has a variety and verve that make it irresistible. Have a look at the opening stanzas of Canto 1:

I want a hero: an uncommon want,
    When every year and month sends forth a new one,
Till, after cloying the gazettes with cant,
    The age discovers he is not the true one;
Of such as these I should not care to vaunt,
    I'll therefore take our ancient friend Don Juan –
We all have seen him, in the pantomime,
Sent to the devil somewhat ere his time.

Vernon, the butcher Cumberland, Wolfe, Hawke,
    Prince Ferdinand, Granby, Burgoyne, Keppel, Howe,
Evil and good, have had their tithe of talk,
    And fill'd their sign posts then, like Wellesley now;
Each in their turn like Banquo's monarchs stalk,
    Followers of fame, 'nine farrow' of that sow:
France, too, had Buonaparte and Dumourier
Recorded in the *Moniteur* and *Courier*.

Barnave, Brissot, Condorcet, Mirabeau,
    Petion, Clootz, Danton, Marat, La Fayette,
Were French, and famous people, as we know:
    And there were others, scarce forgotten yet,
Joubert, Hoche, Marceau, Lannes, Desaix, Moreau,
    With many of the military set,
Exceedingly remarkable at times,
But not at all adapted to my rhymes.

Nelson was once Britannia's god of war,
    And still should be so, but the tide is turn'd;
There's no more to be said of Trafalgar,
    'Tis with our hero quietly inurn'd;
Because the army's grown more popular,
    At which the naval people are concern'd;
Besides, the prince is all for the land-service,
Forgetting Duncan, Nelson, Howe and Jervis.

Brave men were living before Agamemnon
    And since, exceeding valorous and sage,
A good deal like him too, though quite the same none;
    But then they shone not on the poet's page,
And so have been forgotten. I condemn none,
    But can't find any in the present age
Fit for my poem (that is, for my new one);
So, as I said, I'll take my friend Don Juan.

It was a wise choice, and enables Byron to be lyrical, satirical, adventurous and amusing.

Donne, John (1572–1631)

Donne is the greatest of the so-called **'metaphysical poets'**, writers who were able to yoke intellectual argument and emotional feeling as a unified whole, or at least, so the argument goes. Let me give one poem to illustrate what I mean. The poem is called 'The Flea':

Marke but this flea, and marke in this,
How little that which thou deny'st me is;
Me it suck'd first, and now sucks thee,
And in this flea our two bloods mingled bee;
Confesse it, this cannot be said
A sinne, nor shame, nor losse of maidenhead,
    Yet this enjoyes before it wooe,
    And pamper'd swells with one blood made of two,
    And this, alas, is more than wee would doe.

Oh stay, three lives in one flea spare,
When we almost, nay more than maryed are.
This flea is you and I, and this
Our mariage bed, and mariage temple is;
Though parents grudge, and you, w'are met,
And cloyster'd in these living walls of Jet.
    Though use make thee apt to kill mee,
    Let not to this, selfe murder added bee,
    And sacrilege, three sinnes in killing three.

Cruell and sodaine, has thou since
Purpled thy naile, in blood of innocence?
In what could this flea guilty bee,

Except in that drop which it suckt from thee?
Yet thou triumph'st, and saist that thou
Find'st not thyself nor mee the weaker now;
   'Tis true, then learne how false, feares bee;
   Just so much honor, when thou yeeld'st to mee,
   Will wast, as this flea's death tooke life from thee.

Critics would argue that, before the **dissociation of sensibility**, Donne was able to link the sensuous urge to make love to his companion with the intellectual conceit of a flea biting them both and eventually dying for his impertinence. Whatever one makes of this thesis, no one can deny that Donne was supreme in linking disparate images and concepts into a unified whole, and as a consequence he became one of England's greatest poets. But Donne doesn't have to rely on striking images and wayward juxtapositions. He could be a great poet without them, and in his wonderful *Holy Sonnets*, he shows how:

At the round earth's imagin'd corners, blow
Your trumpets, angels, and arise, arise
From death, you numberless infinities
Of souls, and to your scatter'd bodies go;
All whom the flood did, and fire shall o'erthrow,
All whom war, dearth, age, agues, tyrannies,
Despair, law, chance hath slain, and you whose eyes
Shall behold God and never taste death's woe.
But let them sleep, Lord, and me mourn a space,
For if, above all these, my sins abound,
'Tis late to ask abundance of thy grace
When we are there; here on this lowly ground
Teach me how to repent; for that's as good
As if thou hadst seal'd my pardon with thy blood.

I am not a Christian, but the affirmation above moves me to tears. Some of the *Holy Sonnets* have a greatness quite beyond explication.

Doyle, Arthur Conan (1859–1930)

Doyle is best known for the creation of the detective Sherlock Holmes, but he also wrote some very readable adventure novels like *The White Company* (1891) and *The Lost World* (1912). He studied medicine at the University of Edinburgh, was an amateur footballer, played cricket for the MCC, was fascinated by spiritualism, twice stood unsuccessfully for Parliament, had a genuine concern for legal justice, and his gravestone reads:

STEEL TRUE

BLADE STARIGHT

ARTHUR CONAN DOYLE

KNIGHT

PATRIOT, PHYSICIAN & MAN OF LETTERS

The claim that he was a man of letters is almost something of an understatement. Doyle wrote a prodigious amount. There were nine novels or collections of short stories featuring Sherlock Holmes: *A Study in Scarlet* (1887), *The Sign of the Four* (1890), *The Adventures of Sherlock Holmes* (1892), *The Memoirs of Sherlock Holmes* (1894), *The Hound of the Baskervilles* (1902), *The Return of Sherlock Holmes* (1904), *The Valley of Fear* (1915), *His Last Bow* (1917) and *The Case-Book of Sherlock Holmes* (1927). The nature of Holmes is best delineated in *A Study in Scarlet*. First of all, his assistant, Dr Watson, summarises him as follows: 'His ignorance was as remarkable as his knowledge. Of contemporary literature, philosophy and politics he appeared to know next to nothing. Upon my quoting Thomas Carlyle, he inquired in the naïvest way who he might be and what he had done. My surprise reached a climax, however, when I found incidentally that he was ignorant of the Copernican Theory and of the composition of the Solar System. That any civilised human being in this nineteenth century should not be aware that the earth travelled round the sun appeared to be to me such an extraordinary fact that I could hardly realise it.' Holmes then goes on to explain this: 'You see, I consider that a man's brain originally is like a little empty attic, and you have to stock it with such furniture as you choose. A fool takes in all the lumber of every sort that he comes across, so that the knowledge which might be useful to him gets crowded out, or at best is jumbled up with a lot of other things so that he has difficulty in laying his hands upon it. Now the skilful workman is very careful indeed as to what he takes into his brain-attic. He will have nothing but the tools which may help him in doing his work, but of these he has a large assortment, and all in the most perfect order. It is a mistake to think that that little room has elastic walls and can distend to any extent. Depend upon it, there comes a time when for every addition of knowledge you forget something that you knew before. It is of the highest importance, therefore, not to have useless facts elbowing out the useful ones.'

There were five novels featuring Professor Challenger: *The Lost World* (1912), *The Poison Belt* (1913), *The Land of Mist* (1926), *The Disintegration Machine* (1927) and *When the World Screamed* (1928). Professor Challenger is a zoologist, and not known for his patience with the intellectually dim, as this quotation from *The Lost World* indicates: 'You quote an isolated sentence from my lecture, and appear to have some difficulty in understanding it. I should have thought that only a sub-human intelligence could have failed to grasp the point, but if it really needs amplification I shall consent to see you at the hour named . . .' Nor was Challenger hampered by undue modesty. In *When the World Screamed*, he promotes one of his own books as follows: 'I was about to say, before I was interrupted by this unseemly remark, that the whole matter is very fully and lucidly discussed in my forthcoming volume upon the earth, which I may describe with all due modesty as one of the epoch-making books of the world's history.' With such touching diffidence, it is impossible not to warm to the man.

It is, of course, for Sherlock Holmes and, to a lesser extent, Challenger that Doyle is remembered today, but he wrote a great deal more. There were seven historical novels: *Micah Clarke* (1888), *The White Company* (1891), *The Great Shadow* (1892), *The Refugees* (1893), *Rodney Stone* (1896), *Uncle Bernac* (1897) and *Sir Nigel* (1906). Astoundingly, there were at least another forty books, some fiction, some non-fiction. Almost everybody has heard of Conon Doyle; few realise that he was virtually a human book factory.

Drabble, Margaret (1939–)

Apart from being the editor of the 2000 edition of *The Oxford Companion to English Literature*, a volume to which this bastard offspring is much indebted, Margaret Drabble is also a significant novelist in her own right. *The Millstone* (1965) struck me as being particularly good.

dramatic irony

This is the situation in a play when the audience knows more about the situation than the actors on the stage do. For instance, I know that Sir Peter Teazle's wife is hiding behind the screen when Sir Peter is talking about her to Joseph Surface in **Sheridan**'s *School for Scandal*. I know that the letter found by Malvolio in **Shakespeare**'s *Twelfth Night* is not really from Olivia, though he thinks it is. Moments of dramatic irony are very effective, because they make the audience feel superior!

dramatic monologue

A poem thus described is *dramatic* in the sense that it has a theatrical quality, and a *monologue* in that it is spoken by a solitary speaker. This literary technique has been mentioned in connection with **Browning**, but deserves an entry of its own. As the protagonist in a dramatic monologue speaks, he or she not only tells us about the matter that concerns them, but also unwittingly reveals key aspects of their character. It is this latter element that constitutes the major interest of the poem. Although Browning's are probably the most famous examples (*My Last Duchess*, *Fra Lippo Lippi*, *Caliban upon Setebos*, etc.), it is thought that **Tennyson**'s *Ulysses* might be the first example of this genre. In the twentieth century, the influence of Browning's monologues can be seen in the works of **Ezra Pound** and **T. S. Eliot**.

drawing-room comedy

This type of play was quite common in the early twentieth century. The genre concerned itself with middle-class crises enacted often literally in the drawing-room. Well-known examples include **Shaw**'s *Candida* (1895), Coward's *Hay Fever* (1925) and Rattigan's *The Browning Version* (1948).

Drayton, Michael (1563–1631)

It must be extremely irritating to the ghost of a poet for him to discover that he is remembered for only one poem. Such is the case with Michael Drayton. Like so many sixteenth-century men, he produced scores of poems, but is today remembered for only one **sonnet**:

> Since there's no help, come let us kiss and part,
>   Nay, I have done: you get no more of me,
> And I am glad, yea glad with all my heart,
>   That thus so cleanly I myself can free.
> Shake hands for ever, cancel all our vows,
>   And when we meet at any time again
> Be it not seen in either of our brows
>   That we one jot of former love retain.
> Now at the last gasp of Love's latest breath,
>   When his pulse failing, Passion speechless lies,
> When Faith is kneeling by his bed of death,
>   And Innocence is closing up his eyes,
>   Now, if thou wouldst, when all have given him over,
>   From death to life thou might'st him yet recover.

I trust that you agree that it is a splendid sonnet, but all the rest of Drayton's work remains sadly neglected. This does, however, give you ample opportunity to select from it a PhD topic. You could decide to explicate Drayton's obscure satire *The Owle* (1604) or examine his use of legends in *Matilda* (1594). As always, I try to be helpful.

Dryden, John (1631–1700)

Although he did have a small income of his own, John Dryden kept the wolf from the door largely by his writing. So successful was he in producing poems, plays, criticism and translations that his contemporaries began to refer to the second half of the seventeenth century as the Age of Dryden. In 1668 he was made Poet Laureate, largely perhaps because in 1667 he had written *Annus Mirabilis*, a lengthy poem describing the English defeat of the Dutch naval fleet and the Great Fire of London, both events of 1666.

Like most of us, Dryden was a man of many parts. There can be little doubt that he was an extremely skilled translator. He was also an extremely impressive critic. In addition, he was genuinely religious, and in *Religio Laici* (1682), he presented an argument for the faith of the Church of England. He begins it thus:

> Dim, as the borrow'd beams of moon and stars
> To lonely, weary, wand'ring travellers,
> Is reason to the soul; and as on high,
> Those rolling fires discover but the sky
> Not light us here; so reason's glimmering ray
> Was lent not to assure our doubtful way
> But guide us upward to a better day.
> And as those nightly tapers disappear
> When day's bright lord ascends our hemisphere,
> So pale grows reason at religion's sight:
> So dies, and so dissolves in supernatural light.
> Some few, whose lamp shone brighter, have been led
> From cause to cause, to Nature's secret head,
> And found that one first principle must be:
> But what, or who, that Universal He;
> Whether some soul incompassing this ball
> Unmade, unmov'd; yet making, moving all;
> Or various atoms' interfering dance

Leapt into form (the noble work of chance);
Or this great all was from eternity;
Not even the Stagirite himself could see;
And Epicurus guess'd as well as he:
As blindly grop'd they for a future state;
As rashly judg'd of Providence and Fate:
But least of all could their endeavours find
What most concern'd the good of human kind.
For happiness was never to be found;
But vanish'd from 'em, like enchanted ground.
One thought content the good to be enjoy'd:
This, every little accident destroy'd:
The wiser madmen did for virtue toil:
A thorny, or at best a barren soil:
In pleasure some their glutton souls would steep;
But found their line too short, the well too deep;
And leaky vessels which no bliss could keep.
Thus anxious thoughts in endless circles roll,
Without a centre where to fix the soul:
In this wild maze their vain endeavours end:
How can the less the greater comprehend?
Or finite reason reach infinity?
For what could fathom God were more than He.

Yet it is for his satires that Dryden is best known today. One of his earliest, *Mac Flecknoe*, appeared in an unauthorised edition in October 1682; it describes the king of Nonsense, Richard Flecknoe, looking for a successor to his throne and settling on Thomas Shadwell. See separate entry and delight in the sheer fun of the captivating lines. There is also a separate entry on Dryden's masterpiece, *Absalom and Achitophel*, so have a look at that as well. You will notice that what Dryden achieved in his poetry was not the emotional excitement we find in the Romantic poets of the early nineteenth century, nor the intellectual complexities of the **metaphysical poets**. His subject matter was often factual, and he aimed at expressing his thoughts in the most precise way possible. Although he uses formal poetic structures such as heroic stanzas and heroic couplets, he tried to achieve the rhythms of speech. What he does achieve is a relaxed comedy that is as funny as anything in English literature. Here is brief extract from *MacFlecknoe* to whet your appetite:

The rest to some faint meaning make pretence,
But Shadwell never deviates into sense.
Some beams of wit on other souls may fall,
Strike through and make a lucid interval;
But Shadwell's genuine night admits no ray,
His rising fogs prevail upon the day.

No doubt this did not amuse Shadwell, but for the rest of us it is a delight. In addition, if you know anything about the poetry of **Pope**, it is not difficult to see how strongly he was influenced by Dryden. Dryden did not only have an age of his own, but he strongly influenced other ages too.

Dubliners

This volume of short stories was written by **James Joyce** and published in 1914. They are a wonderful achievement, and one can only regret that Joyce lapsed more and more into incomprehensibility until ending with the total enigma of *Finnegans Wake*.

Dunciad, The

This long poem by **Alexander Pope** is the intellectual snob's gospel. In it, Pope celebrated the triumph of Dulness (*sic*) and all her expert practitioners. Book 4 of *The Dunciad* ends as follows:

Religion blushing veils her sacred fires,
And unawares Morality expires.
Nor public flame, nor private, dares to shine;
Nor human spark is left, nor glimpse divine!
Lo! thy dread empire, CHAOS! is restor'd;
Light dies before thy uncreating word:
Thy hand, great Anarch! lets the curtain fall;
And universal darkness buries all.

If you have just been reading about Dryden, you can see that Pope is darker and more savage than Dryden.

Dylan, Bob (1941–)

I am told by friends that I must have Bob Dylan in my encyclopaedia. So I do.

E

eclogue

This word derives from the Greek word for 'selection', and hence originally referred to a short poem or a section extracted from a longer poem. However, later the word was attached to the pastoral poems of Virgil, and has consequently been applied to poems like **Spenser**'s *The Shepheards Calendar* and other rustic rhymes.

Edgeworth, Maria (1767–1849)

Castle Rackrent (1800) is the only Edgeworth novel that I have read – she wrote seven – and so I cannot comment on her skill as a writer, particularly since it is about fifty years since I read *Castle Rackrent* and I can remember nothing about it. However, **Jane Austen** recommends Edgeworth's novel *Belinda* in *Northanger Abbey*, and I operate on the principle that anything that Jane Austen commends ought to be mentioned in this book. In addition, Maria Edgeworth was explicit about the fact that all her stories had a moral purpose behind them, usually pointing out the duty of members of the upper class towards their tenants. Consequently, on moral grounds alone, Maria Edgeworth needs to appear in this book!

Edward II

This is a play by **Christopher Marlowe** that was first performed in 1592. I haven't read it for years, but remember enjoying it. The play is said to have been an important influence on **Shakespeare**'s *Richard II*. It's full title is *The Troublesome Reign and Lamentable Death of Edward the Second, King of England, with the Tragical Fall of Proud Mortimer*.

Edward III

This is a play that was published in 1596. Nobody knows who wrote it, but you can make a reputation for yourself at dinner parties by arguing that its imagery clearly indicates the hand of **Shakespeare**.

MARINER: Near to the coast I have descried, my lord,
                    As I was busy in my watchful charge,

> The proud armada of King Edward's ships,
> Which, at the first, far off when I did ken,
> Seemed as it were a grove of withered pines;
> But, drawing near, their glorious bright aspect,
> Their streaming ensigns wrought of coloured silk,
> Like to a meadow full of sundry flowers,
> Adorns the naked bosom of the earth.

That is an extract from Scene 1, Act 3 of the play. Learn it off by heart; you will be the only person in your town who can quote by memory from *Edward III*. In fact, you may be the only person in the country.

Edwin Drood, The Mystery of

This is the last novel of **Charles Dickens**. Unfortunately Dickens died before he finished it, and sundry people have subsequently attempted to do the job for him. It certainly opens more bizarrely than perhaps any other Dickens novel:

An ancient English cathedral town? How can the ancient English cathedral town be here! The well-known massive grey square tower of its old cathedral? How can that be here! There is no spike of rusty iron in the air, between the eye and it, from any point of the real prospect. What is the spike that intervenes, and who has set it up? Maybe it is set up by the sultan's orders for the impaling of a horde of Turkish robbers, one by one. It is so, for cymbals clash, and the sultan goes by to his palace in long procession. Ten thousand scimitars flash in the sunlight, and thrice ten thousand dancing-girls strew flowers. Then follow white elephants caparisoned in countless gorgeous colours and infinite in number and attendants. Still the cathedral tower rises in the background, where it cannot be, and still no writhing figure is on the grim spike. Stay! Is the spike so low a thing as the rusty spike on the top of a post of an old bedstead that has tumbled all awry? Some vague period of drowsy laughter must be devoted to the consideration of this possibility.

Shaking from head to foot, the man whose scattered consciousness has thus fantastically pieced itself together, at length rises, supports his trembling frame upon his arms, and looks around. He is in the meanest and closest of small rooms. Through the ragged window-curtain, the light of early day steals in from a miserable court. He lies, dressed, across a large unseemly bed, upon a bedstead that has indeed given way under the weight upon it. Lying, also dressed and also across the bed, not longwise, are a Chinaman, a Lascar, and a haggard woman. The two first are in a sleep or stupor; the last is blowing at a kind of pipe, to kindle it. And as she blows, and shading it with her lean hand, concentrates its red spark of light, it serves in the dim morning as a lamp to show him what he sees of her.

In fact we are in an opium den, and the male character whose scattered consciousness we encounter is a choirmaster named John Jasper, who is in love with his pupil, Rosa Bud. Miss Bud is Edwin Drood's fiancée, so obviously we have here a central conflict. Rosa has also caught the eye of the high-spirited and hot-tempered Neville Landless, who comes from Ceylon with his twin sister, Helena. By the end of the novel, Drood has disappeared, and most readers feel that Jasper has killed him. However, the knowledge of what has really happened went with Dickens to the grave.

egotistical sublime

This splendid phrase was used by **Keats** to describe what he felt was the excessively self-centred quality of **Wordsworth**'s poetry. Instead, Keats wanted what he called **negative capability**.

elegy

Somewhat oddly this word has tended to mean different things at different points of time. From the sixteenth century onwards, an elegy has been a poem that is reflective in nature, though over time it has evolved more specifically into a lament on the death of someone deeply mourned. Thus you get **Shelley**'s *Adonais* for **Keats**, **Tennyson**'s *In Memoriam* for **A. H. Hallam** and **Matthew Arnold**'s *Thyrsis* for **Clough**.

Eliot, George (1819–1880)

As you may know, George Eliot was the pen name of Mary Ann Evans, one of the four greatest novelists Britain has ever produced. The twentieth-century writer **Virginia Woolf** declared that the greatest of Eliot's novels, *Middlemarch*, was 'one of the few English novels written for grown-up people'. One may disagree, of course (and I think most people would), but Eliot combines a narrative impetus with a moral direction that render her best novels profound, and very few English novels are that. In order of publication, her novels are:

Adam Bede	1859
The Mill on the Floss	1860
Silas Marner	1861
Romola	1863
Felix Holt the Radical	1866
Middlemarch	1872
Daniel Deronda	1876

They were preceded in 1858 by a volume of short stories called *Scenes of Clerical Life*. Frankly, I think that you can ignore *Scenes of Clerical Life*, but the seven novels are well worth attention. Four of them – *The Mill on the Floss*, *Silas Marner*, *Middlemarch* and *Daniel Deronda* – are masterpieces, and the other three are better than most people ever achieve.

Eliot, Thomas Stearns (1888–1965)

Born in the United States, T. S. Eliot was the greatest poet of the twentieth century. His first major poem, *The Love Song of J. Alfred Prufrock*, was published in 1915, and its combination of lyricism, satire, allusiveness and the elegiac is typical of Eliot:

> Let us go then, you and I,
> When the evening is spread out against the sky
> Like a patient etherised upon a table;
> Let us go, through certain half-deserted streets,
> The muttering retreats
> Of restless nights in one-night cheap hotels
> And sawdust restaurants with oyster-shells:
> Streets that follow like a tedious argument
> Of insidious intent
> To lead you to an overwhelming question . . .
> Oh, do not ask, 'What is it?'
> Let us go and make our visit.
>
> In the room the women come and go
> Talking of Michelangelo.

It was, however, *The Waste Land* in 1922 that propelled Eliot into the stratosphere. This has always puzzled me, largely because I have never understood *The Waste Land*. When confronted by a poem that you do not understand, there are two positions that you can take. You can either say, 'Oh dear, I'm not clever enough to understand this poem', or you can say, 'This poem fails to communicate anything at all to me, so it is clearly a very bad poem.' It probably needs little insight to guess which view I took. Fortunately, between 1935 and 1942, Eliot produced the *Four Quartets*, and they are wondrous poems.

Eliot was, of course, deeply religious, and this permeates many of his poems. It also informs certain of his poetic plays, especially *Murder in the Cathedral*. In addition, Eliot was a penetrating literary critic. For overall impact on the twentieth century, there is perhaps no one more significant.

elision

When you slur one word into another – th'Eternal music of Bach – you are practising elision. In **poetry**, elision is often employed so as to force a line into the required metrical pattern, though sometimes, and more pragmatically, it is used simply to make pronunciation easier.

Elliott, Ebenezer (1781–1849)

Ebenezer Elliot (isn't it a splendid name?) wrote three volumes of poetry, *The Village Patriarch* (1829), *Corn-Law Rhymes* (1831) and *The Splendid Village* (1835). Although he wrote on the side of the angels in attacking the Corn Laws and describing the horrors of rural poverty, he is a dreadful poet. He only appears here because I have never met anyone else who has read Ebenezer Elliott. Doubtless there are thousands of others, but I live a sheltered life. Here is the opening of one of his most emotive poems, *The Ranter*:

> Miles Gordon sleeps; his six days' labour done,
> He dreams of Sunday, verdant fields, and prayer:
> O rise, bless'd morn, unclouded! Let thy sun
> Shine on the artisan – thy purest air
> Breathe on the bread-tax'd labourer's deep despair!
> Poor sons of toil! I grudge them not the breeze
> That plays with Sabbath flowers, the clouds that play
> With Sabbath winds, the hum of Sabbath bees,
> The Sabbath walk, the skylark's Sabbath lay,
> The silent sunshine of the Sabbath day.
> The stars wax pale, the moon is cold and dim;
> Miles Gordon wakes, and grey dawn tints the skies:
> The many-childed widow, who to him

Is as a mother, hears her lodger rise,
And listens to his prayer with swimming eyes.
For her and for her orphans poor he prays,
For all who earn the bread they daily eat:
'Bless them, O God, with useful, happy days,
With hearts that scorn all meanness and deceit;
And round their lowly hearths let freemen meet!'
This morn, betimes, she hastes to leave her bed,
For he must preach beneath th' autumnal tree:
She lights her fire, and soon the board is spread
With Sabbath coffee, toast, and cups for three.
Pale he descends; again she starts to see
His hollow cheek, and feels they soon must part!
But they shall meet again – that hope is sure;
And, oh! she venerates his mind and heart,
For he is pure, if mortal e'er was pure!
His words, his silence, teach her to endure!
And then he helps to feed her orphan'd five!
O God! thy judgments cruel seem to be!
While bad men biggen long, and cursing thrive,
The good, like wintry sunbeams, fade and flee –
That we may follow *them*, and come to thee.

Even so brief an extract induces nausea.

ellipsis

An ellipse or the practice of ellipsis is when you deliberately miss out a word, knowing perfectly well that what you are saying will be understood anyway. **Shakespeare**, for instance, often uses the form, 'I will to Ireland,' because he knows that we will 'hear', 'I will go to Ireland.'

emblem

It would have been better to have omitted 'emblem' because I have never really understood what the word means. Something can be an emblem of something else. Thus the dove can be an emblem of peace. Someone can be an emblem of some quality. Thus a British banker can be an emblem of greed, Othello can be an emblem of jealousy, and Nelson Mandela can be an emblem of almost all the virtues. How, then, does the sense differ from that of the word 'symbol'? You see my problem.

Emma

In my opinion, this is **Jane Austen**'s greatest novel. Jane Austen gives the appearance of being cool, ironic and wise, yet in *Emma* she is much more. Emma the character is an egregious snob, and the whole novel is largely organised around Emma's errors of judgement and her manifest failure to understand her own nature. We ought, therefore, to loathe Emma, to find her tiresome and insufferable. Instead we suffer with her, sympathise with her, and yearn for her well-being. She is introduced to us in the very first chapter:

Emma Woodhouse, handsome, clever, and rich, with a comfortable home and happy disposition, seemed to unite some of the best blessings of existence; and had lived nearly twenty-one years in the world with very little to distress or vex her.

She was the youngest of the two daughters of a most affectionate, indulgent father; and had, in consequence of her sister's marriage, been mistress of his house from a very early period. Her mother had died too long ago for her to have more than an indistinct remembrance of her caresses; and her place had been supplied by an excellent woman as governess, who had fallen little short of a mother in affection.

Sixteen years had Miss Taylor been in Mr Woodhouse's family, less as a governess than a friend, very fond of both daughters, but particularly of Emma. Between *them* it was more the intimacy of sisters. Even before Miss Taylor had ceased to hold the nominal office of governess, the mildness of her temper had hardly allowed her to impose any restraint; and the shadow of authority being now long passed away, they had been living together as friend and friend very mutually attached, and Emma doing just what she liked; highly esteeming Miss Taylor's judgment, but directed chiefly by her own.

The real evils, indeed, of Emma's situation were the power of having rather too much her own way, and a disposition to think a little too well of herself; these were the disadvantages which threatened alloy to her many enjoyments. The danger, however, was at present so unperceived, that they did not by any means rank as misfortunes with her.

Sorrow came – a gentle sorrow – but not at all in the shape of any disagreeable consciousness. Miss Taylor married. It was Miss Taylor's loss which first brought grief. It was on the wedding-day of this beloved friend that Emma first sat in mournful thought of any continuance. The wedding over, and the bride-people gone, her father and herself were left to dine together, with no prospect of a third to cheer a long evening. Her father composed himself to sleep after dinner, as usual, and she had then only to sit and think of what she had lost.

The event had every promise of happiness for her friend. Mr Weston was a man of unexceptionable character, easy fortune, suitable age, and pleasant manners; and there was some satisfaction in considering with what self-denying, generous friendship she had always wished and promoted the match; but it was a black morning's work for her. The want of Miss Taylor would be felt every hour of every day. She recalled her past kindness – the kindness, the affection of sixteen years – how she had taught and how she had played with her from five years old – how she had devoted all her powers to attach and amuse her in health – and how nursed her through the various illnesses of childhood. A large debt of gratitude was owing here; but the intercourse of the last seven years, the equal footing and perfect unreserve which had soon followed Isabella's marriage, on their being left to each other, was yet a dearer, tenderer recollection. She had been a friend and companion such as few possessed: intelligent, well-informed, useful, gentle, knowing all the ways of the family, interested in all its concerns, and peculiarly interested in herself, in every pleasure, every scheme of hers – one to whom she could speak every thought as it arose, and who had such an affection for her as could never find fault.

How was she to bear the change? – It was true that her friend was going only half a mile from them; but Emma was aware that great must be the difference between a Mrs Weston, only half a mile from them, and a Miss Taylor in the house; and with all her advantages, natural and domestic, she was now in great danger of suffering from intellectual solitude. She dearly loved her father, but he was no companion for her. He could not meet her in conversation, rational or playful.

Already we are ensnared. Jane Austen has already made us identify with this opinionated girl, and we follow her growth with the concern of a parent. For Jane Austen to be able to do that is, in itself, a tribute to her style, and it is a style that is a great deal more than simply cool, ironic and wise. It is a style that is humane.

empathy

empathy

Empathy is the ability to share and understand the feelings of someone else. A good writer often induces you to feel empathy for one of his or her characters. *The Penguin Dictionary of Literary Terms and Literary Theory* even suggests that one can feel empathy for inanimate objects, but personally I have always remained unmoved by the burdens of a railway bridge or the stresses of a garden fork.

empiricism

Strictly speaking there should now follow several hundred pages of closely argued philosophy. Empiricism is the belief that knowledge and understanding are derived from observation and experience rather than logical deduction. This has always struck me as absurd. Take the following logical argument:

> All men are mortal.
> Gordon Brown is a man.
> Therefore Gordon Brown is mortal.

That seems to me to be quite clearly a conclusion derived from logical deduction and not dependent on empiricism at all. But then I'm not a philosopher!

end-stopped line

This phrase is used to refer to a line of poetry that expresses a complete thought. Consequently, when reading the poem aloud, there is a natural pause at the end of the line:

> She ey'd the Bard, where supperless he sate,
> And pin'd, unconscious of his rising fate;
> Studious he sate, with all his books around,
> Sinking from thought to thought, a vast profound!

Those lines from **Pope**'s *Dunciad* are all end-stopped. The following lines from **Eliot**'s *East Coker* are not:

> In my beginning is my end. In succession
> Houses rise and fall, crumble, are extended,
> Are removed, destroyed, restored, or in their place
> Is an open field, or a factory, or a by-pass.

Constant end-stopping does tend to render a poem somewhat dull and predictable, though, at the same time, end-stopping does give a poem an appearance of completion, of self-contained sense.

enjambment

Enjambment is the opposite of end-stopping. It is when lines of poetry run into one another as far as coherence is concerned. An end-stopped verse would be like this:

> My love is like a dish of prunes,
> A dish that sings such lovely tunes.
> Without her I would be very sad;
> In fact I think I might go mad.

A poem displaying enjambment might look like this:

> My love could validly be compared
> To a dish of prunes if one fared
> Well upon that taste, but the facts
> Are often otherwise. Yet all the pacts . . .

I'm sure you get the idea, while wincing at the verse that illustrates it.

epic

English poetry does not present us with very many epics. An epic is a long poem devoted to the activities of some heroic figure. **Homer**'s *Odyssey* is devoted to the wanderings of Odysseus and Virgil's *Aeneid* to the adventures of Aeneas. There is nothing comparable in English. **Milton**'s *Paradise Lost* is often cited as an epic, but it is a bit difficult to see who is the heroic figure. **Wordsworth**'s *The Prelude* has been called an epic, but it is hard to see the growth of Wordsworth's mind as quite as heroic as the saga of the Trojan War. **Byron**'s *Don Juan* looks very much like an epic, but its satiric nature debars it; you can't poke fun at your hero. Clearly this presents another opportunity for you: write the first English epic.

epigram

An epigram can be a short, witty poem. Indeed **Coleridge** wrote an epigram in order to define one:

> What is an epigram? A dwarfish whole,
> Its body brevity and wit its soul.

Dryden composed an epigram as an epitaph for his wife's tomb:

> Here lies my wife: here let her lie!
> Now she's at rest – and so am I.

One can, though, also have epigrams in prose. Oscar Wilde's remark, 'I can resist everything except temptation', is a well known example.

epilogue

The epilogue is the conclusion or ending of a written work, yet, though all written works have conclusions or endings, few of them have epilogues. We seem to be caught in an internal contradiction. Let me try to explain. You have been to the theatre. The play has just ended, and it was a delightful comedy about love, loyalty and magic called *A Midsummer Night's Dream*. Yet although the play was splendid, it doesn't somehow seem quite finished. Then, just as you are beginning to clap, the curtain is drawn aside and one of the characters in the play begins to speak:

> If we shadows have offended,
> Think but this, and all is mended:
> That you have but slumber'd here
> While these visions did appear.
> And this weak and idle theme,
> No more yielding but a dream,
> Gentles, do not reprehend:
> if you pardon, we will mend.
> And, as I am an honest Puck,
> If we have unearnèd luck
> Now to 'scape the serpent's tongue,
> We will make amends ere long,
> Else the Puck a liar call.
> So, good night unto you all.
> Give me your hands, if we be friends,
> And Robin shall restore amends.

That is the epilogue. It doesn't advance the action of the play one iota. It doesn't tell you anything that you didn't already know. What it does is graciously send the audience home feeling good. Consequently not all plays or all novels need an epilogue.

Epipsychidion

This is an autobiographical poem by Shelley. It is basically a rapturous tribute to Shelley's libido. He gloriously envisages endless romantic trysts:

> A ship is floating in the harbour now,
> A wind is hovering o'er the mountain's brow;
> There is a path on the sea's azure floor,
> No keel has ever plough'd that path before;
> The halcyons brood around the foamless isles;
> The treacherous Ocean has forsworn its wiles;
> The merry mariners are bold and free:
> Say, my heart's sister, wilt thou sail with me?
> Our bark is as an albatross, whose nest
> Is a far Eden of the purple East;
> And we between her wings will sit, while Night,
> And Day, and Storm, and Calm, pursue their flight.
> Our ministers, along the boundless Sea,
> Treading each other's heels, unheededly.

Personally I find the whole thing adolescently tiresome, but many critics have greatly admired the poem.

epistolary novel

This is a novel written entirely in the form of letters. It was popular in the eighteenth century, and one of its finest exponents was **Samuel Richardson**.

epitaph

Normally speaking, an epitaph is engraved on the tombstone of some-one and summarises their life. Thus a dentist has an epitaph which reads:

> Stranger ! Approach this spot with gravity !
> John Brown is filling his last cavity.

Understandably, few epitaphs are amusing. The majority tend to follow this sort of pattern:

> Here lies One Whose Name was writ in Water.

That is the epitaph of **John Keats**. The one for Rupert Brooke is equally well known:

> If I should die, think only this of me:
> That there's some corner of a foreign
> field that is for ever England.

Some epitaphs even contain a threat, like Shakespeare's:

> Good Frend for Jesus sake forbeare,
> to digg the dust encloased heare.
> Blest be ye man that spares thes stones
> and curst be he that moves my bones.

Since most of us are cremated these days, perhaps the age of epitaphs is drawing to a close.

epithalamion

This is a song or poem sung outside the bride's bedchamber on her wedding night. In the sixteenth and seventeenth centuries, a galaxy of English poets – **Sidney**, **Spenser**, **Donne**, **Jonson**, **Herrick**, **Marvell**, Crashaw, and **Dryden** – all wrote at least one epithalamion, but the form then went out of fashion. **Shelley** and **Tennyson** both wrote one, but they did not stimulate others to do so, and, for most people today, you could explain that an epithalamion was an orange snail found in Egypt and they would believe you. However, among poetry lovers it is almost universally agreed that Spenser wrote one of the finest. It is too long to reproduce in full, but here is a lengthy extract:

> Early, before the world's light-giving lamp
> His golden beam upon the hills doth spread,
> Having dispersed the night's uncheerfull damp,
> Do ye awake; and, with fresh lusty head,
> Go to the bower of my beloved love,
> My truest turtle dove;
> Bid her awake; for Hymen is awake,
> And long since ready forth his mask to move,
> With his bright torch that flames with many a flake,
> And many a bachelor to wait on him,
> In their fresh garments trim.
> Bid her awake therefore, and soon her dight,
> For lo! the wishèd day is come at last,
> That shall, for all the pains and sorrows past,
> Pay to her usury of long delight:

And, whilst she doth her dight,
Do ye to her of joy and solace sing,
That all the woods may answer, and your echo ring.

Bring with you all the Nymphs that you can hear
Both of the rivers and the forests green,
And of the sea that neighbours to her near,
All with gay garlands goodly well beseen.
And let them also with them bring in hand
Another gay garland
For my fair love, of lilies and of roses,
Bound truelove wise, with a blue silk riband.
And let them make great store of bridal posies,
And let them eke bring store of other flowers
To deck the bridal bowers.
And let the ground whereas her foot shall tread,
For fear the stones her tender foot should wrong,
Be strewed with fragrant flowers all along,
And diapered like the discoloured mead.
Which done, do at her chamber door await,
For she will waken straight,
The while do ye this song unto her sing,
The woods shall to you answer, and your echo ring.

Ye Nymphs of Mulla which, with carefull heed,
The silver scaly trouts do tend full well,
and greedy pikes which use therein to feed
(Those trouts and pikes all others do excel);
And ye likewise, which keep the rushy lake,
Where none do fishes take,
Bind up the locks the which hang scattered light,
And in his waters, which your mirror make,
Behold your faces as the crystal bright,
That when you come whereas my love doth lie,
No blemish she may spy.
And eke, ye lightfoot maids, which keepe the deer
That on the hoary mountain use to tower,
And the wild wolves, which seek them to devour,
With your steel darts do chase from coming near,
Be also present here,

To help to deck her and to help to sing,
That all the woods may answer, and your echo ring.

Wake now my love, awake! for it is time;
The Rosy Morn long since left Tithon's bed,
All ready to her silver couch to climb,
And Phoebus gins to shew his glorious head.
Hark how the cheerfull birds do chant their lays
And carol of love's praise.
The merry Lark her matins sings aloft,
The thrush replies, the Mavis descant plays,
The Ouzel shrills, the Ruddock warbles soft;
So goodly all agree, with sweet consent,
To this day's merriment.
Ah! my dear love, why do ye sleep thus long,
When meeter were that ye should now awake,
T'await the coming of your joyous make,
And hearken to the birds' love-learnèd song,
The dewy leaves among.
For they of joy and pleasance to you sing,
That all the woods them answer, and their echo ring.

My love is now awake out of her dreams,
And her fair eyes, like stars that dimmèd were
With darksome cloud, now shew their goodly beams
More bright than Hesperus his head doth rear.
Come now, ye damsels, daughters of delight,
Help quickly her to dight;
But first come ye fair hours, which were begot
In Jove's sweet paradise of Day and Night,
Which do the seasons of the year allot,
And all that ever in this world is fair
Do make and still repair.
And ye three handmaids of the Cyprian Queen,
The which do still adorn her beauty's pride,
Help to adorn my beautifullest bride;
And, as ye her array, still throw between
Some graces to be seen;
And, as ye use to Venus, to her sing,
The whiles the woods shall answer, and your echo ring.

Erewhon

This satirical novel by **Samuel Butler** was published anonymously in 1872. It is fun to read, but I don't think anyone could rate it as a masterpiece.

Setting out to make his fortune in a far-off country, a young traveller called Higgs discovers the remote and beautiful land of Erewhon, and is given a home among its extraordinarily handsome citizens. He soon finds that this seemingly ideal community has its faults – here crime is treated indulgently as a malady to be cured, while illness, poverty and misfortune are cruelly punished, and all machines have been superstitiously destroyed after a bizarre prophecy. Inspired by Samuel Butler's years in colonial New Zealand, and by his reading of Darwin's *Origin of Species*, Erewhon is a highly original, irreverent and humorous satire on conventional virtues, religious hypocrisy and the unthinking acceptance of beliefs. If you are naturally good at anagrams, you will realise where Erewhon actually is.

essay

An essay is a short piece of writing on a specific subject. Most of us wrote vast quantities at school. A number of English writers like Francis Bacon, Leigh Hunt, **Matthew Arnold** and **D. H. Lawrence** have also done so, not for the appraisal of a teacher but for the enlightenment of the general public.

Essay on Man, An

Pope intended this poem as the centrepiece of a proposed system of ethics in which he would, just as **Milton** had tried to do in *Paradise Lost*, justify the ways of God to man. He makes that abundantly clear at the very beginning of the poem:

> Awake, my St John! leave all meaner things
> To low ambition and the pride of kings.
> Let us, since life can little more supply
> Than just to look about us and to die,
> Expatiate free o'er all this scene of man;
> A mighty maze! but not without a plan;
> A wild, where weeds and flowers promiscuous shoot,
> Or garden, tempting with forbidden fruit.
> Together let us beat this ample field,

Try what the open, what the covert yield;
The latent tracts, the giddy heights, explore
Of all who blindly creep or sightless soar;
Eye nature's walks, shoot folly as it flies,
And catch the manners living as they rise;
Laugh where we must, be candid where we can,
But vindicate the ways of God to man.

The 'St John' at the start of the poem is a reference to Lord Bolingbroke, and the poem as a whole consists of four epistles, addressed to Lord Bolingbroke. Pope sets out to demonstrate that no matter how imperfect, complex, inscrutable and disturbingly full of evil the universe may appear to be, it does function in a rational fashion, according to natural laws; and is, in fact, considered as a whole, a perfect work of God. Epistle I concerns itself with the nature of man and with his place in the universe; Epistle II, with man as an individual; Epistle III, with man in relation to human society, to the political and social hierarchies; and Epistle IV, with man's pursuit of happiness in this world. Basically the poem is devoted to demonstrating that all is for the best in the best of all possible worlds. Clearly this is philosophical nonsense, but Pope does it with such skill that one is almost persuaded to join the Conservative Party. Nor can one doubt the intensity of his religious faith:

All are but parts of one stupendous whole,
Whose body nature is, and God the soul;
That, changed thro' all, and yet in all the same;
Great in the earth, as in th'ethereal frame;
Warms in the sun, refreshes in the breeze,
Glows in the stars, and blossoms in the trees;
Lives thro' all life, extends thro' all extent,
Spreads undivided, operates unspent;
Breathes in our soul, informs our mortal part,
As full, as perfect, in a hair as heart;
As full, as perfect, in vile man that mourns,
As the rapt seraph, that adores and burns.
To Him no high, no low, no great, no small;
He fills, He bounds, connects, and equals all!

An Essay on Man may be intellectually spurious, but it is wonderful poetry.

euphemism

The British are very fond of euphemisms. Instead of saying, 'Jack has died', the British will say, 'Jack has passed away.' Instead of saying, 'Sally is under arrest', they will say, 'Sally is helping the police with their enquiries.' Quite what psychological defect forces the British to prevaricate in this fashion, I do not know, but I find euphemisms very irritating. At school Harry is an under-achiever, whereas in fact he is bone from the neck upwards. Private Jones was killed by friendly fire, though I can never see anything friendly about a fatal bullet. I belong to a low socio-economic group, i.e. I'm broke. I'm even getting cross just writing about them. Try to avoid them in your own writing. After all, they are a form of literary dishonesty.

Eve of St Agnes, The

Written in 1819 and published in 1820, this narrative poem by **Keats** is based on the superstition that a girl could see her future husband in a dream if she performed certain rites on the eve of St Agnes. The legend stated that if she went to bed without looking behind her and lay on her back with her hands under her head, the future husband would appear in her dream, kiss her and feast with her. In the original version of this poem, Keats emphasised the young lovers' sexuality, but his publishers, who feared public reaction, forced him to tone down the eroticism. Despite this, the poem is a good one. It opens as follows:

> St Agnes' Eve – Ah, bitter chill it was!
> The owl, for all his feathers, was a-cold;
> The hare limp'd trembling through the frozen grass,
> And silent was the flock in woolly fold:
> Numb were the Beadsman's fingers, while he told
> His rosary, and while his frosted breath,
> Like pious incense from a censer old,
> Seem'd taking flight for heaven, without a death,
>   Past the sweet Virgin's picture, while his prayer he saith.

There are another 41 stanzas to follow, and it has to be admitted that not a great deal happens in those stanzas. Madeline, our heroine, prepares for bed, and follows the commands of the superstition. Her lover, Porphyro, accordingly appears, and the pair flee away into the dark. The Beadsman with whom the poem begins, as we have seen, and Angela, Madeline's nurse, both die:

> And they are gone: ay, ages long ago
> These lovers fled away into the storm.
> That night the Baron dreamt of many a woe,
> And all his warrior-guests, with shade and form
> Of witch, and demon, and large coffin-worm,
> Were long benightmar'd. Angela the old
> Died palsy-twitch'd, with meagre face deform;
> The Beadsman, after thousand aves told,
> For aye unsought for slept among his ashes cold.

And so, in an almost perfunctory manner, the old guard perish, and the world is left to the young lovers. But the sensuous vigour with which Keats paints the alliance of the two lovers makes this a memorable poem.

explication

Literary criticism ought to consist primarily of explication, i.e. the detailed analysis of a piece of writing so as to reveal its merits and its flaws, and hence leave the reader with an increased understanding of the essay, novel, play or poem in question.

F

fable

The trouble with words is that they almost perversely insist on being ambiguous. Once upon a time, a fable was a short story with a pronounced moral meaning. **Aesop**'s fables from the sixth century BC were well known, and in these, animals were used to promulgate some desired virtue or warn against some hateful fault. Since then, the word 'fable' has extended itself to include almost any story that carries some sort of allegorical meaning.

According to Wikipedia, 'A fable differs from a *parable* in that the latter excludes animals, plants, inanimate objects and forces of nature as actors that assume speech and other powers of humankind.'

An author of fables is termed a 'fabulist', and once upon a time the word 'fabulous' meant 'pertaining to a fable'.

Every civilisation has scores, even hundreds, of fables. They are transmitted orally, and are perhaps the most enduring form of folk literature. As a child, living in north-east Shropshire, I could see in the distance the Wrekin. The Wrekin is a large hill, totally isolated, just sitting there between the towns of Wellington and Shrewsbury. There are no other hills in the area, and consequently the Wrekin is very conspicuous. As a child, I soon learnt why the Wrekin was so placed. Apparently a particular giant had a grudge against the mayor of Shrewsbury. Accordingly the giant sank his spade into the ground and dug up a huge clump of earth. He decided that he would throw this clump of earth into the River Severn, and thus drown all the inhabitants of Shrewsbury. He was walking along carrying his spade when he met a man carrying a sack. The giant explained to the man what he intended to do, and asked the man how much farther it was to Shrewsbury. The man was a cobbler, and the sack he was carrying contained shoes given to him for repair. With great presence of mind, the man opened his sack, showed the shoes to the giant, and said, 'I've worn out all these shoes coming from Shrewsbury.' This greatly discouraged the giant. 'Oh, I'm not going that far,' he exclaimed, and accordingly dumped the huge clump of earth and hurried away. So that is how the Wrekin came to be where it is. And no doubt every area of England has local fables just like that.

Fairie Queene, The

Wikipedia begins its article on *The Fairie Queene* as follows:

> *The Faerie Queene* is an English epic poem by Edmund Spenser, published first in three books in 1590, and later in six books in 1596. *The Faerie Queene* is notable for its form: it was the first work written in Spenserian stanzas. It is an allegorical work, written in praise of Queen Elizabeth I. Largely symbolic, the poem follows several knights in an examination of several virtues.

Frankly, it doesn't sound terribly appealing, does it? Then, when you read its opening stanza, it probably seems even less appealing:

> A Gentle Knight was pricking on the plaine,
> Y cladd in mightie armes and siluer shielde,
> Wherein old dints of deepe wounds did remaine,
> The cruell markes of many a bloudy fielde;
> Yet armes till that time did he neuer wield:
> His angry steede did chide his foming bitt,
> As much disdayning to the curbe to yield:
> Full iolly knight he seemd, and faire did sitt,
> As one for knightly giusts and fierce encounters fitt.

Yet, in 1956, when I began studying A-level English, we began Book 1 of *The Fairie Queene* as one of our set books. I knew nothing about **Spenser** and nothing about knights, chivalry, or **stanza** form. This ignorance was probably a blessing. With no preconceptions whatsoever, I came to enjoy studying Book 1 enormously. I enjoyed the allegorical elements in the poem: in Book 1 the knight represents the Church of England, the virgin whom he protects represents Truth, and the evil Duessa and Archimago appear to be aspects of Roman Catholicism. I enjoyed the skill with which Spenser handled the stanza form that he had invented, eight lines of ten syllables each and a ninth line of twelve syllables. I enjoyed the vividness with which Spenser described the environment in which he had placed his characters. Maybe too I enjoyed the fact that the Redcross Knight was engaged on a mission:

> Vpon a great aduenture he was bond,
> That greatest *Gloriana* to him gaue,
> That greatest Glorious Queene of *Faerie* lond,
> To winne him worship, and her grace to haue,

Which of all earthly things he most did craue;
And euer as he rode, his hart did earne
 To proue his puissance in battell braue
Vpon his foe, and his new force to learne;
 Vpon his foe, a Dragon horrible and stearne.

There was also the fact that the English in which the poem was written did pose a few problems. They were not problems of any great difficulty, but they did provide the satisfaction of a challenge.

I doubt if anyone ever studies *The Fairie Queene* for A level these days. I wonder if anyone studies *The Fairie Queene* at any level today. So there you are: if you want to make your name in English literature, become an expert on *The Fairie Queene*. You'll probably enjoy it. However, the entire poem takes 1013 pages in my Penguin edition, so don't expect to do the work over the weekend.

fairy stories

I don't know how prevalent stories like 'Goldilocks', 'Little Red Riding Hood' and 'Jack and the Beanstalk' are today. Once upon a time they seemed to be the common heritage of children. We all knew them. They were useful too. Fairy stories showed us that all stories should have a beginning, a middle and an end. Fairy stories showed us that all stories should have a moral core to them. Above all, fairy stories showed us that everything should have a happy ending, and thus prepared us to swallow all the lies of politicians.

Falkner, John (1858–1932)

John Falkner only wrote three novels, but one of them, *Moonfleet* (1898), has become a children's classic. Indeed it was set for O-level English Literature in 1956, and in retrospect I wish I'd read it.

farce

A farce is normally a play or film in which the characters suffer all sorts of physical misadventures. Thus a farce is a comedy of action, not a comedy of words.

Faulkner, William Cuthbert (1897–1962)

Faulkner was an American novelist. In 1929 he produced *The Sound and the Fury*, one of the most astonishing novels ever written in that about a third of it is narrated by a thirty-three-year-old imbecile whose ramblings appear at first to be entirely incomprehensible. While *The Sound and the Fury* is probably his most significant novel, others, like *As I Lay Dying* (1930) and *Light in August* (1932), are well worth attention.

feminism

Feminism is a movement devoted to securing for women equal rights with men. No sane person could disagree with such an aim, but, like many movements, feminism has become something of a cult. Consequently it has invaded English literature, and there has developed a specific feminist approach to literary works. Perhaps regrettably, I am not wildly in sympathy with this. Men and women have, as human beings, massively more in common than they have dividing them. When I read *Paradise Lost*, the fact that I have a penis does not make me read it differently from Meg who has a vagina.

Festschrift

This is normally a volume of essays presented to someone as a tribute to their life and work. For instance, Daniel Prendergast (whom I've invented) devoted his entire life to an examination of the Cornish language. Since Cornish is dead, and no one now speaks the language, the utility of this study might be questioned, but nevertheless Daniel produced article after article and book after book on the subjunctive in Cornish verbs and the imagery of Cornish metaphors. In tribute to this labour, his colleagues at the University of Empingham cobbled together a collection of essays on dead languages. This was a Festschrift.

Fielding, Henry (1707–54)

I vividly recall an American academic once trying to convince me that Fielding's novel *Tom Jones* (1749) was the greatest novel in the English language. I didn't believe it then, and I don't believe it now. Admittedly, *Tom Jones*, the best of Fielding's novels, is an outstanding work. Certainly every literate person should read it several times. But that doesn't mean that they should ignore *Joseph Andrews* (1742) or *Jonathan Wild* (1743), both of which are great fun. From what I can remember, which isn't much, you can ignore *Amelia* (1751).

As you can tell from his dates, Fielding was one of the earliest English novelists. It is always a matter of astonishment that such mastery should be achieved by someone who was writing in a totally new form. In addition, if you can infer from a novel anything at all about the character and personality of the author, then Fielding seems to have been a remarkably agreeable fellow, someone you'd happily have a pint with. One aspect of Fielding's writing does, though, demand attention. Other pioneers in the new art of novel writing, people like **Defoe** and **Richardson**, presented their works in the form of memoirs or diaries. In this way, they hoped to give an air of verisimilitude to their work. Fielding never bothered, and often overtly reminded the reader that he was making the whole thing up. Perhaps strangely, this just adds an element of charm to the whole thing. Indeed, Fielding's entire style had the air of a man playing games. You see this very plainly in his novel *Joseph Andrews* because this work was an avowed satire on Richardson's novel *Pamela*. Here is an extract from Chapter 2:

Mr Joseph Andrews, the hero of our ensuing history, was esteemed to be the only son of Gaffar and Gammer Andrews, and brother to the illustrious Pamela, whose virtue is at present so famous. As to his ancestors, we have searched with great diligence, but little success; being unable to trace them farther than his great-grandfather, who, as an elderly person in the parish remembers to have heard his father say, was an excellent cudgel-player. Whether he had any ancestors before this, we must leave to the opinion of our curious reader, finding nothing of sufficient certainty to rely on. However, we cannot omit inserting an epitaph which an ingenious friend of ours hath communicated:

> Stay, traveller, for underneath this pew
> Lies fast asleep that merry man Andrew:
> When the last day's great sun shall gild the skies,
> Then he shall from his tomb get up and rise.
> Be merry while thou canst: for surely thou
> Shalt shortly be as sad as he is now.

The words are almost out of the stone with antiquity. But it is needless to observe that Andrew here is writ without an s, and is, besides, a Christian name. My friend, moreover, conjectures this to have been the founder of that sect of laughing philosophers since called Merry-andrews.

To waive, therefore, a circumstance which, though mentioned in conformity to the exact rules of biography, is not greatly material, I proceed to things of more consequence. Indeed, it is sufficiently certain that he had as many ancestors as the best man living, and, perhaps, if we look five or six hundred years backwards, might be related to some persons of very great figure at present, whose ancestors within half the last century are buried in as great obscurity. But suppose, for argument's sake, we should admit that he had no ancestors at all, but had sprung up, according to the modern phrase, out of a dunghill, as the Athenians pretended they themselves did from the earth, would not this αυτοκοπρος have been justly entitled to all the praise arising from his own virtues? Would it not be hard that a man who hath no ancestors should therefore be rendered incapable of acquiring honour; when we see so many who have no virtues enjoying the honour of their forefathers? At ten years old (by which time his education was advanced to writing and reading) he was bound an apprentice, according to the statute, to Sir Thomas Booby, an uncle of Mr Booby's by the father's side. Sir Thomas having then an estate in his own hands, the young Andrews was at first employed in what in the country they call keeping birds. His office was to perform the part the ancients assigned to the god Priapus, which deity the moderns call by the name of Jack o' Lent; but his voice being so extremely musical, that it rather allured the birds than terrified them, he was soon transplanted from the fields into the dog-kennel, where he was placed under the huntsman, and made what the sportsmen term whipper-in. For this place likewise the sweetness of his voice disqualified him; the dogs preferring the melody of his chiding to all the alluring notes of the huntsman, who soon became so incensed at it, that he desired Sir Thomas to provide otherwise for him, and constantly laid every fault the dogs were at to the account of the poor boy, who was now transplanted to the stable. Here he soon gave proofs of strength and agility beyond his years, and constantly rode the most spirited and vicious horses to water, with an intrepidity which surprised everyone. While he was in this station, he rode several races for Sir Thomas, and this with such expertness and success, that the neighbouring gentlemen frequently solicited the knight to permit little Joey (for so he was called) to ride their matches. The best gamesters, before they laid their money, always inquired which horse little Joey was to ride; and the bets were rather proportioned by the rider than by the horse himself; especially after he had scornfully refused a considerable bribe to play booty on such an occasion. This extremely raised his character, and so pleased the Lady Booby, that she desired to have him (being now seventeen years of age) for her own footboy.

It is all so intensely good-humoured. It is difficult to read Fielding without a smile on one's face.

Fitzgerald, Francis Scott (1896–1940)

An American novelist and short-story writer, Scott Fitzgerald is best known for *The Great Gatsby* (1925), a dark and haunting story set in a New York of great wealth and equally great squalor. Of his short stories, *A Diamond as Big as the Ritz* (1922) is one of the most memorable. Fitzgerald was working on a novel, *The Last Tycoon*, when he died at the age of forty-four.

Fleming, Ian (1908–64)

Ian Fleming is not an important or significant novelist, but his stories about a secret agent known as James Bond have been turned into films and comics. As a result, James Bond is better known to most people than the Prime Minister.

folk songs

These are songs of unknown origin, rejoicing in simple tunes and even more simple words. Invariably they possess neither musical merit nor poetic worth, but a small section of the so-called intelligentsia have decided that folk songs link us to a wiser and more profound past. The same spurious sanctity has been bestowed on folklore and folk tales. If you want to achieve fame, compose some folk songs, sing them in a Salopian accent to the accompaniment of a zither, and the world will be yours.

foot

A foot is a unit within a line of verse. If the line is composed of a regular unstressed/stressed pattern (i.e. the **iambic metre**), then each occurrence of that pattern constitutes a foot:

> The cur   few tolls   the knell   of part   ing day

Thus the above line has five feet. If you wish to indicate the stressed and unstressed syllables, you would display the line like this:

> x /   x /   x /   x /   x /
> The cur   few tolls the knell of part   ing day

But of course there can be a number of different sorts of foot. I list the major varieties below:

an **anapaest**	x x /
a **dactyl**	/ x x
an iamb	x /
a trochee	/ x
a **spondee**	/ /

form

It is words like 'form' that make one wonder how anybody ever learns the English language. In my *Dictionary of Homonyms*, I provide six meanings for this word, but in so doing skate over its literary ramifications. First of all, the word means the shape of a literary work – it might be an **essay**, a **novel**, a **sonnet**, an **ode**, an **elegy**, a report, an epic, a play, a **short story** and so on. Each of those words describes the form of the work. But a literary work can also have a conceptual form. A sonnet, for instance, details the fear of death in its octet, but in the sestet pictures the comforts of death. A particular novel has a two-fold form, the first 13 chapters showing the rise of Penelope Snoozby, and the closing 11 chapters showing her decline. Hence you can have a form within a form.

Forster, Edward Morgan (1879–1970)

E. M. Forster was a minor novelist whom one can read with real enjoyment, *Howards End* (1910) and *A Passage to India* (1924) probably being his two best works. Forster was also a literary critic, and his *Aspects of the Novel* (1927) is an agreeable, undemanding survey of the novel form, regarded by **F. R. Leavis** as intellectually non-existent.

Four Quartets

Individually entitled *Burnt Norton*, *East Coker*, *The Dry Salvages* and *Little Gidding*, these four poems by **T. S. Eliot** are a profound reflection on the nature of time and man's position within time. I cannot assess their standing as philosophy, but as poems they are superb. The first of them, *Burnt Norton*, begins like this:

> Time present and time past
> Are both perhaps present in time future,
> And time future contained in time past.
> If all time is eternally present
> All time is unredeemable.
> What might have been is an abstraction

Remaining a perpetual possibility
Only in a world of speculation.
What might have been and what has been
Point to one end, which is always present.
Footfalls echo in the memory
Down the passage which we did not take
Towards the door we never opened
Into the rose-garden. My words echo
Thus, in your mind.
                          But to what purpose
Disturbing the dust on a bowl of rose-leaves
I do not know.
                    Other echoes
Inhabit the garden. Shall we follow?
Quick, said the bird, find them, find them,
Round the corner. Through the first gate,
Into our first world, shall we follow
The deception of the thrush? Into our first world.
There they were, dignified, invisible,
Moving without pressure, over the dead leaves,
In the autumn heat, through the vibrant air,
And the bird called, in response to
The unheard music hidden in the shrubbery,
And the unseen eyebeam crossed, for the roses
Had the look of flowers that are looked at.
There they were as our guests, accepted and accepting.
So we moved, and they, in a formal pattern,
Along the empty alley, into the box circle,
To look down into the drained pool.
Dry the pool, dry concrete, brown edged,
And the pool was filled with water out of sunlight,
And the lotos rose, quietly, quietly,
The surface glittered out of heart of light,
And they were behind us, reflected in the pool.
Then a cloud passed, and the pool was empty.
Go, said the bird, for the leaves were full of children,
Hidden excitedly, containing laughter.
Go, go, go, said the bird: human kind
Cannot bear very much reality.
Time past and time future
What might have been and what has been
Point to one end, which is always present.

free verse

This term does not, alas, refer to poems that you can pick up with your free *Metro* on the bus in the morning. It is a term invented in the early twentieth century to describe poems that do not rhyme and lack a regular metric pulse.

Frost, Robert (1874–1963)

Possibly the USA's most popular poet, Robert Frost can easily be seen as spinning a simple rural philosophy in evocative and accessible verse. Perhaps this is true some of the time, but Frost can be tougher meat than this implies. His most famous poem is *The Road Not Taken*:

> Two roads diverged in a yellow wood,
> And sorry I could not travel both
> And be one traveler, long I stood
> And looked down one as far as I could
> To where it bent in the undergrowth;
>
> Then took the other, as just as fair,
> And having perhaps the better claim,
> Because it was grassy and wanted wear;
> Though as for that the passing there
> Had worn them really about the same,
>
> And both that morning equally lay
> In leaves no step had trodden black.
> Oh, I kept the first for another day!
> Yet knowing how way leads on to way,
> I doubted if I should ever come back.
>
> I shall be telling this with a sigh
> Somewhere ages and ages hence:
> Two roads diverged in a wood, and I –
> I took the one less travelled by,
> And that has made all the difference.

Haven't we all felt something very similar to this?

G

Galsworthy, John (1867–1933)

In the entry on Galsworthy in *The Cambridge Guide to Literature in English*, Ian Ousby concludes by commenting, 'Without remaining in critical favour, his writing has remained popular.' This is one of the besetting problems of literary criticism: members of the general public frequently refuse to take any notice of enlightened guidance. As a result, they continue to read the novels of Jeffrey Archer, Ian Fleming and Barbara Cartland. Yet the situation is a fraction more complicated than this. Archer, Fleming and Cartland are quite simply popular novelists, each of them appealing to a particular sub-section of the literate public. But Galsworthy doesn't fall into this category. He is a 'serious' novelist who wants to be evaluated alongside other writers like **Austen**, **Dickens**, **Eliot**, **Wells**, and so on. The trouble is, he isn't quite good enough. He writes agreeable fiction, but his *Forsyte Saga*, a collection of novels about the Forsyste family, doesn't have the ironic wit of Jane Austen, the compulsion of Dickens, the insight of Eliot or the imagination of Wells. There are plenty of others who inhabit this uneasy middle ground between the great novelists and the popularisers. **Fanny Burney**, **Anthony Trollope**, **Benjamin Disraeli**, **George Gissing** and scores of others get respectful nods from the academics, but don't quite soar into the stratosphere.

Gardner, Erle Stanley (1889–1970)

No one could pretend that Gardner is a monument to English literature. To start with, he wrote eighty-two novels which suggests a production line more than an anguished genius. In addition, each of those novels was written to a formula, and consequently has the originality of a dishcloth. But the vast majority of those novels feature the lawyer Perry Mason, and he has become as well known as Sherlock Holmes or James Bond. Hence Gardner's appearance here.

Gaskell, Elizabeth Cleghorn (1810–65)

Always known as Mrs Gaskell, this nineteenth-century novelist is not as well known among the general public as she deserves to be. *Cranford*, a novel of 1853, is her best known work, but it is different in tone and nature from the rest of her work. *Mary Barton* (1848), *Ruth* (1853), *North and South* (1855), *Sylvia's Lovers* (1863) and *Wives and Daughters* (1866) are much more typical and, for my money, much more interesting. Mrs Gaskell also wrote a biography of her friend Charlotte **Brontë** and a number of short stories.

genre fiction

Most of us have preferences within the field of fiction. Some of us prefer romances, others enjoy science fiction, and so on. Fiction that can be placed within a genre – like spy fiction, detective fiction, adventure fiction, romances, science fiction, westerns, horror fiction, historical fiction and pornographic fiction – is, unsurprisingly, called genre fiction These sub-classes of the novel provide you with the opportunity to make a fortune. *Jaws*, for instance, sold ten million copies. So – decide on your genre, and start writing.

Georgian poetry

I am well aware that this ought be poetry written by George, but in fact the label refers to poetry published between 1912 and 1922 during the reign of George V. Edward Marsh edited five anthologies during that decade, and the major poets appearing in those anthologies included **A. E. Housman**, W. H. Davies, **Walter de la Mare**, John Masefield, Ralph Hodgson, Edward Thomas, James Stephen, James Elroy Flecker, J. C. Squire, Andrew Young, **Siegfried Sassoon**, **Rupert Brooke**, **Wilfred Owen**, **Robert Graves**, Edmund Blunden and **D. H. Lawrence**.

ghost story

It is unlikely to surprise you that a ghost story is a fictional narrative, usually between 1,000 and 25,000 words in length, that features a ghost among its dramatis personae. Dickens's *A Christmas Carol* is probably the best known English ghost story, but it is not a genre that has been much employed by major writers. **Rudyard Kipling**, **R. L. Stevenson** and **Walter de la Mare** all wrote some, and there have been some memorable post-Second World War ones by writers like Muriel Spark, Joan Aiken, Angus Wilson and others.

Gissing, George Robert (1857–1903)

Gissing is a minor novelist, but his best known work, *New Grub Street* (1891), is extremely interesting and quite moving. Another novel, *The Private Papers of Henry Ryecroft* (1903), is semi-autobiographical. He also wrote quite a good critical study of **Dickens**.

Globe Theatre

The Globe Theatre in Southwark was a theatre in which a number of **Shakespeare**'s plays received their first performance. It was destroyed by fire in 1613, but was rebuilt in the same year. It was finally demolished in 1644. In 1996 a replica of it was erected very close to the original site, and Shakespeare's plays are now produced there following as closely as possible the original mode of presentation, though Shakespeare didn't have to struggle against the noise of passing aircraft.

gobbledegook

A splendid word that signifies nonsense. It tends to be used to sneer at people who use any kind of professional jargon.

Golding, William (1911–93)

Golding wrote a number of novels, published criticism and lectures, won the Booker Prize in 1980 for his novel *Rites of Passage*, and in 1983 was awarded the Nobel Prize for Literature. Yet his first novel, *Lord of the Flies* (1954), is still regarded by many as his greatest, and its picture of a group of schoolboys descending into barbarism is very powerful. It also made him enough money to allow him to give up teaching, so life does have the occasional happy ending.

Goldsmith, Oliver (1730–74)

The eighteenth century undoubtedly produced a number of talented all-rounders, and Goldsmith, a writer of novels, poems, plays and essays, certainly filled the bill. His play *She Stoops to Conquer* (1773) is extremely entertaining, his poem *The Deserted Village* (1770) is quite moving, and his novel *The Vicar of Wakefield* (1766) is still very readable. Yet Goldsmith wrote much, much more, and led a life of penury and crisis. His life offers scope for several scholarly disquisitions: 'Sexism in Goldsmith's *Poems for Young Ladies*', 'The Nature of Culture as Revealed by Goldsmith's *Life of Richard Nash*', and so on.

Goodbye to All That

This is a memoir by **Robert Graves**. I've never been very fond of Graves's poetry, but this is a powerful work of autobiography.

Gosse, Sir Edmund (1849–1928)

Gosse was brought up by his father who was a distinguished zoologist and a devout member of a religious sect, the Plymouth Brethren. The pressures imposed by such a background are excellently caught in Gosse's autobiographical account *Father and Son* (1907).

Gothic fiction

This somewhat odd label refers primarily to novels written in the eighteenth century which rely on mystery, horror and the supernatural for their effect. Among the best known are Horace Walpole's *The Castle of Otranto* (1764), **Ann Radcliffe**'s *The Mysteries of Udolpho* (1794) and Matthew Lewis's *The Monk* (1796); they were the sensation fiction of their time. The term Gothic is used occasionally for other novels, like **Stevenson**'s *Dr Jekyll and Mr Hyde* (1886), that make similar attempts to shock. As you might imagine, Gothic novels are easy to mock, and **Thomas Love Peacock** did his best in 1818 with the publication of *Nightmare Abbey*. **Jane Austen** in *Northanger Abbey* also implies that Gothic fiction was rather risible.

Grafton, Sue (1940–)

Sue Grafton has written a series of detective novels with an appealing alphabetical progression: *A is for Alibi, B is for Burglar, C is for Corpse*, and so on. Her detective, Kinsey Millhone, is unusual in being female, and her infectious sense of humour is very engaging.

Grahame, Kenneth (1859–1932)

Grahame is remembered today for only one thing, his work of children's fiction entitled *The Wind in the Willows* (1908). But then most of us are not remembered at all.

Graves, Robert (1895–1985)

Robert Graves was a publishing machine. He wrote numerous volumes of poetry, a memorable autobiography *Goodbye to All That* (1929), several novels, and much non-fiction, the majority of which was concerned with mysticism of some kind or other. Despite this productivity, one cannot help but feel that Graves is doomed to be a footnote in literary history.

Gray, Thomas (1716–71)

Gray's poem *The Bard* has already received an entry in this volume, and frankly there isn't all that much more that one wants to add. Gray's best known poem, *Elegy Written in a Country Churchyard* (1751), trots amiably along in its iambic tedium, and sundry others by him can impart a mild pleasure to the undemanding mind.

great chain of being

This is an interesting idea that has existed for a considerable time, and Arthur Lovejoy's 1936 book on the topic, *The Great Chain of Being: A Study of the History of an Idea*, is fascinating. Briefly, the argument is that everything in the world exists within a great chain. Where something appears within this chain depends on the proportions of spirit and matter that exists in the object concerned. A stone has a lot of matter, but virtually no spirit. Consequently a stone is pretty low down in the great chain. Unsurprisingly, God is at the top of the chain. Thus, in outline, the great chain looks this:

God

angels

human beings

animals

plants

inanimate objects

Needless to say, it's a great deal more complicated than this: gold is higher than iron, shellfish are lower than rabbits, and so on. It is not surprising, therefore, that this all-embracing idea found its reflection in literature. Ulysses in **Shakespeare**'s *Troilus and Cressida* expresses the idea as degree:

> The specialty of rule hath been neglected;
> And look how many Grecian tents do stand
> Hollow upon this plain, so many hollow factions.
> When that the general is not like the hive,
> To whom the foragers shall all repair,
> What honey is expected? Degree being vizarded,

Th'unworthiest shows as fairly in the mask.
The heavens themselves, the planets, and this centre,
Observe degree, priority, and place,
Infixture [fixity], course, proportion, season, form,
Office, and custom, in all line of order;
And therefore is the glorious planet Sol
In noble eminence enthron'd and spher'd
Amidst the other, whose med'cinable eye
Corrects the ill aspects of planets evil,
And posts, like the commandment of a king,
Sans check, to good and bad. But when the planets
In evil mixture to disorder wander,
What plagues and what portents, what mutiny,
What raging of the sea, shaking of earth,
Commotion in the winds, frights, changes, horrors,
Divert and crack, rend and deracinate,
The unity and married calm of states
Quite from their fixture! O, when degree is shak'd,
Which is the ladder of all high designs,
The enterprise is sick! How could communities,
Degrees in schools, and brotherhoods in cities,
Peaceful commerce from dividable shores,
The primogenity and due of birth,
Prerogative of age, crowns, sceptres, laurels,
But by degree, stand in authentic place?
Take but degree away, untune that string,
And hark what discord follows! Each thing melts
In mere oppugnancy: the bounded waters
Should lift their bosoms higher than the shores,
And make a sop of all this solid globe;
Strength should be lord of imbecility,
And the rude son should strike his father dead;
Force should be right; or, rather, right and wrong,
Between whose endless jar justice resides,
Should lose their names, and so should justice too.
Then everything includes itself in power,
Power into will, will into appetite;
And appetite, an universal wolf,

So doubly seconded with will and power,
Must make perforce an universal prey,
And last eat up himself. Great Agamemnon,
This chaos, when degree is suffocate,
Follows the choking.
And this neglection of degree it is
That by a pace goes backward, with a purpose
It hath to climb. The general's disdain'd
By him one step below, he by the next,
That next by him beneath; so every step,
Exampl'd by the first pace that is sick
Of his superior, grows to an envious fever
Of pale and bloodless emulation.
And 'tis this fever that keeps Troy on foot,
Not her own sinews. To end a tale of length,
Troy in our weakness stands, not in her strength.

This is a wonderful speech, and you can see how the entire concept of the great chain of being animates **Ulysses'** concern about the condition among the Greeks.

Pope, in his *Essay on Man*, makes the concept even clearer:

Vast chain of being! which from God began;
Natures ethereal, human, angel, man,
Beast, bird, fish, insect, who no eye can see,
No glass can reach; from infinite to thee;
From thee to nothing. On superior powers
Were we to press, inferior might on ours;
Or in the full creation leave a void,
Where, one step broken, the great scale's destroyed:
From Nature's chain whatever link you like,
Tenth, or ten thousandth, breaks the chain alike.
And if each system in gradation roll,
Alike essential to th'amazing Whole,
The least confusion but in one, not all
That system only, but the Whole must fall.
Let earth unbalanced from her orbit fly,
Planets and stars run lawless thro' the sky;
Let ruling angels from their spheres be hurl'd,

Being on being wreck'd, and world on world;
Heav'n's whole foundations to their centre nod,
And Nature tremble to the throne of God!
All this dread order break – for whom? for thee?
Vile worm! – O madness! pride! impiety!

And, of course, the same concept still has power today. Bankers, for instance, are much higher than teachers.

Great Expectations

This is **Dickens**'s greatest novel, and consequently merits several dozen re-readings.

'The terrible stranger in the churchyard'
by F. W. Pailthorpe, from Charles Dickens's *Great Expectations*

Greene, Graham (1904–91)

A Roman Catholic novelist, Graham Greene was obsessed with moral choice, physical seediness and redemption. At his best (i.e. *The Power and the Glory* [1940] and *The Heart of the Matter* [1948]), Greene is a moving and powerful writer.

Grisham, John (1955–)

Grisham is a best-selling American thriller writer. I have tried on two occasions to read one of his novels. On both occasions, it was a mistake.

Grub Street

There was once a street in London actually called Grub Street, and it became associated with impoverished writers struggling to make a living. Nowadays the term is simply used as shorthand for hack journalism.

Gulliver's Travels

This is a satire by **Jonathan Swift** written in 1726. In it Lemuel Gulliver visits sundry lands, each of which illustrates some imperfection or vagary of mankind. Some of it is very funny, all of it is very interesting, and some of it (i.e. Book Four) is so blistering as to unsettle one's stomach. If you want to irritate, you could always gently enquire as to whether or not *Gulliver's Travels* is a novel.

Gunn, Thom (1929–2004)

Of post-Second World War poets, Gunn must be one of the best. Here is 'Still Life':

> I shall not soon forget
> The greyish-yellow skin
> To which the face had set:
> Lids tight: nothing of his,
> No tremor from within,
> Played on the surfaces.
> He still found breath, and yet
> It was an obscure knack.
> I shall not soon forget
> The angle of his head,
> Arrested and reared back
> On the crisp field of bed.
> Back from what he could neither
> Accept, as one opposed,
> Nor, as a life-long breather,
> Consentingly let go,
> The tube his mouth enclosed
> In an astonished O.

H

hack

This word denotes a person who churns out words for little financial reward. A reference to a person as 'a hack' tends to have a somewhat dismissive tone to it.

Haggard, Henry Rider (1856–1925)

Rider Haggard only appears in this book because, when I was a teenager, I read his *King Solomon's Mines* (1886) and *She* (1887). I enjoyed them hugely, and, if you are fond of adventure stories, it is likely that you will too.

hagiography

If you write about the saints, you are indulging in hagiography. It is not a very flourishing branch of literature.

haiku

This is a Japanese verse form consisting of seventeen syllables in three lines of five, seven and five syllables respectively. From time to time, the English try to write haikus, but their efforts are usually unremarkable.

Hamlet

This is one of **Shakespeare**'s great tragedies, and has probably had more ink expended on it than any other literary work. This is probably because the play concerns itself with sin, virtue, chastity, ambition, revenge, avarice, evil, fidelity, life, death and grave maintenance.

harangue

This word has a slightly disapproving tone to it. An harangue is an impassioned speech designed to persuade a person or group of people to undertake some action. As a result, it is inevitably associated with politicians and trade-union leaders, both normally regarded as lower forms of life. However, there are some examples in literature of inspired harangues. In **Shakespeare**'s play *Henry V*, Henry wants to rouse his soldiers to fever pitch:

Once more unto the breach, dear friends, once more;
Or close the wall up with our English dead!
In peace there's nothing so becomes a man
As modest stillness and humility;
But when the blast of war blows in our ears,
Then imitate the action of the tiger:
Stiffen the sinews, summon up the blood,
Disguise fair nature with hard-favour'd rage;
Then lend the eye a terrible aspect:
Let it pry through the portage of the head
Like the brass cannon; let the brow o'erwhelm it
As fearfully as doth a gallèd rock
O'erhang and jutty his confounded base,
Swill'd with the wild and wasteful ocean.
Now set the teeth and stretch the nostril wide,
Hold hard the breath and bend up every spirit
To his full height. On, on, you noblest English,
Whose blood is fet from fathers of war-proof!
Fathers that, like so many Alexanders,
Have in these parts from morn till even fought,
And sheathed their swords for lack of argument.
Dishonour not your mothers; now attest
That those whom you call'd fathers did beget you.
Be copy now to men of grosser blood,
And teach them how to war. And you, good yeoman,
Whose limbs were made in England, show us here
The mettle of your pasture; let us swear
That you are worth your breeding – which I doubt not;
For there is none of you so mean and base,
That hath not noble lustre in your eyes.
I see you stand like greyhounds in the slips,
Straining upon the start. The game's afoot:
Follow your spirit, and upon this charge
Cry, 'God for Harry, England, and Saint George!'

Antony in Shakespeare's *Julius Caesar* has an even better harangue
over the dead body of Caesar:

Friends, Romans, countrymen, lend me your ears!
I come to bury Caesar, not to praise him.
The evil that men do lives after them,
The good is oft interrèd with their bones:
So let it be with Caesar. The noble Brutus
Hath told you Caesar was ambitious:
If it were so, it was a grievous fault,
And grievously hath Caesar answer'd it.
Here, under leave of Brutus and the rest –
For Brutus is an honourable man;
So are they all, all honourable men –
Come I to speak in Caesar's funeral.
He was my friend, faithful and just to me:
But Brutus says he was ambitious;
And Brutus is an honourable man.
He hath brought many captives home to Rome,
Whose ransoms did the general coffers fill:
Did this in Caesar seem ambitious?
When that the poor have cried, Caesar hath wept:
Ambition should be made of sterner stuff;
Yet Brutus says he was ambitious;
And Brutus is an honourable man.
You all did see that on the Lupercal
I thrice presented him a kingly crown,
Which he did thrice refuse: was this ambition?
Yet Brutus says he was ambitious;
And, sure, he is an honourable man.
I speak not to disprove what Brutus spoke,
But here I am to speak what I do know.
You all did love him once, not without cause:
What cause withholds you, then, to mourn for him?
O judgement! thou art fled to brutish beasts,
And men have lost their reason. Bear with me;
My heart is in the coffin there with Caesar,
And I must pause till it come back to me.

As an example of emotional manipulation, this could not be bettered.
It is an harangue, but an harangue at such a level of genius that one wants
a different word.

Hard Times

This is a novel by **Dickens**, published in 1854. It was hailed by the critic **F. R. Leavis** as the only novel by Dickens worthy of serious attention. Alas, as was not uncommon, Leavis was entirely wrong, but it is true *Hard Times* well deserves considerable attention. It is Dickens's assault on the coercive aspects of utilitarianism, and the novel begins with a savage parody of what Dickens took to be the central message of Benthamism.

'Now, what I want is, Facts. Teach these boys and girls nothing but Facts. Facts alone are wanted in life. Plant nothing else, and root out everything else. You can only form the minds of reasoning animals upon Facts: nothing else will ever be of any service to them. This is the principle on which I bring up my own children, and this is the principle on which I bring up these children. Stick to Facts, sir!'

The scene was a plain, bare, monotonous vault of a schoolroom, and the speaker's square forefinger emphasised his observations by under-scoring every sentence with a line on the schoolmaster's sleeve. The emphasis was helped by the speaker's square wall of a forehead, which had his eyebrows for its base, while his eyes found commodious cellarage in two dark caves, overshadowed by the wall. The emphasis was helped by the speaker's mouth, which was wide, thin, and hard set. The emphasis was helped by the speaker's voice, which was inflexible, dry, and dictatorial. The emphasis was helped by the speaker's hair, which bristled on the skirts of his bald head, a plantation of firs to keep the wind from its shining surface, all covered with knobs, like the crust of a plum pie, as if the head had scarcely warehouse-room for the hard facts stored inside. The speaker's obstinate carriage, square coat, square legs, square shoulders – nay, his very neckcloth, trained to take him by the throat with an unaccommodating grasp, like a stubborn fact, as it was – all helped the emphasis.

'In this life, we want nothing but Facts, sir; nothing but Facts!'

The speaker, and the schoolmaster, and the third grown person present, all backed a little, and swept with their eyes the inclined plane of little vessels then and there arranged in order, ready to have imperial gallons of facts poured into them until they were full to the brim.

It is all unfair, of course. Dickens is distorting the nature of utilitarianism grossly, but he is doing so with a verve that is irresistible.

Hardy, Thomas (1840–1928)

Once or twice in this book it has been stated that England has produced
only four superlatively great novelists. Thomas Hardy is not one of their
number, but he comes very, very close. Set in Wessex, Hardy's best
novels – *The Mayor of Casterbridge* (1886) and *Tess of the D'Urbervilles*
(1891) – have an epic grandeur and a human feeling that makes them
very moving indeed. Yet Hardy is odd. In about five or six novels, he is
very, very impressive; in another seven, like *Two on a Tower* (1882) or *The
Laodicean* (1881), he is close to unreadable.

In his poetry, there is no such disparity. Hardy is always at least
competent in his poems, and at his best is as good as any poet in the
language. Just read 'The Darkling Thrush':

> I leant upon a coppice gate
>   When frost was spectre-grey,
> And winter's dregs made desolate
>   The weakening eye of day.
> The tangled bine-stems scored the sky
>   Like strings of broken lyres,
> And all mankind that haunted nigh
>   Had sought their household fires.
>
> The land's sharp features seemed to be
>   The century's corpse outleant,
> His crypt the cloudy canopy,
>   The wind his death-lament.
> The ancient pulse of germ and birth
>   Was shrunken hard and dry,
> And every spirit upon earth
>   Seemed fervourless as I.
>
> At once a voice arose among
>   The bleak twigs overhead
> In a full-hearted evensong
>   Of joy illimited;
> An aged thrush, frail, gaunt, and small,
>   In blast-beruffled plume,
> Had chosen thus to fling his soul
>   Upon the growing gloom.

So little cause for carolings
     Of such ecstatic sound
Was written on terrestrial things
     Afar or nigh around,
That I could think there trembled through
     His happy good-night air
Some blessed hope, whereof he knew
     And I was unaware.

Of course, we all react differently, but for me there is no finer short poem in English. What is astonishing is that Hardy is almost as good in scores of others. It is amazing that the general public tends to think of Hardy as a novelist, while his real genius was as a poet. Hardy himself would have confirmed this. Very sensibly, he only wrote novels to make money, and when his last novel, *Jude the Obscure* (1896), caused controversy because of its irreligious theme, Hardy stopped writing fiction entirely. He never stopped writing poetry.

Hazlitt, William (1778–1830)

The British don't read a lot of essays, but they ought to make an exception with the essays of William Hazlitt. In a whole series of collections – *Characters of Shakespeare's Plays* (1817), *English Poets* (1818), *English Comic Writers* (1819), *Political Essays* (1819), *Table Talk* (1822) – Hazlitt showed that the essay could be a significant and exciting form.

Hemingway, Ernest Miller (1899–1961)

This American novelist and short-story writer was awarded the Nobel Prize for Literature in 1954, and sensibly wrote virtually nothing thereafter.

Herbert, George (1593–1633)

Herbert was born in Montgomery in Wales. After graduating from Westminster School and Trinity College, Cambridge, Herbert was elected a major fellow of his college. In 1624 he became a Member of Parliament, representing Montgomeryshire. When James I died in 1625, Herbert was less interested in being an MP. Consequently, in 1630, he took holy orders. Suffering from poor health, Herbert died of tuberculosis only three years later. On his deathbed, he reportedly gave the manuscript of *The Temple* to Nicholas Ferrar, the founder of a semi-monastic Anglican religious community at Little Gidding (a name best known today through the poem *Little Gidding* by T. S. Eliot), telling him to publish the poems if he thought they might 'turn to the advantage of any dejected poor soul', and otherwise, to burn them. In less than fifty years, *The Temple: Sacred Poems and Private Ejaculations* had gone through thirteen printings.

As a poet, Herbert could be inventive and even whimsical. His poem, 'Easter Wings', for instance, is constructed in the form of wings:

> Lord, Who createdst man in wealth and store,
> Though foolishly he lost the same,
> Decaying more and more,
> Till he became
> Most poore:

> With Thee
> O let me rise,
> As larks, harmoniously,
> And sing this day Thy victories:
> Then shall the fall further the flight in me.

> My tender age in sorrow did beginne;
> And still with sicknesses and shame
> Thou didst so punish sinne,
> That I became
> Most thinne.

> With Thee
> Let me combine,
> And feel this day Thy victorie;
> For, if I imp my wing on Thine,
> Affliction shall advance the flight in me.

All Herbert's poetry is religiously based. It is not consequently surprising to find one entitled 'Good Friday':

> O my chief good,
> How shall I measure out thy blood?
> How shall I count what thee befell,
> And each grief tell?

> Shall I thy woes
> Number according to thy foes?

Or, since one star show'd thy first breath,
Shall all thy death?

Or shall each leaf,
Which falls in Autumn, score a grief?
Or cannot leaves, but fruit be sign
Of the true vine?

Then let each hour
Of my whole life one grief devour:
That thy distress through all may run,
And be my sun.

Or rather let
My several sins their sorrows get;
That as each beast his cure doth know,
Each sin may so.

Since blood is fittest, Lord, to write
Thy sorrows in, and bloody fight;
My heart hath store, write there, where in
One box doth lie both ink and sin:

That when sin spies so many foes,
Thy whips, thy nails, thy wounds, thy woes
All come to lodge there, sin may say,
'No room for me', and fly away.

Sin being gone, oh fill the place,
And keep possession with thy grace;
Lest sin take courage and return,
And all the writings blot or burn.

In his poetry, Herbert manages something paradoxical: he constructs an entirely artificial entity, a poem, and manages to make it read as something entirely natural.

heroic couplet

The most common type of rhyming couplet is that which consists of two iambic pentameters. It is probably called heroic because **Dryden** used it in his popular plays featuring a heroic leader.

Herrick, Robert (1591–1674)

During the civil war, Herrick supported the Royalist side (which is wrong), probably fathered an illegitimate daughter (which is even wronger) and frequently got into debt (wrongest of all). Hence, from a political infidel, a sexual predator and a financial rogue, we can only expect lyrics of casual immorality with salacious titles:

To the Virgins, to Make Much of Time

Gather ye rosebuds while ye may,
　　Old time is still a-flying:
And this same flower that smiles today
　　Tomorrow will be dying.

The glorious lamp of heaven, the sun,
　　The higher he's a-getting,
The sooner will his race be run,
　　And nearer he's to setting.

That age is best which is the first,
　　When youth and blood are warmer;
But being spent, the worse, and worst
　　Times still succeed the former.

Then be not coy, but use your time,
　　And while ye may go marry:
For having lost but once your prime
　　You may for ever tarry.

The trouble is, these lyrics are delightful, though not the sort of poems one would expect from an Anglican priest.

hexameter

A metrical line of six feet.

Hiawatha, The Song of

This is a narrative poem by an American writer, **Henry Longfellow**. The incantatory **metre** has made it well known and highly popular. Here are a few lines to sample:

> By the shores of Gitche Gumee,
> By the shining Big-Sea-Water,
> Stood the wigwam of Nokomis,
> Daughter of the Moon, Nokomis.
> Dark behind it rose the forest,
> Rose the black and gloomy pine-trees,
> Rose the firs with cones upon them;
> Bright before it beat the water,
> Beat the clear and sunny water,
> Beat the shining Big-Sea-Water.

As you can see, it has an almost hypnotic quality about it, and is liable to induce the sort of sleep usually brought on by drugs.

Hind and the Panther, The

A poem that attempts to reconcile Anglican and Roman Catholic political disagreements doesn't sound the most appealing literary fare, yet this attempt by **Dryden** is both skilful and interesting. Here is an extract:

> The Panther, sure the noblest, next the Hind,
> And fairest creature of the spotted kind:
> Oh, could her inborn stains be wash'd away,
> She were too good to be a beast of prey!
> How can I praise, or blame, and not offend,
> Or how divide the frailty from the friend!
> Her faults and virtues lie so mix'd that she
> Nor wholly stands condemn'd, nor wholly free.
> Then, like her injur'd Lion, let me speak,
> He cannot bend her, and he would not break.
> Unkind already, and estrang'd in part,
> The Wolf begins to share her wand'ring heart.
> Though unpolluted yet with actual ill,
> She half commits, who sins but in her will.
> If, as our dreaming Platonists report,
> There could be spirits of a middle sort,
> Too black for heav'n, and yet too white for hell,
> Who just dropp'd halfway down, nor lower fell;
> So pois'd, so gently she descends from high,
> It seems a soft dismission from the sky.

historical novel

This type of novel has been popular since the eighteenth century, and some notable writers – **Dickens**, **Eliot**, **Thackeray**, **Scott**, etc. – have made their contributions. Today the genre is perhaps more associated with popular writers like Georgette Heyer, and academics have been inclined to look down a little onthe historical novel. Perhaps they forget that Tolstoy's *War and Peace*, the greatest novel of them all, is a historical novel.

Homer

Since Homer was Greek, lived in the ninth century BC, and is not even the certain author of **the *Iliad*** and **the *Odyssey***, he clearly has no place in this book. The trouble is that the *Iliad* and the *Odyssey*, two long epic poems, are the source for scores of Greek myths that centuries ago became incorporated into English culture. As a result, characters like Odysseus, Hector, Achilles, Penelope and sundry gods are often being referred to in works of English literature. So, just as you cannot fully understand English literature without knowing **the Bible**, so you cannot fully understand it without knowing Homer too.

homonym, homograph, homophone

I explain what these words mean in my *Dictionary of Homonyms*, also published by Wordsworth.

Hood, Thomas (1799–1845)

No one will ever pretend that Thomas Hood is a major English poet, but he has the major virtue of frequently being amusing. Here is his comment on the common crime of grave robbery:

> Don't go to weep upon my grave,
> And think that there I be.
> They haven't left an atom there
> Of my anatomie.

Hood was also fond of puns: 'They went and told the sexton and the sexton tolled the bell.' Yet Hood also had a well-developed social conscience, and he is perhaps best known for his *Song of the Shirt*, a blistering attack on working conditions:

With fingers weary and worn,
With eyelids heavy and red,
A woman sat in unwomanly rags,
Plying her needle and thread –
Stitch! stitch! stitch!
In poverty, hunger, and dirt,
And still with a voice of dolorous pitch
She sang the 'Song of the Shirt.'

'Work! work! work!
While the cock is crowing aloof!
And work – work – work,
Till the stars shine through the roof!
It's Oh! to be a slave
Along with the barbarous Turk,
Where woman has never a soul to save,
If this is Christian work!

'Work – work – work
Till the brain begins to swim;
Work – work – work
Till the eyes are heavy and dim.
Seam, and gusset, and band,
Band, and gusset, and seam,
Till over the buttons I fall asleep,
And sew them on in a dream!

'Oh, Men, with Sisters dear!
Oh, Men, with Mothers and Wives!
It is not linen you're wearing out,
But human creatures' lives!
Stitch – stitch – stitch,
In poverty, hunger, and dirt,
Sewing at once, with a double thread,
A shroud as well as a shirt.

'But why do I talk of Death?
That phantom of grisly bone,
I hardly fear his terrible shape,
It seems so like my own –

It seems so like my own,
Because of the fasts I keep;
Oh, God! that bread should be so dear,
And flesh and blood so cheap!

'Work – work – work!
My labour never flags;
And what are its wages? A bed of straw,
A crust of bread – and rags.
That shatter'd roof – and this naked floor –
A table – a broken chair –
And a wall so blank, my shadow I thank
For sometimes falling there.

'Work – work – work!
From weary chime to chime,
Work – work – work,
As prisoners work for crime!
Band, and gusset, and seam,
Seam, and gusset, and band,
Till the heart is sick, and the brain benumb'd,
As well as the weary hand.

'Work – work – work,
In the dull December light,
And work – work – work,
When the weather is warm and bright,
While underneath the eaves
The brooding swallows cling
As if to show me their sunny backs
And twit me with the spring.

'Oh! but to breathe the breath
Of the cowslip and primrose sweet,
With the sky above my head,
And the grass beneath my feet,
For only one short hour
To feel as I used to feel,
Before I knew the woes of want
And the walk that costs a meal.

'Oh, but for one short hour!
A respite however brief!
No blessed leisure for love or hope,
But only time for grief!
A little weeping would ease my heart,
But in their briny bed
My tears must stop, for every drop
Hinders needle and thread!'

With fingers weary and worn,
With eyelids heavy and red,
A woman sat in unwomanly rags,
Plying her needle and thread –
Stitch! stitch! stitch!
In poverty, hunger, and dirt,
And still with a voice of dolorous pitch,
Would that its tone could reach the Rich!
She sang this 'Song of the Shirt'.

One feels that a poem like this is somehow worth more than many
poems that are labelled 'great'.

Hopkins, Gerard Manley (1844–89)

There can be no serious argument that Hopkins is a great poet. In his
poem 'Inversnaid', he could write delightful lyrics like this:

This darksome burn, horseback brown,
His rollrock highroad roaring down,
In coop and in comb the fleece of his foam
Flutes and low to the lake falls home.

A windpuff-bonnet of fáwn-fróth
Turns and twindles over the broth
Of a pool so pitchblack, féll-f017wning,
It rounds and rounds Despair to drowning.

Degged with dew, dappled with dew
Are the groins of the braes that the brook treads through,
Wiry heathpacks, flitches of fern,
And the beadbonny ash that sits over the burn.

What would the world be, once bereft
Of wet and of wildness? Let them be left,
O let them be left, wildness and wet;
Long live the weeds and the wilderness yet.

He could write searing sonnets like 'God's Grandeur':

The world is charged with the grandeur of God.
    It will flame out, like shining from shook foil;
    It gathers to a greatness, like the ooze of oil
Crushed. Why do men then now not reck his rod?
Generations have trod, have trod, have trod;
    And all is seared with trade; bleared, smeared with toil;
    And wears man's smudge and shares man's smell: the soil
Is bare now, nor can foot feel, being shod.

And for all this, nature is never spent;
    There lives the dearest freshness deep down things;
And though the last lights off the black west went
    Oh, morning, at the brown brink eastward, springs –
Because the Holy Ghost over the bent
    World broods with warm breast and with ah! bright wings.

And yet! Hopkins is not an easy poet, and one sometimes feels that the difficulties in understanding Hopkins are not the consequence of theological profundities, but more the failure by Hopkins to render his internal state externally comprehensible.

Take the poem 'That Nature is a Heraclitean Fire and of the Comfort of the Resurrection'. The title itself is forbidding enough, but isn't there a similar excess in the poem?

Cloud-puffball, torn tufts, tossed pillows | flaunt forth, then chevy
    on an air-
built thoroughfare: heaven-roysterers, in gay-gangs | they throng;
    they glitter in marches.
Down roughcast, down dazzling whitewash, | wherever an elm
    arches,
Shivelights and shadowtackle in long | lashes lace, lance, and pair.
Delightfully the bright wind boisterous | ropes, wrestles, beats
    earth bare
Of yestertempest's creases; | in pool and rut peel parches

Squandering ooze to squeezed ' dough, crust, dust; stanches,
    starches
Squadroned masks and manmarks ' treadmire toil there
Footfretted in it. Million-fuelèd, ' nature's bonfire burns on.
But quench her bonniest, dearest ' to her, her clearest-selvèd spark
Man, how fast his firedint, ' his mark on mind, is gone!
Both are in an unfathomable, all is in an enormous dark
Drowned. O pity and indig ' nation! Manshape, that shone
Sheer off, disseveral, a star, ' death blots black out; nor mark
       Is any of him at all so stark
But vastness blurs and time ' beats level. Enough! the Resurrection,
A heart's-clarion! Away grief's gasping, ' joyless days, dejection.
       Across my foundering deck shone
A beacon, an eternal beam. ' Flesh fade, and mortal trash
Fall to the residuary worm; ' world's wildfire, leave but ash:
       In a flash, at a trumpet crash,
I am all at once what Christ is, ' since he was what I am, and
This Jack, joke, poor potsherd, ' patch, matchwood, immortal
    diamond,
            Is immortal diamond.

Don't you get the impression that Hopkins is saying, 'See what a clever fellow I am'? For Hopkins supporters, this sort of remark is heresy, yet it is interesting that a similar verbal diarrhoea infects many who choose to comment on his work. Hopkins is a great poet, and was in many ways a tortured man whose struggles in life were heroic. It is a pity though that his poetry has sometimes been taken as Holy Writ.

horror story

This genre is almost entirely ignored by serious writers, but, on reflection, **Henry James**'s short story *The Turn of the Screw* comes close, and the threat of Room 101 in Orwell's *Nineteen Eighty-Four* is also fairly nasty. A horror story, however, has horror as its *raison d'être*, and serious writers do not want to circumscribe themselves so narrowly.

Housman, Alfred Edward (1859–1936)

A classical scholar and at the time Professor of Latin at University College, London, in 1896 Housman produced a volume of sixty-three poems called *A Shropshire Lad*. I have talked to people who believe that poems like this:

Loveliest of trees, the cherry now
Is hung with bloom along the bough,
And stands about the woodland ride
Wearing white for Eastertide.

Now, of my three score years and ten,
Twenty will not come again,
And take from seventy springs a score,
It only leaves me fifty more.

And since to look at things in bloom
Fifty springs are little room,
About the woodlands I will go
To see the cherry hung with snow.

are works of genius. I don't agree, and *A Shropshire Lad* is full of these pretty truisms. During the First World War, by which time Housman was Kennedy Professor of Latin at Cambridge, *A Shropshire Lad* became massively popular, and Housman was encouraged, in 1922, to produce *Last Poems*. It too became popular, because it contained similar poems of vapid sentiment, like 'Illic Jacet':

Oh hard is the bed they have made him,
    And common the blanket and cheap;
But there he will lie as they laid him:
    Where else could you trust him to sleep?

To sleep when the bugle is crying
    And cravens have heard and are brave,
When mothers and sweethearts are sighing
    And lads are in love with the grave.

Oh dark is the chamber and lonely,
    And lights and companions depart;
But lief will he lose them and only
    Behold the desire of his heart.

And low is the roof, but it covers
    A sleeper content to repose;
And far from his friends and his lovers
    He lies with the sweetheart he chose.

Following his death in 1936, there appeared *More Poems*, and since then, Housman's poetry has retained its appeal for a section of the critically undemanding public.

hubris

This human flaw, much used by the ancient Greeks in their plays, is uppermost when a man ignores the warnings of the gods or his own intuition and is impelled by pride and arrogance to attempt something that eventually secures his doom.

Huckleberry Finn, The Adventures of

This novel, a children's adventure story and the sequel to *Tom Sawyer*, was published in 1884. Its author, **Mark Twain**, manages in this story to present one of the most morally aware novels of all time.

Hughes, Ted (1930–98)

Hughes became Poet Laureate in 1984, but despite this continued to write good poetry. I personally greatly enjoy his *Tales from Ovid* (1997), though his *Birthday Letters* (1998), describing his relationship with the poet **Sylvia Plath**, attracted considerably more attention. Yet it was Hughes' depiction of the natural world that first made him known, and many feel that volumes like *The Hawk in the Rain* (1957) and *Crow* (1970) show the poet at his best. Here is a poem called 'Hawk Roosting':

> I sit in the top of the wood, my eyes closed.
> Inaction, no falsifying dream
> Between my hooked head and hooked feet:
> Or in sleep rehearse perfect kills and eat.
>
> The convenience of the high trees!
> The air's buoyancy and the sun's ray
> Are of advantage to me;
> And the earth's face upward for my inspection.
>
> My feet are locked upon the rough bark.
> It took the whole of Creation
> To produce my foot, my each feather:
> Now I hold Creation in my foot
>
> Or fly up, and revolve it all slowly –
> I kill where I please because it is all mine.

There is no sophistry in my body:
My manners are tearing off heads –

The allotment of death.
For the one path of my flight is direct
Through the bones of the living.
No arguments assert my right:

The sun is behind me.
Nothing has changed since I began.
My eye has permitted no change.
I am going to keep things like this.

Hughes, Thomas (1822–96)

Thomas Hughes is famous for one book, and one book only. Yet *Tom Brown's Schooldays* (1857), the book in question, was the first public-school story, and there have been many since.

Huxley, Aldous (1894–1963)

Rendered nearly blind at the age of sixteen, Huxley was debarred from most professions. He consequently decided to become a writer, and wrote a number of novels and works of social criticism. Perhaps unfortunately, Huxley is today remembered for only one novel, *Brave New World* (1932). A piece of science fiction, the novel envisages a drug called 'soma' that makes everyone happy. Personally, I thought alcohol already did that.

hymn

As we all know, a hymn is a song of praise to God, and an astonishing range of major writers have contributed to the genre. One of the most prolific poetic hymn writers was **William Cowper**, who sought some consolation in his life by writing what have been known as the Olney hymns. Here is an example:

Oh! for a closer walk with God,
A calm and heavenly frame;
A light to shine upon the road
That leads me to the Lamb!

Where is the blessedness I knew
When first I saw the Lord?
Where is the soul-refreshing view
Of Jesus and his word?

What peaceful hours I once enjoy'd!
How sweet their memory still!
But they have left an aching void
The world can never fill.

Return, O holy Dove, return!
Sweet messenger of rest:
I hate the sins that made thee mourn,
And drove thee from my breast.

The dearest idol I have known,
Whate'er that idol be,
Help me to tear it from thy throne,
And worship only thee.

So shall my walk be close with God,
Calm and serene my frame:
So purer light shall mark the road
That leads me to the Lamb.

As you can see, Cowper did not stray from the traditional hymn format. **Milton**, however, in his *Hymn on the Morning of Christ's Nativity* certainly did:

It was the winter wilde,
While the Heav'n-born-childe,
　　All meanly wrapt in the rude manger lies;
Nature in awe to him
Had doff't her gawdy trim,
　　With her great Master so to sympathise:
It was no season then for her
To wanton with the sun, her lusty paramour.

Only with speeches fair
She woos the gentle air
　　To hide her guilty front with innocent snow,
And on her naked shame,
Pollute with sinfull blame,
　　The saintly vail of maiden white to throw,
Confounded, that her Maker's eyes
Should look so neer upon her foul deformities.

But he, her fears to cease,
Sent down the meek-eyed Peace,
    She crown'd with olive green, came softly sliding
Down through the turning sphear
His ready harbinger,
    With turtle wing the amorous clouds dividing,
And waving wide her mirtle wand,
She strikes a universall peace through sea and land.

No war or battail's sound
Was heard the world around,
    The idle spear and shield were high up hung;
The hooked chariot stood
Unstain'd with hostile blood,
    The trumpet spake not to the armed throng,
And kings sate still with awfull eye,
As if they surely knew their sovran Lord was by.

But peacefull was the night
Wherin the Prince of Light
    His raign of peace upon the earth began:
The windes with wonder whist,
Smoothly the waters kist,
    Whispering new joyes to the milde ocean,
Who now hath quite forgot to rave,
While birds of calm sit brooding on the charmeed wave.

The stars with deep amaze
Stand fixt in stedfast gaze,
    Bending one way their pretious influence,
And will not take their flight,
For all the morning light,
    Or Lucifer that often warn'd them thence;
But in their glimmering orbs did glow,
Untill their Lord himself bespake, and bid them go.

And though the shady gloom
Had given day her room,
    The sun himself withheld his wonted speed,
And hid his head for shame,

As his inferiour flame,
    The new enlightn'd world no more should need;
He saw a greater sun appear
Than his bright throne or burning axle-tree could bear.

The Shepherds on the lawn,
Or ere the point of dawn,
    Sate simply chatting in a rustick row;
Full little thought they than
That the mighty Pan
    Was kindly com to live with them below;
Perhaps their loves, or els their sheep,
Was all that did their silly thoughts so busie keep.

When such musick sweet
Their hearts and ears did greet,
    As never was by mortall finger strook,
Divinely-warbled voice
Answering the stringed noise,
    As all their souls in blisfull rapture took:
The air such pleasure loth to lose,
With thousand echoes still prolongs each heav'nly close.

Nature that heard such sound
Beneath the hollow round
    Of Cynthia's seat, the airy region thrilling,
Now was almost won
To think her part was done,
    And that her raign had here its last fulfilling;
She knew such harmony alone
Could hold all Heav'n and Earth in happier union.

At last surrounds their sight
A globe of circular light,
    That with long beams the shame-fac't night array'd,
The helmed cherubim
And sworded seraphim,
    Are seen in glittering ranks with wings displaid,
Harping in loud and solemn quire,
With unexpressive notes to Heav'n's new-born Heir.

Such musick (as 'tis said)
Before was never made,
        But when of old the sons of morning sung,
While the Creator great
His constellations set,
        And the well-ballanc't world on hinges hung,
And cast the dark foundations deep,
And bid the welt'ring waves their oozy channel keep.

Ring out ye crystall sphears,
Once bless our human ears
        (If ye have power to touch our senses so),
And let your silver chime
Move in melodious time;
        And let the base of Heav'n's deep organ blow,
And with your ninefold harmony
Make up full consort to th'angelike symphony.

For if such holy song
Enwrap our fancy long,
        Time will run back, and fetch the age of gold,
And speckl'd vanity
Will sicken soon and die,
        And leprous sin will melt from earthly mould,
And Hell itself will pass away,
And leave her dolorous mansions to the peering day.

Yea, truth and justice then
Will down return to men,
        Th'enameld arras of the rainbow wearing,
And mercy set between,
Thron'd in celestiall sheen,
        With radiant feet the tissued clouds down-stearing,
And Heav'n as at some festivall,
Will open wide the gates of her high palace hall.

But wisest Fate sayes no,
This must not yet be so,
        The Babe lies yet in smiling infancy,
That on the bitter cross

Must redeem our loss;
　　　So both himself and us to glorifie:
Yet first to those ychain'd in sleep,
The wakefull trump of doom must thunder through the deep,

With such a horrid clang
As on mount Sinai rang
　　　While the red fire, and smould'ring clouds out-brake:
The aged Earth agast
With terrour of that blast,
　　　Shall from the surface to the centre shake;
When at the world's last session,
The dreadfull Judge in middle air shall spread his throne.

And then at last our bliss
Full and perfect is,
　　　But now begins; for from this happy day
Th'old Dragon underground
In straiter limits bound,
　　　Not half so far casts his usurped sway,
And, wrath to see his kingdom fail,
Swindges the scaly horrour of his foulded tail.

The oracles are dumm,
No voice or hideous humm
　　　Runs through the arched roof in words deceiving.
Apollo from his shrine
Can no more divine,
　　　With hollow shreik the steep of Delphos leaving.
No nightly trance, or breathed spell,
Inspires the pale-ey'd priest from the prophetic cell.

The lonely mountains o'er,
And the resounding shore,
　　　A voice of weeping heard, and loud lament;
From haunted spring and dale,
Edg'd with poplar pale,
　　　The parting genius is with sighing sent,
With flowre-inwov'n tresses torn
The nymphs in twilight shade of tangled thickets mourn.

In consecrated earth,
And on the holy hearth,
    The lars and lemures moan with midnight plaint,
In urns and altars round,
A drear and dying sound
    Affrights the flamens at their service quaint;
And the chill marble seems to sweat,
While each peculiar power forgoes his wonted seat.

Peor and Baalim
Forsake their temples dim,
    With that twise-batter'd god of Palestine;
And mooned Ashtaroth,
Heav'ns queen and mother both,
    Now sits not girt with tapers' holy shine;
The Libyc Hammon shrinks his horn,
In vain the Tyrian maids their wounded Thamuz mourn.

And sullen Moloch fled,
Hath left in shadows dred,
    His burning idol all of blackest hue;
In vain with cymbals' ring
They call the grisly king,
    In dismall dance about the furnace blue;
The brutish gods of Nile as fast,
Isis and Orus, and the Dog Anubis, haste.

Nor is Osiris seen
In Memphian grove or green,
    Trampling the unshow'r'd grasse with lowings loud:
Nor can he be at rest
Within his sacred chest,
    Naught but profoundest Hell can be his shroud,
In vain with timbrel'd anthems dark
The sable-stoled Sorcerers bear his worshipt Ark.

He feels from Juda's Land
The dredded Infant's hand,
    The rayes of Bethlehem blind his dusky eyn;
Nor all the gods beside,

Longer dare abide,
    Not Typhon huge ending in snaky twine:
Our Babe, to shew his Godhead true,
Can in his swadling bands controul the damned crew.

So when the sun in bed,
Curtain'd with cloudy red,
    Pillows his chin upon an orient wave,
The flocking shadows pale,
Troop to th'infernall jail,
    Each fetter'd ghost slips to his severall grave,
And the yellow-skirted fayes,
Fly after the night-steeds, leaving their moon-lov'd maze.

But see, the Virgin blest
Hath laid her Babe to rest:
    Time is our tedious song should here have ending,
Heav'n's youngest teemed star,
Hath fixt her polisht car,
    Her sleeping Lord with handmaid lamp attending:
And all about the courtly stable,
Bright-harnest angels sit in order serviceable.

It would be a long church service that included hymns with twenty-seven verses.

On the other hand, the British always seem to be singing William Blake's hymn *Jerusalem*, often in entirely non-religious contexts:

And did those feet in ancient time
Walk upon England's mountains green?
And was the holy Lamb of God,
On England's pleasant pastures seen?

And did the Countenance Divine
Shine forth upon our clouded hills ?
And was Jerusalem builded here,
Among these dark Satanic Mills ?

Bring me my Bow of burning gold!
Bring me my Arrows of desire!
Bring me my Spear! O clouds, unfold!
Bring me my Chariot of fire!

> I will not cease from Mental Fight,
> Nor shall my Sword sleep in my hand,
> Till we have built Jerusalem
> In England's green and pleasant Land.

Indeed there seems to be some emotional need within the British soul for hymns, and that is doubtless why so many major British poets have written one or more.

hyperbole

The compilers of guides to English literature are particularly prone to hyperbole, the use of exaggeration in order to arrest attention. Thus they are likely to write, 'The odes of Keats are such perfect poems that they could only have been written by an archangel.' Never trust a writer who employs hyperbole, and, when possible, stone him or her to death. The trouble is, from time to time a writer of genius uses hyperbole, and then it becomes magic. Just look at what Hotspur has to say in *Henry IV*, *Part 1*:

> By heaven, methinks it were an easy leap,
> To pluck bright honour from the pale-faced moon;
> Or dive into the bottom of the deep,
> Where fathom-line could never touch the ground,
> And pluck up drowned honour by the locks;
> So he that doth redeem her thence might wear,
> Without corrival, all her dignities:
> But out upon this half-faced fellowship!

Lovers, too, are prone to use hyperbole when speaking of their loves – *Romeo and Juliet* would be a much shorter play if you cut out all its hyperbole.

iambic metre

One of the things that distinguishes **poetry** from **prose** is that poetry is generally more rhythmic than prose. Indeed, quite often, poems have a very definite and distinct rhythm to them, and the most common of those rhythms is known as the iambic metre. This, quite simply, is a line of poetry in which an unstressed syllable is followed by a stressed one. You consequently get a da-dum da-dum rhythm to the line, just like this:

> The curfew tolls the knell of parting day,
> The lowing herd wind slowly o'er the lea,

Furthermore, if you split each 'da dum' up from its neighbour, you will discover that each line has five 'da dums':

x /	x /	x /	x /	x /
The cur	few tolls	the knell	of part	ing day

Each 'da dum' is called a **foot**, and so the line above has five feet. Consequently the line is referred to as an iambic pentameter because literary critics like to rival their scholarly cousins in physics who are always talking about the top-quark being much heavier than an electron. Hence, in an attempt to be equally incomprehensible, a literary critic can say, 'The monotony of iambic pentameters is relieved by the occasional anapaest.' This makes everyone feel better. Unfortunately, **Thomas Gray**, the opening lines of whose *Elegy Written in a Country Churchyard* I've just quoted, doesn't vary his **metre** with the occasional anapaest or anything else. As a result, the iambic pentameters go on and on:

> Now fades the glimmering landscape on the sight,
> And all the air a solemn stillness holds,
> Save where the beetle wheels his droning flight,
> And drowsy tinklings lull the distant folds:

As a result, the reader slowly slips into sleep. This may be useful to you if you suffer from insomnia. Don't bother with a prescription for sleeping tablets; Gray's *Elegy* will do the trick.

Ideal Husband, An

This 1895 play by **Oscar Wilde** is not as funny as *The Importance of Being Earnest*, but if you go to see it, you will be too busy laughing to notice that.

LORD CAVERSHAM: Good-evening, Lady Chiltern! Has my good-for-nothing young son been here?

LADY CAVERSHAM: [*Smiling.*] I don't think Lord Goring has arrived yet.

MABEL CHILTERN: [*Coming up to* LORD CAVERSHAM.] Why do you call Lord Goring good-for-nothing?

LORD CAVERSHAM: Because he leads such an idle life.

MABEL CHILTERN: How can you say such a thing? Why, he rides in the Row at ten o'clock in the morning, goes to the Opera three times a week, changes his clothes at least five times a day, and dines out every night of the season. You don't call that leading an idle life, do you?

And so it goes on. Very trivial, no doubt, but ideal after changing bedpans, directing traffic or teaching Year Three about German prepositions.

idiom

Every language has idioms. Thus, when we say that it is raining cats and dogs, the French say that it is raining halberds. However, idioms tend to be hackneyed, and therefore should be avoided. Indeed, near synonyms for 'idiom' are '**cliché**', 'colloquialism', '**dead metaphor**' and 'slang', and no self-respecting writer would use any of those.

Idiot Boy, The

This is a poem by **Wordsworth**, first published in the *Lyrical Ballads* of 1798. Since it is 463 lines long, I can't quote it here, but it tells the story of a mentally handicapped boy who is sent by his mother to fetch the doctor for an ailing neighbour. The boy does not reappear, and so the distraught mother goes in search of him. She finds him lounging beside a brook, totally unaware of his erstwhile mission. Meanwhile, the ailing neighbour is so worried about the distraught mother that she recovers and herself goes in search of her. The moral of the story is that the strength of human affections can be all-powerful.

idyll

Normally the word 'idyll' is used to denote a poem that is rural and tranquil in its setting, but **Tennyson** in his *Idylls of the King* and **Browning** in his *Dramatic Idylls* so stretched the word as to render it almost meaningless.

Idylls of the King, The

This is a sequence of poems by **Tennyson**. Published between 1856 and 1885, its twelve books are all centred round King Arthur and his fruitless attempt to create a perfect kingdom. The scene is set in the first book, *The Coming of Arthur*:

> Leodogran, the King of Cameliard,
> Had one fair daughter, and none other child;
> And she was the fairest of all flesh on earth,
> Guinevere, and in her his one delight.
>
> For many a petty king ere Arthur came
> Ruled in this isle, and ever waging war
> Each upon other, wasted all the land;
> And still from time to time the heathen host
> Swarmed overseas, and harried what was left.
> And so there grew great tracts of wilderness,
> Wherein the beast was ever more and more,
> But man was less and less, till Arthur came.
> For first Aurelius lived and fought and died,
> And after him King Uther fought and died,
> But either failed to make the kingdom one.
> And after these King Arthur for a space,
> And through the puissance of his Table Round,
> Drew all their petty princedoms under him.
> Their king and head, and made a realm, and reigned.
>
> And thus the land of Cameliard was waste,
> Thick with wet woods, and many a beast therein,
> And none or few to scare or chase the beast;
> So that wild dog and wolf and boar and bear
> Came night and day, and rooted in the fields,
> And wallowed in the gardens of the King.
> And ever and anon the wolf would steal
> The children and devour, but now and then,

Her own brood lost or dead, lent her fierce teat
To human sucklings; and the children, housed
In her foul den, there at their meat would growl,
And mock their foster mother on four feet,
Till, straightened, they grew up to wolf-like men,
Worse than the wolves. And King Leodogran
Groaned for the Roman legions here again,
And Caesar's eagle; then his brother king,
Urien, assailed him; last a heathen horde,
Reddening the sun with smoke and earth with blood,
And on the spike that split the mother's heart
Spitting the child, brake on him, till, amazed,
He knew not whither he should turn for aid.

But – for he heard of Arthur newly crowned,
Though not without an uproar made by those
Who cried, 'He is not Uther's son' – the King
Sent to him, saying, 'Arise, and help us thou!
For here between the man and beast we die.'

And Arthur yet had done no deed of arms,
But heard the call, and came: and Guinevere
Stood by the castle walls to watch him pass;
But since he neither wore on helm or shield
The golden symbol of his kinglihood,
But rode a simple knight among his knights,
And many of these in richer arms than he,
She saw him not, or marked not, if she saw,
One among many, though his face was bare.
But Arthur, looking downward as he past,
Felt the light of her eyes into his life
Smite on the sudden, yet rode on, and pitched
His tents beside the forest. Then he drave
The heathen; after, slew the beast, and felled
The forest, letting in the sun, and made
Broad pathways for the hunter and the knight
And so returned.

   In the excellent Longman edition of Tennyson, edited by Christopher
Ricks, there then follow 284 pages until the final book, *The Passing of
Arthur*, comes to a melancholy end. The ten books sandwiched between
The Coming of Arthur and *The Passing of Arthur* relate different incidents

or episodes culled from the myths of Arthurian England. It was the longest and most ambitious work of Tennyson's career, and, among other things, attracted the deep admiration of Queen Victoria. It is also a goldmine for interpretations. Each of the tales can be seen as a moral allegory and a vision of a spiritual philosophy of life. No self-respecting literary critic could ignore such an invitation, and many pages have been devoted to *Idylls of the King*. As always, of course, your best tactic would be simply to read the poems. Certainly the Victorians did – in their thousands. *Idylls of the King* was by far his most popular work, yet today it is rarely read, and never by the general public. As Tennyson said in *The Passing of Arthur*: 'The old order changeth, yielding place to new . . . '

Iliad, the

This is a long, epic poem, supposedly by the ancient Greek poet **Homer**. It, and its companion, the *Odyssey*, were once part of the education of every privileged boy at public school. As a result, the stories contained within these poems became well known and part of British culture. Thus everyone knew about Helen of Troy, the anger of Achilles, the wisdom of Odysseus, the death of Hector, and so on. Nowadays, of course, no one reads ancient Greek, but educated people are still expected to be experts on the Trojan War. Thus **W. H. Auden** (1907–73) could write a poem entitled 'The Shield of Achilles' and expect everyone to pick up the reference. Thomas Kinsella (1928–) can write a poem entitled 'Scylla and Charybdis' and expect us all to know who they were.

imagery

Many moons ago I dimly recall writing an MLitt dissertation on the structural role of imagery in four of **Dickens**'s novels. It seems that then I had some almost certain concept as to what imagery was. But that was a long time ago. Today, I haven't a clue. For instance, when I say, 'I can see a buttercup,' I am, in some entirely literal way, using an image. When I say, 'David Cameron is as yellow as a buttercup,' I am once again using an image, but this time it is less literal. Nor does imagery need to be confined to sight. It could be taste: 'I am eating a marshmallow,' or, 'David Cameron is as soft as a marshmallow.' It could be touch: 'I am holding a poker,' or, 'David Cameron thinks that he is as straight as a poker.' And so I could go on. Imagery can be literal, conceptual, meta-phorical or virtually anything else. Whether we like it or not, imagery permeates our speech and our writing. The most non-literary person uses it every day. But, from time to time, a genius arrives, and in his or her hands, imagery is made magical. **Shakespeare**'s play *Macbeth* is so rich in imagery that you do not need to read anything else in order to gain a complete understanding of imagery's power. Here is a famous speech: Macbeth is contemplating the necessary murder of his king, Duncan:

> Is this a dagger which I see before me,
> The handle toward my hand? Come, let me clutch thee:
> I have thee not, and yet I see thee still.
> Art thou not, fatal vision, sensible
> To feeling as to sight? or art thou but
> A dagger of the mind, a false creation,
> Proceeding from the heat-oppressèd brain?
> I see thee yet, in form as palpable
> As this which now I draw.   [*He draws his dagger.*]
> Thou marshall'st me the way that I was going;
> And such an instrument I was to use.
> Mine eyes are made the fools o' the other senses,
> Or else worth all the rest; I see thee still,
> And on thy blade and dudgeon gouts of blood,
> Which was not so before. There's no such thing:
> It is the bloody business which informs
> Thus to mine eyes. Now o'er the one half-world
> Nature seems dead, and wicked dreams abuse
> The curtain'd sleep; witchcraft celebrates
> Pale Hecate's offerings, and wither'd murder,
> Alarum'd by his sentinel, the wolf,
> Whose howl's his watch, thus with his stealthy pace,
> With Tarquin's ravishing strides, towards his design
> Moves like a ghost. Thou sure and firm-set earth,
> Hear not my steps, which way they walk, for fear
> Thy very stones prate of my whereabout,
> And take the present horror from the time,
> Which now suits with it. Whiles I threat, he lives:
> Words to the heat of deeds too cold breath gives.

I could now take you through that speech, identifying as we went every type of image that Shakespeare employs. I shall not do so. Instead, I can only suggest that you learn the speech. I really do mean this. Learn the whole speech by heart. It will teach you more about imagery than I ever can.

imagination

This is what all writers are supposed to have, yet it is surprisingly difficult to say what it is. It might be simpler to say that imagination is the ability to lie.

Importance of Being Earnest, The

This is the title of a trivial play by **Oscar Wilde**. However, it also happens to be almost painfully funny, and should be seen several times by all sentient people.

indirect speech

When you say, 'I'd love a pint of beer now,' you are using what is called direct speech. However, when I say, 'Horace [or whatever your name is] said that he'd love a pint of beer,' then I am using indirect speech. In other words, I am reporting what someone else said, but not quoting directly their precise words. You need to know the difference between direct and indirect speech because you will need such terms when discussing literature.

In Memoriam

This is the title of a series of elegies by **Tennyson** written in memory of A. H. Hallam. It was published in 1850 and became talismanically famous. It was even esteemed by Queen Victoria, though that provides no guidance as to the poetic worth of the work. It is written in iambic tetrameters, and was so popular for a number of non-literary reasons. For instance, it is full of 'sage' pronouncements like this:

> I hold it true, whate'er befall;
>   I feel it when I sorrow most;
>   'Tis better to have loved and lost
> Than never to have loved at all.

It seemed to address current worries, like Darwin's theory of evolution:

> Are God and Nature then at strife,
>   That Nature lends such evil dreams?
>   So careful of the type she seems,
> So careless of the single life;
>
> That I, considering everywhere
>   Her secret meaning in her deeds,

> And finding that of fifty seeds
> She often brings but one to bear,
>
> I falter where I firmly trod,
>   And falling with my weight of cares
>   Upon the great world's altar-stairs
> That slope thro' darkness up to God,
>
> I stretch lame hands of faith, and grope,
>   And gather dust and chaff, and call
>   To what I feel is Lord of all,
> And faintly trust the larger hope.

Indeed, the whole sequence is shot through with the Victorian neurosis about faith and doubt, science and revelation, hope and despair. Consequently, if you want to understand the Victorians, you have to know *In Memoriam*. If you want to read only great poetry, you can probably ignore it. However, you will have noticed that Tennyson uses the rhyming scheme abba. This is unusual, and Tennyson claimed to have invented it. In fact, it had been used earlier by both **Ben Jonson** and Lord Herbert of Cherbury, but it is possible that Tennyson did not know this.

inscape and instress

These words were invented by **Gerard Manley Hopkins** to help explain his poetry. I have never found them of the slightest use.

intentional fallacy

Your friend Peregrine Pedant has just written a long, long poem. He regards it as a masterpiece. It begins as follows:

> We only begin to consider the end
> When we ourselves are approaching death.
> It's enough to drive one round the bend
> And make one lose virtually all one's breath.

And so it goes on. Now you are a close friend of Peregrine's, and your friendship somehow allows you to lose your critical faculties. It so happened that Rebecca was reading Peregrine's poem the other day, and she said, 'Christ, this is awful.' At once you rushed to Peregrine's defence. 'No,' you said, 'the poem is contemplating eternity. It is looking at human transience in the light of time since the big bang. It is a profound meditation on consciousness.' As any semi-conscious person can see from the first four lines alone, Peregrine's poem is appalling. You, however, know that Peregrine intended it to be a philosophical and poetic masterpiece, and, because of your friendship, you take his intention and transpose the intention into an achievement. This is known as the intentional fallacy, and it is quite rightly a crime in literary criticism.

internal rhyme

This occurs when two or more words rhyme within a single line of verse. **Shelley** uses the technique in his poem 'The Cloud':

> I bring fresh showers for the thirsting flowers,
>   From the seas and the streams;
> I bear light shade for the leaves when laid
>   In their noonday dreams.
> From my wings are shaken the dews that waken
>   The sweet buds every one,
> When rocked to rest on their mother's breast,
>   As she dances about the sun.
> I wield the flail of the lashing hail,
>   And whiten the green plains under,
> And then again I dissolve it in rain,
>   And laugh as I pass in thunder.

Intimations of Immortality

To give it its full title, *Intimations of Immortality from Recollections of Early Childhood* is a poem by **William Wordsworth**. It is, if you like, a regret at growing up. Just look at the first two verses:

> There was a time when meadow, grove, and stream,
> The earth, and every common sight,
>   To me did seem
>   Apparelled in celestial light,
> The glory and the freshness of a dream.
> It is not now as it hath been of yore;
>   Turn wheresoe'er I may,
>   By night or day,
> The things which I have seen I now can see no more.

> The Rainbow comes and goes,
> And lovely is the Rose,
> The Moon doth with delight
> Look round her when the heavens are bare,
> Waters on a starry night
> Are beautiful and fair;
> The sunshine is a glorious birth;
> But yet I know, where'er I go,
> That there hath past away a glory from the earth.

Well, yes; most of us have felt like that from time to time. It's mostly spurious, of course. We romanticise our childhoods, but Wordsworth's romanticism is gloriously done, and in his penultimate verse, he finds some consolation:

> What though the radiance which was once so bright
> Be now for ever taken from my sight,
> Though nothing can bring back the hour
> Of splendour in the grass, of glory in the flower;
> We will grieve not, rather find
> Strength in what remains behind;
> In the primal sympathy
> Which having been must ever be;
> In the soothing thoughts that spring
> Out of human suffering;
> In the faith that looks through death,
> In years that bring the philosophic mind.

You do need to know this poem. You may not like it, but it is an important example of the romantic ethos and an important statement in Wordsworth's life.

invective

Invective is when someone fluently insults someone else. Pandarus in **Shakespeare**'s *Troilus and Cressida* is good at it. He comments less than favourably upon the common soldiers passing before him:

> Asses, fools, dolts! chaff and bran, chaff and bran!
> porridge after meat! ... Ne'er look, ne'er look: the eagles
> are gone: crows and daws, crows and daws!

But English literature, both **prose** and **poetry**, is packed with invective. There must be something in the character of the British that makes them delight in abusing others.

irony

Irony is an underhand technique whereby someone or something is made to appear foolish. Socrates in his dialogues assumes total ignorance so as to lure his companions into statements that he then demonstrates to be fallacious. **Jane Austen** in her novels propounds generalisations like, 'It is truth universally acknowledged, that a single man in possession of a good fortune, must be in want of a wife', but those generalisations are at best only half true. **Pope**, in *The Rape of a Lock*, inflates a trivial incident to earth-shattering proportions. In doing so, of course, he is poking fun at those who took any notice of the incident in the first place.

In one sense, irony is intelligent and restrained sarcasm, but irony can be so oblique that it becomes a tone. Jonathan Swift has it in *Gulliver's Travels*. For example, when Gulliver visited Lilliput, he learnt that years ago, people broke eggs at the big end. However, the present king's grandfather once cut himself breaking an egg in this manner, so the king at the time, the father of the present king's grandfather, issued an edict that all were to break eggs at the small end. Some of the people resisted, and they found refuge in Blefuscu, and 'for six and thirty moons past' the two sides have been at war. To Gulliver, of course, fighting for thirty-six years over at which end to crack an egg is absurd, but Swift is obliquely pointing out that England's wars against France are no less absurd. Gibbon, in *The Decline and Fall of the Roman Empire*, adopts a similarly ironic tone about Christianity.

What I have been talking about is known as verbal irony, but there are other brands. There is dramatic irony, most frequently seen in a play, where the audience knows more than the character on the stage. As a result, the audience have to watch the character making mistakes because of his ignorance while, at the same time, desperately wanting to tell him the real state of affairs. There can also be cosmic irony where the characters in the play, novel or poem are combating, not ignorance, but a malevolent universe. In *Tess of the D'Urbervilles*, **Hardy** makes this overt at the end of the novel by commenting that, 'Justice was done, and the President of the Immortals, in Aeschylean phrase, had ended his sport with Tess.'

ivory tower

This phrase is used disapprovingly to indicate that someone lives in a world of their own, and consequently is woefully ill equipped to cope with the real world. Personally living in an ivory tower seems to be markedly better than living in a world where cruelty and deceit are the norm, but each to his or her own.

J

jabberwocky

In *Alice Through the Looking Glass*, Lewis Carroll introduced a poem called 'Jabberwocky'. It is often regarded as the greatest nonsense poem in the English language:

> 'Twas brillig, and the slithy toves
>   Did gyre and gimble in the wabe:
> All mimsy were the borogoves,
>   And the mome raths outgrabe.
>
> 'Beware the Jabberwock, my son!
>   The jaws that bite, the claws that catch!
> Beware the Jubjub bird, and shun
>   The frumious Bandersnatch!'
>
> He took his vorpal sword in hand:
>   Long time the manxome foe he sought –
> So rested he by the Tumtum tree,
>   And stood awhile in thought.
>
> And, as in uffish thought he stood,
>   The Jabberwock, with eyes of flame,
> Came whiffling through the tulgey wood,
>   And burbled as it came!
>
> One, two! One, two! And through and through
>   The vorpal blade went snicker-snack!
> He left it dead, and with its head
>   He went galumphing back.

'And, has thou slain the Jabberwock?
　　Come to my arms, my beamish boy!
O frabjous day! Callooh! Callay!'
　　He chortled in his joy.

'Twas brillig, and the slithy toves
　　Did gyre and gimble in the wabe;
All mimsy were the borogoves,
　　And the mome raths outgrabe.

Jaberwocky by John Tenniel, from Lewis Carroll's *Alice Through the Looking Glass*

As a result, if someone appears to be talking nonsense, you might say that he or she is talking jabberwocky.

Jacobean

The writing that took place in England during the reign of James I (1603–25) is known as Jacobean. The term has no stylistic connotations. It just happens to be shorter than saying 'the first quarter of the seventeenth century'.

James I

Read the entry immediately above. After all, you don't really want or need to know that James I was also James VI of Scotland and that he was the author of a short work on the rules for writing Scots poetry.

James, Henry (1843–1916)

James was an American novelist, though from 1876 he made his home in England. As you will know if you have read any other entries in this work, my comments on topics are always fair, balanced and sagacious. You will therefore accept as gospel truth my statement that James is a great novelist only marginally diminished by being unreadable. When I was an undergraduate, I read *Portrait of a Lady*. When I had finished it, I said to myself, 'That is clearly a great novel; why didn't I enjoy it?' And this is the trouble with James. His style is wordy, diffuse, full of double negatives, and packed with complex imagery. Some of the later novels, like *The Wings of the Dove* (1902) and *The Golden Bowl* (1904), I've never managed to finish. His friend **Edith Wharton**, who admired him greatly, said that there were passages in his work that were all but incomprehensible. **Oscar Wilde** said that James wrote fiction as if it were a painful duty. **H. G. Wells** harshly portrayed James as a hippopotamus laboriously attempting to pick up a pea that has got into a corner of its cage. I am therefore comforted that I am not alone in finding James impenetrable. It does, however, mean that I cannot say anything very positive in this entry.

Jane Eyre

This is Charlotte Brontë's best known novel, though not, in my opinion, her best. However, it is certainly dramatic, and perhaps played a not dishonourable part in fostering women's rights. (See **the Brontës**.)

jargon

This is the word used to signify the unintelligible vocabulary of others when they are conversing about something that uses its own technical terms. Hence, if you are not a computer scientist, you might not understand people talking about normalising a database. If you are not a historian, you might be baffled by someone wanting to steer a middle way between the Whig approach and the Marxist one. We all of us use jargon in some way or other.

Jerome, Jerome Klapka (1859–1927)

The humble son of an ironmonger in Walsall, Jerome improbably became an actor and reporter and, in addition, wrote *Three Men in a Boat* (1889), an entirely trivial but very funny novel.

Jew of Malta, The

This is a play by **Christopher Marlowe**. Do not take your seven-year-old daughter to see it. It contains financial extortion, the poisoning of nuns and the boiling to death of the Jew. Unsurprisingly, the play was very popular in early-seventeenth-century England.

Johnson, Dr Samuel (1709–84)

It is difficult to be concise about Samuel Johnson. It is even more difficult to be restrained about him, because Johnson had the sort of intelligence that makes most of us in comparison look moronic. He was poor, ugly, plagued with ill health, and should, like millions of others, have passed his days in total obscurity. Instead he became a considerable poet, an interesting playwright, an essay writer of genius, a biographer of insight, a literary critic who has rarely been equalled, a political pamphleteer, one of England's earliest novelists, and a lexicographer of such magnitude that his *Dictionary of the English Language* (1755) has been ranked as one of the greatest single achievements of scholarship the world has ever known. He could also come out with aphorisms like these:

'Tis better to remain silent and be thought a fool, than open one's mouth and remove all doubt.

What is written without effort is in general read without pleasure.

Love is the wisdom of the fool and the folly of the wise.

Prejudice not being founded on reason cannot be removed by argument.

Consequently it is better to ignore Dr Johnson. One stands no chance of summarising his work adequately or of assessing his influence fully. The Great Cham, as he was sometimes known, is too massive for any reference book to encompass.

Jonson, Ben (1572–1637)

Tact and diplomacy were not striking traits of Ben Jonson. Highly intelligent himself, he tended to scorn those less gifted, something that did not endear him to all his contemporaries. He also tended to speak or write first without considering the possible consequences of his words. As a result, he was more than once imprisoned for sedition. Yet Jonson was a brilliant dramatist, and it is a pity that his plays are no longer presented. Some of his comedies, *Volpone* and *The Alchemist* in particular, are still very funny, and his tragedy, *Sejanus*, I remember studying with considerable enjoyment as an undergraduate. Jonson was also a poet and 'To Celia' has quite rightly achieved lasting fame:

> Drink to me only with thine eyes,
>   And I will pledge with mine ;
> Or leave a kiss but in the cup
>   And I'll not look for wine.
> The thirst that from the soul doth rise
>   Doth ask a drink divine:
> But might I of Jove's nectar sup,
>   I would not change for thine.
>
> I sent thee late a rosy wreath,
>   Not so much honouring thee
> As giving it a hope that there
>   It could not wither'd be.
> But thou thereon didst only breathe,
>   And sent'st it back to me:
> Since when it grows, and smells, I swear,
>   Not of itself but thee!

Jonson also said when **Shakespeare** died: 'He was not of an age, but for all time.' For that perception alone, Jonson deserves to be remembered.

Journey's End

This is a play by R. C. Sherriff that was first produced in 1928. It is a study of bravery and cowardice in First World War trenches, and is extremely moving.

Joyce, James (1882–1941)

When I began this dictionary, I did not realise that there were going to be so many topics that I was quite incapable of writing about. James Joyce is another of them. Let me just give you an extract from one of Joyce's novels, *Finnegans Wake*:

> Sir Tristram, violer d'amores, fr'over the short sea, had passen-core rearrived from North Armorica on this side the scraggy isthmus of Europe Minor to wielderfight his penisolate war: nor had top-sawyer's rocks by the stream Oconee exaggerated themselse to Laurens County's gorgios while they went doublin their mumper all the time: nor avoice from afire bellowsed mishe mishe to tauftauf thuartpeatrick: not yet, though venissoon after, had a kidscad buttended a bland old isaac: not yet, though all's fair in vanessy, were sosie sesthers wroth with twone nathandjoe. Rot a peck of pa's malt had Jhem or Shen brewed by arclight and rory end to the regginbrow was to be seen ringsome on the aquaface.

Now you see why I cannot comment intelligibly about Joyce. The whole novel is written in this sort of gobbledegook. It is a great shame.

In 1914 Joyce published a collection of short stories under the title *Dubliners*, and excellent short stories they are. In the same year a quasi-autobiographical piece called *A Portrait of the Artist as a Young Man* also appeared, and that too is very good. But then Joyce became ensnared by his own linguistic bravura. In 1922 came *Ulysses*, and although *Ulysses* is a very, very impressive novel, it is not exactly easy reading. It took me three attempts before I finally succeeded in completing it. Then, in 1939, came *Finnegans Wake*, and world war was the result, though I am prepared to admit that there may be no causal connection between the two events. All that one can say is that Joyce was Irish, and this perhaps explains everything.

Jude the Obscure

This is the last of **Thomas Hardy**'s novels and was published in 1895. It aroused outrage, partly because of its unrelieved pessimism and partly because Jude had a sex drive.

Julius Caesar

I include *Julius Caesar* because it often seems to me that this **Shakespeare** play is underrated. It can hardly be accused of triviality, being concerned with ambition, government, love, loyalty, public service and treachery. The play is intensely gripping, and you leave a good performance emotionally and intellectually drained.

juvenilia

This word relates to work done in one's youth.

K

Kafka, Franz (1883–1924)

Since Kafka was a German-speaking Jew whose novels were not translated into English until after his death, his appearance in this dictionary might occasion some surprise. But Kafka has given us a word: Kafkaesque. No one can pretend to be literate if he or she doesn't know what Kafkaesque means. The trouble is, the word is quite tricky to define. Wikipedia does it as follows:

'Kafkaesque' is an auctorial descriptive which is used to describe concepts, situations, and ideas which are reminiscent of the literary work of Prague writer Franz Kafka, particularly his novels *The Trial*, *The Castle* and *Metamorphosis*.

The term, which is quite fluid in definition, has also been described as meaning 'marked by a senseless, disorienting, often menacing complexity: Kafkaesque bureaucracies', and 'marked by surreal distortion and often a sense of impending danger: Kafkaesque fantasies of the impassive interrogation, the false trial, the confiscated passport . . . haunt his innocence' – *New Yorker*.

It can also describe an intentional distortion of reality by powerful but anonymous bureaucrats. 'Lack of evidence is treated as a pesky inconvenience, to be circumvented by such Kafkaesque means as depositing unproven allegations into sealed files . . . ' Another definition would be an existentialist state of ever-elusive freedom while existing under unmitigatable control.

The adjective refers to anything suggestive of Kafka, especially his nightmarish type of narration, in which characters lack a clear course of action, the ability to see beyond immediate events, and the possibility of escape. The term's meaning has transcended the literary realm to apply to real-life occurrences and situations that are incomprehensibly complex, bizarre, or illogical.

Much more briefly, one may content oneself with a dictionary definition:

> Characterised by surreal distortion and a sense of impending danger – 'the kafkaesque terror of the endless interrogations'

The ideal thing, of course, is to read *The Trial* (1925), Kafka's best novel. Then you'll really know what Kafkaesque means.

Keats, John (1795–1821)

As you can see, Keats did not live long, but, in a life marked by pain, tragedy and despair, he succeeded in writing some of the most magical poems ever produced in English. Indeed, Keats poses a problem. Those who like his poetry tend to like it with a passion that makes the average football supporter seem lukewarm. Self-evidently, I like Keats's poetry, and my immediate impulse is simply to reproduce here his twelve greatest poems and leave you to glory in them. In fact, I've already quoted one of Keats's poems, since I used his *La Belle Dame Sans Merci* as an example of a **ballad**. If you look up **sonnet**, you'll find another one.

Consequently here I can concentrate on his mastery of the **ode**. Keats wrote a number of odes, and at least four of them – 'Nightingale', 'Grecian Urn', 'Melancholy' and 'Autumn' – defy belief in their loveliness. Here is the one to autumn:

> Season of mists and mellow fruitfulness,
>   Close bosom-friend of the maturing sun;
> Conspiring with him how to load and bless
>   With fruit the vines that round the thatch-eves run;
> To bend with apples the moss'd cottage-trees,
>   And fill all fruit with ripeness to the core;
>   To swell the gourd, and plump the hazel shells

With a sweet kernel; to set budding more,
And still more, later flowers for the bees,
Until they think warm days will never cease,
For Summer has o'er-brimm'd their clammy cells.

Who hath not seen thee oft amid thy store?
    Sometimes whoever seeks abroad may find
Thee sitting careless on a granary floor,
    Thy hair soft-lifted by the winnowing wind;
Or on a half-reap'd furrow sound asleep,
    Drows'd with the fume of poppies, while thy hook
        Spares the next swath and all its twinèd flowers:
And sometimes like a gleaner thou dost keep
    Steady thy laden head across a brook;
    Or by a cyder-press, with patient look,
        Thou watchest the last oozings hours by hours.
Where are the songs of Spring? Ay, where are they?
    Think not of them, thou hast thy music too, –
While barred clouds bloom the soft-dying day,
    And touch the stubble-plains with rosy hue;
Then in a wailful choir the small gnats mourn
    Among the river sallows, borne aloft
        Or sinking as the light wind lives or dies;
And full-grown lambs loud bleat from hilly bourn;
    Hedge-crickets sing; and now with treble soft
    The red-breast whistles from a garden-croft;
        And gathering swallows twitter in the skies.

I am not going to attempt an analysis of this poem, but just have another look at the first stanza. It almost suffers from overload. Keats is so determined to paint a concrete picture of autumn that the vivid, visual images jostle against each other as in the Underground at rush hour. Look at the verbs: load, bless, run, bend, fill, swell, plump, set, o'er-brim. Virtually every one is a verb of excess. Yet I bet you haven't noticed that the whole verse lacks a main verb. In grammatical terms, the first stanza isn't a proper sentence. Yet by doing this, Keats forces us to be sucked into the processes of that stanza, the ripening, the swelling, the sheer abundance of summer. He does it so superbly that you don't even notice the absence of a main verb, something that you were doubtless taught at primary school. That is a good illustration of a truth too often ignored:

poetry is magic. Great poetry sucks you into its own universe, and the rules of everyday life no longer apply.

Although Keats is at his best in odes, sonnets and ballads, he did also write some quite long poems, and two of them, *The Eve of St Agnes* and *Lamia*, are well worth attention.

Kerouac, Jack (1922–69)

On the Road, Kerouac's semi-autobiographical 1957 novel, achieved fame in its day as a searing exposé of 'the Beat Generation'. Accordingly, in my late teens, I read it. I remember thinking that rarely could so much fuss have been generated by something so vapid.

King Lear

Hailed by many as the greatest play in the English language, *King Lear* is a **tragedy** by **Shakespeare**. It deals with love, ambition, revenge, treason and maturity, but does so in so painful a manner that many people cannot read the play or see it without tears.

Kingsley, Charles (1819–75)

Charles Kingsley was a social reformer, which is to his credit, and a novelist, which, on the whole, is not. I remember as a child reading *The Water Babies* (1863), *Westward Ho!* (1855) and *Hereward the Wake* (1866). I quite enjoyed *The Water Babies* but I am not sure that at the age of seven my critical faculties were fully developed. The other two I read at secondary school, and don't recall being very impressed with either of them. As an adult, I read *Yeast* (1848) and *Alton Locke* (1850), and can only advise you not to. Kingsley appears in this dictionary mainly because the town Westward Ho! was named after his novel, thus becoming the only British town to have an exclamation mark.

Kipling, Rudyard (1865–1936)

Kipling poses something of a problem. In his lifetime, he was praised and celebrated in a manner rare for a writer. He was awarded the Noble Prize for Literature in 1907, and offered a knighthood and the Poet Laureateship, both of which he declined. Today, however, he is often scorned and derided. The truth, as is often the case, lies somewhere in between. Kipling was a superb writer for children, and I remember at about the age of eight being totally entranced by his story 'Rikki-Tikki-Tavi'. Kipling was also a poet, but here he commits at least a couple of unforgiveable sins: he is easy to read, and he points a moral.

Here, for instance, is 'If', one of his most famous poems:

> If you can keep your head when all about you
> Are losing theirs and blaming it on you;
> If you can trust yourself when all men doubt you,
> But make allowance for their doubting too;
> If you can wait and not be tired by waiting,
> Or, being lied about, don't deal in lies,
> Or being hated, don't give way to hating,
> And yet don't look too good, nor talk too wise;
>
> If you can dream – and not make dreams your master;
> If you can think – and not make thoughts your aim;
> If you can meet with Triumph and Disaster
> And treat those two impostors just the same;
> If you can bear to hear the truth you've spoken
> Twisted by knaves to make a trap for fools,
> Or watch the things you gave your life to, broken,
> And stoop and build 'em up with worn-out tools;
>
> If you can make one heap of all your winnings
> And risk it on one turn of pitch-and-toss,
> And lose, and start again at your beginnings,
> And never breathe a word about your loss;
> If you can force your heart and nerve and sinew
> To serve your turn long after they are gone,
> And so hold on when there is nothing in you
> Except the Will which says to them: 'Hold on!'
>
> If you can talk with crowds and keep your virtue,
> Or walk with Kings – nor lose the common touch;
> If neither foes nor loving friends can hurt you,
> If all men count with you, but none too much;
> If you can fill the unforgiving minute
> With sixty seconds' worth of distance run,
> Yours is the Earth and everything that's in it,
> And – which is more – you'll be a Man, my son!

There are many people around for whom 'If' is an inspiring poem. There are also many for whom it is an example of trite, sentimental and unthinking verbiage. Kipling also possessed a strong vein of patriotism that partook in full of imperial arrogance:

Take up the White Man's burden –
Send forth the best ye breed –
Go bind your sons to exile
To serve your captives' need . . .

And yet, Kipling accomplished so much. He was a journalist, an editor, a poet, a short-story writer, a novelist, and even perhaps a thinker. He was rarely first class at anything, but he was a good second class in a number of fields. And anyway, one can hardly fail to honour someone who said:

Borrow trouble for yourself, if that's your nature, but don't lend it to your neighbours.

Everyone is more or less mad on one point.

For the female of the species is more deadly than the male.

God could not be everywhere, and therefore he made mothers.

Never look backwards or you'll fall down the stairs.

Never scorn the writer who provides you with aphorisms: it saves so much time, not having to think for oneself!

'He put his nose into the ink'
from 'Rikki-Tikki-Tavi' in Rudyard Kipling's *The Jungle Book*

Kubla Khan

This is the title of a poem by Coleridge. The entry on Coleridge largely consists of a reading of this poem. It is a magical poem, so turn at once to **Coleridge**.

L

La Belle Dame sans Merci

See **Keats, John** and **ballad**

Lady Chatterley's Lover

This is a novel by **D. H. Lawrence**. It is a long way from being his best novel, but it deserves mention because, though written in 1928, it was not allowed to be published in Britain until 1960. This was because the novel was judged obscene – after all, you can't have people reading about a lady having sex with a gamekeeper, can you? – and it was not until the publishers Penguin produced an unexpurgated version and forced a change in the law that it became legally permissible to read it. The court case surrounding that publication was deeply comic.

Lady of Shalott, The

Tennyson is a great poet, yet it is not *Ulysses*, ***In Memoriam*** or *Locksley Hall* that the general public have taken to their hearts. Instead it is this atmospheric chant, *The Lady of Shalott*:

PART I

On either side the river lie
Long fields of barley and of rye,
That clothe the wold and meet the sky;
And through the field the road runs by
   To many-tower'd Camelot;
And up and down the people go,
Gazing where the lilies blow
Round an island there below,
   The island of Shalott.

Willows whiten, aspens quiver,
Little breezes dusk and shiver
Through the wave that runs for ever
By the island in the river
   Flowing down to Camelot.
Four grey walls, and four grey towers,
Overlook a space of flowers,
And the silent isle imbowers
   The Lady of Shalott.

By the margin, willow veil'd,
Slide the heavy barges trail'd
By slow horses; and unhail'd
The shallop flitteth silken-sail'd
      Skimming down to Camelot:
But who hath seen her wave her hand?
Or at the casement seen her stand?
Or is she known in all the land,
      The Lady of Shalott?

Only reapers, reaping early,
In among the bearded barley,
Hear a song that echoes cheerly
From the river winding clearly
      Down to tower'd Camelot;
And by the moon the reaper weary,
Piling sheaves in uplands airy,
Listening, whispers, ' 'Tis the fairy
      Lady of Shalott.'

PART 2

There she weaves by night and day
A magic web with colours gay.
She has heard a whisper say
A curse is on her if she stay
      To look down to Camelot.
She knows not what the curse may be,
And so she weaveth steadily,
And little other care hath she,
      The Lady of Shalott.

And moving through a mirror clear
That hangs before her all the year,
Shadows of the world appear.
There she sees the highway near
      Winding down to Camelot;
There the river eddy whirls,
And there the surly village churls
And the red cloaks of market girls
      Pass onward from Shalott.

Sometimes a troop of damsels glad,
An abbot on an ambling pad,

227

Sometimes a curly shepherd lad
Or long-hair'd page in crimson clad
      Goes by to tower'd Camelot;
And sometimes through the mirror blue
The knights come riding two and two:
She hath no loyal knight and true,
      The Lady of Shalott.

But in her web she still delights
To weave the mirror's magic sights,
For often through the silent nights
A funeral, with plumes and lights
      And music, went to Camelot;
Or when the moon was overhead,
Came two young lovers lately wed.
'I am half sick of shadows,' said
      The Lady of Shalott.

PART 3

A bow-shot from her bower-eaves,
He rode between the barley sheaves,
The sun came dazzling thro' the leaves
And flamed upon the brazen greaves
      Of bold Sir Lancelot.
A red-cross knight for ever kneel'd
To a lady in his shield
That sparkled on the yellow field,
      Beside remote Shalott.

The gemmy bridle glitter'd free,
Like to some branch of stars we see
Hung in the golden Galaxy.
The bridle bells rang merrily
      As he rode down to Camelot:
And from his blazon'd baldric slung
A mighty silver bugle hung,
And as he rode his armour rung
      Beside remote Shalott.

All in the blue unclouded weather,
Thick-jewell'd shone the saddle-leather,
The helmet and the helmet-feather
Burn'd like one burning flame together,
      As he rode down to Camelot.

As often thro' the purple night,
Below the starry clusters bright,
Some bearded meteor, burning bright,
      Moves over still Shalott.

His broad clear brow in sunlight glow'd;
On burnish'd hooves his war-horse trode;
From underneath his helmet flow'd
His coal-black curls, as on he rode,
      As he rode down to Camelot.
From the bank and from the river
He flashed into the crystal mirror,
'Tirra lirra,' by the river
      Sang Sir Lancelot.

She left the web, she left the loom,
She made three paces through the room,
She saw the water-lily bloom,
She saw the helmet and the plume,
      She look'd down to Camelot.
Out flew the web and floated wide;
The mirror crack'd from side to side;
'The curse is come upon me,' cried
      The Lady of Shalott.

PART 4

In the stormy east-wind straining,
The pale yellow woods were waning,
The broad stream in his banks complaining.
Heavily the low sky raining
      Over tower'd Camelot;
Down she came and found a boat
Beneath a willow left afloat,
And around about the prow she wrote
      The Lady of Shalott

And down the river's dim expanse –
Like some bold seer in a trance,
Seeing all his own mischance –
With a glassy countenance
      Did she look to Camelot.
And at the closing of the day
She loosed the chain, and down she lay;

The broad stream bore her far away,
        The Lady of Shalott.

Lying, robed in snowy white
That loosely flew to left and right –
The leaves upon her falling light –
Thro' the noises of the night,
        She floated down to Camelot:
And as the boat-head wound along
The willowy hills and fields among,
They heard her singing her last song,
        The Lady of Shalott.

Heard a carol, mournful, holy,
Chanted loudly, chanted lowly,
Till her blood was frozen slowly,
And her eyes were darkened wholly,
        Turn'd to tower'd Camelot.
For ere she reach'd upon the tide
The first house by the water-side,
Singing in her song she died,
        The Lady of Shalott.

Under tower and balcony,
By garden-wall and gallery,
A gleaming shape she floated by,
Dead-pale between the houses high,
        Silent into Camelot.
Out upon the wharfs they came,
Knight and burgher, lord and dame,
And around the prow they read her name,
        THE LADY OF SHALOTT.

Who is this? And what is here?
And in the lighted palace near
Died the sound of royal cheer;
And they crossed themselves for fear,
        All the knights at Camelot;
But Lancelot mused a little space
He said, 'She has a lovely face;
God in his mercy lend her grace,
        The Lady of Shalott.'

The separation between image and reality, the nature of poetic inspiration, the states of liberty and imprisonment, whatever it is that you decide *The Lady of Shalott* is really about, there can be little doubting that its almost incantatory tone exerts a magical grip.

Lady Windermere's Fan

Performed in 1892, this play by **Oscar Wilde** has the abundance of witty paradox that makes Wilde so irresistible.

Lake Poets

This is a label given to **Wordsworth**, **Coleridge** and Southey because they lived for some years in the Lake District.

Lamia

This is a poem by **Keats** in which a serpent is transformed into a beautiful maiden. The operation is not an entire success, and the poem could, I suppose, be regarded as yet another attempt to probe the differences between appearance and reality.

Langland, William (c. 1330–86)

A contemporary of **Chaucer**, Langland is famous for his poem *Piers Plowman*. The poem begins as follows:

> In a somer seson, whan softe was the sonne,
> I shoop me into shroudes as I a sheep were,
> In habite as an heremite unholy of werkes,
> Wente wide in this world wondres to here.
> Ac on a May morwenynge on Malverne hilles
> Me bifel a ferly, of Fairye me thoghte.
> I was wery forwandred and wente me to reste
> Under a brood bank by a bourne syde;
> And as I lay and lenede and loked on the watres,
> I slombred into a slepyng, it sweyed so murye.

As you can see, it poses considerable problems for a twenty-first-century reader. In addition, we know absolutely nothing about Langland. Consequently, my silence is not only convenient but academically necessary.

Larkin, Philip Arthur (1922–85)

Larkin was a librarian, novelist, jazz critic and one of the few outstanding poets of the twentieth century. Hardly surprisingly, therefore, that it is to his poetry that most attention has been paid. There is an excellent biography of Larkin by Andrew Motion, and that in itself is a major achievement because nothing startling or heroic ever happened in Larkin's life. But quite a lot of startling and heroic things happened inside Larkin's mind, and it is these that the poetry reflects. Just read 'Church Going', and you will see what I mean:

> Once I am sure there's nothing going on
> I step inside, letting the door thud shut.
> Another church: matting, seats, and stone,
> And little books; sprawlings of flowers, cut
> For Sunday, brownish now; some brass and stuff
> Up at the holy end; the small neat organ;
> And a tense, musty, unignorable silence,
> Brewed God knows how long. Hatless, I take off
> My cycle-clips in awkward reverence.
>
> Move forward, run my hand around the font.
> From where I stand, the roof looks almost new –
> Cleaned, or restored? Someone would know: I don't.
> Mounting the lectern, I peruse a few
> Hectoring large-scale verses, and pronounce
> 'Here endeth' much more loudly than I'd meant.
> The echoes snigger briefly. Back at the door
> I sign the book, donate an Irish sixpence,
> Reflect the place was not worth stopping for.
>
> Yet stop I did: in fact I often do,
> And always end much at a loss like this,
> Wondering what to look for; wondering, too,
> When churches will fall completely out of use
> What we shall turn them into, if we shall keep
> A few cathedrals chronically on show,
> Their parchment, plate and pyx in locked cases,
> And let the rest rent-free to rain and sheep.
> Shall we avoid them as unlucky places?

Or, after dark, will dubious women come
To make their children touch a particular stone;
Pick simples for a cancer; or on some
Advised night see walking a dead one?
Power of some sort will go on
In games, in riddles, seemingly at random;
But superstition, like belief, must die,
And what remains when disbelief has gone?
Grass, weedy pavement, brambles, buttress, sky,

A shape less recognisable each week,
A purpose more obscure. I wonder who
Will be the last, the very last, to seek
This place for what it was; one of the crew
That tap and jot and know what rood-lofts were?
Some ruin-bibber, randy for antique,
Or Christmas-addict, counting on a whiff
Of gown-and-bands and organ-pipes and myrrh?
Or will he be my representative,

Bored, uninformed, knowing the ghostly silt
Dispersed, yet tending to this cross of ground
Through suburb scrub because it held unspilt
So long and equably what since is found
Only in separation – marriage, and birth,
And death, and thoughts of these – for which was built
This special shell? For, though I've no idea
What this accoutred frowsty barn is worth,
It pleases me to stand in silence here;

A serious house on serious earth it is,
In whose blent air all our compulsions meet,
Are recognised, and robed as destinies.
And that much never can be obsolete,
Since someone will forever be surprising
A hunger in himself to be more serious,
And gravitating with it to this ground,
Which, he once heard, was proper to grow wise in,
If only that so many dead lie round.

Diffident, uncertain, semi-embarrassed: all very Larkinesque qualities. Yet there is a searching for a meaning that is noble, and the last stanza is both touching and profound. For some, such a conclusion is unacceptable. Larkin was a racist, or at least sometimes appeared to be so. He also greatly enjoyed pornography, which some regard as a grievous sin. Hence it follows that Larkin cannot be a significant poet. It hardly seems worth arguing against such idiocy. Just read his poems. They will demonstrate beyond doubt that Larkin was certainly a significant poet.

Lawrence, David Herbert (1885–1930)

D. H. Lawrence was virtually the only twentieth-century novelist to receive the approval of the literary critic **F. R. Leavis**. As a result, Lawrence became something of a cult figure. As Wikipedia expresses it, 'Lawrence is now generally valued as a visionary thinker and significant representative of **modernism** in English literature, although some **feminists** object to the attitudes toward women and sexuality found in his works.' I am not even sure what that means, and the idea of Lawrence as a visionary thinker strikes me as ludicrous. None the less, Lawrence cannot be ignored. Some of his novels are outstanding, some of his poetry is impressive, and some of his posturing is not without dignity.

In 1930, Lawrence's friend Catherine Carswell summed up his life:

In the face of formidable initial disadvantages and life-long delicacy, poverty that lasted for three quarters of his life and hostility that survives his death, he did nothing that he did not really want to do, and all that he most wanted to do he did. He went all over the world, he owned a ranch, he lived in the most beautiful corners of Europe, and met whom he wanted to meet and told them that they were wrong and he was right. He painted and made things, and sang, and rode. He wrote something like three dozen books, of which even the worst page dances with life that could be mistaken for no other man's, while the best are admitted, even by those who hate him, to be unsurpassed. Without vices, with most human virtues, the husband of one wife, scrupulously honest, this estimable citizen yet managed to keep free from the shackles of civilisation and the cant of literary cliques. He would have laughed lightly and cursed venomously in passing at the solemn owls – each one secretly chained by the leg – who now conduct his inquest. To do his work and lead his life in spite of them took some doing, but he did it, and long after they are forgotten, sensitive and innocent people – if any are left – will turn Lawrence's pages and will know from them what sort of a rare man Lawrence was.

One has to salute this attempt to be balanced and fair. In the twentieth century, such an attempt seemed almost impossible, and the publication of *Lady Chatterley's Lover* in 1928 ensured that Lawrence would be notorious for at least fifty years after his death. That novel seems to suggest that human beings have a sex drive, and such a scurrilous idea led to Lawrence being denounced and reviled. Lawrence was also an atheist, never a good thing in a world which worships Mammon so devoutly. Anyway, the upshot of all this was that, for the bulk of the twentieth century, Lawrence was either adored as a prophet or reviled as an infidel. In the twenty-first century, he seems largely to be ignored.

Lear, Edward (1812–88)

Edward Lear can hardly be seen as a significant literary figure, but it cannot be denied that he contributed greatly to the gaiety of nations, and this is no mean feat. Lear did this by writing poems, of an entirely ludicrous and comic nature, which delight through their absurdity and their wit. The limerick was a favourite form, and Lear produced gems like this:

> 'I perceive a young bird in this bush!'
>   When they said, 'Is it small?'
>   He replied, 'Not at all!
> It is four times as big as the bush!'

The limerick does not lend itself to profundity, but even Lear's poetic self-portrait lacks gravitas:

'How pleasant to know Mr Lear!'
    Who has written such volumes of stuff.
Some think him ill-tempered and queer,
    But a few find him pleasant enough.

His mind is concrete and fastidious,
    His nose is remarkably big;
His visage is more or less hideous,
    His beard it resembles a wig.

He has ears, and two eyes, and ten fingers
    (Leastways if you reckon two thumbs);
He used to be one of the singers,
    But now he is one of the dumbs.

He sits in a beautiful parlour,
    With hundreds of books on the wall;
He drinks a great deal of Marsala,
    But never gets tipsy at all.

He has many friends, laymen and clerical,
    Old Foss is the name of his cat;
His body is perfectly spherical,
    He weareth a runcible hat.

When he walks in waterproof white,
    The children run after him so!
Calling out, 'He's come out in his night-
    gown, that crazy old Englishman, oh!'

He weeps by the side of the ocean,
    He weeps on the top of the hill;
He purchases pancakes and lotion,
    And chocolate shrimps from the mill.

He reads, but he does not speak, Spanish,
    He cannot abide ginger beer;
Ere the days of his pilgrimage vanish,
    How pleasant to know Mr Lear!

And perhaps it was pleasant to know Mr Lear, for his 'poetry' is a constant source of delight to people in their pre-teen years.

Leavis, Frank Raymond (1895–1978)

F. R. Leavis was probably the most significant literary critic of the twentieth century. Based for virtually the whole of his academic career at Downing College, Cambridge, Leavis emphasised the moral significance of literature, and insisted on the closest analysis of the text under consideration. Humility, however, was not a Leavis trait, and critics whose approach was different from his were denounced as apostles of the devil.

Lewes, George Henry (1817–78)

Lewes was an essayist, comic dramatist, actor and philosopher, but his real importance in English literature is that he lived with **George Eliot**, and greatly encouraged her writing.

limerick

A usually comic five-line verse of no literary importance:

> There was a young author from Main
> Whose prose was exceedingly plain.
> So he learned how to dance
> But tripped on his pants,
> And now he must walk with a cane.

Now you can see why. All the same, the limerick can be succinctly amusing, as this example by **Edward Lear** illustrates:

> There was a young lady of Clyde,
> 'Twas of eating green apples she died.
> The apples fermented
> Inside the lamented
> And made cider inside her inside.

Indeed, this entry is a tribute to my self-restraint. In writing this brief explanation, I have read large numbers of limericks, and have found it very difficult not to include at least six more.

literature

One of the relatively few things that make life meaningful.

litotes

This is a figure of speech in which something positive is expressed in a negative fashion. Hence you may say that Mary is no mean actress or that Bristol is no mean city, meaning, of course, that Mary is an excellent actress and that Bristol is a noteworthy city.

Little Women

This novel by **L. M. Alcott** was published in 1868–9, and has been one of the most popular children's books ever published. Since I was about eight when I read it, my memory of the plot is somewhat vague.

Lodge, David John (1935–)

In 1976, Lodge became Professor of English Literature at Birmingham University but had already made his name with some excellent critical works like *Language of Fiction* (1966) and *The Novelist at the Crossroads* (1971) and the entertaining novel *The British Museum is Falling Down* (1965). Since then there have been more critical works and more novels. In all his writing, Lodge has consistently displayed humour, intelligence and balance.

London, Jack (1876–1916)

A drifting teenager in San Francisco, London joined a sealing ship which took him to the Arctic and Japan. On arriving back in the States, he began a chaotic time of self-education and political agitation, took part in the Klondike gold rush and tried his hand at writing short stories. This last endeavour proved successful, and London moved on to writing novels. His third, *The Call of the Wild* (1903), brought him recognition and made London rich. Yet he could never reconcile the contradictions within himself, and his death at the age of forty was possibly suicide. Given the confusion and disorder of his childhood – an absent father, a mentally unstable mother – it is amazing that London ever produced anything, let alone stories and novels of considerable power.

Longfellow, Henry Wadsworth (1807–82)

Longfellow was the most popular American poet of his day, but his popularity rapidly declined. Frankly, there always seems to me to be something spurious about Longfellow. His rhythms, his repetitions, his facilely portentous vocabulary and his almost mystic tone make the poems sound insincere and mannered. Here, for instance, is the beginning of his massively long *Song of Hiawatha* (see also lines quoted under *Hiawatha, Song of*):

> Should you ask me, whence these stories?
> Whence these legends and traditions,
> With the odors of the forest,
> With the dew and damp of meadows,

With the curling smoke of wigwams,
With the rushing of great rivers,
With their frequent repetitions,
And their wild reverberations
As of thunder in the mountains?
  I should answer, I should tell you,
'From the forests and the prairies,
From the great lakes of the Northland,
From the land of the Ojibways,
From the land of the Dacotahs,
From the mountains, moors, and fenlands
Where the heron, the Shuh-shuh-gah,
Feeds among the reeds and rushes.
I repeat them as I heard them
From the lips of Nawadaha,
The musician, the sweet singer.'

Oh dear! This seems to me to ooze pretention.

Lorna Doone

This is the title of a novel by R. D. Blackmore that was published in 1869. Blackmore doesn't have an entry to himself in this dictionary, but *Lorna Doone* is such a gripping adventure story that I felt it ought to make an appearance. Set in the late seventeenth century, it follows the attempt by a yeoman called John Ridd to avenge his father's death at the hands of the Doones. As you have doubtless already guessed, Ridd encounters a Doone daughter with whom he falls in love. I shall not reveal any more, but it is an enthralling tale.

Lost World, The

Everybody knows that **Conan Doyle** wrote about Sherlock Holmes, but his excellent adventure stories are less well known. *The Lost World*, starring Professor George Edward Challenger, is one of the best.

Lowell, Robert Traill Spence (1917–77)

When I was an undergraduate, Lowell published a volume of poetry entitled *Life Studies* (1959) and I became an enthusiast. I did not know then that Lowell was a manic depressive, a fanatical Roman Catholic, a conscientious objector, a drunkard, and had been hospitalised for mania.

I don't suppose that it would have made any difference if I had known. Here is one of his most famous poems, *For the Union Dead*. It is far too long to quote in a book of this nature, but since I'm making the rules, here it is:

The old South Boston Aquarium stands
in a Sahara of snow now. Its broken windows are boarded.
The bronze weathervane cod has lost half its scales.
The airy tanks are dry.

Once my nose crawled like a snail on the glass;
my hand tingled
to burst the bubbles
drifting from the noses of the cowed, compliant fish.

My hand draws back. I often sigh still
for the dark downward and vegetating kingdom
of the fish and reptile. One morning last March,
I pressed against the new barbed and galvanized

fence on the Boston Common. Behind their cage,
yellow dinosaur steamshovels were grunting
as they cropped up tons of mush and grass
to gouge their underworld garage.

Parking spaces luxuriate like civic
sandpiles in the heart of Boston.
A girdle of orange, Puritan-pumpkin-colored girders
braces the tingling Statehouse,

shaking over the excavations, as it faces Colonel Shaw
and his bell-cheeked Negro infantry
on St Gaudens' shaking Civil War relief,
propped by a plank splint against the garage's earthquake.

Two months after marching through Boston,
half the regiment was dead;
at the dedication,
William James could almost hear the bronze Negroes breathe.

Their monument sticks like a fishbone
in the city's throat.
Its Colonel is as lean
as a compass-needle.

He has an angry wrenlike vigilance,
a greyhound's gently tautness;
he seems to wince at pleasure,
and suffocate for privacy.

He is out of bounds now. He rejoices in man's lovely,
peculiar power to choose life and die –
when he leads his black soldiers to death,
he cannot bend his back.

On a thousand small-town New England greens,
the old white churches hold their air
of sparse, sincere rebellion; frayed flags
quilt the graveyards of the Grand Army of the Republic.

The stone statues of the abstract Union Soldier
grow slimmer and younger each year –
wasp-waisted, they doze over muskets
and muse through their sideburns . . .

Shaw's father wanted no monument
except the ditch,
where his son's body was thrown
and lost with his 'niggers'.

The ditch is nearer.
There are no statues for the last war here;
on Boylston Street, a commercial photograph
shows Hiroshima boiling

over a Mosler Safe, the 'Rock of Ages'
that survived the blast. Space is nearer.
When I crouch to my television set,
the drained faces of Negro school-children rise like balloons.

Colonel Shaw
is riding on his bubble,
he waits
for the blessèd break.

The Aquarium is gone. Everywhere,
giant finned cars nose forward like fish;
a savage servility
slides by on grease.

Lucky Jim

This, the first novel of Kingsley Amis, was published in 1954 and caused a sensation. It is very funny, and devastatingly attacks phoniness in university life. Certainly Amis never went on to publish anything else that was as popular as this novel.

Lucy poems, The

This is the name given to a group of poems written by **William Wordsworth**. They are among the most beautiful and moving poems ever written by anyone. Here is one of them:

> She dwelt among the untrodden ways
>   Beside the springs of Dove;
> A maid whom there were none to praise,
>   And very few to love.
>
> A violet by a mossy stone
>   Half-hidden from the eye!
> Fair as a star, when only one
>   Is shining in the sky.
>
> She lived unknown, and few could know
>   When Lucy ceased to be;
> But she is in her grave, and, oh!
>   The difference to me!

If that doesn't almost move you to tears, you are an insensitive clod and will doubtless make a fortune as a financier.

Lycidas

This is a pastoral elegy of 193 lines by **John Milton** published in 1638. For many years I regarded it as the greatest poem in the English language. Do read it and make your own judgement.

lyric poetry

Most of us think of lyric poetry as being relatively short, possibly even set to music, and concerned with the expression of personal feelings. Something like this:

> I heard a fly buzz when I died;
>   The stillness round my form

Was like the stillness in the air
    Between the heaves of storm.

The eyes beside had wrung them dry,
    And breaths were gathering sure
For that last onset, when the king
    Be witnessed in his power.

I willed my keepsakes, signed away
    What portion of me I
Could make assignable,-and then
    There interposed a fly,

With blue, uncertain, stumbling buzz,
    Between the light and me;
And then the windows failed, and then
    I could not see to see.

That was by **Emily Dickinson** and might not quite have been what you think of as a lyric. Perhaps these few lines by **Robert Herrick** are more traditional:

Here a solemn fast we keep,
While all beauty lies asleep;
Hush'd be all things, no noise here
But the toning of a tear;
Or a sigh of such as bring
Cowslips for her covering.

But lyric poetry can come in all sorts of shapes and sizes. Originally the word 'lyric' meant 'for the lyre', so lyric poetry was poetry that could be sung to the accompaniment of a lyre. Depending on the stamina of your lyre player, that could mean almost anything.

Lyrical Ballads

In 1798 a volume of poems called *Lyrical Ballads with a Few Other Poems* was published. The poems within the book were written by **William Wordsworth** and **Samuel Taylor Coleridge**, and the volume is often taken as marking a revolution in English literature. If such things could be dated, the book might be seen as marking the beginning of the Romantic movement. The second paragraph of the Preface to the volume explains to some extent the object of the exercise:

243

The majority of the following poems are to be considered as experiments. They were written chiefly with a view to ascertain how far the language of conversation in the middle and lower classes of society is adapted to the purposes of poetic pleasure. Readers accustomed to the gaudiness and inane phraseology of many modern writers, if they persist in reading this book to its conclusion, will perhaps frequently have to struggle with feelings of strangeness and aukwardness: they will look round for poetry, and will be induced to enquire by what species of courtesy these attempts can be permitted to assume that title. It is desirable that such readers, for their own sakes, should not suffer the solitary word Poetry, a word of very disputed meaning, to stand in the way of their gratification; but that, while they are perusing this book, they should ask themselves if it contains a natural delineation of human passions, human characters, and human incidents; and if the answer be favorable to the author's wishes, that they should consent to be pleased in spite of that most dreadful enemy to our pleasures, our own pre-established codes of decision.

Since 1798, *Lyrical Ballads* has come to be accepted as one of the most striking and outstanding volumes of poetry ever to have been published. Within it are poems that almost every literate person knows: ***The Rime of the Ancient Mariner***, ***The Idiot Boy***, ***Tintern Abbey***. Here is one that would have done very well as an example of a lyric poem in the entry immediately preceding this. It is called 'Lines Written in Early Spring':

> I heard a thousand blended notes,
> While in a grove I sate reclined,
> In that sweet mood when pleasant thoughts
> Bring sad thoughts to the mind.

> To her fair works did nature link
> The human soul that through me ran;
> And much it griev'd my heart to think
> What man has made of man.

> Through primrose-tufts, in that sweet bower,
> The periwinkle trail'd its wreathes;
> And 'tis my faith that every flower
> Enjoys the air it breathes.

> The birds around me hopp'd and play'd:

Their thoughts I cannot measure,
But the least motion which they made,
It seem'd a thrill of pleasure.

The budding twigs spread out their fan,
To catch the breezy air;
And I must think, do all I can,
That there was pleasure there.

If I these thoughts may not prevent,
If such be of my creed the plan,
Have I not reason to lament
What man has made of man?

Summing up the volume as a whole, Andrew Motion states:

The Lyrical Ballads, the great collaborate collection of poetry written by Wordsworth and Coleridge, and first published in 1798, is one of the defining documents of the Romantic movement. Not only because it has a wonderfully democratic range of subjects and interests, but also because it arises from the kind of self-consciousness we recognise as being modern. The book is more than two hundred years old now, but still feels wonderfully fresh and new: it's a beacon, as well as an icon.

No one with a love for poetry will fail to return again and again to this masterpiece.

M

Macbeth

This is the title of a play by **Shakespeare**. I personally think that it is poetically the richest play that Shakespeare ever wrote. I shall not explain the plot here, but Macbeth and his wife plan to kill Duncan, the current king of Scotland, and thus ensure that Macbeth himself becomes king. Here are Lady Macbeth's thoughts on Duncan's impending visit to their home:

> The raven himself is hoarse
> That croaks the fatal entrance of Duncan
> Under my battlements. Come, you spirits
> That tend on mortal thoughts, unsex me here,
> And fill me, from the crown to the toe, top-full
> Of direst cruelty: make thick my blood;
> Stop up the access and passage to remorse,
> That no compunctious visitings of nature
> Shake my fell purpose, nor keep peace between
> The effect and it! Come to my woman's breasts,
> And take my milk for gall, you murdering ministers,
> Wherever in your sightless substances
> You wait on nature's mischief! Come, thick night,
> And pall thee in the dunnest smoke of hell,
> That my keen knife see not the wound it makes,
> Nor heaven peep through the blanket of the dark
> To cry, 'Hold, hold!'

I could have chosen a passage just as rich from virtually every scene in the play. Of course, the verse does not exist in a vacuum. It exists because it illuminates a story of ambition, revenge and loyalty that is one of the most harrowing experiences the British theatre has to offer. If you have never read or seen *Macbeth*, do so as soon as you can. It is immeasurably great.

Mac Flecknoe

From time to time this book will contain an entry that you may feel belongs more properly to the magisterial volumes of scholarship to which I refer in the Preface. This is such an entry. *Mac Flecknoe* is a mock-epic poem by **John Dryden**. To start with, Dryden is not a common topic of conversation in the pub. I am sure that in your local public house they frequently talk about **Wordsworth**'s *Prelude* or **Keats**'s *Odes*, but I bet you've never heard anyone chat about Dryden. Still less will you have heard them discuss *Mac Flecknoe*. This is a pity, because, as I point out in the entry under Dryden, the poem is great fun. Dryden had quarrelled with a contemporary dramatist called Thomas Shadwell, and in *Mac Flecknoe*, Dryden paints Shadwell as the apostle of dullness:

> All human things are subject to decay,
> And, when Fate summons, monarchs must obey:
> This Flecknoe found, who, like Augustus, young
> Was call'd to empire, and had govern'd long:
> In prose and verse, was own'd, without dispute
> Through all the realms of Non-sense, absolute.
> This aged prince now flourishing in peace,
> And blest with issue of a large increase,
> Worn out with business, did at length debate
> To settle the succession of the State:
> And pond'ring which of all his sons was fit
> To reign, and wage immortal war with wit,
> Cry'd, 'tis resolv'd; for nature pleads that he
> Should only rule, who most resembles me:
> Shadwell alone my perfect image bears,
> Mature in dullness from his tender years.
> Shadwell alone, of all my sons, is he
> Who stands confirm'd in full stupidity.
> The rest to some faint meaning make pretence,
> But Shadwell never deviates into sense.
> Some beams of wit on other souls may fall,
> Strike through and make a lucid interval;
> But Shadwell's genuine night admits no ray,
> His rising fogs prevail upon the day . . .

And so it continues. I defy you to read it without an almost permanent smile.

So that is one reason that I mention it in this volume: I think that you will enjoy it. There is, though, a secondary reason. The primary purpose of this book is to give help through the thickets of English literature, but, like every other subject, English literature is subject to snobberies and pretences. There is a scoring system. If you mention Dryden at all, you will score 2 points. If you mention *Mac Flecknoe*, you will score 4 points. If you mention that **Pope**'s ***Dunciad*** was massively indebted to *Mac Flecknoe* you will score 8 points. Try it tonight. When you are in the Red Lion or whatever, try saying, 'Well, let's face it, Pope's *Dunciad* is not much more than an elongation of Dryden's *Mac Flecknoe*.' Your intellectual standing will soar, and people will clamour to buy you a pint. Alternatively, of course, you might find yourself ignored as a pretentious poseur.

McGonagall, William (1825–1902)

William McGonagall is a major asset in English literature. He is often cited as the worst poet who ever existed, but he is an asset for two reasons. First of all, although McGonagall frequently writes about tragedies and disasters, his poetry is so dire that it reduces most people to helpless laughter. Just sample the touching story of the Tay Bridge disaster:

> Beautiful Railway Bridge of the Silv'ry Tay!
> Alas! I am very sorry to say
> That ninety lives have been taken away
> On the last Sabbath day of 1879,
> Which will be remember'd for a very long time.
>
> 'Twas about seven o'clock at night,
> And the wind it blew with all its might,
> And the rain came pouring down,
> And the dark clods seem'd to frown,
> And the Demon of the air seem'd to say –
> 'I'll blow down the Bridge of Tay.'
>
> When the train left Edinburgh
> The passengers' hearts were light and felt no sorrow,
> But Boreas blew a terrific gale,
> Which made their hearts for to quail,
> And many of the passengers with fear did say –
> 'I hope God will send us safe across the Bridge of Tay.'

But when the train came near to Wormit Bay,
Boreas he did loud and angry bray
And shook the central girders of the Bridge of Tay,
On the last Sabbath day of 1879,
Which will be remember'd for a very long time.

So the train sped on with all its might,
And Bonnie Dundee soon hove in sight,
And the passengers' hearts felt light,
Thinking they would enjoy themselves on the New Year,
With their friends at home they lov'd most dear,
And wish them all a happy New Year.

So the train mov'd slowly along the Bridge of Tay
Until it was about midway,
Then the central girders with a crash gave way,
And down went the train and passengers into the Tay!
The Storm Fiend did loudly bray,
Because ninety lives had been taken away,
On the last Sabbath day of 1879,
Which will be remember'd for a very long time.

As soon as the catastrophe came to be known
The alarm from mouth to mouth was blown,
And the cry rang out all o'er the town,
Good Heavens! the Tay Bridge is blown down,
And a passenger train from Edinburgh!
Which fill'd all the people's hearts with sorrow,
And made them for to turn pale,
Because none of the passengers were sav'd to tell the tale –
How the disaster happen'd on the last Sabbath day of 1879,
Which will be remember'd for a very long time.

It must have been an awful sight,
To witness in the dusky moonlight,
While the Storm Fiend did laugh, and angry did bray,
Along the Railway Bridge of the Silv'ry Tay.
Oh! ill-fated Bridge of the Silv'ry Tay,
I must now conclude my lay
By telling the world, fearlessly without the least dismay,
That your central girders would not have given way,

> At least many sensible men do say,
> Had they been supported on each side with buttresses,
> At least many sensible men confesses,
> For the stronger we our houses do build,
> The less chance we have of being killed.

When you have recovered from your hilarity, try to work out why this poem is so bad, because this is McGonagall's second asset: he provides a convenient means of distinguishing between success and failure in poetry. If you can work out why McGonagall is so bad, it will greatly help you in working out why **Browning** or **Yeats** is so good.

MacNeice, Frederick Louis (1907–63)

Born in Ulster, MacNeice went to Oxford and thereafter became a university lecturer in classics. Early in his career, MacNeice was identified with a group of politically committed poets like Spender, **Auden** and Isherwood, though MacNeice himself was never very good at sticking to any party line. As a result, his poems tend to be reflections rather than sermons, considerations rather than conclusions. Typical of this is 'Prayer Before Birth':

> I am not yet born; O hear me.
> Let not the bloodsucking bat or the rat or the stoat or the club-
> footed ghoul come near me.
>
> I am not yet born, console me.
> I fear that the human race may with tall walls wall me, with strong
> drugs dope me, with wise lies lure me, on black racks rack me, in
> blood-baths roll me.
>
> I am not yet born; provide me
> With water to dandle me, grass to grow for me, trees to talk to me,
> sky to sing to me, birds and a white light in the back of my mind
> to guide me.
>
> I am not yet born; forgive me
> For the sins that in me the world shall commit, my words when they
> speak me, my thoughts when they think me, my treason
> engendered by traitors beyond me, my life when they murder by
> means of my hands, my death when they live me.

I am not yet born; rehearse me.
In the parts I must play and the cues I must take when old men
    lecture me, bureaucrats hector me, mountains frown at me,
    lovers laugh at me, the white waves call me to folly and the desert
    calls me to doom and the beggar refuses my gift and my children
    curse me.

I am not yet born; O hear me.
Let not the man who is beast or who thinks he is God come near me.

I am not yet born; O fill me
With strength against those who would freeze my humanity, would
    dragoon me into a lethal automaton, would make me a cog in a
    machine, a thing with one face, a thing, and against all those
    who would dissipate my entirety, would blow me like thistle-
    down hither and thither or hither and thither like water held in
    the hands would spill me.

Let them not make me a stone and let them not spill me.
Otherwise kill me.

I like this. I hope you did.

malapropism

In **Sheridan**'s play *The Rivals* (1775) there appears a delightful character called Mrs Malaprop. She is anxious to appear cultivated and learned, but unfortunately her vocabulary often betrays her. The Internet conveniently provided these examples from the play:

- ' . . . promise to forget this fellow – to illiterate him, I say, quite from your memory.' [obliterate]

- 'Oh, he will dissolve my mystery!' [resolve]

- 'He is the very pineapple of politeness!' [pinnacle]

- 'I have since laid Sir Anthony's preposition before her.' [proposition]

- 'Oh! it gives me the hydrostatics to such a degree.' [hysterics]

- 'I hope you will represent her to the captain as an object not altogether illegible.' [eligible]

- ' . . . she might reprehend the true meaning of what she is saying.' [comprehend]

- ' . . . she's as headstrong as an allegory on the banks of Nile.' [alligator]

- 'I am sorry to say, Sir Anthony, that my affluence over my niece is very small.' [influence]

- 'Why, murder's the matter! slaughter's the matter! killing's the matter! – but he can tell you the perpendiculars.' [particulars]

- 'Nay, no delusions to the past – Lydia is convinced.' [allusions]

- ' . . . behold, this very day, I have interceded another letter from the fellow.' [intercepted]

- 'I thought she had persisted from corresponding with him.' [desisted]

- 'His physiognomy so grammatical!' [phraseology]

- 'I am sure I have done everything in my power since I exploded the affair.' [exposed]

- 'I am sorry to say, she seems resolved to decline every particle that I enjoin her.' [article]

- ' . . . if ever you betray what you are entrusted with . . . you forfeit my malevolence for ever . . . ' [benevolence]

- 'Your being Sir Anthony's son, captain, would itself be a sufficient accommodation.' [recommendation]

- 'Sure, if I reprehend anything in this world it is the use of my oracular tongue, and a nice derangement of epitaphs!' [apprehend, vernacular, arrangement, epithets]

As a consequence of Sheridan's inventiveness, such vocabulary errors have since been known as malapropisms, though, of course, **Shakespeare**'s Dogberry in *Much Ado about Nothing* makes similar errors.

Mansfield Park

This is a novel by **Jane Austen**, published in 1814. Its heroine, Fanny Price, is too passive to be very interesting, but some of the other characters almost compensate for this, and anyway the novel has a happy ending which for some people is all that matters.

Marlowe, Christopher (1564–93)

Marlowe had the misfortune to live at the same time as **Shakespeare**. Had he not done so, his plays, *Tamburlaine the Great* (Parts 1 and 2), *The Jew of Malta*, *Dr Faustus* and *Edward II*, would be hailed as the finest verse plays in the English language. Here is Tamburlaine trying to persuade an opponent to join him:

> In thee, thou valiant man of Persia,
> I see the folly of thy emperor.
> Art thou but captain of a thousand horse,
> That, by characters graven in thy brows
> And by thy martial face and stout aspect,
> Deserv'st to have the leading of an host?
> Forsake thy king, and do but join with me,
> And we will triumph over all the world.
> I hold the Fates bound fast in iron chains,
> And with my hand turn Fortune's wheel about;
> And sooner shall the sun fall from his sphere
> Than Tamburlaine be slain or overcome.
> Draw forth thy sword, thou mighty man-at-arms,
> Intending but to race my charméd skin,
> And Jove himself will stretch his hand from heaven
> To ward the blow and shield me safe from harm.
> See how he rains down heaps of gold in showers,
> As if he meant to give my soldiers pay!
> And, as a sure and grounded argument
> That I shall be the monarch of the East,
> He sends this soldan's daughter, rich and brave,
> To be my queen and portly emperess.
> If thou wilt stay with me, renownéd man,
> And lead thy thousand horse with my conduct,
> Besides thy share of this Egyptian prize,
> Those thousand horse shall sweat with martial spoil
> Of conquered kingdoms and of cities sacked.
> Both we will walk upon the lofty cliffs;
> And Christian merchants that with Russian stems
> Plow up huge furrows in the Caspian sea
> Shall vail to us as lords of all the lake.
> Both we will reign as consuls of the earth,

And mighty kings shall be our senators.
Jove sometime maskéd in a shepherd's weed;
And by those steps that he hath scaled the heavens
May we become immortal like the gods!
Join with me now in this my mean estate
(I call it mean because, being yet obscure,
The nations far removed admire me not),
And, when my name and honour shall be spread
As far as Boreas claps his brazen wings,
Or fair Boötes sends his cheerful light,
Then shalt thou be competitor with me,
And sit with Tamburlaine in all his majesty.

This is verse of the highest quality, and all five of the plays that I have mentioned contain at least some verse of this standard.

Nor was Marlowe less talented as a poet. His best known poem is 'The Passionate Shepherd to his Love' and it is a delight:

Come live with me and be my love,
And we will all the pleasures prove,
That valleys, groves, hills and fields,
Woods or steepy mountains yield.

And we will sit upon the rocks,
Seeing the shepherds feed their flocks
By shallow rivers, to whose falls
Melodious birds sing madrigals.

And I will make thee beds of roses,
And a thousand fragrant posies,
A cap of flowers and a kirtle
Embroidered all with leaves of myrtle;

A gown made of the finest wool,
Which from our pretty lambs we pull;
Fair-lined slippers for the cold,
With buckles of the purest gold;

A belt of straw and ivy buds,
With coral clasps and amber studs;
And if these pleasures may thee move,
Come live with me and be my love.

The shepherd swains shall dance and sing
For thy delight each May morning;
If these delights thy mind may move,
Then live with me and be my love.

But on top of being a poet and playwright, Marlowe was also a spy, an atheist, and got killed in a pub brawl. It has also been argued that he wasn't really killed in the brawl, but went off and wrote all of Shakespeare's plays. Hence, if you fancy writing a biography, Marlowe provides you with all the material necessary, and you can sell the rights afterwards to Hollywood.

Marsh, Dame Ngaio (1899–1982)

My own passion for detective fiction accounts for at least three of the entries in this book, and this is one of them. Ngaio Marsh, a New Zealander, introduced us to Superintendent Roderick Alleyn in the 1934 novel *A Man Lay Dead*, and just over another thirty were to follow. Alleyn, very much in the Holmes and Wimsey tradition, is a delightful creation, and Marsh's detective fiction is excellently constructed.

Marvell, Andrew (1621–78)

Marvell was a seventeenth-century poet who wrote a number of poems of the highest quality. Unfortunately, one of his poems, *To His Coy Mistress*, superbly expresses the arguments of a man trying to get a woman into bed, and consequently this poem alone is well known:

Had we but world enough, and time,
This coyness, Lady, were no crime
We would sit down and think which way
To walk and pass our long love's day.
Thou by the Indian Ganges' side
Shouldst rubies find: I by the tide
Of Humber would complain. I would
Love you ten years before the Flood,
And you should, if you please, refuse
Till the conversion of the Jews.
My vegetable love should grow
Vaster than empires, and more slow;
An hundred years should go to praise

Thine eyes and on thy forehead gaze;
Two hundred to adore each breast,
But thirty thousand to the rest;
An age at least to every part,
And the last age should show your heart.

For, Lady, you deserve this state,
Nor would I love at lower rate.
  But at my back I always hear
Time's wingèd chariot hurrying near;
And yonder all before us lie
Deserts of vast eternity.
Thy beauty shall no more be found,
Nor, in thy marble vault, shall sound
My echoing song: then worms shall try
That long preserved virginity,
And your quaint honour turn to dust,
And into ashes all my lust:
The grave's a fine and private place,
But none, I think, do there embrace.
  Now therefore, while the youthful hue
Sits on thy skin like morning dew,
And while thy willing soul transpires
At every pore with instant fires,
Now let us sport us while we may,
And now, like amorous birds of prey,
Rather at once our time devour
Than languish in his slow-chapt power.
Let us roll all our strength and all
Our sweetness up into one ball,
And tear our pleasures with rough strife
Thorough the iron gates of life:
Thus, though we cannot make our sun
Stand still, yet we will make him run.

As you can see, it is the randy man's perfect poem, but try 'An Horation Ode upon Cromwell's Return from Ireland' or 'Upon Appleton House' or 'The Garden'. They don't have the sex appeal of 'To My Coy Mistress', but they are very good poems.

Mary Barton

This is an excellent novel of 1848 by **Mrs Gaskell**. When I tell you that it was violently attacked by Manchester mill owners and the Tory press when it was published, you will realise that this is a virtual guarantee of the novel's quality. Its power stems from Mrs Gaskell's own outrage at the poverty she saw among the uneducated factory workers of Manchester. It opens with a picture of the working classes that is entirely sympathetic and without pretention.

A Mysterious Disappearance

Oh! 'tis hard, 'tis hard to be working
The whole of the live-long day,
When all the neighbours about one
Are off to their jaunts and play.

There's Richard he carries his baby,
And Mary takes little Jane,
And lovingly they'll be wandering
Through fields and briery lane.

MANCHESTER SONG

There are some fields near Manchester, well known to the inhabitants as 'Green Heys Fields', through which runs a public footpath to a little village about two miles distant. In spite of these fields being flat, and low, nay, in spite of the want of wood (the great and usual recommendation of level tracts of land), there is a charm about them which strikes even the inhabitant of a mountainous district, who sees and feels the effect of contrast in these commonplace but thoroughly rural fields, with the busy, bustling manufacturing town he left but half an hour ago. Here and there an old black-and-white farmhouse, with its rambling outbuildings, speaks of other times and other occupations than those which now absorb the population of the neighbourhood. Here in their seasons may be seen the country business of haymaking, ploughing, etc., which are such pleasant mysteries for townspeople to watch: and here the artisan, deafened with noise of tongues and engines, may come to listen awhile to the delicious sounds of rural life: the lowing of cattle, the milkmaid's call, the clatter and cackle of poultry in the farmyards. You cannot wonder, then, that these fields are popular places of resort at every holiday time; and you would not wonder, if you could see, or I properly describe, the charm of one particular stile, that it should be, on such

257

occasions, a crowded halting place. Close by it is a deep, clear pond, reflecting in its dark green depths the shadowy trees that bend over it to exclude the sun. The only place where its banks are shelving is on the side next to a rambling farmyard, belonging to one of those old world, gabled, black-and-white houses I named above, overlooking the field through which the public footpath leads. The porch of this farmhouse is covered by a rose tree; and the little garden surrounding it is crowded with a medley of old-fashioned herbs and flowers, planted long ago, when the garden was the only druggist's shop within reach, and allowed to grow in scrambling and wild luxuriance – roses, lavender, sage, balm (for tea), rosemary, pinks and wallflowers, onions and jessamine, in most republican and indiscriminate order. This farmhouse and garden are within a hundred yards of the stile of which I spoke, leading from the large pasture field into a smaller one, divided by a hedge of hawthorn and blackthorn; and near this stile, on the farther side, there runs a tale that primroses may often be found, and occasionally the blue sweet violet on the grassy hedge bank.

I do not know whether it was on a holiday granted by the masters, or a holiday seized in right of Nature and her beautiful springtime by the workmen, but one afternoon (now ten or a dozen years ago) these fields were much thronged. It was an early May evening – the April of the poets: for heavy showers had fallen all the morning, and the round, soft, white clouds which were blown by a west wind over the dark blue sky, were sometimes varied by one blacker and more threatening. The softness of the day tempted forth the young green leaves, which almost visibly fluttered into life; and the willows, which that morning had had only a brown reflection in the water below, were now of that tender grey-green which blends so delicately with the spring harmony of colours.

Groups of merry and somewhat loud-talking girls, whose ages might range from twelve to twenty, came by with a buoyant step. They were most of them factory girls, and wore the usual out-of-doors dress of that particular class of maidens: namely, a shawl, which at midday or in fine weather was allowed to be merely a shawl, but towards evening, if the day was chilly, became a sort of Spanish mantilla or Scotch plaid, and was brought over the head and hung loosely down, or was pinned under the chin in no unpicturesque fashion.

Their faces were not remarkable for beauty: indeed, they were below the average, with one or two exceptions; they had dark hair, neatly and classically arranged, dark eyes, but sallow complexions and irregular features. The only thing to strike a passer-by was an acuteness and intelligence of countenance, which has often been noticed in a manufacturing population.

There were also numbers of boys, or rather young men, rambling among these fields, ready to bandy jokes with anyone, and particularly ready to enter into conversation with the girls, who, however, held themselves aloof, not in a shy, but rather in an independent way, assuming an indifferent manner to the noisy wit or obstreperous compliments of the lads. Here and there came a sober, quiet couple, either whispering lovers, or husband and wife, as the case might be; and if the latter, they were seldom unencumbered by an infant, carried for the most part by the father, while occasionally even three or four little toddlers had been carried or dragged thus far, in order that the whole family might enjoy the delicious May afternoon together.

Sometime in the course of that afternoon, two working men met with friendly greeting at the stile so often named. One was a thorough specimen of a Manchester man: born of factory workers, and himself bred up in youth, and living in manhood, among the mills. He was below the middle size and slightly made; there was almost a stunted look about him; and his wan, colourless face gave you the idea, that in his childhood he had suffered from the scanty living consequent upon bad times and improvident habits. His features were strongly marked, though not irregular, and their expression was extreme earnestness: resolute either for good or evil, a sort of latent stern enthusiasm. At the time of which I write, the good predominated over the bad in the countenance, and he was one from whom a stranger would have asked a favour with tolerable faith that it would be granted. He was accompanied by his wife, who might, without exaggeration, have been called a lovely woman, although now her face was swollen with crying, and often hidden behind her apron. She had the fresh beauty of the agricultural districts; and somewhat of the deficiency of sense in her countenance, which is likewise characteristic of the rural inhabitants in comparison with the natives of the manufacturing towns. She was far advanced in pregnancy, which perhaps occasioned the over-powering and hysterical nature of her grief. The friend whom they met was more handsome and less sensible-looking than the man I have just described; he seemed hearty and hopeful, and although his age was greater, yet there was far more of youth's buoyancy in his appearance. He was tenderly carrying a baby in arms, while his wife, a delicate, fragile-looking woman, limping in her gait, bore another of the same age; little, feeble twins, inheriting the frail appearance of their mother.

I have quoted this at some length so that you can judge it adequately. Have you not already been sucked into Mrs Gaskell's world? Has not this beguiling description roused your interest? There is an honesty and a care about Elizabeth Gaskell's writing that always strikes me as admirable. She is an author whom one trusts.

Massinger, Philip (1583–1640)

Shakespeare's reputation is under no danger from the plays of Philip Massinger, but he deserves mention here because he wrote fifty-five plays which is remarkable in itself, and because a number of them have a lucidity and directness that is eminently praiseworthy.

Maurice

This is a novel by **E. M. Forster**. It was published in 1971, a year after Forster died, though he wrote it in 1913–14. The reason for the delay is that *Maurice* is a homosexual novel, and Forster did not dare publish it during his lifetime. There are times when one weeps because of the prudish, sanctimonious and hypocritical nature of the British.

Mayor of Casterbridge, The

This is one of **Hardy**'s finest novels, but do not read it if you need cheering up. It is an unrelieved saga of misery. But it contains some of Hardy's finest prose writing:

> One evening of late summer, before the nineteenth century had reached one-third of its span, a young man and woman, the latter carrying a child, were approaching the large village of Weydon-Priors, in Upper Wessex, on foot. They were plainly but not ill clad, though the thick hoar of dust which had accumulated on their shoes and garments from an obviously long journey lent a disadvantageous shabbiness to their appearance just now.
>
> The man was of fine figure, swarthy, and stern in aspect; and he showed in profile a facial angle so slightly inclined as to be almost perpendicular. He wore a short jacket of brown corduroy, newer than the remainder of his suit, which was a fustian waistcoat with white horn buttons, breeches of the same, tanned leggings, and a straw hat overlaid with black glazed canvas. At his back he carried by a looped strap a rush basket, from which protruded at one end the crutch of a

hay-knife, a wimble for hay-bonds being also visible in the aperture. His measured, springless walk was the walk of the skilled countryman as distinct from the desultory shamble of the general labourer; while in the turn and plant of each foot there was, further, a dogged and cynical indifference, personal to himself, showing its presence even in the regularly interchanging fustian folds, now in the left leg, now in the right, as he paced along.

What was really peculiar, however, in this couple's progress, and would have attracted the attention of any casual observer otherwise disposed to overlook them, was the perfect silence they preserved. They walked side by side in such a way as to suggest afar off the low, easy, confidential chat of people full of reciprocity; but on closer view it could be discerned that the man was reading, or pretending to read, a ballad sheet which he kept before his eyes with some difficulty by the hand that was passed through the basket strap. Whether this apparent cause were the real cause, or whether it were an assumed one to escape an intercourse that would have been irksome to him, nobody but himself could have said precisely; but his taciturnity was unbroken, and the woman enjoyed no society whatever from his presence. Virtually she walked the highway alone, save for the child she bore. Sometimes the man's bent elbow almost touched her shoulder, for she kept as close to his side as was possible without actual contact, but she seemed to have no idea of taking his arm, nor he of offering it; and far from exhibiting surprise at his ignoring silence she appeared to receive it as a natural thing. If any word at all were uttered by the little group, it was an occasional whisper of the woman to the child – a tiny girl in short clothes and blue boots of knitted yarn – and the murmured babble of the child in reply.

As you can see, the air of menace is established from the outset. If you do read this novel, you will never forget it.

melodrama

A melodrama is a play (or situation) marked by exaggerated reactions, sensational incidents and violent emotions. Today melodrama is often used for comic effect, but in the nineteenth century in particular it was a staple ingredient of repertory theatres. In addition, of course, most of us know someone who is prone to melodrama: Alex gets a speck of dirt on her dress and instantly proclaims that her life is ruined or Henry can't find his library book and immediately declares that Scilla has stolen it.

Melville, Herman (1819–91)

I have only read three works by Melville, the outstanding short stories 'Bartleby the Scrivener' and '**Billy Budd**', and the 1852 novel *Pierre, or The Ambiguities*. I greatly enjoyed all three. Unfortunately Melville also wrote the greatest American novel, *Moby Dick* (1851) which I find tedious beyond endurance, and hence have never finished it. At the time, a critic for the *London Athenaeum* described it as: 'An ill-compounded mixture of romance and matter-of-fact. The idea of a connected and collected story has obviously visited and abandoned its writer again and again in the course of composition. The style of his tale is in places disfigured by mad (rather than bad) English; and its catastrophe is hastily, weakly, and obscurely managed.' Since then, of course, *Moby Dick* has been exalted as an American epic almost equal in genius to the works of **Homer**. Personally I'm more on the side of the *London Athenaeum*.

Men and Women

If you read no other **Robert Browning**, do try at least some poems in his 1855 volume, *Men and Women*. My own favourite is *Andrea del Sarto*, but *Fra Lippo Lippi*, 'One Word More', 'Love Among the Ruins' and a number of others are among the glories of English writing.

Merchant of Venice, The

This wonderful play by **Shakespeare** is perhaps most famous for the embittered Jew, Shylock, but there are other fascinating characters too, some wonderful verse, and enough moral dilemmas to keep a philosophy class going for months. As you may know, the 'hate' figure in the play is Shylock, but he is a long way from being unequivocally evil in the way that Iago is in *Othello*. He defends, for instance, his enmity towards Antonio:

> He hath disgraced me, and hindered me half a million; laughed at my losses, mocked at my gains, scorned my nation, thwarted my bargains, cooled my friends, heated mine enemies – and what's his reason? I am a Jew. Hath not a Jew eyes? hath not a Jew hands, organs, dimensions, senses, affections, passions? fed with the same food, hurt with the same weapons, subject to the same diseases, healed by the same means, warmed and cooled by the same winter and summer, as a Christian is? If you prick us, do we not bleed? if you tickle us, do we not laugh? if you poison us, do we not die? and if you wrong us, shall we not

revenge? If we are like you in the rest, we will resemble you in that. If a Jew wrong a Christian, what is his humility? Revenge. If a Christian wrong a Jew, what should his sufferance be by Christian example? Why, revenge. The villany you teach me, I will execute, and it shall go hard but I will better the instruction.

The play is littered with dilemmas of this nature. The whole thing is an exercise in moral ambiguity, and an excellent case can be made that the Christians in the play are morally more culpable than Shylock.(See also **blank verse**, for another of Shylock's speeches.)

metaphor

Metaphors seem central to language itself. Basically a metaphor is when, by implication, object 1 is equivalent to object 2. If you say, 'The headmaster is like a pig,' you are using a simile. If, however, you say, 'The headmaster is a pig,' you are using a metaphor. It is almost impossible to speak or write without using metaphors. People who don't know what a metaphor is, use them constantly: 'Mary's an angel'; 'Peter's a swine'; 'That programme's a knockout.' People who do know what a metaphor is, also use them constantly in much the same way. **Shakespeare** used them magically. Here are a couple from *Romeo and Juliet*:

> This *bud of love* by summer's ripening breath
> May prove a beauteous flower when next we meet.

> Thou knowest the *mask of night* is on my face
> Else would a maiden blush bepaint my cheek.

One should, however, beware of mixed metaphors. They occur when one metaphor is shown as doing something which is literally impossible. For instance, let us just imagine that you have just been betrayed by your colleagues. You exclaim in anger, 'Those vipers stabbed me in the back.' That is a mixed metaphor because vipers can't stab anything. Needless to say, mixed metaphors are frequently the source of considerable amusement. The following is supposed to have been said in the Irish Parliament:

'Mr Speaker, I smell a rat. I see him floating in the air. But mark me, sir, I will nip him in the bud.'

An American politician is supposed to have said this:

metaphor

'Rather than wallowing in tears, let this passionate community strike while the iron is hot.'

The metaphor is indispensable as a figure of speech, but, as with all language, care should be taken in its use.

metaphysical poets

This is a label given to a number of seventeenth-century poets – **Donne**, **Marvell**, Vaughan, **Herbert** and others. Although the term was first used by **Samuel Johnson** to characterise poets who used absurd comparisons, lacked feeling and were academically pretentious, it had no validity when Johnson used it, and naturally has had no validity since. The poets mentioned have never had very much in common anyway, and certainly did not lack feeling. It is true that their comparisons were sometimes unusual – comparing love to a pair of compasses, for example, in Donne's 'A Valediction: Forbidding Mourning' (see **conceit**) – but most of us see this as a merit, and certainly not as an example of academic pretention.

metonymy

This is a figure of speech in which the name of an attribute or thing is substituted for the thing itself. Some examples will make it clear:

'My career is on the stage,' means, 'My career is in the theatre.'

'I was before the bench,' means, 'I was in court.'

'The Crown is innocent,' means, 'The Queen is innocent.'

metre

The one thing that distinguishes **poetry** from **prose** is that poetry has a more pronounced rhythmic base than prose. Indeed, a lot of poetry has a very regular rhythm, and this is because it is written in a particular metre. All that this means is that some syllables are stressed and others are not. If the stressed and unstressed syllables occur in a regular pattern, then you have a metre. Compare

I wandered, lonely as a cloud
That floats on high, o'er vales and hills . . .

with

The Assyrian came down like a wolf on the fold,
And his cohorts were gleaming in purple and gold . . .

The rhythmic difference is obvious. The first, by **Wordsworth**, is in **iambic metre**; the second, by **Byron**, is in **anapaestic**. Both of them are different from **Longfellow**'s rhythm in *The Song of Hiawatha*:

> From the waterfall he named her,
> Minnehaha, Laughing Water.

That is in trochaic metre. And so I could go on, but none of it matters very much. What does matter is that you hear the rhythm. Being able to name it as anapaestic, iambic or trochaic is only handy for pub quizzes.

Middlemarch

This is **George Eliot**'s greatest novel. Published in 1871–2, it is one of the supreme novelistic achievements in English.

Milton, John (1608–74)

John Milton was a poet, pamphleteer and political propagandist. Clearly in this book it is going to be his poetry in which we are primarily interested, but that in itself poses problems. For many people, Milton is Britain's greatest poet, and *Paradise Lost* England's greatest poem. For others, Milton is Britain's greatest bore. **T. S. Eliot**, no mean poet himself, said that what Milton wrote was 'not serious poetry', and that his imagery was merely distracting. **F. R. Leavis** claimed that there was a 'looseness about meaning' in Milton's poetry and a 'remoteness . . . from any English that was ever spoken', and indeed a 'callousness to the intrinsic nature of English'. One can hardly get more damning. Yet, celebrated though Eliot and Leavis both are, they are in a small minority here. Most people interested in English literature regard Milton as a very great poet indeed, and on this occasion, for a change, most people are right.

On 1 March 2008, Claire Tomalin published an article about Milton in the *Guardian*. She began her article as follows:

> When I was invited by my publishers to choose any English poet for a 'selected poems' I found myself saying, almost without a pause to think, 'Milton'. I confess I was surprised that they took the idea on board so readily. John Milton is a great name, but today he is not a popular poet. To me the early poems are sumptuous, the sonnets witty, magnificent and moving by turns, and *Paradise Lost* as thrilling as a novel. Yet I suspect that he does not fit easily into our age of

performance poetry, and that he may be read less than he deserves to be. His reputation as a bad-tempered husband and father is held against him. But it seems to me that the man who emerges from the poems is a man possessed by natural and human beauty, by dreams, myths and legends, a man full of ideas that are sometimes in conflict with one another; who was prepared to give up his vocation as a poet for years in order to serve a political cause; and who overcame blindness to write his greatest work, full of exquisitely imagined scenes. However gnarled and crusty a man, he is a poet who commands attention.

Clearly this is not pretending to be the last word on Milton, but it is eminently right: Milton is a poet who commands attention. Why? I cannot answer this question here, but let us just have a look at one of his sonnets. As you may know, Milton went blind in 1651, and this is what he wrote:

> When I consider how my light is spent,
>   Ere half my days, in this dark world and wide,
>   And that one talent which is death to hide
>   Lodged with me useless, though my soul more bent
> To serve therewith my Maker, and present
>   My true account, lest He returning chide;
>   'Doth God exact day-labour, light denied?'
>   I fondly ask. But Patience, to prevent
> That murmur, soon replies, 'God doth not need
>   Either man's work or His own gifts. Who best
>   Bear His mild yoke, they serve Him best. His state
> Is kingly: thousands at His bidding speed,
>   And post o'er land and ocean without rest;
>   They also serve who only stand and wait.'

Now if, like me, you find the combination of personal feeling and rational control a compelling amalgam in the above sonnet, then move on to *Lycidas*. For many years I regarded *Lycidas* as the greatest elegy in the English language, and I still regard it as one of the supreme poetic achievements. If you don't like it, then I fear that Milton is not for you.

mixed metaphor

See **metaphor**.

Moby-Dick

See **Melville**.

Modest Proposal, A

'A Modest Proposal for Preventing the Children of Poor People in Ireland from being a Burden to Their Parents, or the Country, and for Making Them Beneficial to the Public' was a pamphlet written by **Jonathan Swift** and published in 1729. In it Swift proposes that the children of poor people should be sold to rich people so as to add variety to the rich people's diet.

> I have been assured by a very knowing American of my acquaintance in London, that a young healthy child well nursed, is, at a year old, a most delicious, nourishing and wholesome food, whether stewed, roasted, baked, or boiled; and I make no doubt that it will equally serve in a fricasie, or a ragout.
>
> I do therefore humbly offer it to publick consideration, that of the hundred and twenty thousand children, already computed, twenty thousand may be reserved for breed, whereof only one fourth part to be males; which is more than we allow to sheep, black cattle, or swine; and my reason is, that these children are seldom the fruits of marriage, a circumstance not much regarded by our savages, therefore, one male will be sufficient to serve four females. That the remaining hundred thousand may, at a year old, be offered in sale to the persons of quality and fortune, through the kingdom, always advising the mother to let them suck plentifully in the last month, so as to render them plump, and fat for a good table. A child will make two dishes at an entertainment for friends, and when the family dines alone, the fore or hind quarter will make a reasonable dish, and seasoned with a little pepper or salt, will be very good boiled on the fourth day, especially in winter.

This deadpan advocacy of cannibalism superbly highlights how the poor people of Ireland were being exploited by the rich landowners.

Morris, William (1834–96)

Educated at Marlborough College and Exeter College, Oxford, William Morris was the son of a successful businessman. Brought up as he was amidst money and privilege, it is somewhat surprising to discover that Morris turned into a radical socialist. Consequently Morris, as a writer, produced two socialist fantasies, *A Dream of John Ball* (1888) and *News from Nowhere* (1891), the latter of which is well worth reading.

Much Ado about Nothing

This is one of Shakespeare's most delightful plays, a charade of sexual alliances and misalliances with a dash of political intrigue thrown in for good measure. The chequered relationship between Beatrice and Benedick is one of Shakespeare's major triumphs, and strikes a chord with anyone who has ever had any sort of relationship with a member of the opposite sex. This is their conversation when they first meet in the play:

BEATRICE: I wonder that you will still be talking, Signior Benedick: nobody marks you.

BENEDICK: What, my dear Lady Disdain! are you yet living?

BEATRICE: Is it possible Disdain should die while she hath such meet food to feed it as Signior Benedick? Courtesy itself must convert to Disdain, if you come in her presence.

BENEDICK: Then is Courtesy a turncoat. But it is certain I am loved of all ladies, only you excepted: and I would I could find in my heart that I had not a hard heart; for, truly, I love none.

BEATRICE: A dear happiness to women: they would else have been troubled with a pernicious suitor. I thank God and my cold blood, I am of your humour for that: I had rather hear my dog bark at a crow than a man swear he loves me.

BENEDICK: God keep your ladyship still in that mind, so some gentleman or other shall 'scape a predestinate scratched face.

BEATRICE: Scratching could not make it worse, an 'twere such a face as yours were.

BENEDICK: Well, you are a rare parrot-teacher.

BEATRICE: A bird of my tongue is better than a beast of yours.

BENEDICK: I would my horse had the speed of your tongue, and so good a continuer. But keep your way, i' God's name; I have done.

BEATRICE: You always end with a jade's trick: I know you of old.

Needless to say, Beatrice and Benedick end the play by agreeing to marry each other.

Murdoch, Dame Iris Jean (1919–99)

Although professionally a philosopher, Iris Murdoch, in 1954, produced a novel, *Under the Net*. She then went on to produce twenty more, and although some of them are marred by being too intellectually pretentious, a considerable number depict with wit, compassion and skill the sexual conundrums experienced by intelligent people.

muse

Zeus and Mnemosyne had nine daughters who became the Muses, each one presiding over a separate activity:

CALLIOPE	epic poetry	CLIO	history
ERATO	love poetry	EUTERPE	lyric poetry
MELPOMENE	tragedy	TERPSICHORE	dancing
THALIA	comedy	URANIA	astronomy
	POLYHYMNIA	songs of praise to the gods	

Mysteries of Udolpho, The

This is the title of a novel by **Ann Radclliffe** published in 1794. It is over forty years since I read it, and I can remember nothing whatsoever about it. It appears in this book for two reasons. First of all, it is an example of a group of novels that are often referred to as Gothic novels. These are novels that depict scenes of bizarre and extreme horror and rely on plot mechanisms like family curses, witches' spells and supernatural apparitions. The second reason is that **Jane Austen** pokes fun at Gothic novels in general and *The Mysteries of Udolpho* in particular in her novel *Northanger Abbey*. I provide a little more information in the entry **Gothic fiction**, but so little that it isn't really worth your looking it up.

mystery plays

For me the term 'mystery plays' refers to the plays of Sir Alan Ayckbourn because it is always a mystery to me why they are so popular, but more accurately the term refers to plays of the Middle Ages that recreated some incident or action from **the Bible**.

myth

Like so many words, 'myth' now carries a variety of meanings. The one that concerns us is that whereby a story has been invented in order to explain something else. Thus there are, for instance, a number of creation myths explaining how the earth came into being, and how mankind originated. Every community tends to develop its own myths. As a result, you have Greek myths about Zeus, Roman myths about Jupiter, and so on. I live in the south-west of England, and that area seems to have engendered a series of myths about animals, big panther-like cats, monster black dogs, and so on.

N

Nabokov, Vladimir (1899–1977)

Born in Russia, Nabokov had a fascinating life in the course of which he lived in Russia, England, France, Germany and the United States, and wrote seventeen novels and several volumes of short stories. Yet for most of us, Nabokov is famous for one novel only; in 1955, he published *Lolita*. A mock sententious foreword to the book explains that the manuscript which follows is the confession of one Humbert Humbert, who died in captivity in 1952 just before his trial was due to start. Humbert introduces himself as a European of mixed stock who, at the age of twelve, 'in a princedom by the sea', loved and lost a *petite fille fatale* named Annabel Leigh, and has thereafter remained in sexual bondage to 'the perilous magic' of subteen sirens – he calls them 'nymphets'. There follows a sketch of his tortured career up to the time when, in his late thirties, he settles in a quiet New England town under the same roof as a fatally seductive nymphet, Dolores Haze. This 'Lolita' is the daughter of his landlady, whom he marries with murderous intent. But an accident eliminates Mrs Haze, and Humbert finds himself the guardian of his darling, who, on their first night together, turns out to be utterly depraved and plays the role of seducer. Their weird affair – which carries them on a frenzied motel-hopping trek across the American continent – is climaxed by Lolita's escape with a playwright and Humbert's eventual revenge on his rival. As you might imagine, this novel created outrage in Britain, the United States and other areas where a spurious Puritanism still reigns. Inevitably it became a best-seller, though many of its readers must have been disappointed by the novel's decorous restraint.

narrative

A narrative is simply the telling of an event. It can be extremely short: 'I bought some flowers.' It can be extremely long, e.g. *War and Peace*. It can be a first-person narrative: 'The story that I'm going to tell you began long ago on a damp Thursday morning . . . ' More commonly, it can be a third-person narrative: 'The story began long ago on a damp Thursday morning . . . ' Needless to say, much has been written on the art of the narrative, but there is only one prime criterion: it must be interesting. If a narrative does not interest the reader, then it stands no chance of doing anything else. You might write a short story designed to convert people to vegetarianism, but if your narrative does not interest, it will convert no one to anything.

narrative verse

Poetry does many things, and one of the things that it can do is tell a story. As a result, most nations have such poems, and they can vary widely in type. A **ballad**, for instance, will be relatively short, and will recount an episode that is self-contained. An **epic** will be very long, and may well be open-ended. There are numerous types that lie between these extremes. Let me just list in chronological order some well-known narrative poems, and you can see how different they can be from each other:

Chaucer	*The Canterbury Tales*
Spenser	*The Fairie Queene*
Milton	*Paradise Lost*
Pope	*The Rape of the Lock*
Cowper	*The Task*
Wordsworth	*The Prelude*
Byron	*Don Juan*
Arnold	*Sohrab and Rustum*
Browning	*My Last Duchess*

But listing examples of narrative verse is foolish: there are so many, that a remotely adequate list would take many, many pages. But at least the nine listed above are all good ones!

Nash, Ogden (1902–71)

No self-respecting reference book would include Ogden Nash. After all, one can hardly laud someone who comes out with a **limerick** like this:

> There was a young belle of old Natchez
> Whose garments were always in patchez.
> When comment arose
> On the state of her clothes,
> She replied, 'When Ah itchez, Ah scratchez'.

Or even this:

There once was a man from Calcutta,
Who coated his tonsils with butta,
    Thus converting his snore
    From a thunderous roar,
To a soft, oleaginous mutta.

Nash also wrote longer poems of a frivolous nature, and was well known for dropping pearls of wisdom like this:

Parents were invented to make children happy by giving them something to ignore.

Hence we can safely say that Ogden Nash does not belong in any serious work devoted to English literature. Yet he delighted the American public for over thirty years, and that is no mean achievement.

negative capability

This is a phrase that was used by **Keats** in 1817 in a letter to his brothers George and Thomas. By it Keats seems to have meant the ability to accept the sundry uncertainties, contradictions and puzzles that life presents without neurotically searching for a resolution to them. He cited **Shakespeare** as someone who had abundant negative capability, and **Milton** as someone who had virtually none. In his own poetry, Keats exemplifies negative capability in *La Belle Dame Sans Merci* and in his 'Ode to a Nightingale'.

nemesis

If you do anything wrong, then you will be punished for it. This punishment is your nemesis. Hence, if you cut down Neptune's sacred bush, then you run a real risk of being drowned at sea. As you can see, the concept of nemesis was a meaningful one when people believed in a plurality of gods. Doing X would offend Venus, doing Y would anger Athene, and so on. Today the concept is not normally taken seriously, though it is frequently invoked as a doom for cheating bankers, conniving politicians and estate agents in general.

neo-classicism

This label refers to writing carried out between 1660 and 1780, give or take a decade either side. In other words, the writing of **Dryden**, **Swift**, **Addison**, Steele, **Pope**, **Fielding**, **Johnson**, **Goldsmith** and Gibbon is all neo-classical writing. As is the case with most labels, it disguises more than it reveals. After all, there is not much in common between the writing of Pope and the writing of Fielding. In theory though, all these writers believed in reason, practised decorum and wrote with proportion, balance and restraint. In theory!

Newbolt, Sir Henry John (1862–1938)

I flippantly argued in the entry on Nash that Ogden Nash should not be allowed to appear in a 'serious' work of reference. More seriously, Newbolt shouldn't be allowed in either, simply because he isn't very good. Yet one of his poems, *Drake's Drum*, has attained an almost mythic status:

> Drake he's in his hammock an' a thousand miles away
> (Capten, art tha sleepin' there below?),
> Slung atween the round shot in Nombre Dios Bay,
> An' dreamin' arl the time o' Plymouth Hoe.
> Yarnder lumes the Island, yarnder lie the ships,
> Wi' sailor lads a-dancing' heel-an'-toe,
> An' the shore-lights flashin', an' the night-tide dashin',
> He sees et arl so plainly as he saw et long ago.
>
> Drake he was a Devon man, an' ruled the Devon seas
> (Capten, art tha' sleepin' there below?),
> Rovin' tho' his death fell, he went wi' heart at ease,
> A' dreamin' arl the time o' Plymouth Hoe.
> 'Take my drum to England, hang et by the shore,
> Strike et when your powder's runnin' low;
> If the Dons sight Devon, I'll quit the port o' Heaven,
> An' drum them up the Channel as we drumm'd them long ago.'
>
> Drake he's in his hammock till the great Armadas come
> (Capten, art tha sleepin' there below?),
> Slung atween the round shot, listenin' for the drum,
> An' dreamin arl the time o' Plymouth Hoe.
> Call him on the deep sea, call him up the Sound,
> Call him when ye sail to meet the foe;
> Where the old trade's plyin', an' the old flag's flyin',
> They shall find him ware an' wakin', as they found him long ago!

Personally I find the above poem contrived, sentimental and spurious, but lots of Tories seem to love it.

New Grub Street

This is almost certainly the best known novel by **George Gissing**. It is a novel that greatly appeals to me because within it are at least two characters who deserve literary fame but who are denied it.

Nigger of the 'Narcissus', The

This novel is **Conrad**'s first masterpiece, and is also notable for having a Preface which explains Conrad's artistic aims and intentions.

Nightmare Abbey

This is a novel of 1818 by **Peacock**. It is probably only comprehensible to someone of a reasonable literary background because Peacock is, to some extent, satirising **Byron**, **Coleridge** and **Shelley**. He is also confronting the issues raised by **Milton** in *L'Allegro* and *Il Penseroso*. However, if you brave this literary atmosphere, the novel is great fun.

Nineteen Eighty-Four

This novel by **George Orwell** was written in 1949. Its major aim, I suppose, is to demonstrate the terrifying possibilities of totalitarian government. In terms of influence and impact, therefore, it can be judged a total failure, since the world has witnessed and is witnessing a plethora of totalitarian regimes. It is, however, an excellent novel.

nom de plume

A pen name, or, in other words, a name adopted by a writer because he or she doesn't want to use his or her real name. **George Eliot**, **Lewis Carroll** and **George Orwell** are all *noms de plume*.

nonsense verse

This is verse that is designed to amuse by means of paradoxical situations, ludicrous outcomes and employing invented words. **Lewis Carroll** and **Edward Lear** were two masters of the genre, but this little gem is from Conrad Parker:

> Sometimes I eat porridge
> Sometimes I eat wheat
> But I prefer to eat bananas
> Because I eat them with my feet.

The British are peculiarly partial to nonsense verse, presumably because the British are themselves absurd. Christopher Isherwood, for instance, can produce this piece of idiocy:

> The common cormorant or shag
> Lays eggs inside a paper bag.
> The reason you will see no doubt
> It is to keep the lightning out.
> But what these unobservant birds
> Have never noticed is that herds
> Of wandering bears may come with buns
> And steal the bags to hold the crumbs.

And this is the charm of nonsense verse: it envisages something so totally insane and illogical that one is reduced to helpless hysteria.

North and South

As always, individual judgements can very considerably. I'm not very fond of *North and South* – I found it a bit schematic – but for some people it is their favourite **Gaskell** novel. As the title suggests, the novel makes a contrast between the industrial north and the more refined and leisured south of England.

novel

The novel is an extended piece of fictitious **prose** that tells a more or less coherent story. You will have instantly spotted sundry ambiguities in that definition. How long, for instance, is 'extended'; what distinguishes a short story from a novel? There is, of course, no hard and fast rule about this, but it does lead to absurdities like having a long short story. Secondly, how do you measure 'coherent'? In one of **Faulkner**'s novels, for instance, an entire section is told by an idiot, and that is a long way from being coherent. Finally, what counts as a story? Not much happens, for instance, in **Sterne**'s *Tristram Shandy*. One might argue that 'the novel' is rather like love; no one can define it, but everyone knows what it is. Anyway, the novel is without doubt the literary form that most people today actually encounter, yet it didn't exist until the eighteenth century. Then, all of a sudden, a galaxy of outrageous talent began writing novels: **Defoe, Fielding, Richardson, Smollett, Sterne**. One can account for this rise of the novel by a whole series of socio-economic factors, yet it is a sobering thought that, for thousands of years, mankind had to exist without role models like Tom Jones, Oliver Twist or 007.

nursery rhyme

Many of us had our first introduction to poetry by means of the nursery rhyme, a traditional verse or set of verses often chanted to us at bedtime in the hope that Jack and Jill or Little Bo Peep would aid our passage into sleep. Does this seem conducive to sleep?

> A little boy ran to the end of the sky
> With a rag and a pole and a gooseberry pie.
> He cried: 'Three cheers for the Fourth of July!'
> With a rag and a pole and a gooseberry pie.
> He saw three little donkeys at play,
> He tickled their noses to make them bray,
> And he didn't come back until Christmas Day –
> With a rag and a pole and a gooseberry pie.

Or this?

> A prince came down from Pepperville
> In satin and in lace,
> He wore a bonnet on his head
> And whiskers on his face.
> And when he came to Battleburg
> This is what befell:
> He gave the king and cabinet
> A half a peanut shell.

Ironically, a study in 2004 showed that nursery rhymes exposed children to far more violent incidents than an average evening watching television. Now there's another PhD thesis for you!

O

objective correlative

This term was invented in 1919 by **T. S. Eliot** to signify that any emotion expressed in a play should have a clearly identifiable origin, i.e. an objective correlative. Eliot was complaining at the time that Hamlet, in **Shakespeare**'s play of the same name, expressed more emotion than the facts seemed to justify. Hamlet's father had recently been murdered, and Hamlet's mother was just about to marry Claudius, the man who had killed her husband, so one does feel that Hamlet is allowed a certain amount of emotional reaction. Admittedly Hamlet doesn't actually know that his father had been killed by Claudius, but he did suspect it, and anyway was outraged that his mother should marry again so quickly. Such a context seems to me to justify quite a lot of emotional turmoil, but Eliot disagreed and saw fit to invent this entirely unnecessary piece of jargon. I am fairly sure that you can have an illustrious career as a literary critic without ever once using it. However, if you have a spare decade to throw away, you could devote the time to reading the critical disquisitions that this piece of pretention has engendered.

obscurity

An 'obscure' writer is one whose meaning is difficult to apprehend. Most people are likely to agree with that statement. The trouble is, what is obscure to one person, may not be obscure to another. Of course, one can always comfort oneself by arguing that a writer one finds obscure is, by definition, a poor writer.

occasional verse

This is verse that has been written to mark a particular occasion. There is a lot of it. **Milton**'s *Lycidas* was written to mark the occasion of Edward King's death. **Hopkins**'s *The Wreck of the Deutschland* was written to mark the sinking of a ship carrying a group of nuns. The list could continue for many pages.

ode

An ode is a lyric poem, but it is difficult to say very much more. If one wanted to be technical, one could distinguish between Pindaric odes and Horatian ones, but I doubt if you'd remember the difference, particularly since it barely matters. Wikipedia tells me: 'A classic ode is structured in three parts: the strophe, the antistrophe, and the epode. Different forms such as the homostrophic ode and the irregular ode also exist.' Frankly, I don't care. All that really matters is that **Keats** wrote some marvellous ones, and that there have been some excellent efforts too from **Marvell**, **Dryden**, **Gray**, **Coleridge**, **Wordsworth**, **Shelley**, **Tennyson** and virtually everybody else. Indeed, one gains the impression that a person can barely be termed a poet unless he or she has written at least one ode. One can, though, make that a self-fulfilling prophecy. A poem doesn't need to have the word 'Ode' in its title to be regarded as an ode. Keats's 'To Autumn' is always regarded as an ode. So is W. H. Auden's 'In Memory of W. B. Yeats'. Consequently, if someone comes up to you and says, '**Edmund Spenser** didn't write any odes,' you can reply, 'Ah, but "An Hymne in Honour of Love" is an ode in all but name.'

Odyssey, the

This is an epic Greek poem possibly written by **Homer**. You need to know it because English writers of poems, plays and novels tend to assume that you do, and are consequently prone to make references to Scylla and Charybdis, Penelope or Circe. Failure to comprehend such references will label you as not belonging to the elite!

Old Curiosity Shop, The

This is a novel by **Charles Dickens**. I single it out only because it contains a character called Little Nell whose death evinces perhaps the most sentimental wallowing in English literature. Oscar Wilde claimed that no one could read the death of Little Nell without bursting into uncontrollable laughter.

Oliver Twist

This is also a novel by **Dickens**. It is massively flawed and psychologically unbelievable, but contains so much of Dickens's genius that it is almost impossible not to respond to it. One can feel Dickens's anger as he recounts the circumstances of Oliver's birth:

Although I am not disposed to maintain that the being born in a workhouse is in itself the most fortunate and enviable circumstance that can possibly befall a human being, I do mean to say that in this particular instance it was the best thing for Oliver Twist that could by possibility have occurred. The fact is, that there was considerable difficulty in inducing Oliver to take upon himself the office of respiration – a troublesome practice, but one which custom has rendered necessary to our easy existence; and for some time he lay gasping on a little flock mattress, rather unequally poised between this world and the next: the balance being decidedly in favour of the latter. Now, if during this brief period Oliver had been surrounded by careful grandmothers, anxious aunts, experienced nurses, and doctors of profound wisdom, he would most inevitably and indubitably have been killed in no time. There being nobody by, however, but a pauper old woman, who was rendered rather misty by an unwonted allowance of beer; and a parish surgeon, who did such matters by contract; Oliver and Nature fought out the point between them. The result was that, after a few struggles, Oliver breathed, sneezed, and proceeded to advertise to the inmates of the workhouse the fact of a new burden having been imposed upon the parish by setting up as loud a cry as could reasonably have been expected from a male infant who had not been possessed of that very useful appendage, a voice, for a much longer space of time than three minutes and a quarter.

As Oliver gave this first proof of the free and proper action of his lungs, the patchwork coverlet which was carelessly flung over the iron bedstead rustled; the pale face of a young woman was raised feebly from the pillow; and a faint voice imperfectly articulated the words, 'Let me see the child, and die.'

The surgeon had been sitting with his face turned towards the fire, giving the palms of his hands a warm and a rub alternately. As the young woman spoke, he rose, and advancing to the bed's head, said, with more kindness than might have been expected of him, 'Oh, you must not talk about dying yet.'

'Lor bless her heart, no!' interposed the nurse, hastily depositing in her pocket a green glass bottle, the contents of which she had been tasting in a corner with evident satisfaction. 'Lor bless her dear heart, when she has lived as long as I have, sir, and had thirteen children of her own, and all on 'em dead except two, and them in the wurkus with me, she'll know better than to take on in that way, bless her dear heart! Think what it is to be a mother, there's a dear young lamb, do.'

Apparently this consolatory perspective of a mother's prospects failed in producing its due effect. The patient shook her head, and stretched out her hand towards the child.

The surgeon deposited it in her arms. She imprinted her cold white lips passionately on its forehead; passed her hands over her face; gazed wildly round; shuddered; fell back – and died. They chafed her breast, hands, and temples; but the blood had stopped for ever. They talked of hope and comfort. They had been strangers too long.

'It's all over, Mrs Thingummy!' said the surgeon at last.

'Ah, poor dear, so it is!' said the nurse, picking up the cork of the green bottle, which had fallen out on the pillow as she stooped to take up the child. 'Poor dear!'

'You needn't mind sending up to me, if the child cries, nurse,' said the surgeon, putting on his gloves with great deliberation. 'It's very likely it *will* be troublesome. Give it a little gruel if it is.' He put on his hat, and, pausing by the bedside on his way to the door, added, 'She was a good-looking girl, too; where did she come from?'

'She was brought here last night,' replied the old woman, 'by the overseer's order. She was found lying in the street. She had walked some distance, for her shoes were worn to pieces; but where she came from, or where she was going to, nobody knows.'

The surgeon leaned over the body, and raised the left hand. 'The old story,' he said, shaking his head: 'no wedding ring, I see. Ah! Good-night!'

The medical gentleman walked away to dinner; and the nurse, having once more applied herself to the green bottle, sat down on a low chair before the fire and proceeded to dress the infant.

What an excellent example of the power of dress young Oliver Twist was! Wrapped in the blanket which had hitherto formed his only covering, he might have been the child of a nobleman or a beggar; it would have been hard for the haughtiest stranger to have assigned him his proper station in society. But now that he was enveloped in the old calico robes which had grown yellow in the same service, he was badged and ticketed, and fell into his place at once – a parish child – the orphan of a workhouse – the humble, half-starved drudge – to be cuffed and buffeted through the world – despised by all, and pitied by none. Oliver cried lustily. If he could have known that he was an orphan, left to the tender mercies of churchwardens and overseers, perhaps he would have cried the louder.

The story that follows is absurd, inconsistent and unbelievable – but powerful.

Omar Khayyam, The Rubáiyát of

This work is an outstanding example of the oddity of the British people. Omar Khayyam was a Persian poet and astronomer of the eleventh century. His four-line verses (*rubáiyát*) were 'translated' into English verse by Edward Fitzgerald (1809–83), and have since been taken as a mystical compendium of Eastern wisdom. This is odd because the verse is mediocre and the wisdom non-existent.

onomatopoeia

This impossible-to-spell term refers to words that sound like the thing they are describing. Thus the word 'cuckoo' is onomatopoeic because the name of the bird sounds like the cry of the bird. The words *buzz*, *whizz*, *whoosh*, *zoom*, *crackle*, *pop* and *moo* are all onomatopoeic.

Orley Farm

This was a 1862 novel by **Trollope**. I haven't read all of Trollope's novels – few people have – but of the dozen or so that I've managed, *Orley Farm* is probably the best.

Orwell, George (1903–50)

This is the pen name of Eric Arthur Blair, whose real name very few people will recognise, but almost everyone has heard of George Orwell. This is because, in *Animal Farm* and *Nineteen Eighty-Four*, Orwell created two of the most biting political satires in English literature. He also wrote some excellent essays, some political journalism and a couple of novels, but it is for his satire that he is best remembered – but not, alas, heeded.

Othello

Othello is one of Shakespeare's greatest plays, showing, as it does, a paradigm of evil in Iago, and the devastating power of jealousy in Othello. In the final act, Othello unjustly kills the woman he loves. His speech before doing so is heartbreaking:

> It is the cause, it is the cause, my soul,
> Let me not name it to you, you chaste stars!

It is the cause. Yet I'll not shed her blood,
Nor scar that whiter skin of hers than snow
And smooth as monumental alabaster.
Yet she must die, else she'll betray more men.
Put out the light, and then put out the light:
If I quench thee, thou flaming minister,
I can again thy former light restore,
Should I repent me; but once put out thy light,
Thou cunning'st pattern of excelling nature,
I know not where is that Promethean heat
That can thy light relume. When I have pluck'd the rose,
I cannot give it vital growth again:
It must needs wither. I'll smell it on the tree. [*Kissing her*]
Ah balmy breath, that dost almost persuade
Justice to break her sword! One more, one more.
Be thus when thou art dead, and I will kill thee,
And love thee after. One more, and this the last:
So sweet was ne'er so fatal. I must weep,
But they are cruel tears; this sorrow's heavenly:
It strikes where it doth love. She wakes.

ottava rima

This is the name given to a specific **stanza** which comprises eight iambic lines, and which has the rhyming scheme abababcc. **Byron** uses it in his *Don Juan*:

I want a hero: an uncommon want,
When every year and month sends forth a new one,
Till, after cloying the gazettes with cant,
The age discovers he is not the true one;
Of such as these I should not care to vaunt,
I'll therefore take our ancient friend Don Juan –
We all have seen him, in the pantomime,
Sent to the Devil somewhat ere his time.

Yeats uses it in 'Sailing to Byzantium':

That is no country for old men. The young
In one another's arms, birds in the trees –
Those dying generations – at their song,
The salmon-falls, the mackerel-crowded seas,

Fish, flesh, or fowl, commend all summer long
Whatever is begotten, born, and dies.
Caught in that sensual music all neglect
Monuments of unageing intellect.

An aged man is but a paltry thing,
A tattered coat upon a stick, unless
Soul clap its hands and sing, and louder sing
For every tatter in its mortal dress,
Nor is there singing school but studying
Monuments of its own magnificence;
And therefore I have sailed the seas and come
To the holy city of Byzantium.

O sages standing in God's holy fire
As in the gold mosaic of a wall,
Come from the holy fire, perne in a gyre,
And be the singing-masters of my soul.
Consume my heart away; sick with desire
And fastened to a dying animal
It knows not what it is; and gather me
Into the artifice of eternity.

Once out of nature I shall never take
My bodily form from any natural thing,
But such a form as Grecian goldsmiths make
Of hammered gold and gold enamelling
To keep a drowsy Emperor awake;
Or set upon a golden bough to sing
To lords and ladies of Byzantium
Of what is past, or passing, or to come.

The form was first introduced into England by **Wyatt** in the early sixteenth century, and, although not commonly used, there have been works in ottava rima by **Spenser**, **Drayton**, **Shelley**, **Keats**, **Byron** and **Yeats**.

Owen, Wilfred (1893–1918)

The almost unimaginable horrors of the First World War stimulated a number of young men involved in that war to write poems to describe the hell that surrounded them. The greatest of those poets was Wilfred Owen, and here is a small snapshot of that hell:

Anthem for Doomed Youth

What passing-bells for these who die as cattle?
  Only the monstruous anger of the guns.
Only the stuttering rifles' rapid rattle
  Can patter out their hasty orisons.
No mockeries now for them; no prayers nor bells;
    Nor any voice of mourning save the choirs –
The shrill, demented choirs of wailing shells;
    And bugles calling for them from sad shires.

What candles may be held to speed them all?
  Not in the hands of boys, but in their eyes
  Shall shine the holy glimmers of good-byes.
The pallor of girls' brows shall be their pall;
    Their flowers the tenderness of patient minds,
    And each slow dusk a drawing-down of blinds.

Again, of course, reactions vary, but I find that so unbearably moving that I am instantly convinced that Owen was the greatest English poet of the twentieth century.

Oxford English Dictionary, The

This is one of the wonders of the world. It contains about 400,000 words, and for the majority of those words, the *OED* provides a historical conspectus of its usage over the centuries that the word has existed. No person interested in language can afford to be without it. However, if you have never encountered the *OED*, you may be in for something of a surprise when you look up a word. Here, for instance, is the word 'tug':

1. An act or the action of tugging; a forcible or violent pull; a severe strain or drag.
1500–20 Dunbar *Poems* xxxiii. 81 The tarsall gaif him tug for tug. **1635** Quarles *Embl.* IV. iii. 28 The idle vessell slides that watry lay, Without the blast, or tug, of wind, or Oare. 1697 Dryden *Æneid* ix. 759 Downward by the feet he drew The trembling dastard: at the tug he falls. **1754** Mrs. Delany in *Life & Corr.* (1861) III. 307 Lady Harriet had a tooth drawn by Rutter . . . and he gave three tugs before he got it out! **1815** *Hist. J. Decastro* IV. 111 The door stuck to the posts so fast that I was forced to take three or four good tugs at it before it would come open. **1886** Fenn *Master of Cerem.* xiv, Morton felt a tug at his line.

2. Labour, toil (*obs. rare*); *esp.* a determined effort to accomplish or attain something; a hard try; a struggle; a 'go'.

1504 *Plumpton Corr.* (Camden) 191 It ryseth on my owne mynd to give over grett tuggs of husbandry which I had, and take me to lesse charge. **1673** Ld. Conway in *Essex Papers* (Camden) I. 141, I shall yet have a tug for the M^r of the Ordnance place. **1764** *Mem. G. Psalmanazar* 84, I . . . found it a very hard tug to keep up my credit. **1856** Bryant *Autumn Woods* xii, The vain low strife That makes men mad, the tug for wealth and power.

3.a. A strenuous contest between two forces or persons.

1660 Gower in *5th Rep. Hist. MSS. Comm.* (1876) 204/1 The only tug is between Episcopacy and Presbytery. **1830** Scott *Demonol.* i. 11 Amid the mortal tug of combat. **1868** Freeman *Norm. Conq.* II. viii. 269 On this day . . . William began that career of good fortune in the mere tug of battle. **1897** *Westm. Gaz.* 8 Dec. 2/3 The tug of will between the overbearing Kaiser and his hitherto subservient people.

b. *tug of war.* (*a*) The decisive contest; the real struggle or tussle; a severe contest for supremacy. (*b*) An athletic contest between two teams who haul at the opposite ends of a rope, each trying to drag the other over a line marked between them. Also *attrib.*

1677 N. Lee *Alex. Gt.* IV. ii, When Greeks joined Greeks, then was the tug of war. **1822** Byron *Juan* VIII. li, At last [the mob] takes to weapons. Then comes 'the tug of war'. **1876** *World* V. No. 108. 13 The tug of war was the most popular item in Saturday's entertainment. **1893** E. H. Barker *Wand. Southern Waters* 263 He [the devil] therefore lost no time in entering upon a tug-of-war with the saintly interloper. **1902** *Westm. Gaz.* 6 June 7/1 Their tug-of-war team pulled over two teams of British Tommies.

c. *tug of love*, a conflict of affections; *spec.* a contest for custody of a minor; also (with hyphens) *attrib.* Perh. infl. by the title of a comedy 'The Tug of Love' by I. Zangwill (1907).

1973 *Times* 9 Nov. 20/7 The Houghton committee was set up after some highly-publicized 'tug of love' cases, and recommended making it easier for long-term foster-parents to adopt. **1977** *Daily Mirror* 21 Mar. 13/1 Back home in the arms of her mother, a tiny tug-of-love girl sleeps peacefully. The girl had been taken to California after being snatched by her father. **1984** *Times* 12 Oct. 2/2 'Tug of love' cases where a child is seized by one parent from another.

4. In harness: **a**. (Chiefly *pl.*) A pair of short chains attached to the hames, by which the collar is connected with the shafts. **b**. A trace. **c**. A short strap sewn on various parts of the harness and serving to keep it in position; also (*pl.*) the loops of the back-strap which support the shafts. **d**. A metal stud or pin on the shaft to prevent it running too far forward through the loops of the back-strap. **e**. See quot. 1844. Also *locally* applied to other parts of harness: see quot. 1888.

*c*1250 *MS. Barlow 49* (2) lf. 16 In carucis . . . emendandis . . . In iugis et tuggis ad idem emptis ix. d.] **1417–18** in *Archæol. Jrnl.* (1881) XXXVIII. 78 Item in vij Teugys, xijd. **1481–3** *Acc. Exch. K.R.* File 496 No. 26 Tuggis et hamis.

1497 *Naval Acc. Hen. VII* (1896) 96 Tugges for horsharnesse, ij baskettes. **1562** W. Bullein *Bulwark, Dial. Soarnes & Chir.* 7b, Banishe them from Chyrurgi, commende them to the Carte. To the flaile and the rake, the trace and the togge. **1589** Puttenham *Eng. Poesie* III. xxiii. (Arb.) 281 Which word tugge signifieth the pull or draught of the oxen or horses, and therefore the leathers that beare the chiefe stresse of the draught, the cartars call them tugges. **1786** Burns *To Auld Mare* xi, Thou was a noble fittie-lan', As e'er in tug or tow was drawn! **1794** W. Felton *Carriages* (1801) II. x. 134 Tugs to hold up the traces. *Ibid.* 135 The hipstrap buckles to the tugs of the breeching to hold it up. *Ibid.* 147 In the middle [of each of a pair of hames] other loops are hung, to which the tugs for the draught are fixed. **1808–18** Jamieson, *Tug*, raw-hide, of which formerly plough-traces were made. **1844** Stephens *Bk. Farm* II. 695 The pace of the old horse should be subdued by the rein and tug; which the short reins are called, that pass from the head of one horse to the collar of the other. **1862** *Catal. Internat. Exhib., Brit.* II. No. 4708, The collars, hames, and tugs are suited to give the horse the least fatigue in drawing the vehicle. **1888** Elworthy *W. Somerset Word-bk.*, *Tug*, the hook or other iron on the carriage, or on the whipple-tree, to which the trace is attached. The end of the leather trace at the part where it is attached to the vehicle. A loose loop buckled round the shaft, to which (when used) is fastened the kicking-strap.

f. *Mining.* The iron hoop of a corf or hoisting bucket.

1858 Simmonds *Dict. Trade*, *Tug* a hoop of iron to hold a tackle. **1877** in Knight *Dict. Mech.* **1881** Raymond *Mining Gloss.*, *Tug* (Derb.), the iron hook of a hoisting bucket, to which the tacklers are attached.

g. A rope. *U.S.* 1805 M. Lewis *Jrnl.* in *Lewis & Clark Exped.* (1904) I. 369 The white perogue [was] refitted in a few minutes with some tugs of raw hides and nales. 1852 H. C. Watson *Nights in Block-House* 445 They took a strong tug, made from the raw hide of the buffalo or elk. 1910 W. M. Raine *B. O'Connor* xiv. 216 He stopped as if to fasten a tug.

5. A timber-wagon. *south.* and *east. dial.*

1706 PHILLIPS (ed. Kersey), *Tug*, a Country-Word for a Waggon to carry Timber. **1724** DEFOE *Tour Gt. Brit.* I. 59, I have seen one tree on a carriage which they call here [Lewes] a tug, drawn by two and twenty oxen. **1791** GILPIN *Forest Scenery* I. 116 A sort of wain, which in that deep country [Sussex], is expressively called a tugg. **1829** HOR. SMITH *New Forest* I. i. 3 A timber-wain, in Hampshire called a tug.

6.a. A small, stoutly built, and powerful steamer used to tow other vessels; a tug-boat.

1817 *Chron.* in *Ann. Reg.* 101 This vessel, appropriately named the Tug, is meant to track ten other vessels . . . The utility of the Tug is not confined to tracking. **1840** *Evid. Hull Docks Comm.* 73 You use the tug to tow them from the harbour. **1908** [MISS FOWLER] *Betw. Trent & Ancholme* 12 The smoke of a tug drawing vessels.

b. Any other towing craft or vehicle, *spec.* (*a*) = *tug aircraft* below; (*b*) a tractor used to tow aircraft on the ground or unpowered road vehicles.

1942 *Jrnl. R. Aeronaut. Soc.* XLVI. 7 Aircraft towing as a method for launching high-performance gliders is a relatively recent development. Up till now, no specially designed aircraft 'tug' has become available. **1945** *Amer. Speech* XX. 227/2 *Tug,* a four- or six-wheeled tractor used for towing planes on the ground or for towing warehouse trailers. **1960** *Times Rev. Industry* Nov. 20/3 A tractor can be a tug for two vans. **1981** *Times* 14 Dec. 22/8 Tugs could not move the big jets because of ice.

7. Phrases. *to hold tug* (also *hold a tug*), *to hold one tug,* to keep one strenuously occupied, or fully engaged; *in tug, upon a tug,* in conflict or contest (*with*).

1577 GRANGE *Golden Aphrod.* Iiv, Whiche twoo pretie poyntes [for discussion] helde them tugge with hard holde vntill aboute dinner tyme. **1659** *Burton's Diary* (1828) IV. 317 The debate held such tug that it was moved to adjourn. **1667** WOOD *Life* 18 July (O.H.S.) II. 113 There was work enough that would hold him tugg for a whole yeare. **1672** *Westminster Drollery* II. 94 No Tankerd, Flaggon, Bottle, nor Jugg so well can hold Tugg. **1681** R. L'ESTRANGE *Apol. Prot.* IV. i. 99 The Popes were at that time upon a Tugg with the Emperor. **1700** MOTTEUX *Quix.* I. IV. iv. II. 398 The Barber held tugg with her till the Curate advis'd him to return it. **1791** GOUV. MORRIS in Sparks *Life & Writ.* (1832) I. 355 Lafayete will hold a good tug, being as cunning as any body. **1849** C. BRONTË *Shirley* xx, She had seen from the window Tartar in full tug with two carriers' dogs.

8. [Perh. a different word.] *Public School slang.* At Eton College, a student on the foundation, a colleger as distinguished from an oppidan. In wider use, a studious or academic type, a swot.

1864 *Eton School Days* ii. 21 That building on the right is Tuggery, where the Tug-Muttons live; you'll hate the Tugs like anything: all the Oppidans hate the Tugs. **1922** S. LESLIE *Oppidan* iv. 48 *Tugs* or Scholars were separated from Oppidans by the same gulf that lay between Professionals and Gentlemen in the world of sport. **1976** R. POUND *A. P. Herbert* i. 23 In Wykehamist parlance, he was a 'tug', a clever chap, whose achievement was held worthier than any playing-field victory. **1977** A. J. AYER *Part of My Life* ii. 34 Traditionally, the Oppidans despised the Collegers, who tended to come from a lower social stratum, and spoke of them as Tugs, because they were believed to engage in tugs of war for the few pieces of mutton which was all that they were given to eat. **1982** BARR & YORK *Official Sloane Ranger Handbk.* 71/1 Swots are weeds (at Eton: 'tugs don't wash').

9. *attrib.* and *Comb.*: in sense 6, as *tug-boat* (whence *tug-boatman*), *-captain,* *-man, -master, -owner, -service, -steamer, traffic;* also *tug-like* adj.; **tug aircraft**, a powered aircraft used to tow a glider or train of gliders; **tug-boating** *U.S.,* working on a tug-boat; **tug-buckle,** a trace-buckle; **tug-carrier,** each of a pair of loops through which the tugs or traces pass (Knight *Dict. Mech.* 1877); **tug-chain,** a chain trace; also a short chain by which a leather trace is attached to the splinter-bar (*Funk's Stand. Dict.* 1895); **tug-hole:** cf. sense 4f; **tug-hook,** a hook on the hame to which the trace is attached; **tug-iron:** see quot.; **tug-mutton** = sense 8 above; **tug pilot,** the pilot of a tug aircraft; **tug-plate:** see quot.; **tug-rope** *Obs.* exc. *U.S.,* a trace of rope; **tug-slide,** a tongueless trace-buckle: cf. SLIDE *n.* 6; **tug-spring**, a spring connexion for traces to reduce the strain of starting a load; **tug-strap**, a leather trace; **tug-whiting**, a whiting caught by a handline (*Sc.*). See also Tugwithe.

1931 *Flight* 26 June 578/2 The *tug aircraft, as it will probably be called. **1962** [see *parachute aircraft* s.v. PARACHUTE *n.* 5]. **1976** J. COLVILLE *Footprints in Time* xxxiii. 185 Soon there were fleets of gliders too. As each was released over the river, its tug-aircraft turned steeply away for home.

1832 BABBAGE *Econ. Manuf.* vi. (ed. 3) 44 A kind of *tug-boat for vessels which have occasion to ascend the rapid. **1860** *Merc. Marine Mag.* VII. 73 One ship was waiting to be towed out by the tugboat.

1941 E. P. O'DONNELL *Great Big Doorstep* xxi. 310 If it wasn't for rain, I wooden have a job to hole down. You'd see me *tugboatin on the river or some kinda ordinary work. 1973 *Publ. Amer. Dial. Soc.* LX. 1 The coastal fringes are ideally suited to those who make their living from the seafishing, whaling.., boat~building, tugboating.

1891 *Daily News* 3 Feb. 3/5 The *tug-boatmen who struck on Friday at Liverpool were still out yesterday.

1851 MAYHEW *Lond. Labour* I. 359 His foreman says to me, 'Give that *tug-buckle a file'. 1862 *Catal. Internat. Exhib.*, *Brit.* II. No. 4686 Set of carriage harness, with improved tug buckles.

1897 *Westm. Gaz.* 26 May 4/3 A *tug captain from Limehouse was called by the police.

1797 J. CURR *Coal Viewer* 18 Should the corves be made to draw by conductors, the chains from the center of the *tug hole to the center of the ring that connects them, should measure 22 inches.

1417–18 in *Archæol. Jrnl.* (1881) XXXVIII. 78 Item in *Teughookys. vijd **1844** W. BARNES *Poems Rur. Life* Gloss., *Tugiron of shafts*, an iron on the shafts [of a wagon] to hitch the traces to.

1890 'R. BOLDREWOOD' *Col. Reformer* (1891) 155 Energetic people have certain advantages. Their *tuglike, unremitting habit of doing something keeps the machine going.

1891 *Scott. Leader* 24 Jan. 6 Over 80 per cent. of the *tugmen at Liverpool have joined the Sailors' Union.

1896 *Pall Mall Mag.* Nov. 386 The responsibilities and anxieties of a *tug-master.

1864 *Tug-mutton [see sense 8 above].

1901 *Westm. Gaz.* 26 Aug. 5/2 They were *tug-owners, and worked the ferry between Hobbs's Point and the Neyland Ordnance Stores.

1948 PARTRIDGE *Dict. Forces' Slang* 197 *Tug pilot*, the pilot of an aeroplane towing a glider. (Colloquial.)

1978 A. WELCH *Bk. of Airsports* iii. 48/2 When experienced as a tug pilot, you will probably be given the occasional cross-country retrieve from a field or private airstrip.

1794 W. FELTON *Carriages* (1801) II. Gloss., *Tug Plate*, a plate, fixed on the shafts, in which the tugs of a one horse harness is placed.

1417–18 in *Archæol. Jrnl.* (1881) XXXVIII. 78 Item in cordis vocatis *Teugropis, viij^d.

1852 J. REYNOLDS *Pioneer Hist. Illinois* 236 They often pack their meat by running a tug rope through each piece. **1891** *Century Mag.* Mar. 774/2 We began by eating the rawhide tug ropes and parfleches.

1877 KNIGHT *Dict. Mech.*, *Tug-slide..*Tug-spring.

1861 *Wheat & Tares* 252 *Tug steamers flashed hither and thither, panting and groaning with their heavy train of stone-laden barges.

1882 *Cassell's Encycl. Dict.* s.v. *Breast-strap*, The breast-collar at its rear ends receives the *tug-straps.

1906 *Daily Tel.* 1 Feb., The Thames and London Rowing Clubs have never complained of the general, business *tug-traffic.

*a***1670** SPALDING *Troub. Chas. I* (1851) II. 174 About this tyme [1642], sum *tug-quhytinges [were] takin.

Hence **Tuggery** *Eton College slang*, the collegers' boarding-house; the position or status of a colleger.

1864 [see TUG *n.* 8].

1883 J. BRINSLEY-RICHARDS *Seven Yrs. at Eton* xii. 112 [A boy] who had come from Aberdeen 'to try for Tuggery', that is, to try and pass on to the foundation as a King's scholar.

As you can see, the *OED* brings a depth and comprehensiveness to defining a word that is almost frightening.

oxymoron

An oxymoron is a contradiction in terms, or an expression in which two incompatible ideas are simultaneously propounded. **Milton** uses one in his description of hell:

> no light, but rather darkness visible

Pope uses two in his description of man:

> a being darkly wise, and rudely great

P

paean

A song or chant of rejoicing. Thus you sing a paean of triumph when the British army has overcome the opposition and advanced 200 yards.

Pair of Blue Eyes, A

This is a novel by **Thomas Hardy**. I mention it because, unlike *The Mayor of Casterbridge* or *Tess of the D'Urbervilles*, it is not very well known, but deserves to be. It has exactly those ironies of plot that are so characteristic of Hardy.

palindrome

A palindrome is a word or phrase that reads exactly the same backwards as it does forwards. 'Madam, I'm Adam' is a palindromic phrase. I believe there have even been competitions in which people attempt to compose palindromic sentences. Such an activity makes cricket look rational by comparison. However, I would be remiss if I didn't give you some of the best palindromes:

> A man, a plan, a canal – Panama
>
> Able was I ere I saw Elba
>
> Sums are not set as a test on Erasmus
>
> Amy, must I jujitsu my ma?
>
> A new order began: a more Roman age bred Rowena.
>
> Are we not drawn onward to new era?
>
> Do geese see God?
>
> No, Mel Gibson is a casino's big lemon.
>
> No, sir, panic is a basic in a prison.

You can find hundreds on the Internet, but I shouldn't imagine you feel the need for more.

Palliser novels, the

Anthony Trollope wrote six novels in which the political character Plantagenet Palliser plays a leading role.

Pamela

This is the title of **Samuel Richardson**'s first novel, published in 1740, and consequently one of the very earliest English novels. Written in epistolary form, the novel is very long, and traces the fortunes of an innocent girl, Pamela, whose virtue is threatened by an unscrupulous nobleman, Mr B. She rejects him continually, and her virtue is eventually rewarded when he shows his sincerity by proposing an equitable marriage to her. In the second part of the novel, Pamela attempts to accommodate herself to upper-class society and to build a successful relationship with him. The novel is unremittingly moral, and ought to be unreadable. Indeed its nauseating morality is lampooned in **Henry Fielding**'s *Shamela* (1741) and *Joseph Andrews* (1742). Even so, *Pamela* is not unreadable, and even possesses a kind of narrative compulsion that drives you on. Judge for yourself; here is the first letter that Pamela writes:

> Dear Mother and Father – I have great trouble, and some comfort, to acquaint you with. The trouble is, that my good lady died of the illness I mentioned to you, and left us all much grieved for the loss of her; for she was a dear good lady, and kind to all us her servants. Much I feared that as I was taken by her ladyship to wait upon her person, I should be quite destitute again, and forced to return to you my poor parents, who have enough to do to maintain yourselves; and, as my lady's goodness had put me to write and cast accounts, and made me a little expert at my needle, and otherwise qualified above my degree, it was not every family that could have found a place that your poor Pamela was fit for: but God, whose graciousness to us we have so often experienced at a pinch, put it into my good lady's heart, on her death-bed, just an hour before she expired, to recommend to my young master all her servants, one by one; and when it came to my turn to be recommended (for I was sobbing and crying at her pillow), she could only say, My dear son! – and so broke off a little; and then recovering – Remember my poor Pamela – And these were some of her last words! Oh how my eyes run – Don't wonder to see the paper so blotted.
>
> Well, but God's will must be done! – And so comes the comfort, that I shall not be obliged to return back to be a clog upon my dear parents! For my master said, I will take care of you all, my good

maidens; and for you, Pamela (and took me by the hand; yes, he took my hand before them all), for my dear mother's sake, I will be a friend to you, and you shall take care of my linen. God bless him! and pray with me, my dear father and mother, for a blessing upon him, for he has given mourning and a year's wages to all my lady's servants; and I having no wages as yet, my lady having said she should do for me as I deserved, ordered the housekeeper to give me mourning with the rest; and gave me with his own hand four golden guineas, and some silver, which were in my old lady's pocket when she died; and said, if I was a good girl, and faithful and diligent, he would be a friend to me, for his mother's sake. And so I send you these four guineas for your comfort; for Providence will not let me want: And so you may pay some old debt with part, and keep the other part to comfort you both. If I get more, I am sure it is my duty, and it shall be my care, to love and cherish you both; for you have loved and cherished me, when I could do nothing for myself. I send them by John, our footman, who goes your way: but he does not know what he carries; because I seal them up in one of the little pill-boxes, which my lady had, wrapt close in paper, that they mayn't chink; and be sure don't open it before him.

I know, dear father and mother, I must give you both grief and pleasure; and so I will only say, Pray for your Pamela; who will ever be

Your most dutiful daughter.

One can see why Henry Fielding was moved to publish a parody of this novel, yet, if one continues, the novel begins to exert an almost hypnotic effect. Try it.

Pandarus

For an entirely fictional and not altogether agreeable character, Pandarus has a surprising role in world literature. He first appears in Homer's *Iliad* as a famous archer, but in English literature, Pandarus reappears in Chaucer's *Troilus and Criseyde* (1370), where he is an active go-between for his niece Criseyde and the Trojan prince Troilus. He plays a similar role in Shakespeare's *Troilus and Cressida*, and consequently became the origin of the verb 'pander' in its original meaning of 'to act as go-between'. Shakespeare's character, though, is more devious and under-hand than Chaucer's, and as a result, the verb 'to pander' and the noun 'a panderer' both have distasteful tinges to them. Indeed, in the Shakespeare play, Pandarus ends the drama by wishing upon the audience all his many diseases:

A goodly medicine for my aching bones! O world!
world! world! thus is the poor agent despised!
O traitors and bawds, how earnestly are you set
a-work, and how ill requited! why should our
endeavour be so loved and the performance so loathed?
what verse for it? what instance for it? Let me see:

> Full merrily the humble-bee doth sing,
> Till he hath lost his honey and his sting;
> And being once subdued in armed tail,
> Sweet honey and sweet notes together fail.

Good traders in the flesh, set this in your painted cloths.
As many as be here of Pander's hall,
Your eyes, half out, weep out at Pandar's fall;
Or if you cannot weep, yet give some groans,
Though not for me, yet for your aching bones.
Brethren and sisters of the hold-door trade,
Some two months hence my will shall here be made:
It should be now, but that my fear is this,
Some galled goose of Winchester would hiss;
Till then I'll sweat and seek about for eases,
And at that time bequeathe you my diseases.

panegyric

This is a speech or essay devoted to praising someone or something. The word carries a suggestion of effusiveness, and we tend to associate panegyrics with politicians buttering up another corrupt state, actors praising each other, and mothers talking about the abilities of their children. In literature, Antony's funeral oration over the body of Caesar in **Shakespeare**'s *Julius Caesar* could be described as a panegyric.

Pangloss

Dr Pangloss is a character in Voltaire's *Candide*. He is a quasi-philosopher who holds, despite abundant evidence to the contrary, that all is for the best in the best of all possible worlds. He only appears here because Pangloss has become an **archetype**, and you sometimes find references to Panglossian attitudes. All prime ministers, presidents, etc. are Panglossian because they always assert that their government is working for the good of the country.

pantomime

This is another quaint British custom. At Christmas and into the New Year, most theatres in Britain put on a ludicrous dramatic entertainment centring round some **nursery-rhyme** character like Jack (he of the Beanstalk), Little Red Riding-Hood or Snow White. Such entertainments are called pantomimes and are characterised by slapstick, meaningless songs, and gross overacting. Aimed primarily at audiences of children, pantomimes provide abundant evidence that Britain has not yet become an educated society.

parable

A parable is a story intended to illustrate a moral or a spiritual lesson. Jesus, for instance, told a number of parables to this end, that of the Good Samaritan being one of the best known.

paradigm

If something is a paradigm, it illustrates some quality superbly. Thus the Nonsuch Bank is a paradigm in the handling of mortgages, James Patterson is a paradigm of punctuality and the *Knowle Gazette* is a paradigm in its accurate reporting of the south Bristol football league. (All three of these examples are an invention. In real life, nothing is ever a paradigm.)

Paradise Lost

Paradise Lost is an epic poem by **Milton** published in 1667. Regarded by many as the greatest poem in the English language, it seeks (and fails) to justify the ways of God to man. Like every other poem in the language, it arouses differing views. A friend of mine regards it as the greatest poem in the language, and this is not an unusual view. Others find it an prolix example of verbosity. Just have a look at its opening sentence:

> Of Man's first disobedience, and the fruit
> Of that forbidden tree, whose mortal taste
> Brought death into the world, and all our woe,
> With loss of Eden, till one greater Man
> Restore us, and regain the blissful seat,
> Sing heav'nly Muse, that on the secret top
> Of Oreb, or of Sinai, didst inspire
> That shepherd, who first taught the chosen seed,

In the beginning how the Heav'ns and Earth
Rose out of Chaos; or if Sion hill
Delight thee more, and Siloa's brook that flow'd
Fast by the oracle of God: I thence
Invoke thy aid to my advent'rous song,
That with no middle flight intends to soar
Above th' Aonian mount, while it pursues
Things unattempted yet in prose or rhyme.

That is one sentence, and Milton sustains this for twelve books, each book having 700 to 1,000 lines. Not everyone can manage such a diet. Yet I first encountered Milton at A level, when we 'did' Books 9 and 10 of *Paradise Lost*. I have to confess that I loved it.

Paradise Regained

Centred round Christ's temptation in the wilderness, this long poem by **Milton** purports to show how Adam's sin was nullified by Christ's perfection. It isn't as good as ***Paradise Lost***.

paradox

Something is a paradox when it appears to exhibit two contradictory things. A document may contain a page on which is printed: 'This page is intentionally left blank', thereby making the page not blank. If there is an exception to every rule, then every rule must have at least one exception, the exception to this one being that it has no exception. If truth does not exist, the statement 'truth does not exist' is a truth, thereby proving itself incorrect. And, of course, the biggest paradox of them all, how can you reconcile a loving God with the cruel world in which we live? **Pope**, in his ***Essay on Man***, catalogues the paradoxes of human kind:

Placed on this isthmus of a middle state,
A being darkly wise and rudely great:
With too much knowledge for the Sceptic side,
With too much weakness for the Stoic's pride,
He hangs between, in doubt to act or rest;
In doubt to deem himself a God or Beast;
In doubt his mind or body to prefer;
Born but to die, and reas'ning but to err;
Alike in ignorance, his reason such,

Whether he thinks too little or too much;
Chaos of thought and passion, all confused;
Still by himself abused or disabused;
Created half to rise, and half to fall:
Great lord of all things, yet a prey to all;
Sole judge of truth, in endless error hurl'd;
The glory, jest, and riddle of the world!

paraphrase

If you paraphrase something, you express the same meaning as the original but do so in different words. Thus you could express the sentence 'People apprehended in purloining artifacts will be incarcerated' as 'People caught stealing objects will be imprisoned.' The second sentence is a paraphrase of the first. However, some things cannot be paraphrased. If you try to paraphrase a great poem, you lose everything of value about the original.

parody

A parody is when something resembles something else, but the resemblances are meant to deride the original. Gulliver's visit to Laputa in *Gulliver's Travels*, for instance, is a parody of the scientific method. **Pope**'s *The Rape of the Lock* is a parody of the poetic epic. Cervantes' *Don Quixote* is a parody of the knight's pursuit of chivalry. *Peter Bell the Third* is a parody by **Shelley** of **Wordsworth**'s *Peter Bell*. Parody is difficult to do well.

Passage to India, A

This is a novel by **E. M. Forster**, published in 1924. It is a skilful depiction of the clash of two cultures. Wikipedia tells us: 'It was selected as one of the 100 great works of English literature by the Modern Library and won the 1924 James Tait Black Memorial Prize for fiction. *Time Magazine* included the novel in its "*Time*'s 100 best English-language novels from 1923 to 2005".' Despite this, it is well worth reading.

pathetic fallacy

I was standing in the school library one day looking at the novels of **Thomas Hardy** when my English teacher passed by me. 'Ah,' he said, 'in search of the pathetic fallacy are you, David?' I didn't then know what the pathetic fallacy was, but I looked it up there and then and discovered that it is the attribution of human emotions to works of nature. Thus, when you describe the wind as pitiless, you are employing the pathetic fallacy. Hardy, of course, imbues Wessex with a series of stark human attitudes. Nor is usage of the pathetic fallacy confined to Hardy. You and I employ it, and so does every English writer:

> The stars will awaken
> Though the moon sleep a full hour later. SHELLEY

> The fruitful field
> Laughs with abundance. COWPER

> Nature must be gladsome when I was so happy. C. BRONTË

> The red rose, cries, 'She is near, she is near,'
> And the white rose weeps, 'She is late.' TENNYSON

> The rain set early in tonight;
> Sullen wind was soon awake,
> Tore the elm-tops down for spite,
> And did its worst to vex the lake. BROWNING

Peacock, Thomas Love (1785–1866)

I doubt if Peacock is much read now, but I recently reread his satirical novels *Headlong Hall* (1816), *Melincourt* (1817) and *Nightmare Abbey* (1818) and they still have the power to amuse. Peacock was also an essayist and poet.

pentameter

This is a line of **poetry** consisting of five feet. It is the most common line in English verse.

Perdita

Perdita is the heroine of **Shakespeare**'s play *The Winter's Tale*. She only appears here because her name means 'The lost one', and my wife refused to allow our daughter to be called Perdita.

personification

Personification is a figure of speech in which an inanimate object or an abstraction is given human qualities or abilities. We tend to encounter personification very early in a **nursery rhyme** like this:

> Hey diddle, diddle,
> The cat and the fiddle,
> The cow jumped over the moon;
> The little dog laughed
> To see such sport,
> And the dish ran away with the spoon.

But the figure of speech is endemic in English, and poets and prose writers employ it constantly. **Emily Dickinson**'s personification of a train is amusing:

> I like to see it lap the miles,
> And lick the valleys up,
> And stop to feed itself at tanks;
> And then, prodigious, step
>
> Around a pile of mountains,
> And, supercilious, peer
> In shanties by the sides of roads;
> And then a quarry pare
>
> To fit its sides, and crawl between,
> Complaining all the while
> In horrid, hooting stanza;
> Then chase itself downhill
>
> And neigh like Boanerges;
> Then, punctual as a star,
> Stop – docile and omnipotent –
> At its own stable door.

More prosaically, we talk about the light dancing on the wall, about the cows grumbling in the field, and about the bed welcoming one back at the end of the day.

Peter Grimes

This is probably Benjamin Britten's best known opera, but the title and content of that opera were stolen from **George Crabbe**'s poem 'The Borough' (1810).

Peter Pan

This play by J. M. Barrie, first performed in 1904, has become a British tradition, and is put on in most towns every Christmas.

philistine

This is a term of abuse used by cultivated and literate people like you to refer to materialistic, semi-literate people like bankers, footballers and business executives. Its origin lies in **the Bible**. The Philistines were a people who constantly attempted to dislodge the Jews from Palestine. However, there is no suggestion in the Bible that the Philistines were massively bovine and uncultured, and so its present derogatory meaning has probably come from the German word *Philister* which means 'townsman'. The idea was that people living in a town were busy making money and selling goods. As a result, they had little time for aesthetic delights like music, poetry and painting.

picaresque novel

A picaresque novel is a novel which recounts in a series of episodes the story of its hero. Thus **Fielding**'s *Tom Jones* or **Mark Twain**'s *Huckleberry Finn* are both picaresque novels.

Pierre

This is the title of a novel by **Herman Melville**. I personally think that it is an excellent novel, but it makes its appearance here because the question, 'What is the sub-title of Melville's novel *Pierre*?' will make you deeply loved in your local pub quiz. The answer, if you care, is *The Ambiguities*.

Pilgrim's Progress, The

This is a prose allegory by **John Bunyan**, and I quote quite extensively from it in the entry on Bunyan himself. Briefly, Bunyan has a dream in which Christian sets out on a journey. He fails to persuade his wife and children to join him, but in Part 2, they also leave their city and embark on a similar journey. On their respective journeys, they encounter sundry temptations and obstacles and various allegorical characters like Giant Despair. As you will have realised, the work is a fictitious account of the Christian's path to salvation. Part 1 was written in 1679 while Bunyan was in jail for having conducted unauthorised religious services. Part 2 was not written until 1684, and is frequently not included in versions of the text. Part 1 though has been translated into over a hundred languages, which doubtless explains why self-sacrifice, humility and fortitude are so widespread.

Pinter, Harold (1930–2008)

Pinter was a dramatist whose plays frequently demonstrate the sheer difficulty of communicating anything at all. Since most of us share this difficulty, Pinter's plays, like *The Birthday Party* (1958) and *The Caretaker* (1960), have become popular and celebrated. The Pinter pause, while the characters on the stage search for something to say, has become a well-known element of his technique.

plagiarism

When one author pinches material from another author without acknowledgment, the activity is known as plagiarism. It is not an activity that can be defended, and practitioners should be forced to recite in the market square all of **Wordsworth**'s ecclesiastical sonnets.

Plath, Sylvia (1932–63)

Sylvia Path was a poet who, in 1956, married a far greater poet, **Ted Hughes**. In 1963 she committed suicide.

platitude

This is a truth that is so commonplace that it has become stale and hackneyed. Most of us use 581 platitudes a day, saying things like, 'You can't keep a good man down,' and, 'You can't have your cake and eat it.' Platitudes are merely the short change of speech, but one wants to avoid them in writing.

plot

A plot is an account of fictional events with some attempt made to explain why those events took place. Hence we don't just witness Macbeth killing Duncan, we also know why he killed Duncan. The plot is very important in detective fiction, because it is its entire *raison d'être* and culminates in the detective explaining how and why the murder took place and who wielded the fatal knife.

Poe, Edgar Allan (1809–49)

An American poet and short-story writer, Poe is best known today for his mastery of the macabre and mysterious. Thus his stories *The Murders in the Rue Morgue* and *The Purloined Letter*, both featuring the detective Dupin, are still widely read, and his poem *The Raven* still chills some timid hearts.

poetry

Poetry is one of those things that is almost impossible to define but that we, on the whole, almost instantly recognise. My favourite definition is that poetry is the best words in the best order, but as a means of identifying poetry, that is so subjective as to be useless. So is almost everything else. **Matthew Arnold** stated that 'Poetry is simply the most beautiful, impressive, and widely effective mode of saying things, and hence its importance.' **Wordsworth** famously said that 'Poetry is the spontaneous overflow of powerful feelings: it takes its origin from emotion recollected in tranquillity.' **Dr Johnson** claimed that 'The essence of poetry is invention.' **Keats** affirmed that 'Poetry should surprise by a fine excess.' And so I could go on. The only definition that seems to me to provide any meaningful content is that which argues that poetry has a firmer and more regular rhythmic basis to it than prose. One might, perhaps, argue that poetry has a more frequent recourse to **imagery** and **metaphor** than **prose** does, but how do you gauge 'more frequent', and anyway, I'm not sure that it's true. In addition, of course, one needs to distinguish between poetry and verse. Verse contains the elements of poetry – rhythm, **rhyme**, imagery – but lacks talent. **Coleridge** summed up what every poet doubtless feels about every versifier:

> Swans sing before they die – t'were no bad thing
> Did certain persons die before they sing.

poets

Misguided beings who write poetry.

Polonius

Polonius is a character in **Shakespeare**'s play *Hamlet*. I mention him only because he gets a bad press as a garrulous know-all, ladling out unwanted advice, particularly to his children, Laertes and Ophelia. Such a view is, of course, a slander on all elderly fathers!

Pope, Alexander (1688–1744)

I can remember as a teenager first discovering **Pope**. I thought he was magic. Of course, as teenagers tend to be, I was delighted by the amount of sheer malice that Pope could pack into half a dozen lines. Now that I am less enchanted by vituperation for its own sake, I still admire Pope greatly. He has a wit, a concision, an intelligence and learning that is virtually unparalleled in English poetry. He needs to be quoted at considerable length because Pope's poems almost invariably are propounding a sustained argument, with his four-volume *Dunciad* being the summit of his art. Here, however, are the opening 26 lines of 'An Epistle from Mr Pope to Dr Arbuthnot'.

> Shut, shut the door, good John! fatigu'd, I said,
> Tie up the knocker, say I'm sick, I'm dead.
> The dog-star rages! nay 'tis past a doubt,
> All Bedlam, or Parnassus, is let out:
> Fire in each eye, and papers in each hand,
> They rave, recite, and madden round the land.
> What walls can guard me, or what shades can hide?
> They pierce my thickets, through my grot they glide;
> By land, by water, they renew the charge;
> They stop the chariot, and they board the barge.
> No place is sacred, not the church is free;
> Ev'n Sunday shines no Sabbath-day to me:
> Then from the Mint walks forth the man of rhyme,
> Happy! to catch me just at dinner-time.
>   Is there a parson, much bemus'd in beer,
> A maudlin poetess, a rhyming peer,
> A clerk, foredoom'd his father's soul to cross,
> Who pens a stanza, when he should engross?
> Is there, who, lock'd from ink and paper, scrawls
> With desp'rate charcoal round his darken'd walls?
> All fly to Twic'nam, and in humble strain
> Apply to me, to keep them mad or vain.
> Arthur, whose giddy son neglects the laws,
> Imputes to me and my damn'd works the cause:
> Poor Cornus sees his frantic wife elope,
> And curses wit, and poetry, and *Pope*.

This is typical Pope, but two impediments can already be detected, even in these introductory lines. Pope is prone to make classical allusions and even more prone to refer to contemporary figures. Hence, to understand Pope fully, one does need a reasonable acquaintance with classical myths and at least a moderate awareness of eighteenth-century literature and politics. Few of us have that these days, and so the sensible course is to get oneself a good edition of the poet. It is tiresome having to read notes of explication, but Pope is certainly worth it.

pornography

This is writing that is designed to arouse sexual feelings. Literary criticism disapproves of such writing, and so when great writers like **Shakespeare** or **Joyce** indulge in pornography we are told that they are extending the parameters of human awareness – or some such guff.

Pound, Ezra Weston Loomis (1885–1972)

T. S. Eliot and **F. R. Leavis** both praised the poetry of Ezra Pound, and both were wiser and more learned men than myself. I, alas, have never found Pound comprehensible. Eliot and Leavis both regarded *Hugh Selwyn Mauberley* as Pound at his best, so here is the beginning of that poem:

> For three years, out of key with his time,
> He strove to resuscitate the dead art
> Of poetry; to maintain 'the sublime'
> In the old sense. Wrong from the start –
>
> No, hardly, but, seeing he had been born
> In a half-savage country, out of date;
> Bent resolutely on wringing lilies from the acorn;
> Capaneus; trout for factitious bait:
>
> *'Idmen gar toi panth, os eni Troie*
> Caught in the unstopped ear;
> Giving the rocks small leeway
> The chopped seas held him, therefore, that year.
>
> His true Penelope was Flaubert,
> He fished by obstinate isles;
> Observed the elegance of Circe's hair
> Rather than the mottoes on sundials.
>
> Unaffected by 'the march of events',
> He passed from men's memory in *l'an trentième*
> *De son âge*; the case presents
> No adjunct to the Muses' diadem.

I cannot see the renaissance that Leavis and others saw over fifty years ago, but maybe you can.

practical criticism

These two unassuming words are critical jargon for an entertaining form of torture. A student is given a **poem** or a short **prose** passage and asked to analyse it. Since the student does not know the author or the date at which the work was written, the chance of the student making a total fool of him- or herself is greatly magnified. The technique was invented by I. A. Richards at Cambridge University in the 1920s, and has been much used by sadistic teachers ever since.

Prelude, The

This is an autobiographical poem by **Wordsworth**. Its subtitle, *Growth of a Poet's Mind*, indicates its nature, and it is essential reading for anyone who wishes to understand the Romantic movement or William Wordsworth. Since it exists in three versions, it also provides excellent training material for proof-readers.

Pride and Prejudice

While I do not think that this is **Jane Austen**'s greatest novel, *Pride and Prejudice* is such a masterpiece of wit, irony, romance and characterisation that it would be criminal to omit it. Published in 1813, this novel is a delight from beginning to end.

problem play

This term is used by **Shakespeare** scholars to designate a small group of plays by Shakespeare that have a comic structure and plot, but are far from comic in their dark and sombre handling of that plot. Normally the term is confined to three plays, *Troilus and Cressida*, *Measure for Measure* and *All's Well That Ends Well*.

propaganda

Propaganda is the attempt to influence people in support of some person, event, creed or attribute. It consequently is relatively rare in literature. Or it is omnipresent. Both views are sustainable. Literature does not go in for blatant propaganda of the type that you see in a party-political speech or a pamphlet from the RSPCA. On the other hand, since every writer carries around an entire matrix of beliefs, assumptions, prejudices and attitudes, it is inevitable that the matrix will reveal itself in their writing, sometimes more overtly than at others. **Dickens** makes it fairly plain in *Little Dorrit* that he is not wildly in favour of debtors' prisons. **George Orwell** in *Nineteen Eighty-Four* seems to suggest that a free society is preferable to a tyranny. **George Eliot** is never as overt as that, but her novels (and those of countless others) seem to indicate that love is a desirable emotion. So, although a poem, play or novel is unlikely to urge you directly to support Amnesty International, that poem, play or novel is more subtly guiding you towards an overall attitude in life.

prose

Prose is the unadorned, straightforward way of communicating in words. The moment one reads such a statement, its entire falsity becomes evident. Just have a look at this:

> Stately, plump Buck Mulligan came from the stairhead, bearing a bowl of lather on which a mirror and a razor lay crossed. A yellow dressinggown, ungirdled, was sustained gently behind him by the mild morning air. He held the bowl aloft and intoned:
> – *Introibo ad altare Dei.*
> Halted, he peered down the dark winding stairs and called out coarsely:
> – Come up, Kinch! Come up, you fearful jesuit!
> Solemnly he came forward and mounted the round gunrest. He faced about and blessed gravely thrice the tower, the surrounding land and the awaking mountains. Then, catching sight of Stephen Dedalus, he bent towards him and made rapid crosses in the air, gurgling in his throat and shaking his head. Stephen Dedalus, displeased and sleepy, leaned his arms on the top of the staircase and looked coldly at the shaking gurgling face that blessed him, equine in its length, and at the light untonsured hair, grained and hued like pale oak.

Those are the opening lines of *Ulysses* by **James Joyce**. The language is plain and unvarnished by Joyce's standards, but no one could say that it was unadorned and straightforward. But it is prose. So is this:

2 Grace be to you and peace from God our Father, and from the Lord Jesus Christ.

3 Blessed be God, even the Father of our Lord Jesus Christ, the Father of mercies, and the God of all comfort;

4 Who comforteth us in all our tribulation, that we may be able to

> comfort them which are in any trouble, by the comfort wherewith
> we ourselves are comforted of God.
>
> 5 For as the sufferings of Christ abound in us, so our consolation also
> aboundeth by Christ.
>
> 6 And whether we be afflicted, it is for your consolation and salvation,
> which is effectual in the enduring of the same sufferings which we
> also suffer: or whether we be comforted, it is for your consolation
> and salvation.
>
> 7 And our hope of you is stedfast, knowing, that as ye are partakers of
> the sufferings, so shall ye be also of the consolation.

These verses are from the first chapter of Paul's Second Epistle to the
Corinthians in the **Authorised Version** of **the Bible**. And I could
continue giving examples for page after page. Few write prose that is
unadorned and straightforward. Most of us have our own individual
style. It is just that in prose we do not use a distinctive rhythm or have the
words rhyming.

pun

This is a play on words where two words have the same sound, and
possibly the same spelling, but mean two very different things. 'There is
no place for plaice in this banquet.' Many people are inveterate punsters,
and if you wish to join them, my *Dictionary of Homonyms* (Wordsworth
Editions 2007) will be invaluable to you. However, it doesn't include this
pun from **Saul Bellow**:

> She was what we used to call a suicide blonde – dyed by her own hand.

Would that all puns were so amusing.

punctuation

As you doubtless know, punctuation is the usage of strange marks like
! , : ? – and ;. The correct usage of these marks helps to make one's
writing clearer. But, inevitably, since punctuation is not a science,
individual writers can have somewhat individual ways of handling their
punctuation. **Emily Dickinson**, for instance, seemed to regard the
dash as virtually all she ever needed. For us lesser mortals, however,
punctuation is an essential aid to clear communication. People who
leave school not knowing how to use the colon and the semicolon, for
instance, are a disgrace to the British education system.

Pygmalion

This play by **G. B. Shaw** is the delightful story of Henry Higgins turning a cockney flower girl, Eliza Doolittle, into a lady of society through elocution lessons. Its transformation into the musical comedy *My Fair Lady* has made the story massively well known.

Q

There are number of possible entrants for the letter Q. One might mention *Queen Mab*, an imaginative poem by **Shelley**, or *Quentin Durward*, a novel by **Sir Walter Scott**. Sir Arthur Quiller-Couch deserves to appear because of his work in editing **Shakespeare**, and a number of fictional characters like Peter Quince, Quilp and Mistress Quickly could also be included. Perhaps it is wicked not to tell you that a quatrain is a **stanza** of four lines. In the end, however, I decided that none of them quite made the degree of significance necessary to appear within these pages. The same is true for the letters X and Z, but those letters don't even get an apology for their non-appearance.

R

Rabelaisian

François Rabelais (*c.* 1494–1553) was a French Renaissance writer, doctor and humanist. He was a writer of fantasy, satire, the grotesque, dirty jokes and bawdy songs, and hence the adjective Rabelaisian has come to be a synonym for 'ribald'. Thus, according to Pierre Beaudry, to be Rabelaisian means 'to be totally outrageous, raunchy, crude in every way, absolutely stubborn in matters of truth, relentless against hypocrisy, and against all forms of popular opinion; but, also, in a more profound way, it means *axiom busting*'.

Radcliffe, Ann (1764–1823)

Ann Radcliffe's most famous novel *The Mysteries of Udolpho* has its own entry and is referred to in the brief entry on Gothic fiction because its publication in 1794 made its author England's most popular novelist. What seemed frightening and exciting in the 1790s, however, alas, merely seems quaint in the twenty-first century.

Raleigh, Sir Walter (1554–1618)

Best known perhaps for his work as an explorer, adventurer and introducer of tobacco to England, Raleigh was also a skilled poet. He didn't write a great deal – it is difficult to find the time when you are busy killing Spanish mercenaries or searching for gold in Guiana – but this prefatory sonnet to **Spenser**'s *Faerie Queene* is a delight:

> Methought I saw the grave, where Laura lay,
> Within that temple, where the vestal flame
> Was wont to burn, and passing by that way,
> To see that buried dust of living fame,
> Whose tomb fair Love and fairer Virtue kept,
> All suddenly I saw the Faerie Queene;
> At whose approach the soul of Petrarch wept,
> And from thenceforth those graces were not seen,
> For they this Queen attended, in whose stead
> Oblivion laid him down on Laura's hearse.

Hereat the hardest stones were seen to bleed,
And groans of buried ghosts the heavens did pierce;
Where Homer's spright did tremble all for grief,
And cursed th'access of that celestial thief.

Raleigh wrote a number of other gems too, though it is always difficult to be sure who wrote what in sixteenth-century England. As you may know, he died by having his head cut off on the orders of James I. This, of course, makes him a martyr, and one is only allowed to say nice things about him.

Ralph Roister Doister

Although this play by Nicholas Udall is the first known English comedy, it makes its appearance here largely because its name is irresistible. Written round about 1553, but not published until 1567, it concerns Ralph Roister Doister's unavailing attempts to seduce a rich widow. Well, would you marry anyone called Ralph Roister Doister?

Ransome, Arthur (1884–1967)

In 1930, Arthur Ransome published *Swallows and Amazons*, the first in a series of children's fiction that eventually totalled twelve books. I consumed all of them when I was a child, so I can only assume that they are excellent.

Rape of the Lock, The

This is one of **Pope**'s most delightful poems. Apparently a Lord Petre snipped off a lock of Arabella Fermor's hair. The two families quarrelled over this outrage, and so Pope constructed a mock epic over the incident. It begins as follows:

What dire offence from am'rous causes springs,
What mighty contests rise from trivial things,
I sing – This verse to Caryl, muse! is due;
This, ev'n Belinda may vouchfafe to view:
Slight is the subject, but not so the praise,
If she inspire, and he approve my lays.
    Say what strange motive, goddess! cou'd compel
A well-bred lord t'assault a gentle belle?
Oh say what stranger cause, yet unexplor'd,
Cou'd make a gentle belle reject a lord?

> And dwells such rage in softest bosoms then?
> And lodge such daring souls in little men?

And so it continues. Pope eulogises the locks in question:

> This nymph, to the destruction of mankind,
> Nourish'd two locks, which graceful hung behind
> In equal curls, and well conspir'd to deck
> With shining ringlets her smooth iv'ry neck.
> Love in these labyrinths his slaves detains,
> And mighty hearts are held in slender chains.

He then, at considerable length, meditates on how the sylphs guarding the maiden's hair could be so remiss as to allow unhallowed hands to approach the sacred locks. But they do, and the rape is consummated. The poem is a masterpiece of irony, and should be read every week by all journalists.

Rasselas

This is a novel written in 1759 by **Samuel Johnson**. It deserves a mention here if only because it is the only novel that I know that was written in order to pay for a mother's funeral. But it deserves a mention for purely literary reasons too. *Rasselas* is a remarkable novel in that virtually nothing whatsoever happens in it. Instead, it is a series of quasi-philosophical vignettes of much charm and considerable sense. I do assure you, *Rasselas* never gets boring.

realism

This word is much used in literary **criticism**. You may consequently expect it to be massively ambiguous. And you would be right. *The Penguin Dictionary of Literary Terms and Literary Theory* provides two definitions of the word 'thrush'. The first comes from Collins's *Field Guide to Birds of Britain and Europe* and the second comes from Ted Hughes's poem *Thrushes*. They are both specimens of 'realism', but, as you would expect, they are very dissimilar. It might, therefore, be sensible to forget that the word even exists.

Reed, Henry (1914–86)

Reed was a poet, translator and dramatist who appears here simply because he wrote the wondrous poem, 'Naming of Parts', a poem inspired by his experiences in the Second World War:

Today we have naming of parts. Yesterday,
We had daily cleaning. And tomorrow morning,
We shall have what to do after firing. But today,
Today we have naming of parts. Japonica
Glistens like coral in all of the neighbouring gardens,
        And today we have naming of parts.

This is the lower sling swivel. And this
Is the upper sling swivel, whose use you will see,
When you are given your slings. And this is the piling swivel,
Which in your case you have not got. The branches
Hold in the gardens their silent, eloquent gestures,
        Which in our case we have not got.

This is the safety-catch, which is always released
With an easy flick of the thumb. And please do not let me
See anyone using his finger. You can do it quite easy
If you have any strength in your thumb. The blossoms
Are fragile and motionless, never letting anyone see
        Any of them using their finger.

And this you can see is the bolt. The purpose of this
Is to open the breech, as you see. We can slide it
Rapidly backwards and forwards: we call this
Easing the spring. And rapidly backwards and forwards
The early bees are assaulting and fumbling the flowers:
        They call it easing the Spring.

We call it easing the spring: it is perfectly easy
If you have any strength in your thumb: like the bolt,
And the breech, and the cocking-piece, and the point of balance,
Which in our case we have not got; and the almond-blossom
Silent in all of the gardens and the bees going backwards
                                and forwards,
        For today we have naming of parts.

Irony has rarely been so delicate, so amusing and so heart-stoppingly
sad. The poem is a masterpiece.

refrain

A refrain is a repeated part of a poem, particularly when it comes either at the end of a stanza or between two stanzas. In his poem 'Easter 1916', **W. B. Yeats** used the refrain 'A terrible beauty is born.' Another famous refrain line is 'Sweet Thames! run softly, till I end my song', from **Spenser**'s *Prothalamion*. There is even a poem called *Refrain* by the American poet Allen Ginsberg:

> The air is dark, the night is sad,
> I lie sleepless and I groan.
> Nobody cares when a man goes mad:
> He is sorry, God is glad.
> Shadow changes into bone.
>
> Every shadow has a name;
> When I think of mine I moan,
> I hear rumors of such fame.
> Not for pride, but only shame,
> Shadow changes into bone.
>
> When I blush I weep for joy,
> And laughter drops from me like a stone:
> The aging laughter of the boy
> To see the ageless dead so coy.
> Shadow changes into bone.

However, it is only fair to point out that most 'refrains' occur as a repeated chorus in some popular song. They are common, too, in **ballads**.

Renaissance, the

This was a period of artistic efflorescence in Europe, but since no one can agree as to when it started or finished, you are probably best advised to forget about it entirely.

Rendell, Ruth (1930–)

As you may have realised, in order to secure entry in this book, all that you need to do is write detective fiction. This Ruth Rendell has done since 1965, and her Chief Inspector Reginald Wexford deserves to join the ranks of Campion, Daziel, Holmes and Wimsey.

repartee

This is conversation composed of witty or clever rejoinders. At a 1912 dinner party, Lady Astor became annoyed at an inebriated Churchill, who was pontificating on some topic. Reaching the end of her patience, she snapped, 'Winston, if you were my husband, I'd put poison in your coffee.' Churchill famously replied: 'Nancy, if you were my wife, I'd drink it.' A reporter was sent to interview a woman on her 104th birthday. Expecting the usual **clichéd** responses customary at these occasions, the reporter had to smile when he asked, 'What's the best thing about being 104?' and the woman replied, 'No peer pressure.' For most of us, however, the witty response occurs to us five hours after the event.

Restoration comedy

The restoration of Charles II to the English throne took place in 1660, and over the years that followed a group of talented dramatists wrote a number of witty, urbane and often sexy comedies. The best known are Wycherley's *The Country Wife* (1673), Congreve's *The Way of the World* (1700) and Farquhar's *The Recruiting Officer* (1706).

revenge tragedy

This is a genre that flourished in sixteenth- and early-seventeenth-century England and involved plays in which a crime has been committed and the progress of the drama depends on the steps for revenge that are taken. Well-known examples include Kyd's *Spanish Tragedy*, **Marlowe**'s *The Jew of Malta*, and **Shakespeare**'s *Hamlet*. Perhaps the goriest and bloodiest of them all is *Titus Andronicus*, and although this is a long way from being Shakespeare's best play, it is essential reading for lovers of the gruesome.

revue

This describes a theatrical entertainment that incorporates song, dance and comic sketches. By its nature, it is a transient form.

rhyme

I assume that we all know what a rhyme is: main and gain, flutter and mutter, creep and sleep, and so on. Many children mistakenly believe that rhyme is what distinguishes poetry from prose. There are, however, masculine rhymes and feminine rhymes. The former have an accented final syllable, while the latter don't. I think that is probably about the most irrelevant piece of information that this book contains, so I won't define wrenched rhymes, semantic rhymes, mosaic rhymes or any other types. Your soul would not be enriched by your knowing.

Richard II

I studied this **Shakespeare** play for O level, and fell in love with it. It isn't one of Shakespeare's greatest plays – it isn't even the greatest of the history plays – but the picture that Shakespeare paints of this hapless king losing control and eventually his life is very moving. Nor can Shakespeare resist making his characters soliloquise from time to time on philosophical topics. Here is Bolingbroke in Act 1, Scene 3:

> O, who can hold a fire in his hand
> By thinking on the frosty Caucasus?
> Or cloy the hungry edge of appetite
> By bare imagination of a feast?
> Or wallow naked in December snow
> By thinking on fantastic summer's heat?
> O, no! the apprehension of the good
> Gives but the greater feeling to the worse:
> Fell sorrow's tooth doth never rankle more
> Than when he bites, but lanceth not the sore.

It is impossible not to glory in writing as superb as this.

Richardson, Samuel (1689–1761)

Richardson is one of the founders of the English novel. His own ventures into this new form – *Pamela*, *Clarissa*, *Sir Charles Grandison* – were all written in the epistolary form, which means that the action is somewhat slower than would suit a James Bond novel. The themes are also intensely moral, and are deliberately designed to guide you along the paths of righteousness. Despite this, Richardson is astoundingly readable, and his novels have genuine psychological interest. One almost feels that this was inevitable: Richardson had two wives who, between them, gave birth to twelve children, of whom eight died in infancy. To experience personally infant mortality at this rate must, one feels, challenge one's philosophy and make one psychologically stronger – or bitter, and Richardson never sounds bitter.

Rime of the Ancient Mariner, The

There can be few more famous poems in the English language than
Coleridge's *Rime of the Ancient Mariner*. Just look at how it begins; it has
an hypnotic compulsion about it:

> It is an ancient Mariner,
> And he stoppeth one of three.
> 'By thy long grey beard and glittering eye,
> Now wherefore stopp'st thou me?
>
> The bridegroom's doors are opened wide,
> And I am next of kin;
> The guests are met, the feast is set:
> Mayst hear the merry din.'
>
> He holds him with his skinny hand,
> 'There was a ship –' quoth he.
> 'Hold off! unhand me, grey-beard loon!'
> Eftsoons his hand dropped he.
>
> He holds him with his glittering eye –
> The Wedding-Guest stood still,
> And listens like a three years' child:
> The Mariner hath his will.
>
> The Wedding-Guest sat on a stone:
> He cannot choose but hear;
> And thus spake on that ancient man,
> The bright-eyed Mariner.

What follows, I will leave you to discover, but there can be few **ballads**
that are more imbued with important themes, like sacrifice, redemption,
innocence and guilt.

Ring and the Book, The

This is a long poem by **Robert Browning**. Published in 1869, it became
a best-seller and established Browning's reputation. This is astonishing
because the poem is over 21,000 lines long, and comprises versions of
the same story told by several different people.

Robinson Crusoe

Published in 1719, *Robinson Crusoe* by **Daniel Defoe** is one of those very, very few novels of which everyone knows the story though very few have actually read it. It is, though, very well worth reading, and Ian Watt in his excellent book *The Rise of the Novel* (1957) virtually makes the shipwrecked Crusoe a paradigm of modern man.

Rochester, John Wilmot (1647–80)

As a dirty-minded schoolboy, I became interested in Rochester when I discovered that he wrote a number of sexually explicit poems. But I also discovered that he was witty and really quite complex. His judgement of Charles II is well known:

> God bless our good and gracious king,
> Whose promise none relies on;
> Who never said a foolish thing,
> Nor ever did a wise one.

Rochester also had an amusingly jaundiced view of mankind as he reveals in his poem 'A Satyre Against Man':

> Were I – who to my cost already am
> One of those strange, prodigious creatures, man –
> A spirit free to choose for my own share
> What sort of flesh and blood I pleased to wear,
> I'd be a dog, a monkey, or a bear,
> Or anything but that vain animal,
> Who is so proud of being rational.
> His senses are too gross; and he'll contrive
> A sixth, to contradict the other five;
> And before certain instinct will prefer
> Reason, which fifty times for one does err.

Nor was Rochester's view of woman an over-rosy one either, as we can see from the final stanza of 'A Woman's Honour':

> Consider real honour then,
> You'll find hers cannot be the same;
> 'Tis noble confidence in men,
> In women, mean, mistrustful shame.

As you may already have deduced from these brief extracts, Rochester is far from being a major poet, but he is an interesting and amusing one.

roman-à-clef

From time to time an author writes a novel in which some (or all) of the fictitious characters actually represent real and living persons. This is known as a *roman-à-clef* or 'novel with a key'. There is a surprising number of these in existence, and it is likely that you have read some, like *Scott Fitzgerald*'s *The Great Gatsby* or *On the Road* by **Jack Kerouac**, without realising that they were *romans-à-clef*. Fortunately you missed nothing because of your ignorance.

romance

Like so many English words, 'romance' can serve a variety of functions. At one end of the literary scale, it can mean a pallid novel of love published by Mills and Boon. At the other end, it can signify a stirring story of knights, chivalry and quest. Prosaically, to the average person, a 'romance' signifies a novel focused on the romantic love between two people which culminates in the obligatory happy ending. However, there are romantic novels where there is a tragic result, romantic novels set in an historical context, paranormal romances and novels where the emphasis is so strongly on sexual description that they become pornographic. There is also an odd quirk of definition. **Jane Austen**'s *Pride and Prejudice* is a romance because it concentrates on the relationship between Elizabeth and Darcy, but no one would dream of calling *Pride and Prejudice* a romance because it is work of genius. Somehow the term 'romance' has a tinge of the second-rate attached to it. In a romance, the characters are good or bad, the plot is hackneyed and the readers are female. Yet the format is successful. Mills and Boon, for instance, release five hundred titles a month in twenty-five different languages.

romanticism

Once upon a time, in the decorous and ordered eighteenth century, people used to write like this:

> 'Tis hard to say, if greater Want of Skill
> Appear in Writing or in Judging ill;
> But, of the two, less dang'rous is th' Offence
> To tire our Patience than mislead our Sense.

But by the early years of the nineteenth century, they had begun to write like this:

Hail to thee, blithe Spirit!
    Bird thou never wert –
That from Heaven, or near it,
    Pourest thy full heart
In profuse strains of unpremediatated art.

The first example is the opening lines of **Pope**'s *Essay on Criticism*; the second is the opening lines of **Shelley**'s *To a Skylark*. Even with such brief extracts, the difference between the two poems is evident. The first is disciplined, rational and ordered; the second is spontaneous, impressionistic and rhapsodic. As you have doubtless assumed, the specimen from Shelley is an example of romanticism.

So much has been written about romanticism that I am reluctant to add very much more. And anyway, my two extracts virtually do it for me. The Romantics wanted to escape from the ordered and disciplined mode of the eighteenth century, and to introduce more feeling, more emotion, more adventure and more immediacy into their writing. The results were profound, and no writer today can escape from the effects of the Romantic movement. Yet for all that, Augustan writing and Romantic writing are both concerned with the same entity: human nature. There is a difference in their modes of expression. There is even a difference in their conceptual understanding. Yet **Dryden** and **Wordsworth** are both talking about the same issues. **Johnson** and **Byron** both grapple with the same problems. Romanticism was a profound change in English literature, but the readers who read **Keats** were much the same sort of people as those who had read **Swift**. We can get so excited about romanticism that we forget that it was merely a change of emphasis, not a change of species.

Rushdie, Salman (1947–)

Regrettably Salman Rushdie is most famous for being condemned to death by the ruler of Iran. In 1988, Rushdie published his fifth novel, *The Satanic Verses*. That novel contains references to Islam which the Ayatollah of Iran took exception to. Accordingly, the people of Iran were informed that they would be doing a service to their religion if they killed Rushdie. This edict has now been lifted, but for some years Rushdie needed to have police protection. The event also distracted everyone from questions about Rushdie's skill as a novel writer, but many place him very high indeed among contemporary novelists.

S

saga

Basically the word 'saga' means 'story', but it has come to mean a specific kind of story. You can have a family saga whereby the story of the Rothwells shows how, beginning as unlettered peasants in the thirteenth century, they rose to become kitchen maids and car-park attendants in the twentieth century. You can have national sagas in which a land is shown escaping the tyranny of British imperialism and rising to the benefits of native despotism. You can even have individual sagas in which David the Dreadnaught is shown killing the dragon and going on to marry Susan the Succulent. Yet English literature has virtually no sagas. I suppose **Milton**'s *Paradise Lost* can be described as a saga, but it is extremely difficult to think of any others. Perhaps you could make that your mission, to write a saga about the rise and fall of Woolworths. I suggest anapaestic couplets.

Saki [Munro, Hector Hugh] (1870–1916)

Saki is best known for his short stories which are delightful though wry confections.

Salinger, Jerome David (1919–2010)

In 1951, Salinger published his first novel, *The Catcher in the Rye*. Its picture of the adolescent Holden Caulfield captured the hearts and minds of the young in the 1950s and 1960s to an astounding degree. Nothing that Salinger wrote subsequently had anything like the same impact, and anyway, the man became a reclusive hermit, barely communicating at all with the outside world.

Samson Agonistes

I was once asked to tutor a girl in **Milton**'s poem *Samson Agonistes*. Since I had never read the poem, I undertook the task with glee. My delight was eminently justified. Recounting the story of Samson uprooting the pillars of the temple and thereby destroying himself and all the assembled Philistines, the poem has dignity, grace and vision. It begins with deceptive calm:

A little onward lend thy guiding hand
To these dark steps, a little further on,
For yonder bank hath choice of sun or shade;
There I am wont to sit, when any chance
Relieves me from my task of servile toil,
Daily in the common prison else enjoined me,
Where I, a prisoner chain'd, scarce freely draw
The air, imprison'd also, close and damp,
Unwholesome draught. But here I feel amends,
The breath of Heav'n fresh-blowing, pure and sweet,
With day-spring born; here leave me to respire.

Just over a thousand lines later, the blind Samson is less quiescent:

I know no spells, use no forbidden arts;
My trust is in the living God who gave me
At my nativity this strength, diffus'd
No less through all my sinews, joints and bones,
Than thine, while I preserv'd these locks unshorn,
The pledge of my unviolated vow.
For proof hereof, if Dagon be thy god,
Go to his temple, invocate his aid
With solemnest devotion, spread before him
How highly it concerns his glory now
To frustrate and dissolve these magic spells,
 Which I to be the power of Israel's God
Avow, and challenge Dagon to the test,
Offering to combat thee, his champion bold,
With th' utmost of his godhead seconded:
Then thou shalt see, or rather to thy sorrow
Soon feel, whose God is strongest, thine or mine.

Sanditon

This is the title of a novel that **Jane Austen** was working on in the year of her death. It is consequently unfinished.

Sassoon, Siegfried Loraine (1886–1967)

The First World War was so overwhelmingly awful an event that it led a number of people to try to purge their nightmares by writing poetry. Sassoon was one of those people. He continued to write after the war, but it is only his war poems that have lasted. Here is one called 'Suicide in the Trenches':

I knew a simple soldier boy
Who grinned at life in empty joy,
Slept soundly through the lonesome dark,
And whistled early with the lark.

In winter trenches, cowed and glum,
With crumps and lice and lack of rum,
He put a bullet through his brain.
No one spoke of him again.

You smug-faced crowds with kindling eye
Who cheer when soldier lads march by,
Sneak home and pray you'll never know
The hell where youth and laughter go.

That is too painful to make any comment either possible or desirable.

satire

Satire is when someone or something is held up to ridicule. In *Candide*, Voltaire satirises the philosophy of utilitarianism. In *Oliver Twist*, **Dickens** satirises the workhouse system. In *Gulliver's Travels*, **Swift** satirises the human race. Some works of satire have been subtle enough to convince the public at large that they were intended literally. Swift's *A Modest Proposal* is a good example. In that work, Swift suggests that the problems of poverty and over-population in Ireland could both be solved if the Irish were to eat their children. Today, however, satire is rare. The idiocies and crassness of the human race have rendered satire irrelevant. But it was Swift who provided the best definition of satire: 'Satire is a sort of glass, wherein beholders do generally discover everybody's face but their own.'

Sayers, Dorothy Leigh (1893–1957)

No one could pretend that Dorothy L. Sayers was a major writer, but her urbane detective, Lord Peter Wimsey, is a civilised delight, and her plots in novels like *The Nine Taylors* (1934) are masterly. She also translated Dante and wrote a sequence of radio plays about the life of Christ.

scansion

Scansion is the process of marking the stressed and unstressed syllables in a poem, and dividing each line into **feet**. The matter is dealt with briefly in the entry **metre**, but a scanned line of a poem in the **iambic metre** would look something like this:

x /	x /	x /	x /	x /
Perhaps	in this	neglect	ed spot	is laid

As you will have deduced, an x indicates an unstressed syllable, a / indicates a stressed syllable, and the above line of poetry consists of five feet. It is, therefore, an iambic pentameter. Exactly the same sort of operation can be carried out for any and all lines of **poetry**. It makes a change from Suduko.

scene

In a play, a scene is a section of the action which takes place at a particular time and in a particular locality. One can apply the same word to a section of a novel or short story where the same criteria apply.

science fiction

In the campus of novel writing, there are many mansions. Some read only **romance**, where the talented but troubled heroine eventually attains salvation by marrying the charismatic baronet. Others are wedded to the **detective novel**, where the perceptive sleuth (Holmes, Dalziel, Poirot, etc.) ensures that virtue is rewarded and vice punished. Few, however, are as devoted as the science-fiction aficionados, and it is not difficult to see the attraction. Like romances or detective stories, science fiction has the appeal of character development, ingenious plotting and structural integrity, with the addition of prophetic power. Will we in the future really be able to travel to other galaxies? Will we really be able to send David Cameron to a black hole?

school

This word is used to refer to a group of writers who share a common attitude, technique or purpose. Since writers tend to be strongly individualistic, schools are rare and short-lived.

Scott, Sir Walter (1771–1832)

Scott began his literary life as a poet, and *The Lay of the Last Minstrel* (1805) was the first poem by which he attracted national attention. Following it up with *Marmion* (1808), *The Lady of the Lake* (1810) and two or three other long poems, Scott considerably increased his popularity, and in 1813 was offered the Laureateship, an honour he declined. Yet today Scott is hardly thought of as a major poet. Why is this? Let us have a look. *The Lady of the Lake* marked the pinnacle of Scott's achievement as a poet. With 25,000 copies sold in eight months, it broke all records for the sale of poetry, and Scott's fame spread beyond Great Britain to the United States. The critics almost matched the public in their enthusiasm.

Here is the Boat Song from Canto 2 of *The Lady of the Lake*:

Hail to the chief who in triumph advances!
Honoured and blessed be the evergreen pine!
Long may the tree in his banner that glances
Flourish the shelter and grace of our line!
Heaven send it happy dew,
Earth lend it sap anew,
Gaily to burgeon, and broadly to grow;
While every Highland glen
Sends our shout back agen,
Roderigh Vich Alpine dhu, ho! ieroe!

Ours is no sapling, chance-sown by the fountain,
Blooming at Beltane, in winter to fade;
When the whirlwind has stripped every leaf on the mountain,
The more shall Clan Alpine exult in her shade.
Moored on the rifted rock,
Proof to the tempest's shock,
Firmer he roots him the ruder it blow;
Menteith and Breadalbane, then
Echo his praise agen,
Roderigh Vich Alpine dhu, ho! ieroe!

Proudly our pibroch has thrilled in Glen Fruin,
And Banochar's groans to our slogan replied:
Glen Luss and Ross-dhu, they are smoking in ruin,
And the best of Loch Lomond lie dead on her side.
Widow and Saxon maid,
Long shall lament our raid,
Think of Glen Alpine with fear and with woe;

> Lennox and Leven Glen
> Shake when they hear agen,
> Roderigh Vich Alpine dhu, ho! ieroe!
>
> Row, vassals, row, for the pride of the Highlands!
> Stretch to your oars, for the evergreen pine!
> Oh! that the rosebud that graces yon islands
> Were wreathed in a garland around him to twine!
> Oh! that some seedling gem
> Worthy such noble stem,
> Honoured and blessed in their shadow might grow!
> Loud should Clan Alpine then
> Ring from her deepmost glen,
> Roderigh Vich Alpine dhu, ho! ieroe!

It is not really difficult to see why this was popular. First of all, it panders to Scottish national sentiments. Secondly, it has a rousing martial sound and rhythm. But no one could say that it was significant poetry.

Scott's first real poetic success was with *The Lay of the Last Minstrel*. Just have a look at how that opens:

> The way was long, the wind was cold,
> The Minstrel was infirm and old;
> His withered cheek and tresses grey,
> Seemed to have known a better day;
> The harp, his sole remaining joy,
> Was carried by an orphan boy.
> The last of all the Bards was he,
> Who sung of Border chivalry;
> For, well-a-day! their date was fled,
> His tuneful brethren all were dead;
> And he, neglected and oppressed,
> Wished to be with them, and at rest.
> No more, on prancing palfrey borne,
> He carolled, light as lark at morn . . .

It is, let us face it, pretty humdrum stuff. It's pleasant enough, and it's easy to read, and, who knows, maybe we'll get interested in the story it has to tell, but it is versifying, not poetry. One is, perhaps, surprised at the enthusiasm that Scott's poetry aroused, but contemporary judgements are always, by their nature, provisional. It takes at least three hundred years to arrive at a fairly secure judgement!

However, the rise of **Byron** seems to have dispirited Scott's poetic ambitions, and he turned instead to novel-writing, and it is for this that he is largely remembered today. I have pinched a chronological list from Wikipedia:

TITLE	PUBLISHED	MAIN SETTING	PERIOD
Waverley, or, 'Tis Sixty Years Since	1814	Perthshire (Scotland)	1745–6
Guy Mannering, or, The Astrologer	1815	Galloway (Scotland)	1760–5, 1781–2
The Antiquary	1816	Angus (Scotland)	1790s
The Black Dwarf	1816	Scottish Borders	1707
The Tale of Old Mortality	1816	Southern Scotland	1679–89
Rob Roy	1818	Loch Lomond and environs (Scotland)	1715–16
The Heart of Midlothian	1818	Edinburgh &Richmond, London	1736
The Bride of Lammermoor	1819	East Lothian (Scotland)	1709–11
A Legend of Montrose	1819	Scottish Highlands	1644–5
Ivanhoe	1819	Yorkshire and Leicestershire (England)	1194
The Monastery	1820	Scottish Borders	1547–57
The Abbot	1820	Various in Scotland	1567–8
Kenilworth	1821	Southern England	1575
The Pirate	1822	Shetland and Orkney	late 17th century
The Fortunes of Nigel	1822	London and Greenwich	1616–19
Peveril of the Peak	1822	Derbyshire, the Isle of Man, and London	1658–80
Quentin Durward	1823	Tours and Péronne (France) Liège (Wallonia/Belgium)	1468
St Ronan's Well	1824	Southern Scotland	1800s
Redgauntlet	1824	Southern Scotland, & Cumberland (England)	1766
The Betrothed	1825	Wales & Gloucester	1187–92
The Talisman	1825	Syria	1191
Woodstock, or, The Cavalier	1826	Woodstock & Windsor Brussels, in the Spanish Netherlands	1652
St Valentine's Day, or, The Fair Maid of Perth	1828	Perthshire (Scotland)	1396
Anne of Geierstein, or, The Maiden in the Mist	1829	Switzerland & Eastern France	1474–77
Count Robert of Paris	1831	Constantinople and Scutari	1097
Castle Dangerous	1831	Kirkcudbrightshire	1307

As you can see, it is a formidable catalogue, and few of us have read them all. But Scott is an important writer. He virtually invented both the short story and the historical novel. And some of those stories and novels are good. Scott will probably never again be as popular as he was during the nineteenth century, but novels of the quality of *Guy Mannering* or *The Heart of Midlothian* will never, I trust, entirely disappear.

Scrutiny

This was a literary magazine published in Cambridge from 1932 to 1953. It had a number of distinguished editors, but was dominated by **F. R. Leavis**, and became the flagship for Leavis's moral and aesthetic Puritanism.

seer

A seer is someone who sees visions of divine things. Poets are often called seers by those who believe that they couldn't have written such wonderful poems without being divinely inspired. **William Blake**, I suspect, honestly thought that he was a seer.

sense and sensibility

As you may well know, this is the title of a novel by **Jane Austen**, but I am not concerned here with the novel. Sense and sensibility are two differing traits in human beings. Sense is rational, sensible and ordered. Sensibility is intuitive, emotional and wayward. The Augustans tended to write with sense, the Romantics with sensibility. Needless to say, of course, the well-balanced person has them both.

sentimentality

In writing, sentimentality is a grievous crime. It occurs when emotion is ladled into a scene gratuitously instead of the emotion being a product of the event. In *The Old Curiosity Shop*, Dickens is so determined to reduce us to tears with the death of Little Nell that he becomes ludicrous in the process. Yet in *Bleak House*, Dickens manages the death of Jo, the road sweeper, with admirable restraint. As a result, one is moved to tears rather than laughter.

sestet

A group of six lines that form the second part of a **sonnet**.

Sewell, Anna (1820–78)

Anna Sewell, a Norfolk Quaker, only wrote one novel, and she was over fifty when she did so. The novel was called **Black Beauty**, was published in 1877 and is one of the most delightful and poignant of children's novels.

Shakespeare, William (1564–1616)

Shakespeare is a problem. Anyone who has ever studied Shakespeare, read Shakespeare or seen Shakespeare is quite often possessed by the view that he was the greatest dramatist of all time. Hazlitt wrote, 'If we wish to know the force of human genius we should read Shakespeare.' Emerson commented, 'It is difficult not to be intemperate in speaking of Shakespeare.' Carlyle affirmed, 'If I say that Shakespeare is the greatest of all intellects, I have said all concerning him.' **Pope**, almost despairingly, said, 'He seems to have known the world by intuition, to have looked through nature at one glance.' Shakespeare was a supreme dramatist, and those of us who are lucky enough to enjoy him are blessed beyond measure.

Of course, one of the consequences of Shakespeare's greatness is that he has become an industry. Critical monographs are published on him virtually every week, dire productions of his plays can be seen in places as diverse as the Old Vic in London and Child's Ercall village hall, and occasional attempts are made to prove that Shakespeare didn't write any plays at all. They were all written by **Marlowe**, **Raleigh**, Queen Elizabeth or the tooth fairy. None of this matters very much, but the plays of Shakespeare do matter. In 1950, when I was ten, I had never heard of Shakespeare, since I came from a completely non-literary family. However, having just arrived at secondary school, I was cast as Puck in *A Midsummer Night's Dream*. A new and magic world was opened up for me. I then appeared in every Shakespeare production that the school did, and a lifetime's obsession was born.

So then, why is Shakespeare so good? He is supreme because his plays are superbly structured. He is unrivalled because he's funnier than any other dramatist. He is unparalleled because his characterisation reveals human nature in a way no psychologist can match. He is matchless because his handling of **imagery** gives a magical richness to his work. He is stupendous because he depicts human conflict with an insight that is uncanny. He is great because he shows the **tragedy** of existence more movingly and meaningfully than anyone else. He is as near perfect as it is possible for a human being to be because he handles themes that are profound. Whether you are an English scholar or a chemist, a gardener or an airline pilot, Shakespeare needs to be part of your world because, more than any other writer who has ever lived, Shakespeare enables you to understand yourself.

Shaw, George Bernard (1856–1950)

It is appropriate that Bernard Shaw should follow **Shakespeare** because Shaw was a dramatist who actually thought that he was markedly better than Shakespeare. He was wrong, but then Shaw was born in Dublin which may explain his delusion. What is astonishing is that anyone with such a degree of misplaced arrogance should have produced works of real value. Yet Shaw did. Many of his plays are extremely amusing, one of them at least (*Saint Joan*) is a real **tragedy**, and all of them are marked by a blistering and exciting intelligence.

Shelley, Percy Bysshe (1792–1822)

Shelley is a member of that group of Romantic poets active at the turn of the eighteenth century. Expelled from Oxford for writing a pamphlet entitled *The Necessity of Atheism*, he then quarrelled with his father and promptly eloped to Scotland with a sixteen-year-old girl. After that, life continued at the same disordered and frenetic pace, and it is amazing that Shelley ever found the time to write any poetry. Yet he wrote a great deal, and a surprising amount of it is extremely good. His elegy on the death of **Keats**, *Adonais*, is marvellous, and some of his shorter poems like 'Ode to the West Wind', *To a Skylark* and 'The Cloud' have genius stamped all over them. Maybe his political radicalism, his bizarre sex life, and his own neuroses have detracted from appreciation of his poetry, but here is a sonnet, 'Ozymandias', that ranks with the best in the language:

> I met a traveller from an antique land
> Who said: Two vast and trunkless legs of stone
> Stand in the desert. Near them on the sand,
> Half sunk, a shattered visage lies, whose frown
> And wrinkled lip and sneer of cold command
> Tell that its sculptor well those passions read
> Which yet survive, stamped on these lifeless things,
> The hand that mocked them and the heart that fed.
> And on the pedestal these words appear:
> 'My name is Ozymandias, king of kings:

Look on my works, ye mighty, and despair!'
Nothing beside remains. Round the decay
Of that colossal wreck, boundless and bare,
The lone and level sands stretch far away.

If anyone ever tells you that Shelley was not a great poet, read them this.

Sheridan, Richard Brinsley (1751–1816)

For three plays, *The Rivals* (1775), *The School for Scandal* (1777) and *The Critic* (1779), Sheridan will be remembered for ever. They are pinnacles of comic drama. Yet he despised the theatre, wanted to devote his life to politics and died in abject poverty.

short story

All good reference books should have something that is indefinable, and 'short story' will do very well. A short story is a piece of prose fiction that is shorter than a novel. At what point a long short story becomes a novel or a short novel becomes a short story it is impossible to say.

Sidney, Sir Philip (1554–86)

I suppose that Sidney is best remembered as the fatally wounded soldier who, upon seeing another dying soldier gazing at his water bottle, handed the flask over with the words, 'Thy need is greater than mine.' For our purposes, however, Sidney is notable for having written an exceptionally good sequence of sonnets under the title *Astrophel and Stella*. Here is one of them:

With how sad steps, O Moon, thou climb'st the skies!
How silently, and with how wan a face!
What! may it be that even in heavenly place
That busy archer his sharp arrows tries?
Sure, if that long-with-love-acquainted eyes
Can judge of love, thou feel'st a lover's case:
I read it in thy looks; thy languish'd grace
To me, that feel the like, thy state descries.
Then, even of fellowship, O Moon, tell me,
Is constant love deemed there but want of wit?
Are beauties there as proud as here they be?
Do they above love to be loved, and yet
    Those lovers scorn whom that love doth possess?
    Do they call virtue there, ungratefulness?

Taken as a whole, I think *Astrophel and Stella* a greater achievement than Shakespeare's collection of sonnets, but clearly I cannot admit to such heresy here. Sidney also produced other literary works, including *A Defence of Poetry*, and was also active in aiding other poets like **Spenser**.

simile

A simile is simply when you say that A is like B:

> Tom is like a tiger.

This does not mean that Tom has yellow-and-black-striped skin, walks on four legs and kills other animals. It means that Tom is watchful, active and fully aware.

Smollett, Tobias George (1721–71)

I suspect that Smollett is little read these days, but he is an entertaining novelist and three novels in particular – *The Adventures of Roderick Random*, *The Adventures of Peregrine Pickle* and *The Expedition of Humphry Clinker* – are well worth while. A friend of mine recollected a word discovered when reading *Humphry Clinker*: 'In fact it was early in the book that I first came across the word *stercoracious*. I seem to recall a reference to a *stercoracious fume*.' My friend went on to say, 'If you haven't read it, *Humphry Clinker* is an absolute cracker.' I would echo this, and it also does wonders for your street cred if you mention in passing, 'Oh, I'm just reading Tobias Smollett at the moment.'

soap opera

This term is used to signify a long-running drama on television that one watches regularly every week or three times a week or whatever. The on-screen events do become a substitute for life, and one hears people saying, 'Eh, I never thought Elsie would do that to Trevor.'

social-problem novel

This is a label often used to particularise certain nineteenth-century novels, like **Dickens**'s *Oliver Twist*, **Gaskell**'s *North and South* and **Kingsley**'s *Yeast*, that isolate a social problem and imply that reform is needed.

soliloquy

A soliloquy is a speech, usually quite lengthy, delivered by a character who is alone onstage. They are common in Elizabethan and Jacobean drama, and give the audience the opportunity of seeing into the mind of a particular character. **Shakespeare**'s *Richard III* opens with Richard himself delivering a soliloquy, and thus, from the start, we are given an insight into his tortured mind:

> Now is the winter of our discontent
> Made glorious summer by this sun of York;
> And all the clouds that lour'd upon our house
> In the deep bosom of the ocean buried.
> Now are our brows bound with victorious wreaths;
> Our bruised arms hung up for monuments;
> Our stern alarums changed to merry meetings,
> Our dreadful marches to delightful measures.
> Grim-visaged war hath smooth'd his wrinkled front,
> And now, instead of mounting barded steeds
> To fright the souls of fearful adversaries,
> He capers nimbly in a lady's chamber
> To the lascivious pleasing of a lute.
> But I, that am not shaped for sportive tricks,
> Nor made to court an amorous looking-glass;
> I, that am rudely stamp'd, and want love's majesty
> To strut before a wanton ambling nymph;
> I, that am curtail'd of this fair proportion,
> Cheated of feature by dissembling nature,
> Deformed, unfinish'd, sent before my time
> Into this breathing world, scarce half made up,
> And that so lamely and unfashionable
> That dogs bark at me as I halt by them;
> Why, I, in this weak piping time of peace,
> Have no delight to pass away the time,
> Unless to spy my shadow in the sun
> And descant on mine own deformity:
> And therefore, since I cannot prove a lover,
> To entertain these fair well-spoken days,
> I am determined to prove a villain,
> And hate the idle pleasures of these days.
> Plots have I laid, inductions dangerous,
> By drunken prophecies, libels and dreams,
> To set my brother Clarence and the king
> In deadly hate the one against the other:

> And if King Edward be as true and just
> As I am subtle, false and treacherous,
> This day should Clarence closely be mew'd up,
> About a prophecy, which says that 'G'
> Of Edward's heirs the murderer shall be.
> Dive, thoughts, down to my soul – here
> Clarence comes.

Notice, though, that it is not just an insight into Richard's mind that we gain here. We are also told about his plans. This is of great dramatic importance because it means that we, the audience, know, from the outset, lots of things that the other characters in the play don't know. This privileged position makes us suffer the more as we watch Richard duping others. So a soliloquy is not only useful for revealing a character, but can also be vital in involving the audience even more intimately in the fabric of the drama.

sonnet

The sonnet is a fourteen-line poem, and it is almost difficult to find a bearably respectable poet who hasn't written at least one sonnet. Some of them, particularly in the sixteenth century, wrote nothing else.

Any decent reference book will tell you that sonnets can be divided into two types, Petrarchan and Shakespearian. I'm not totally convinced that the distinction matters all that much, and I am fairly sure that you won't remember it anyway, but, just to be scholarly, this is the difference:

PETRARCHAN – Named, of course, after the fourteenth-century Italian poet, this form has the following rhyming scheme:

abba abba cde cde

The first eight lines are called the octave, and the concluding six lines are called the sestet. Occasionally the sestet had the rhyming scheme ccd ccd. Metrically, the sonnet was virtually always written in iambic pentameters.

SHAKESPEARIAN – A much more common form than the Petrarchan, it is named after our greatest poet and has the following rhyme scheme:

abab bcbc cdcd ee

It too is written in iambic pentameters, and its concluding rhyming couplet tends to give the Shakespearian form a more definite feeling of conclusion.

The sonnet in England seems to have been introduced by **Sir Thomas Wyatt** (1503–42), who used the basic Petrarchan form, though he did adopt the couplet ending:

> Farewell, Love, and all thy laws for ever:
>   Thy baited hooks shall tangle me no more.
> Senec and Plato call me from thy lore,
>   To perfect wealth my wit for to endeavour.
> In blind error when I did persevere,
>   Thy sharp repulse, that pricketh aye so sore,
> Hath taught me to set in trifles no store,
>   And scape forth, since liberty is liever.
> Therefore farewell, so trouble younger hearts,
>   And in me claim no more authority:
> With idle youth go use thy property,
>   And thereon spend thy many brittle darts.
>   For, hitherto tho' I've lost all my time,
>   Me lusteth no longer rotten boughs to climb.

Now compare that with one in the Shakespearian form, written, unsurprisingly, by **Shakespeare** himself:

> Let me not to the marriage of true minds
>   Admit impediments. Love is not love
> Which alters when it alteration finds,
>   Or bends with the remover to remove:
> O no! it is an ever-fixèd mark
>   That looks on tempests and is never shaken;
> It is the star to every wandering bark,
>   Whose worth's unknown, although his height be taken.
> Love's not Time's fool, though rosy lips and cheeks
>   Within his bending sickle's compass come:
> Love alters not with his brief hours and weeks,
>   But bears it out even to the edge of doom.
>   If this be error and upon me proved,
>   I never writ, nor no man ever loved

Both the Wyatt and Shakespeare examples demonstrate that the sonnet is an excellent form for encapsulating an argument or emotion within an adaptable though constricting structure. Love, of course, is often the emotion chosen, and **Keats** provides a perfect instance in 'Last Sonnet':

> Bright star, would I were steadfast as thou art –
>   Not in lone splendour hung aloft the night,
> And watching, with eternal lids apart,
>   Like nature's patient sleepless eremite,
> The moving waters at their priestlike task
>   Of pure ablution round earth's human shores,
> Or gazing on the new soft-fallen mask
>   Of snow upon the mountains and the moors –
> No, yet still steadfast, still unchangeable,
>   Pillow'd upon my fair love's ripening breast,
> To feel for ever its soft fall and swell,
>   Awake for ever in a sweet unrest,
>   Still, still to hear her tender-taken breath,
>   And so live ever or else swoon to death.

Yet the sonnet is also admirably able to express an emotional opposite, as 'On seeing a piece of our heavy artillery brought into action' by **Wilfred Owen** demonstrates:

> Be slowly lifted up, thou long black arm,
> Great gun towering towards Heaven, about to curse;
> Sway steep against them, and for years rehearse
> Huge imprecations like a blasting charm!
> Reach at that arrogance which needs thy harm,
> And beat it down before its sins grow worse.
> Spend our resentment, cannon – yea, disburse
> Our gold in shapes of flame, our breaths in storm.
>
> Yet, for men's sakes whom thy vast malison
> Must wither innocent of enmity,
> Be not withdrawn, dark arm, thy spoilure done,
> Safe to the bosom of our prosperity.
> But when thy spell be cast complete and whole,
> May God curse thee, and cut thee from our soul!

Only 14 lines, but for over 500 years the sonnet has shown itself capable of creating worlds.

Spenser, Edmund (c.1552–99)

Spenser is chiefly celebrated for writing a very long poem published in six books and entitled *The Faerie Queene*, yet even if that magnum opus did not exist, Spenser would still be a major poet. He wrote a sonnet sequence of 89 sonnets entitled *Amoretti*, and many of them, like number 79, are of extremely high quality:

> Men call you fayre, and you doe credit it,
>> For that your selfe ye daily such doe see:
> But the trew fayre, that is the gentle wit,
>> And vertuous mind, is much more prays'd of me.
> For all the rest, however fayre it be,
>> Shall turne to nought and loose that glorious hew:
> But onely that is permanent and free
> From frayle corruption that doth flesh ensew.
> That is true beautie: that doth argue you
>> To be divine and borne of heavenly seed:
>> Deriv'd from that fayre Spirit, from whom all true
>> And perfect beauty did at first proceed.
> He onely fayre, and what he fayre hath made,
> All other fayre lyke flowres untymely fade.

In addition, Spenser wrote *The Shepheardes Calender*, a series of twelve eclogues, each one devoted to a specific month, and each one relating some tale of love or life. Each is relatively short – none reaches 300 lines – and Spenser appends notes to each eclogue in order to explain his classical references or underline his moral meaning. *The Shepheardes Calender* was dedicated to **Sir Philip Sidney**, and Spenser wrote an elegy on the death of Sidney touchingly entitled *Astrophel*. Furthermore, a shepherd's boy called Colin Clout occasionally appears in *The Shepheardes Calender*, and one of Spenser's most successful short poems (955 lines) is entitled *Colin Clouts Come Home Againe*. Other poems deserve mention, but there is little purpose in providing a list, and it is to *The Faerie Queene* that we must turn.

Few people today read *The Faerie Queene*. There are good reasons for this. First of all, it is an allegory, and who wants to be bothered learning that a bearded goat is a symbol of lechery or that the Faerie Queene herself is an emblem of Elizabeth I? Secondly, the language of the poem does pose some problems. They are not major problems, but verse like this does demand more concentration than some of us are willing to give:

> Eftsoones his cruell hand Sir Guyan stay'd,
> Tempering the passion with aduizement slow,
> And maistring might on enemy dismayd:
> For th'euall dye of warre he well did know;

Thirdly, *The Faerie Queene* is pretty long. Each book is divided into 12 cantos, each canto has between 40 and 60 verses, and each verse has 9 lines. You can do the maths for yourself, but clearly *The Faerie Queene* is not something that you will polish off this evening. As a result, one can do a degree in English at a British university and not encounter *The Faerie Queene* at all, and one certainly won't encounter Spenser at school unless one is lucky enough to have a wild eccentric in charge of the English department. This is a pity. Spenser is one of Britain's great poets. Like the other three great poets, **Chaucer**, **Shakespeare** and **Milton**, he has become the preserve of the scholar, and scholars, as a race, are facing the fate of the dodo.

spondee

A metrical unit or **foot** that consists of two stressed syllables. Clearly, in English metrics, a spondee is always going to come as a divergence from the basic **metre** of the poem, be it iambic, trochaic, anapaestic or dactylic. As a result, a spondee gives an extra emphasis to the syllables concerned. Just look at this example from a poem by **Gerard Manley Hopkins**:

> And áll trádes, their gear and tackle and trim.

Spoonerism

Spoonerisms give great enjoyment. The Reverend William Archibald Spooner (1844–1930), Warden of New College, Oxford, was prone to switch the opening syllables of some of his words. Thus, when announcing a hymn, instead of saying 'Conquering kings their titles take', he would say, 'Kinquering congs their titles take'. Other examples include the following:

- 'Three cheers for our queer old dean!' (dear old queen, referring to Queen Victoria)

- 'Is it kisstomary to cuss the bride?' (customary to kiss)
- 'The Lord is a shoving leopard.' (a loving shepherd)
- 'A blushing crow.' (crushing blow)
- 'A well-boiled icicle' (well-oiled bicycle)
- 'You were fighting a liar in the quadrangle.' (lighting a fire)
- 'Is the bean dizzy?' (dean busy)
- 'Someone is occupewing my pie. Please sew me to another sheet.' (occupying my pew . . . show me to another seat)

Unfortunately it is probable that the majority of these were invented by others, and not uttered by the Reverend Spooner at all. Be that as it may, we owe him a debt for introducing us to a delightful linguistic quirk.

sprung rhythm

This is a term that was invented by **G. M. Hopkins** in order to describe his own idiosyncratic metrical mode. As you know, rhythm in poetry depends upon a pattern of stressed and unstressed syllables. Hopkins couldn't be bothered with this, and so abandoned regular rhythm completely. The free verse that consequently ensued he termed sprung rhythm, but the term neither defines nor explains anything.

stanza

Poems are often divided into verses or stanzas (the two words appear to be synonymous). Each stanza has the same number of lines and the same **rhyme** scheme as all the other stanzas in the same poem. It will also have, roughly, the same metre. Self-evidently stanzas can come in all sorts of shapes and sizes. Here is a stanza from **Blake**:

> Little Lamb, who made thee?
>   Dost thou know who made thee,
> Gave thee life and bid thee feed
> By the stream and o'er the mead;
> Gave thee clothing of delight,
> Softest clothing, woolly, bright;
> Gave thee such a tender voice,
> Making all the vales rejoice?
>   Little Lamb who made thee?
>   Dost thou know who made thee?

Here is another from Charlotte Mew:

> Sometimes I know the way
> You walk, up over the bay;
> It is a wind from that far sea
> That blows the fragrance of your hair to me

Most hymns are also composed of four-line stanzas:

> Our God, our help in ages past,
> Our hope for years to come,
> Our shelter from the stormy blast,
> And our eternal home.

Some stanzas are even named after the poet who first used them. Here, for example, is a Spenserian stanza:

> Lo I the man, whose Muse whilome did maske,
>   As time her taught, in lowly Shepheards weeds,
>   Am now enforst a far unfitter taske,
>   For trumpets sterne to chaunge mine oaten reeds,
>   And sing of Knights and Ladies gentle deeds;
>   Whose prayses having slept in silence long,
>   Me, all too meane, the sacred Muse areeds
>   To blazon broad amongst her learned throng:
> Fierce warres and faithfull loves shall moralise my song.

Steinbeck, John Ernst (1902–68)

Whether this American novelist will endure, I cannot tell, but I remember that as an undergraduate I greatly enjoyed *Of Mice and Men* (1937) and *The Grapes of Wrath* (1939).

Sterne, Laurence (1713–68)

Sterne is a man whom one is obliged to deplore greatly. To start with, he found women very attractive and had affairs with several of them. Secondly, despite being a parish priest, he frequently poked fun at the church. Thirdly, even though the novel was itself a relatively new form, Sterne published a massive novel himself that satirised the conventions of earlier writers. In fact, **Tristram Shandy**, which was the title of his novel, seems to foreshadow the **stream of consciousness** technique of the twentieth century. Here is its opening paragraph:

I wish either my father or my mother, or indeed both of them, as they were in duty both equally bound to it, had minded what they were about when they begot me; had they duly consider'd how much depended upon what they were then doing; – that not only the production of a rational Being was concerned in it, but that possibly the happy formation and temperature of his body, perhaps his genius and the very cast of his mind; – and, for aught they knew to the contrary, even the fortunes of his whole house might take their turn from the humours and dispositions which were then uppermost; – had they duly weighed and considered all this, and proceeded accordingly, – I am verily persuaded I should have made a quite different figure in the world, from that in which the reader is likely to see me. – Believe me, good folks, this is not so inconsiderable a thing as many of you may think it; – you have all, I dare say, heard of the animal spirits, how they are transfused from father to son, &c. &c. – and a great deal to that purpose – Well, you may take my word, that nine parts in ten of a man's sense or his nonsense, his successes and miscarriages in this world depend upon their motions and activity, and the different tracks and trains you put them into, so that when they are once set a-going, whether right or wrong, 'tis not a halfpenny matter, – away they go cluttering like hey-go mad; and by treading the same steps over and over again, they presently make a road of it, as plain and as smooth as a garden-walk, which, when they are once used to, the Devil himself sometimes shall not be able to drive them off it.

I suspect that paragraph alone is enough to tell you whether or not you will enjoy Sterne's novel. He did, however, write another and much shorter novel, *A Sentimental Journey Through France and Italy*, and this is less idiosyncratic than *Tristram*.

Stevenson, Robert Louis (1850–94)

As a child, I read Stevenson's *Treasure Island* (1883) and *The Master of Ballantrae* (1889), and as a result grew up assuming that Stevenson was a writer of children's fiction. In fact, of course, he is much more varied. *The Strange Case of Dr Jekyll and Mr Hyde* (1886) is well known, but is hardly children's fiction. Stevenson also wrote poetry, travel books, plays and historical fiction. He died while writing *Weir of Hermiston*, and in many ways that does look a most impressive novel. He was greatly admired by **Henry James** and **Graham Greene**, so perhaps we ought to give Stevenson rather more attention that we currently do.

stream of consciousness

This is a technique used occasionally by some writers of fiction. It purports to be a realistic mode of narration because it portrays exactly what is happening inside a human mind at one time. Probably first used by Joyce, it has also been employed by **Virginia Woolf** and **William Faulkner**. Here is a sample from *Ulysses* by James Joyce:

– It's not fair to tease you like that, Kinch, is it? he said kindly. God knows you have more spirit than any of them.

Parried again. He fears the lancet of my art as I fear that of his. The cold steelpen.

– Cracked lookingglass of a servant! Tell that to the oxy chap downstairs and touch him for a guinea. He's stinking with money and thinks you're not a gentleman. His old fellow made his tin by selling jalap to Zulus or some bloody swindle or other. God, Kinch, if you and I could only work together we might do something for the island. Hellenise it.

Cranly's arm. His arm.

– And to think of your having to beg from these swine. I'm the only one that knows what you are. Why don't you trust me more? What have you up your nose against me? Is it Haines? If he makes any noise here I'll bring down Seymour and we'll give him a ragging worse than they gave Clive Kempthorpe.

Young shouts of moneyed voices in Clive Kempthorpe's rooms. Palefaces: they hold their ribs with laughter, one clasping another. O, I shall expire! Break the news to her gently, Aubrey! I shall die! With slit ribbons of his shirt whipping the air he hops and hobbles round the table, with trousers down at heels, chased by Ades of Magdalen with the tailor's shears. A scared calf's face gilded with marmalade. I don't want to be debagged! Don't you play the giddy ox with me!

Shouts from the open window startling evening in the quadrangle. A deaf gardener, aproned, masked with Matthew Arnold's face, pushes his mower on the sombre lawn watching narrowly the dancing motes of grasshalms.

Ulysses was published over eighty years ago, yet stream of consciousness is still an alien technique in Britain.

style

This word is extremely difficult to define. If you give someone an extract from a novel by **Jane Austen**, they are likely to say, 'Well the style seems to suggest Jane Austen.' Present someone with a poem that they do not know but which happens to be by **Gerard Manley Hopkins**, and they are likely to identify the author immediately. Style, then, is the idiosyncratic way in which a person writes. It consists of many things: the way they use **imagery**, the way they construct sentences, the nature of their vocabulary, and so on. Interestingly, style is not simply individual. Everyone does have their individual style, but they will exercise it within the parameters of the age in which they are writing. Thus you can be given a piece of writing, and you may end up saying, 'I don't know who wrote this, but clearly it's eighteenth century.'

Swift, Jonathan (1667–1745)

Swift was perhaps the greatest satirist that Britain has produced. In some ways one needs to be a historian to appreciate Swift fully, simply because so many of his works were responses to the social, economic and political events of his day. *Gulliver's Travels* (1726), however, is more a general examination of the problems of being human, and can be read today with as much delight as it gave its readers in the eighteenth century.

I lay down on the grass, which was very short and soft, where I slept sounder than ever I remembered to have done in my life, and, as I reckoned, about nine hours; for when I awaked, it was just daylight. I attempted to rise, but was not able to stir: for, as I happened to lie on my back, I found my arms and legs were strongly fastened on each side to the ground; and my hair, which was long and thick, tied down in the same manner. I likewise felt several slender ligatures across my body, from my armpits to my thighs. I could only look upwards; the sun began to grow hot, and the light offended my eyes. I heard a confused noise about me; but in the posture I lay, could see nothing except the sky. In a little time I felt something alive moving on my left leg, which advancing gently forward over my breast, came almost up to my chin; when, bending my eyes downwards as much as I could, I perceived it to be a human creature not six inches high, with a bow and arrow in his hands, and a quiver at his back. In the meantime, I felt at least forty more of the same kind (as I conjectured) following the first. I was in the utmost astonishment, and roared so loud, that they all ran back in

341

a fright; and some of them, as I was afterwards told, were hurt with the falls they got by leaping from my sides upon the ground. However, they soon returned, and one of them, who ventured so far as to get a full sight of my face, lifting up his hands and eyes by way of admiration, cried out in a shrill but distinct voice, *Hekinah Degul*: the others repeated the same words several times, but then I knew not what they meant. I lay all this while, as the reader may believe, in great uneasiness. At length, struggling to get loose, I had the fortune to break the strings, and wrench out the pegs that fastened my left arm to the ground; for, by lifting it up to my face, I discovered the methods they had taken to bind me, and at the same time with a violent pull, which gave me excessive pain, I a little loosened the strings that tied down my hair on the left side, so that I was just able to turn my head about two inches. But the creatures ran off a second time, before I could seize them; whereupon there was a great shout in a very shrill accent, and after it ceased I heard one of them cry aloud *Tolgo Phonac*; when in an instant I felt above a hundred arrows discharged on my left hand, which pricked me like so many needles; and besides, they shot another flight into the air, as we do bombs in Europe, whereof many, I suppose, fell on my body (though I felt them not), and some on my face, which I immediately covered with my left hand. When this shower of arrows was over, I fell a groaning with grief and pain; and then striving again to get loose, they discharged another volley larger than the first, and some of them attempted with spears to stick me in the sides; but by good luck I had on a buff jerkin, which they could not pierce. I thought it the most prudent method to lie still, and my design was to continue so till night, when, my left hand being already loose, I could easily free myself: and as for the inhabitants, I had reason to believe I might be a match for the greatest army they could bring against me, if they were all of the same size with him that I saw. But fortune disposed otherwise of me. When the people observed I was quiet, they discharged no more arrows; but, by the noise I heard, I knew their numbers increased; and about four yards from me, over against my right ear, I heard a knocking for above an hour, like that of people at work; when turning my head that way, as well as the pegs and strings would permit me, I saw a stage erected about a foot and a half from the ground, capable of holding four of the inhabitants, with two or three ladders to mount it: from whence one of them, who seemed to be a person of quality, made me a long speech, whereof I understood not one syllable. But I should have mentioned, that before the principal person began his oration, he cried out three times, *Langro Dehul San* (these words and the former were afterwards repeated and explained to me); whereupon, immediately, about fifty of the inhabitants came and cut the strings that fastened the left side of my head, which gave me the liberty of turning it to the right, and of observing the person and gesture of him that was to speak.

As you may have realised, this is an extract from the first chapter of *Gulliver's Travels* where the shipwrecked Gulliver finds himself in the land of Lilliput. His adventures there are most amusing, and the book as a whole is fascinating and very thought provoking.

It is, of course, a gross distortion to represent someone as significant as Swift with only one book, but I expect that he'd have taken the injustice with a casual shrug.

Swinburne, Algernon Charles (1837–1909)

For a Victorian, Swinburne did not err on the side of respectability. He was a poet, but instead of confining himself to the likes of **Idylls of the King** as **Tennyson** did, Swinburne repeatedly referred to sado-masochism, lesbianism, irreligion and a death-wish. His *Hymn to Proserpine*, for instance, laments the arrival of Christianity:

I have lived long enough, having seen one thing, that love hath an
    end;
Goddess and maiden and queen, be near me now and befriend.
Thou art more than the day or the morrow, the seasons that laugh
    or that weep;
For these give joy and sorrow; but thou, Proserpina, sleep.
Sweet is the treading of wine, and sweet the feet of the dove;
But a goodlier gift is thine than foam of the grapes or love.
Yea, is not even Apollo, with hair and harpstring of gold,
A bitter god to follow, a beautiful god to behold?
I am sick of singing: the bays burn deep and chafe. I am fain
To rest a little from praise and grievous pleasure and pain.
For the gods we know not of, who give us our daily breath,
We know they are cruel as love or life, and lovely as death.

O gods dethroned and deceased, cast forth, wiped out in a day,
From your wrath is the world released, redeemed from your
    chains, men say.

New gods are crowned in the city; their flowers have broken your
      rods;
They are merciful, clothed with pity, the young compassionate gods.
But for me their new device is barren, the days are bare;
Things long past over suffice, and men forgotten that were.
Time and the gods are at strife; ye dwell in the midst thereof,
Draining a little life from the barren breasts of love.
I say to you, cease, take rest; yea, I say to you all, be at peace,
Till the bitter milk of her breast and the barren bosom shall cease.
Wilt thou yet take all, Galilean ? but these thou shalt not take,
The laurel, the palms and the paean, the breasts of the nymphs in
      the brake;
Breasts more soft than a dove's, that tremble with tenderer breath;
And all the wings of the Loves, and all the joy before death;
All the feet of the hours that sound as a single lyre,
Dropped and deep in the flowers, with strings that flicker like fire.

And so Swinburne continues, very melodiously, but treating Christianity as an arrogant upstart. One cannot imagine Queen Victoria
warming to that as she warmed to Tennyson's pious *In Memoriam*.
Even worse was a poem like *Anactoria*, a poem so shocking that it is not
often included in collections. In it, Sappho describes the carnal pleasures
she has shared with her lover and the pain her lover's rejection has
caused her:

My life is bitter with thy love; thine eyes
Blind me, thy tresses burn me, thy sharp sighs
Divide my flesh and spirit with soft sound,
And my blood strengthens, and my veins abound.
I pray thee sigh not, speak not, draw not breath;
Let life burn down, and dream it is not death.
I would the sea had hidden us, the fire
(Wilt thou fear that, and fear not my desire?)
Severed the bones that bleach, the flesh that cleaves,
And let our sifted ashes drop like leaves.
I feel thy blood against my blood: my pain
Pains thee, and lips bruise lips, and vein stings vein.
Let fruit be crushed on fruit, let flower on flower,
Breast kindle breast, and either burn one hour.
Why wilt thou follow lesser loves? are thine

Too weak to bear these hands and lips of mine?
I charge thee for my life's sake, O too sweet
To crush love with thy cruel faultless feet,
I charge thee keep thy lips from hers or his,
Sweetest, till theirs be sweeter than my kiss:
Lest I too lure, a swallow for a dove,
Erotion or Erinna to my love.
I would my love could kill thee; I am satiated
With seeing thee live, and fain would have thee dead.
I would earth had thy body as fruit to eat,
And no mouth but some serpent's found thee sweet.
I would find grievous ways to have thee slain,
Intense device, and superflux of pain;
Vex thee with amorous agonies, and shake
Life at thy lips, and leave it there to ache;
Strain out thy soul with pangs too soft to kill,
Intolerable interludes, and infinite ill;
Relapse and reluctation of the breath,
Dumb tunes and shuddering semitones of death.

This mixture of lesbianism and sadism is still too shocking for many, and it can hardly be said that sadism ever ennobles art or anything else. It is a pity, for Swinburne had considerable poetic gifts.

syllogism

This is a three-part logical argument. You start off with two premisses:

> All men are mortal.
> Tom Soper is a man.

And from those two premisses, you draw an inevitable conclusion:

> Tom Soper is mortal.

The result is a syllogism.

synaesthesia

This is a literary device in which one kind of sensation is described in terms normally confined to another. Hence you might describe a colour as being warm, a tune as being glacial or a view of the valley below as being delicious.

T

Tale of a Tub, A

There are two works of English literature with this title, neither of which you are very likely to read. The first chronologically is a play by **Ben Jonson** about a girl whose hand in marriage is sought by sundry suitors. The second is a satire in prose by **Jonathan Swift** largely poking fun at religious division.

taste

This is a pliable word. Taste is aesthetic discernment and it is what you have. Unfortunately most people don't possess any. In other words, 'taste' is an approval word entirely devoid of meaning. In preferring Mozart's G Minor String Quintet to Elvis Presley singing 'Hound Dog', you display taste, but no doubt the admirer of Presley sees it differently. In admiring **Pope**'s *Moral Essays*, you display excellent taste, but in the eyes of an **Ogden Nash** addict the reverse is true. **Leavis** and his followers seemed to think that works of literature could be graded like exam marks: 98% for **Shakespeare**'s *King Lear* but only 33% for *Kim* by **Kipling**. I think this is absurd, and content myself with self-evident truth:

I have taste, and so do all those whose judgements agree with mine.

If you cling to this tenet, you need never be worried about matters of evaluation.

Tempest, The

This is probably **Shakespeare**'s last play. Whether it was or not, it is unalloyed magic, and many have seen Prospero's speech towards the end of the play abjuring his magic powers as being Shakespeare's farewell to the theatre:

Ye elves of hills, brooks, standing lakes and groves,
And ye that on the sands with printless foot
Do chase the ebbing Neptune and do fly him
When he comes back; you demi-puppets that
By moonshine do the green sour ringlets make,
Whereof the ewe not bites, and you, whose pastime

Is to make midnight mushrumps, that rejoice
To hear the solemn curfew; by whose aid,
Weak masters though ye be, I have bedimm'd
The noontide sun, call'd forth the mutinous winds,
And 'twixt the green sea and the azured vault
Set roaring war: to the dread rattling thunder
Have I given fire and rifted Jove's stout oak
With his own bolt; the strong-based promontory
Have I made shake and by the spurs pluck'd up
The pine and cedar: graves at my command
Have waked their sleepers, oped, and let 'em forth
By my so potent art. But this rough magic
I here abjure; and, when I have required
Some heavenly music, which even now I do,
To work mine end upon their senses that
This airy charm is for, I'll break my staff,
Bury it certain fathoms in the earth,
And deeper than did ever plummet sound
I'll drown my book.

In addition, the magic of *The Tempest* has stimulated other writers like
Shelley, **Browning** and **Auden** to produce works of their own based on
the play.

Tennyson, Alfred Lord (1809–92)

Most people are somewhat divided about Tennyson. There is no doubt
that he wrote some exquisite lyrics. *Mariana*, for instance, is a gem:

With blackest moss the flower-plots
     Were thickly crusted, one and all;
The rusted nails fell from the knots
     That held the pear to the gable-wall.
The broken sheds look'd sad and strange:
     Unlifted was the clinking latch;
     Weeded and worn the ancient thatch
Upon the lonely moated grange.
          She only said, 'My life is dreary,
               He cometh not,' she said;
          She said, 'I am aweary, aweary,
               I would that I were dead!'

Her tears fell with the dews at even;
   Her tears fell ere the dews were dried;
She could not look on the sweet heaven,
   Either at morn or eventide.
After the flitting of the bats,
   When thickest dark did trance the sky,
   She drew her casement-curtain by,
And glanced athwart the glooming flats.
      She only said, 'The night is dreary,
         He cometh not,' she said;
      She said, 'I am aweary, aweary,
         I would that I were dead!'

Upon the middle of the night,
   Waking she heard the night-fowl crow:
The cock sung out an hour ere light;
   From the dark fen the oxen's low
Came to her; without hope of change,
   In sleep she seem'd to walk forlorn,
   Till cold winds woke the grey-eyed morn
About the lonely moated grange.
      She only said, 'The day is dreary,
         He cometh not,' she said;
      She said, 'I am aweary, aweary,
         I would that I were dead!'

About a stone-cast from the wall
   A sluice with blacken'd waters slept,
And o'er it many, round and small,
   The cluster'd marish-mosses crept.
Hard by a poplar shook alway,
   All silver-green with gnarlèd bark:
   For leagues no other tree did mark
The level waste, the rounding grey.
      She only said, 'My life is dreary,
         He cometh not,' she said;
      She said, 'I am aweary, aweary,
         I would that I were dead!'

And ever when the moon was low,
   And the shrill winds were up and away,

In the white curtain, to and fro,
    She saw the gusty shadow sway.
But when the moon was very low,
    And wild winds bound within their cell,
    The shadow of the poplar fell
Upon her bed, across her brow.
        She only said, 'The night is dreary,
            He cometh not,' she said;
        She said, 'I am aweary, aweary,
            I would that I were dead!'

All day within the dreamy house,
    The doors upon their hinges creak'd;
The blue fly sung in the pane; the mouse
    Behind the mouldering wainscot shriek'd,
Or from the crevice peer'd about.
        Old faces glimmer'd thro' the doors,
        Old footsteps trod the upper floors,
Old voices call'd her from without.
        She only said, 'My life is dreary,
            He cometh not,' she said;
        She said, 'I am aweary, aweary,'
            I would that I were dead!'

The sparrow's chirrup on the roof,
    The slow clock ticking, and the sound
Which to the wooing wind aloof
    The poplar made, did all confound
Her sense; but most she loathed the hour
    When the thick-moted sunbeam lay
    Athwart the chambers, and the day
Was sloping toward his western bower.
        Then, said she, 'I am very dreary,
            He will not come,' she said;
        She wept, 'I am aweary, aweary,
            O God, that I were dead!'

Nor is there any doubt that in *In Memoriam* Tennyson produced a
masterpiece of elegiac fragments, as well as reflecting superbly the
ethical and religious doubts of Victorian England:

Are God and Nature then at strife,
 That Nature lends such evil dreams?
 So careful of the type she seems,
So careless of the single life;

That I, considering everywhere
 Her secret meaning in her deeds,
 And finding that of fifty seeds
She often brings but one to bear,

I falter where I firmly trod,
 And falling with my weight of cares
 Upon the great world's altar-stairs
That slope thro' darkness up to God,

I stretch lame hands of faith, and grope,
 And gather dust and chaff, and call
 To what I feel is Lord of all,
And faintly trust the larger hope.

But among the gold, there is a distressing amount of dross. Not many of us today can wade through *Idylls of the King*, and a fair number of the verses that Tennyson dutifully produced as Poet Laureate are best forgotten. Aren't you, for instance, glad that I only quote eleven lines of *On the Jubilee of Queen Victoria*?

I

Fifty times the rose has flower'd and faded,
Fifty times the golden harvest fallen,
Since our Queen assumed the globe, the sceptre.

II

She beloved for a kindliness
Rare in fable or history,
Queen, and Empress of India,
Crown'd so long with a diadem
Never worn by a worthier,
Now with prosperous auguries
Comes at last to the bounteous
Crowning year of her Jubilee.

And so it goes on for another sixty lines. Tennyson could be very wearisome indeed. But his gold is wondrous.

Tess of the D'Urbervilles

Hardy's greatest novel. Published in 1891 and subtitled *A Pure Woman*, it outraged sensibilities at the time because Tess, the pure woman, was seen as little better than a prostitute and was certainly a murderer. Yet the book closes with Tess's lover, Angel Clare, and Tess's sister looking towards the prison in which Tess is being hanged:

> Against these far stretches of country rose, in front of the other city edifices, a large red-brick building, with level grey roofs, and rows of short barred windows bespeaking captivity, the whole contrasting greatly by its formalism with the quaint irregularities of the Gothic erections. It was somewhat disguised from the road in passing it by yews and evergreen oaks, but it was visible enough up here. The wicket from which the pair had lately emerged was in the wall of this structure. From the middle of the building an ugly flat-topped octagonal tower ascended against the east horizon, and viewed from this spot, on its shady side and against the light, it seemed the one blot on the city's beauty. Yet it was with this blot, and not with the beauty, that the two gazers were concerned.
>
> Upon the cornice of the tower a tall staff was fixed. Their eyes were riveted on it. A few minutes after the hour had struck something moved slowly up the staff, and extended itself upon the breeze. It was a black flag.
>
> 'Justice' was done, and the President of the Immortals, in Aeschylean phrase, had ended his sport with Tess. And the d'Urberville knights and dames slept on in their tombs unknowing. The two speechless gazers bent themselves down to the earth, as if in prayer, and remained thus a long time, absolutely motionless: the flag continued to wave silently. As soon as they had strength they arose, joined hands again, and went on.

Taken out of context, those concluding paragraphs have less than a tenth of their power, but coming as they do at the end of a desperately moving story, they wring the heart.

Thackeray, William Makepeace (1811–63)

Thackeray was a novelist, a very good novelist, but he suffers because one of his novels, *Vanity Fair*, is a masterpiece. It also contains one of the great characters of English literature, Becky Sharp. The novel opens with Amelia Sedley and Becky Sharp leaving the boarding establishment run by Miss Pinkerton. Amelia is a delightful character, thoughtful, considerate, attractive and rich. Becky is quick witted, but of a very lowly background and not rich at all. One gains an excellent impression of her nature upon first meeting her:

'You'll go in and say goodbye to Miss Pinkerton, Becky!' said Miss Jemima to a young lady of whom nobody took any notice, and who was coming downstairs with her own bandbox.

'I suppose I must,' said Miss Sharp calmly, and much to the wonder of Miss Jemima; and the latter having knocked at the door, and receiving permission to come in, Miss Sharp advanced in a very unconcerned manner, and said in French, and with a perfect accent, 'Mademoiselle, je viens vous faire mes adieux.'

Miss Pinkerton did not understand French; she only directed those who did: but biting her lips and throwing up her venerable and Roman-nosed head (on the top of which figured a large and solemn turban), she said, 'Miss Sharp, I wish you a good morning.' As the Hammersmith Semiramis spoke, she waved one hand, both by way of adieu and to give Miss Sharp an opportunity of shaking one of the fingers of the hand which was left out for that purpose.

Miss Sharp only folded her own hands with a very frigid smile and bow, and quite declined to accept the proffered honour; on which Semiramis tossed up her turban more indignantly than ever. In fact, it was a little battle between the young lady and the old one, and the latter was worsted. 'Heaven bless you, my child,' said she, embracing Amelia, and scowling the while over the girl's shoulder at Miss Sharp. 'Come away, Becky,' said Miss Jemima, pulling the young woman away in great alarm, and the drawing-room door closed upon them for ever.

Then came the struggle and parting below. Words refuse to tell it. All the servants were there in the hall – all the dear friends – all the young ladies – the dancing-master who had just arrived; and there was such a scuffling, and hugging, and kissing, and crying, with the hysterical *yoops* of Miss Swartz, the parlour-boarder, from her room, as no pen can depict, and as the tender heart would fain pass over. The embracing was over; they parted – that is, Miss Sedley parted from her friends. Miss Sharp had demurely entered the carriage some minutes before. Nobody cried for leaving *her*.

Sambo of the bandy legs slammed the carriage door on his young weeping mistress. He sprang up behind the carriage. 'Stop!' cried Miss Jemima, rushing to the gate with a parcel.

'It's some sandwiches, my dear,' said she to Amelia. 'You may be hungry, you know; and Becky, Becky Sharp, here's a book for you that my sister – that is, I – Johnson's Dixonary, you know; you mustn't leave us without that. Goodbye. Drive on, coachman. God bless you!'

And the kind creature retreated into the garden, overcome with emotion.

But, lo! and just as the coach drove off, Miss Sharp put her pale face out of the window and actually flung the book back into the garden.

Becky Sharp isn't going to be patronised by anyone, not even the kind and self-effacing Jemima.

Certainly everyone should read *Vanity Fair*, and *The History of Henry Esmond* (1852) is well worth attention too. But Thackeray was a Victorian, and consequently wrote far more than anyone can be expected to read:

- *The Yellowplush Papers*, 1838
- *Catharine*, 1839
- *The Paris Sketch Book*, 1840
- *A Shabby Genteel Story*, 1840
- *The History of Samuel Titmarsh and the Great Hoggarty Diamond*, 1841
- *The Irish Sketch Book*, 1843
- *The Luck of Barry Lyndon*, 1844
- *Notes on a Journey from Cornhill to Grand Cairo*, 1846
- *The Book of Snobs*, 1848
- *Vanity Fair*, 1847–8
- *The History of Pendennis*, 1848–50
- *Rebecca and Rowena*, 1850
- *The History of Henry Esmond*, 1852
- *The English Humourists of the Eighteenth Century*, 1853
- *The Newcomes*, 1853–5
- *The Rose and the Ring*, 1855
- *Miscellanies*, 4 vols, 1855–7
- *The Virginians*, 1857–9
- *The Four Georges*, 1860
- *Lovel the Widower*, 1860
- *Poems and Essays*, 1860
- *The Adventures of Philip on his Way through the World*, 1862
- *Roundabout Papers*, 1860–3
- *Denis Duval*, 1864
- *Letters and Private Papers* (edited by Gordon Ray), 1945–6

For a life of fifty-two years, it does seem a remarkable output. Yet it was almost the norm for a Victorian man of letters. I suspect that days had more than twenty-four hours in them then.

Thomas, Dylan Marlais (1914–53)

Because of his drunken, disordered life and the constant pose of the wayward genius, Thomas attracted a great deal of attention during his life. He also had a marvellous voice, a voice so seductive that it could persuade you that the Swansea telephone directory was great poetry. As a result, thousands became convinced that Thomas was the Welsh bard for which Wales had been waiting for over a thousand years. This verse, declaimed by his sonorous voice, could sound like the words of the Messiah transposed to the metrics of **Tennyson**:

> And death shall have no dominion.
> Dead men naked they shall be one
> With the man in the wind and the west moon;
> When their bones are picked clean and the clean bones gone,
> They shall have stars at elbow and foot;
> Though they go mad they shall be sane,
> Though they sink through the sea they shall rise again,
> Though lovers be lost love shall not;
> And death shall have no dominion.

Yet although Thomas could be pretentious and a sham, he had a genuine lyrical gift. A poem like *Fern Hill*, for instance, is a delight:

> Now as I was young and easy under the apple boughs
> About the lilting house and happy as the grass was green,
> The night above the dingle starry,
> Time let me hail and climb
> Golden in the heydays of his eyes,
> And honoured among wagons I was prince of the apple towns
> And once below a time I lordly had the trees and leaves
> Trail with daisies and barley
> Down the rivers of the windfall light.
>
> And as I was green and carefree, famous among the barns
> About the happy yard and singing as the farm was home,
> In the sun that is young once only,
> Time let me play and be
> Golden in the mercy of his means,

And green and golden I was huntsman and herdsman, the calves
Sang to my horn, the foxes on the hills barked clear and cold,
        And the sabbath rang slowly
     In the pebbles of the holy streams.

All the sun long it was running, it was lovely, the hay
Fields high as the house, the tunes from the chimneys, it was air
        And playing, lovely and watery
          And fire green as grass.
        And nightly under the simple stars
As I rode to sleep the owls were bearing the farm away,
All the moon long I heard, blessed among stables, the nightjars
          Flying with the ricks, and the horses
     Flashing into the dark.

And then to awake, and the farm, like a wanderer white
With the dew, come back, the cock on his shoulder: it was all
        Shining, it was Adam and maiden,
          The sky gathered again
     And the sun grew round that very day.
So it must have been after the birth of the simple light
 n the first, spinning place, the spellbound horses walking warm
          Out of the whinnying green stable
     On to the fields of praise.

And honoured among foxes and pheasants by the gay house
Under the new made clouds and happy as the heart was long,
        In the sun born over and over,
          I ran my heedless ways,
        My wishes raced through the house high hay
And nothing I cared, at my sky blue trades, that time allows
In all his tuneful turning so few and such morning songs
        Before the children green and golden
     Follow him out of grace,

Nothing I cared, in the lamb white days, that time would take me
Up to the swallow thronged loft by the shadow of my hand,
        In the moon that is always rising,
          Nor that riding to sleep
        I should hear him fly with the high fields
And wake to the farm forever fled from the childless land.
Oh as I was young and easy in the mercy of his means,
          Time held me green and dying
     Though I sang in my chains like the sea.

Certainly too, whatever one's personal view of Thomas may be, he was invaluable to Wales. Hundreds of people, purely for research, of course, toured the pubs frequented by Thomas to see if they too could capture his lilting ease. They couldn't; and, at least once, Thomas reached greatness. Watching his father grow old and frail, Thomas wrote this:

> Do not go gentle into that good night,
> Old age should burn and rave at close of day;
> Rage, rage against the dying of the light.
>
> Though wise men at their end know dark is right,
> Because their words had forked no lightning they
> Do not go gentle into that good night.
>
> Good men, the last wave by, crying how bright
> Their frail deeds might have danced in a green bay,
> Rage, rage against the dying of the light.
>
> Wild men who caught and sang the sun in flight,
> And learn, too late, they grieved it on its way,
> Do not go gentle into that good night.
>
> Grave men, near death, who see with blinding sight
> Blind eyes could blaze like meteors and be gay,
> Rage, rage against the dying of the light.
>
> And you, my father, there on the sad height,
> Curse, bless me now with your fierce tears, I pray.
> Do not go gentle into that good night.
> Rage, rage against the dying of the light.

Anyone who can read that without tears welling in his or her eyes deserves to be forced to attend an eisteddfod.

Thurber, James Grover (1894–1961)

Thurber was an American humorist. With stories like *The Secret Life of Walter Mitty*, Thurber amused the world for decades. Now, if you are planning a speech at the annual convention of undertakers or the AGM of Rutland florists, you could do worse than ransack Thurber for an appropriate quote:

Boys are beyond the range of anybody's sure understanding, at least when they are between the ages of 18 months and 90 years.

Early to rise and early to bed makes a man healthy, wealthy and dead.

He who hesitates is sometimes saved.

The most dangerous food is wedding cake.

We all have faults, and mine is being wicked.

Well, if I called the wrong number, why did you answer the phone?

Tintern Abbey, Lines written a few miles above

This is one of **Wordsworth**'s greatest poems. If you want to understand what the Romantic movement was, read *Tintern Abbey*. If you want to understand why the Romantics idolised Nature, read *Tinten Abbey*. If you want to understand Wordsworth, read *Tintern Abbey*:

> Five years have past; five summers, with the length
> Of five long winters! and again I hear
> These waters, rolling from their mountain-springs
> With a soft inland murmur. – Once again
> Do I behold these steep and lofty cliffs,
> That on a wild secluded scene impress
> Thoughts of more deep seclusion; and connect
> The landscape with the quiet of the sky.
> The day is come when I again repose
> Here, under this dark sycamore, and view
> These plots of cottage-ground, these orchard-tufts,
> Which at this season, with their unripe fruits,
> Are clad in one green hue, and lose themselves
> 'Mid groves and copses. Once again I see
> These hedgerows, hardly hedgerows, little lines
> Of sportive wood run wild: these pastoral farms,
> Green to the very door; and wreaths of smoke
> Sent up, in silence, from among the trees,
> With some uncertain notice, as might seem,
> Of vagrant dwellers in the houseless woods,
> Or of some hermit's cave, where by his fire
> The hermit sits alone.
>   These beauteous forms,

Through a long absence, have not been to me
As is a landscape to a blind man's eye:
But oft, in lonely rooms, and 'mid the din
Of towns and cities, I have owed to them
In hours of weariness, sensations sweet,
Felt in the blood, and felt along the heart;
And passing even into my purer mind,
With tranquil restoration: – feelings too
Of unremembered pleasure: such, perhaps,
As have no slight or trivial influence
On that best portion of a good man's life,
His little, nameless, unremembered, acts
Of kindness and of love. Nor less, I trust,
To them I may have owed another gift,
Of aspect more sublime; that blessed mood,
In which the burthen of the mystery,
In which the heavy and the weary weight
Of all this unintelligible world,
Is lightened: – that serene and blessed mood,
In which the affections gently lead us on, –
Until, the breath of this corporeal frame
And even the motion of our human blood
Almost suspended, we are laid asleep
In body, and become a living soul:
While with an eye made quiet by the power
Of harmony, and the deep power of joy,
We see into the life of things.
                                        If this
Be but a vain belief, yet, oh! how oft –
In darkness and amid the many shapes
Of joyless daylight; when the fretful stir
Unprofitable, and the fever of the world,
Have hung upon the beatings of my heart –
How oft, in spirit, have I turned to thee,
O sylvan Wye! thou wanderer thro' the woods,
How often has my spirit turned to thee!

    And now, with gleams of half-extinguished thought,
With many recognitions dim and faint,

And somewhat of a sad perplexity,
The picture of the mind revives again:
While here I stand, not only with the sense
Of present pleasure, but with pleasing thoughts
That in this moment there is life and food
For future years. And so I dare to hope,
Though changed, no doubt, from what I was when first
I came among these hills; when like a roe
I bounded o'er the mountains, by the sides
Of the deep rivers, and the lonely streams,
Wherever nature led: more like a man
Flying from something that he dreads, than one
Who sought the thing he loved. For nature then
(The coarser pleasures of my boyish days,
And their glad animal movements all gone by)
To me was all in all. – I cannot paint
What then I was. The sounding cataract
Haunted me like a passion: the tall rock,
The mountain, and the deep and gloomy wood,
Their colours and their forms, were then to me
An appetite; a feeling and a love,
That had no need of a remoter charm,
By thought supplied, nor any interest
Unborrowed from the eye. – That time is past,
And all its aching joys are now no more,
And all its dizzy raptures. Not for this
Faint I, nor mourn nor murmur, other gifts
Have followed; for such loss, I would believe,
Abundant recompence. For I have learned
To look on nature, not as in the hour
Of thoughtless youth; but hearing oftentimes
The still, sad music of humanity,
Nor harsh nor grating, though of ample power
To chasten and subdue. And I have felt
A presence that disturbs me with the joy
Of elevated thoughts; a sense sublime
Of something far more deeply interfused,
Whose dwelling is the light of setting suns,

And the round ocean and the living air,
And the blue sky, and in the mind of man;
A motion and a spirit, that impels
All thinking things, all objects of all thought,
And rolls through all things. Therefore am I still
A lover of the meadows and the woods,
And mountains; and of all that we behold
From this green earth; of all the mighty world
Of eye, and ear, – both what they half create,
And what perceive; well pleased to recognise
In nature and the language of the sense,
The anchor of my purest thoughts, the nurse,
The guide, the guardian of my heart, and soul
Of all my moral being.
                              Nor perchance,
If I were not thus taught, should I the more
Suffer my genial spirits to decay:
For thou art with me here upon the banks
Of this fair river; thou my dearest Friend,
My dear, dear Friend; and in thy voice I catch
The language of my former heart, and read
My former pleasures in the shooting lights
Of thy wild eyes. Oh! yet a little while
May I behold in thee what I was once,
My dear, dear Sister! and this prayer I make,
Knowing that Nature never did betray
The heart that loved her; 'tis her privilege,
Through all the years of this our life, to lead
From joy to joy: for she can so inform
The mind that is within us, so impress
With quietness and beauty, and so feed
With lofty thoughts, that neither evil tongues,
Rash judgments, nor the sneers of selfish men,
Nor greetings where no kindness is, nor all
The dreary intercourse of daily life,
Shall e'er prevail against us, or disturb
Our cheerful faith, that all which we behold
Is full of blessings. Therefore let the moon

Shine on thee in thy solitary walk;
And let the misty mountain-winds be free
To blow against thee: and, in after years,
When these wild ecstasies shall be matured
Into a sober pleasure; when thy mind
Shall be a mansion for all lovely forms,
Thy memory be as a dwelling-place
For all sweet sounds and harmonies; oh! then,
If solitude, or fear, or pain, or grief,
Should be thy portion, with what healing thoughts
Of tender joy wilt thou remember me,
And these my exhortations! Nor, perchance –
If I should be where I no more can hear
Thy voice, nor catch from thy wild eyes these gleams
Of past existence – wilt thou then forget
That on the banks of this delightful stream
We stood together; and that I, so long
A worshipper of Nature, hither came
Unwearied in that service: rather say
With warmer love – oh! with far deeper zeal
Of holier love. Nor wilt thou then forget,
That after many wanderings, many years
Of absence, these steep woods and lofty cliffs,
And this green pastoral landscape, were to me
More dear, both for themselves and for thy sake!

There is no excuse in a reference book for quoting such a long poem in full, but if you have actually read the poem, no excuse will be needed.

Tom Jones

As you know, tastes vary and opinions differ. Be that as it may, *Tom Jones* is one of the three or four English novels that you *must* read. Written by **Henry Fielding** and published in 1749, *Tom Jones* must be the most entirely pleasurable novel in the language. *Emma* is more penetrating, **Great Expectations** more absorbing, **Tess of the D'Urbervilles** more dramatic, but *Tom Jones* is the most fun. Just read this passage from Chapter 11; it has the relaxed irony and tolerant amusement that make Fielding such delightful company:

It hath been observed, by wise men or women, I forget which, that all persons are doomed to be in love once in their lives. No particular season is, as I remember, assigned for this; but the age at which Miss Bridget was arrived seems to me as proper a period as any to be fixed on for this purpose: it often, indeed, happens much earlier; but when it doth not, I have observed it seldom or never fails about this time. Moreover, we may remark that at this season love is of a more serious and steady nature than what sometimes shows itself in the younger parts of life. The love of girls is uncertain, capricious, and so foolish that we cannot always discover what the young lady would be at; nay, it may almost be doubted whether she always knows this herself. Now we are never at a loss to discern this in women about forty; for as such grave, serious, and experienced ladies well know their own meaning, so it is always very easy for a man of the least sagacity to discover it with the utmost certainty.

Miss Bridget is an example of all these observations. She had not been many times in the captain's company before she was seized with this passion. Nor did she go pining and moping about the house, like a puny, foolish girl, ignorant of her distemper: she felt, she knew, and she enjoyed, the pleasing sensation, of which, as she was certain it was not only innocent but laudable, she was neither afraid nor ashamed.

And to say the truth, there is, in all points, great difference between the reasonable passion which women at this age conceive towards men, and the idle and childish liking of a girl to a boy, which is often fixed on the outside only, and on things of little value and no duration; as on cherry-cheeks, small, lily-white hands, sloe-black eyes, flowing locks, downy chins, dapper shapes; nay, sometimes on charms more worthless than these, and less the party's own; such are the outward ornaments of the person, for which men are beholden to the taylor, the laceman, the periwig-maker, the hatter, and the milliner, and not to nature. Such a passion girls may well be ashamed, as they generally are, to own either to themselves or others.

The love of Miss Bridget was of another kind. The captain owed nothing to any of these fop-makers in his dress, nor was his person much more beholden to nature. Both his dress and person were such as, had they appeared in an assembly or a drawing-room, would have been the contempt and ridicule of all the fine ladies there. The former of these was indeed neat, but plain, coarse, ill-fancied, and out of fashion. As for the latter, we have expressly described it above. So far was the skin on his cheeks from being cherry-coloured, that you could not discern what the natural colour of his cheeks was, they being totally overgrown by a black beard, which ascended to his eyes. His shape and limbs were indeed exactly proportioned, but so large that they denoted the strength rather of a ploughman than any other. His shoulders were broad beyond all size, and the calves of his legs larger than those of a common chairman. In short, his whole person wanted all that elegance and beauty which is the very reverse of clumsy strength, and which so agreeably sets off most of our fine gentlemen; being partly owing to the high blood of their ancestors, viz., blood made of rich sauces and generous wines, and partly to an early town education.

Though Miss Bridget was a woman of the greatest delicacy of taste, yet such were the charms of the captain's conversation, that she totally overlooked the defects of his person. She imagined, and perhaps very wisely, that she should enjoy more agreeable minutes with the captain than with a much prettier fellow; and forwent the consideration of pleasing her eyes, in order to procure herself much more solid satisfaction.

I can never read Fielding without wanting to share a pint with him. What agreeable company he must have been.

tone

You are aware when you having a conversation with some people that tone adds an extra dimension to the words being spoken. Peter sounds very disenchanted about the revue, while Margaret is as bubbly as ever. It was interesting too that Lionel sounded less bored than usual. In other words, our intonation, our emphasis, our volume and our pitch all help in communicating our full meaning. You can do the same with written words. Just read this:

A Saturday afternoon in November was approaching the time of twilight, and the vast tract of unenclosed wild known as Egdon Heath embrowned itself moment by moment. Overhead the hollow stretch of whitish cloud shutting out the sky was as a tent which had the whole heath for its floor.

The heaven being spread with this pallid screen and the earth with the darkest vegetation, their meeting-line at the horizon was clearly marked. In such contrast the heath wore the appearance of an instalment of night which had taken up its place before its astronomical hour was come: darkness had to a great extent arrived hereon, while day stood distinct in the sky. Looking upwards, a furze-cutter would have been inclined to continue work; looking down, he would have decided to finish his faggot and go home. The distant rims of the world and of the firmament seemed to be a division in time no less than a division in matter. The face of the heath by its mere complexion added half an hour to evening; it could in like manner retard the dawn, sadden noon, anticipate the frowning of storms scarcely generated, and intensify the opacity of a moonless midnight to a cause of shaking and dread.

In fact, precisely at this transitional point of its nightly roll into darkness the great and particular glory of the Egdon waste began, and nobody could be said to understand the heath who had not been there at such a time. It could best be felt when it could not clearly be seen, its complete effect and explanation lying in this and the succeeding hours before the next dawn; then, and only then, did it tell its true tale. The spot was, indeed, a near relation of night, and when night showed itself, an apparent tendency to gravitate together could be perceived in its shades and the scene. The sombre stretch of rounds and hollows seemed to rise and meet the evening gloom in pure sympathy, the heath exhaling darkness as rapidly as the heavens precipitated it. And so the obscurity in the air and the obscurity in the land closed together in a black fraternisation towards which each advanced halfway.

The place became full of a watchful intentness now; for when other things sank brooding to sleep the heath appeared slowly to awake and listen. Every night its Titanic form seemed to await something; but it had waited thus, unmoved, during so many centuries, through the crises of so many things, that it could only be imagined to await one last crisis – the final overthrow.

That is taken from the opening chapter of **Thomas Hardy**'s novel *The Return of the Native*. Would you describe its tone as light hearted? Of course you wouldn't. The tone is dark, forbidding, threatening. Now compare the piece with the extract from *Tom Jones* quoted in the entry immediately preceding it. Its tone could hardly be more different.

tradition

We are all of us influenced and moulded by the past. Clearly I don't mean that we wake up every morning brooding about the Black Hole of Calcutta. But our surroundings have been shaped by the past, and we consequently are to some extent the prisoners of that past. When you travel to work on the bus in the morning, you don't suddenly sing a Mozart aria because that is not the sort of thing one does in our culture. When you are introduced to the managing director of Paltry Plastics Ltd, you shake his hand and say how pleased you are to meet him. This is the sort of thing one does.

It is the same for writers. Most writers tend to be reasonably well read in other writers, and as a result, most writers are conditioned by the work of their predecessors. No one writes like **Pope** today because **Wordsworth** and the rest made it impossible. Even if a writer decides to kick against the prevailing tradition, that writer is still responding to tradition. One has no alternative.

tragedy

If you want to know what 'tragedy' means, look it up in the dictionary. You'll find a definition something like this:

> A drama or literary work in which the main character is brought to ruin or suffers extreme sorrow, especially as a consequence of a tragic flaw, moral weakness or inability to cope with unfavourable circumstances.

But if you want to know what the word 'tragedy' *really* means, read **Shakespeare**'s *King Lear*.

Traherne, Thomas (1637–74)

Having died in 1674, Traherne had to wait until 1903 and 1908 before his poems were published. Once they were published, Traherne was grouped as belonging to the **metaphysical poets**, though that tells us little. Just have a look at one of his poems, one called *Shadows in the Water*.

> In unexperienced infancy
> Many a sweet mistake doth lie:
> Mistake though false, intending true;
> A seeming somewhat more than view;
> That doth instruct the mind
> In things that lie behind,

And many secrets to us show
Which afterwards we come to know.

Thus did I by the water's brink
Another world beneath me think;
And while the lofty spacious skies
Reversèd there, abused mine eyes,
    I fancied other feet
    Came mine to touch or meet;
As by some puddle I did play
Another world within it lay.

Beneath the water people drowned,
Yet with another heaven crowned,
In spacious regions seemed to go
As freely moving to and fro:
    In bright and open space
    I saw their very face;
Eyes, hands, and feet they had like mine;
Another sun did with them shine.

'Twas strange that people there should walk,
And yet I could not hear them talk:
That through a little watery chink,
Which one dry ox or horse might drink,
    We other worlds should see,
    Yet not admitted be;
And other confines there behold
Of light and darkness, heat and cold.

I called them oft, but called in vain;
No speeches we could entertain:
Yet did I there expect to find
Some other world, to please my mind.
    I plainly saw by these
    A new antipodes,
Whom, though they were so plainly seen,
A film kept off that stood between.

By walking men's reversèd feet
I chanced another world to meet;
Though it did not to view exceed

A phantom, 'tis a world indeed;
    Where skies beneath us shine,
    And earth by art divine
Another face presents below,
Where people's feet against ours go.

Within the regions of the air,
Compassed about with heavens fair,
Great tracts of land there may be found
Enriched with fields and fertile ground;
    Where many numerous hosts
    In those far distant coasts,
For other great and glorious ends
Inhabit, my yet unknown friends.

O ye that stand upon the brink,
Whom I so near me through the chink
With wonder see: what faces there,
Whose feet, whose bodies, do ye wear?
    I my companions see
    In you another me.
They seemèd others, but are we;
Our second selves these shadows be.

Look how far off those lower skies
Extend themselves! scarce with mine eyes
I can them reach. O ye my friends,
What secret borders on those ends?
    Are lofty heavens hurled
    'Bout your inferior world?
Are yet the representatives
Of other people's distant lives?

Of all the playmates which I knew
That here I do the image view
In other selves, what can it mean?
But that below the purling stream
    Some unknown joys there be
    Laid up in store for me;
To which I shall, when that thin skin
Is broken, be admitted in.

I find this poem, and many others by Traherne, curiously modern. Here was a man steeped in the seventeenth-century religious consciousness who yet has an almost mystical awareness. Traherne is not, like **Milton**, **Wordsworth** or **Tennyson**, a very well-known poet, but he is one that I would encourage you to explore.

Tristram Shandy

This is a novel by **Laurence Sterne**, published between 1759 and 1767, that seems to employ the twentieth-century technique of **stream of consciousness** two centuries before Virginia Woolf made it fashionable.

Trollope, Anthony (1815–82)

Trollope is a problem. To start with, he wrote too much. There are several volumes of short stories, three travel books, two biographies, several books of sketches and an autobiography. And then there are the novels. Just look at the list:

- *The Macdermots of Ballycloran*, 1847
- *The Kellys and the O'Kellys*, 1848
- *La Vendée: An Historical Romance*, 1850
- *The Warden*, 1855
- *Barchester Towers*, 1857
- *The Three Clerks*, 1858
- *Doctor Thorne*, 1858
- *The Bertrams*, 1859
- *Castle Richmond*, 1860
- *Framley Parsonage*, 1861
- *Orley Farm*, 1862
- *The Struggles of Brown, Jones & Robinson*, 1862
- *Rachel Ray*, 1863
- *The Small House at Allington*, 1864
- *Can You Forgive Her?*, 1865
- *Miss Mackenzie*, 1865
- *The Belton Estate*, 1866
- *The Claverings*, 1867
- *Nina Balatka*, 1867
- *The Last Chronicle of Barset*, 1867
- *Linda Tressel*, 1868
- *Phineas Finn*, 1869

- *He Knew He Was Right*, 1869
- *The Vicar of Bullhampton*, 1870
- *Sir Harry Hotspur of Humblethwaite*, 1871
- *Ralph the Heir*, 1871
- *The Golden Lion of Granpère*, 1872
- *The Eustace Diamonds*, 1873
- *Harry Heathcote of Gangoil*, 1874
- *Lady Anna*, 1874
- *Phineas Redux*, 1874
- *The Way We Live Now*, 1875
- *The Prime Minister*, 1876
- *The American Senator*, 1877
- *Is He Popenjoy?*, 1878
- *John Caldigate*, 1879
- *An Eye for an Eye*, 1879
- *Cousin Henry*, 1879
- *The Duke's Children*, 1880
- *Ayala's Angel*, 1881
- *Doctor Wortle's School*, 1881
- *The Fixed Period*, 1882
- *Kept in the Dark*, 1882
- *Marion Fay*, 1882
- *Mr Scarborough's Family*, 1883
- *The Landleaguers* (unfinished novel), 1883
- *An Old Man's Love*, 1884

I make that forty-seven novels, and I doubt whether many people have read them all. Secondly, he wrote for money, and real artists are supposed to write because the **Muse** drives them. Instead, Trollope wrote to a timetable, knocking out a 1,000 words every morning. Thirdly, Trollope is very uneven. If one takes the six novels that form the popular Barsetshire series, the first, *The Warden*, is dire, but the last, *The Last Chronicle of Barset*, is superb. As a result, critics have never really known what to do with Trollope. **Henry James** and **Graham Greene** both liked him; **F. R. Leavis** didn't. Unsurprisingly, a valid assessment lies between the extremes. Trollope at his best is very good – try *Orley Farm*, for instance – and is never unreadable, but fundamentally Trollope is a pleasant, civilised and intelligent author, but not a great one.

Turn of the Screw, The

This is a superb short story by **Henry James**, a short story that was used by Benjamin Britten as the basis for his opera of the same name.

Twain, Mark (1835–1910)

This is the pen name of Samuel Langhorne Clemens, a writer who, in *Tom Sawyer* (1876) and *Huckleberry Finn* (1884), wrote novels that can be equally enjoyed by children and adults.

Twelfth Night

It is difficult to believe that a play can be as good as *Twelfth Night* actually is. It is funny, charming, touching, probing and almost, at times, tragic. Two of its characters, Malvolio and Sir Andrew Aguecheek, are among the most memorable that **Shakespeare** ever created. And who can resist the gentle wistfulness of the song with which the play ends:

> When that I was and a little tiny boy,
>   With a heigh-ho, the wind and the rain:
> A foolish thing was but a toy,
>   For the rain it raineth ev'ry day.
>
> But when I came to man's estate,
>   With a heigh-ho, the wind and the rain:
> 'Gainst thieves and knaves men shut their gate,
>   For the rain it raineth ev'ry day.
>
> But when I came alas! to wive,
>   With a heigh-ho, the wind and the rain:
> By swaggering never could I thrive,
>   For the rain it raineth ev'ry day.
>
> But when I came unto my beds,
>   With a heigh-ho, the wind and the rain:
> With toss-pots still had drunken heads,
>   For the rain it raineth ev'ry day.
>
> A great while ago the world begun,
>   With a heigh-ho, the wind and the rain;
> But that's all one, our play is done
>   And we'll strive to please you ev'ry day.

U

Ulysses

This is the title of a good poem by **Tennyson** and a great but unreadable novel by **James Joyce**. They both, of course, take their inspiration from **Shakespeare**'s portrayal of Ulysses, the Greek commander in *Troilus and Cressida*. Shakespeare, in turn, took his inspiration from **Homer**. There must, therefore, be several potential PhDs on the topic of Ulysses. One could, for instance, examine Ulysses' great speech on order in *Troilus and Cressida* and compare it to Molly Bloom's final speech in *Ulysses*.

V

Vanity Fair

In **Bunyan**'s *Pilgrim's Progress*, there is a fair in the town of Vanity where everything conceivable is for sale, including souls. Bunyan was satirising Restoration society, but his barbs are appropriate for every human society since the emergence of man. Thackeray then borrowed the concept for his novel entitled *Vanity Fair*. Set in the time of the Napoleonic Wars, the novel is much concerned with the corrupting power of money. You can find a quote from the novel in the entry on **Thackeray**.

Vanity of Human Wishes, The

This is a poem by **Samuel Johnson** that, on its publication in 1749, attracted widespread praise. It is too long to quote in full here, but its tone is perfectly well established from the beginning:

> Let Observation with extensive View,
> Survey Mankind, from China to Peru;
> Remark each anxious Toil, each eager Strife,
> And watch the busy Scenes of crowded Life;
> Then say how Hope and Fear, Desire and Hate,
> O'er spread with Snares the clouded Maze of Fate,
> Where wav'ring Man, betray'd by vent'rous Pride,
> To tread the dreary Paths without a Guide;

> As treach'rous Phantoms in the Mist delude,
> Shuns fancied Ills, or chases airy Good.
> How rarely Reason guides the stubborn Choice,
> Rules the bold Hand, or prompts the suppliant Voice,
> How Nations sink, by darling Schemes oppres'd,
> When Vengeance listens to the Fool's Request.
> Fate wings with ev'ry Wish th' afflictive Dart,
> Each Gift of Nature, and each Grace of Art,
> With fatal Heat impetuous Courage glows,
> With fatal Sweetness Elocution flows,
> Impeachment stops the Speaker's pow'rful Breath,
> And restless Fire precipitates on Death.
>
> But scarce observ'd, the Knowing and the Bold
> Fall in the gen'ral Massacre of Gold;
> Wide-wasting Pest! that rages unconfin'd,
> And crowds with Crimes the Records of Mankind;
> For Gold his Sword the Hireling Ruffian draws,
> For Gold the hireling Judge distorts the Laws;
> Wealth heap'd on Wealth, nor Truth nor Safety buys,
> The Dangers gather as the Treasures rise.

As you might well surmise, Johnson suffered from depression, and this poem is surely the most superbly structured and articulated example of that emotion.

Vicar of Wakefield, The

This is the only novel that Oliver Goldsmith wrote. Published in 1766, it does possess a magical charm, and the characters within it are un-confusingly either good or evil. It also, of course, has a happy ending.

Villette

This novel, published in 1853, is widely (and correctly) taken to be the best of the four novels written by Charlotte Brontë.

Vivian Grey

This was the first novel published by Disraeli. I only include it here because this is a convenient question for a pub quiz.

Volpone

This comic play by **Ben Jonson** is often regarded as his masterpiece.

war poets

Bellicose Britain has been in many wars, and for them all there have been poets around. Yet the phrase 'war poets' only refers to poets who wrote about the First World War. Presumably this is because a number of them actually fought in the trenches, and also because the First World War exceeded in horror any previous war, and consequently stimulated poetry that was starker and more heartbreaking than ever. One wants to give 200 examples, but here is just one, '*A Dead Boche*' by **Robert Graves**:

> To you who'd read my songs of war
> And only hear of blood and fame,
> I'll say (you've heard it said before),
> 'War's Hell!' and if you doubt the same,
> Today I found in Mametz Wood
> A certain cure for lust of blood:
> Where, propped against a shattered trunk,
> In a great mess of things unclean,
> Sat a dead Boche; he scowled and stunk
> With clothes and face a sodden green,
> Big-bellied, spectacled, crop-haired,
> Dribbling black blood from nose and beard.

Waste Land, The

This is a poem by **T. S. Eliot**. It is widely hailed as the most significant poem of the twentieth century. I would happily concur in this view if it were not for the fact that I have never understood it. The poem is divided into five unequal sections. The first is called 'The Burial of the Dead'. Here it is. See what you make of it.

> April is the cruellest month, breeding
> Lilacs out of the dead land, mixing
> Memory and desire, stirring
> Dull roots with spring rain.
> Winter kept us warm, covering
> Earth in forgetful snow, feeding
> A little life with dried tubers.
> Summer surprised us, coming over the Starnbergersee

With a shower of rain; we stopped in the colonnade,
And went on in sunlight, into the Hofgarten,
And drank coffee, and talked for an hour.
Bin gar keine Russin, stamm' aus Litauen, echt deutsch.
And when we were children, staying at the archduke's,
My cousin's, he took me out on a sled,
And I was frightened. He said, Marie,
Marie, hold on tight. And down we went.
In the mountains, there you feel free.
I read, much of the night, and go south in the winter.

What are the roots that clutch, what branches grow
Out of this stony rubbish? Son of man,
You cannot say, or guess, for you know only
A heap of broken images, where the sun beats,
And the dead tree gives no shelter, the cricket no relief,
And the dry stone no sound of water. Only
There is shadow under this red rock
(Come in under the shadow of this red rock),
And I will show you something different from either
Your shadow at morning striding behind you
Or your shadow at evening rising to meet you;
I will show you fear in a handful of dust.
> *Frisch weht der Wind*
> *Der Heimat zu.*
> *Mein Irisch Kind,*
> *Wo weilest du?*
'You gave me hyacinths first a year ago;
'They called me the hyacinth girl.'

– Yet when we came back, late, from the hyacinth garden,
Your arms full, and your hair wet, I could not
Speak, and my eyes failed, I was neither
Living nor dead, and I knew nothing,
Looking into the heart of light, the silence.
Oed' und leer das Meer.

Madame Sosostris, famous clairvoyante,
Had a bad cold, nevertheless
Is known to be the wisest woman in Europe,
With a wicked pack of cards. Here, said she,
Is your card, the drowned Phoenician Sailor.

(Those are pearls that were his eyes. Look!)
Here is Belladonna, the Lady of the Rocks,
The lady of situations.
Here is the man with three staves, and here the Wheel,
And here is the one-eyed merchant, and this card,
Which is blank, is something he carries on his back,
Which I am forbidden to see. I do not find
The Hanged Man. Fear death by water.
I see crowds of people, walking round in a ring.
Thank you. If you see dear Mrs Equitone,
Tell her I bring the horoscope myself:
One must be so careful these days.

Unreal City,
Under the brown fog of a winter dawn,
A crowd flowed over London Bridge, so many,
I had not thought death had undone so many.
Sighs, short and infrequent, were exhaled,
And each man fixed his eyes before his feet.
Flowed up the hill and down King William Street,
To where Saint Mary Woolnoth kept the hours
With a dead sound on the final stroke of nine.
There I saw one I knew, and stopped him, crying: 'Stetson!
'You who were with me in the ships at Mylae!
'That corpse you planted last year in your garden,
'Has it begun to sprout? Will it bloom this year?
'Or has the sudden frost disturbed its bed?
'Oh keep the Dog far hence, that's friend to men,
'Or with his nails he'll dig it up again!
'You! hypocrite lecteur! – mon semblable – mon frère!'

'Watsons, The'

This entry is probably useful for a pub quiz. The question is, 'Which British novelist began a novel entitled "The Watsons" but left it in an unfinished state?' The answer is **Jane Austen**. Some people see 'The Watsons' as the precursor of her novel *Emma*, though there is no evidence whatsoever to support this view.

Waugh, Evelyn Arthur St John (1903–66)

The trouble with including Evelyn Waugh in a reference book is that one virtually needs a doctorate in psychology to write anything meaningful about this complex and impossible man. I shall therefore content myself by saying that Waugh wrote a number of extremely amusing novels of which his first, *Decline and Fall* (1928), and *Brideshead Revisited* (1945) are probably the best.

Way of All Flesh, The

This is a novel by **Samuel Butler** that was posthumously published in 1903. It is a searing attack on religious piety, and should therefore be read by all vicars.

Webster, John (c. 1578–c. 1626)

If Shakespeare hadn't existed, if that tragically had been the case, then dramatists like John Webster would be celebrated throughout the English-speaking world. With plays like *The White Devil* and *The Duchess of Malfi*, Webster created bloody and horrific masterpieces that I advise no one to read just before going to bed.

Weir of Hermiston

As a piece of advice, try to ensure that you have an unfinished novel beside you when you die. **Robert Louis Stevenson** left, when he died in 1894, the manuscript of *Weir of Hermiston*; there is too little of it to make any valid judgement, but that has not prevented some critics from hailing it as Stevenson's masterpiece.

Wells, Herbert George (1866–1946)

H. G. Wells is probably most remembered today for being one of the earliest writers of science fiction, with *The Time Machine* (1895), *The Invisible Man* (1897) and *The War of the Worlds* (1898) being his most successful ventures in this field. He did, though, write two quite impressive novels of social manners, *Kipps* (1905) and *The History of Mr Polly* (1910), as well as a number of other novels, two history books, some short stories, an autobiography and some works of scientific and political comment.

West, Nathanael (1903–40)

This American novelist had a somewhat jaundiced view of life. His two most successful novels, *Miss Lonelyhearts* (1933) and *The Day of the Locust* (1939), reveal, in turn, the spuriousness of a lonely-hearts newspaper column and the falsity of Hollywood.

Wharton, Edith (1862–1937)

I am always amazed that Edith Wharton is not much better known than she is. Of course, she was an American which is a disadvantage, but some of her novels – *The House of Mirth* (1905), *Ethan Frome* (1911), *The Age of Innocence* (1920) – are very impressive.

Wilde, Oscar Fingal O'Flahertie Wills (1854–1900)

The most important thing about Wilde is that he gave us the funniest plays that have ever been written. *Lady Windermere's Fan* (1892), *A Woman of No Importance* (1893) and *An Ideal Husband* (1895) would all be acclaimed as masterpieces if Wilde hadn't written *The Importance of Being Earnest* (1895), a play that can lead to laughter so violent as to cause physical injury. Wilde also wrote one very impressive novel, *The Picture of Dorian Gray* (1891), lots of stories and some poetry of which one, *The Ballad of Reading Gaol* (1898), is great. It is too long to quote in full, but here is Part One:

> He did not wear his scarlet coat,
>   For blood and wine are red,
> And blood and wine were on his hands
>   When they found him with the dead,
> The poor dead woman whom he loved,
>   And murdered in her bed.
>
> He walked amongst the trial men
>   In a suit of shabby grey;
> A cricket cap was on his head,
>   And his step seemed light and gay;
> But I never saw a man who looked
>   So wistfully at the day.
>
> I never saw a man who looked
>   With such a wistful eye
> Upon that little tent of blue
>   Which prisoners call the sky,
> And at every drifting cloud that went
>   With sails of silver by.
>
> I walked, with other souls in pain,
>   Within another ring,
> And was wondering if the man had done
>   A great or little thing,

When a voice behind me whispered low,
  '*That fellow's got to swing.*'

Dear Christ! the very prison walls
  Suddenly seemed to reel,
And the sky above my head became
  Like a casque of scorching steel;
And, though I was a soul in pain,
  My pain I could not feel.

I only knew what hunted thought
  Quickened his step, and why
He looked upon the garish day
  With such a wistful eye;
The man had killed the thing he loved
  And so he had to die.

Yet each man kills the thing he loves
  By each let this be heard,
Some do it with a bitter look,
  Some with a flattering word,
The coward does it with a kiss,
  The brave man with a sword!

Some kill their love when they are young,
  And some when they are old;
Some strangle with the hands of lust,
  Some with the hands of gold:
The kindest use a knife, because
  The dead so soon grow cold.
Some love too little, some too long,
  Some sell, and others buy;
Some do the deed with many tears,
  And some without a sigh:
For each man kills the thing he loves,
  Yet each man does not die.

He does not die a death of shame
  On a day of dark disgrace,
Nor have a noose about his neck,
  Nor a cloth upon his face,
Nor drop feet foremost through the floor
  Into an empty place.

He does not sit with silent men
  Who watch him night and day;
Who watch him when he tries to weep,
  And when he tries to pray;
Who watch him lest himself should rob
  The prison of its prey.

He does not wake at dawn to see
  Dread figures throng his room,
The shivering chaplain robed in white,
  The sheriff stern with gloom,
And the governor all in shiny black,
  With the yellow face of doom.

He does not rise in piteous haste
  To put on convict-clothes,
While some coarse-mouthed doctor gloats, and notes
  Each new and nerve-twitched pose,
Fingering a watch whose little ticks
  Are like horrible hammer-blows.

He does not know that sickening thirst
  That sands one's throat, before
The hangman with his gardener's gloves
  Slips through the padded door,
And binds one with three leathern thongs,
  That the throat may thirst no more.
He does not bend his head to hear
  The Burial Office read,
Nor, while the terror of his soul
  Tells him he is not dead,
Cross his own coffin, as he moves
  Into the hideous shed.

He does not stare upon the air
  Through a little roof of glass;
He does not pray with lips of clay
  For his agony to pass;
Nor feel upon his shuddering cheek
  The kiss of Caiaphas.

Wordsworth, William (1770–1850)

Appropriately, Wordsworth Editions publish Wordsworth's collected poems. Their edition runs to 1,082 pages and of necessity the print is small. This is off-putting. Then, by chance, you open the volume at page 514 and read the 14th sonnet in Part 2 of the Ecclesiastical Sonnets:

> Those had given earliest notice, as the lark
> Springs from the ground the morn to gratulate;
> Or rather rose the day to antedate,
> By striking out a solitary spark,
> When all the world with midnight gloom was dark. –
> Then followed the Waldensian bands, whom Hate
> In vain endeavours to exterminate,
> Whom Obloquy pursues with hideous bark:
> But they desist not; – and the sacred fire,
> Rekindled thus, from dens and savage woods
> Moves, handed on with never-ceasing care,
> Through courts, through camps, o'er limitary floods;
> Nor lacks this sea-girt Isle a timely share
> Of the new Flame, not suffered to expire.

Let's face it, it isn't very good, is it? Quite sensibly you decide that you can't stand another 1,081 pages of this. You put the book down, and silently creep away. This is a pity. Wordsworth is a great poet.

Just imagine that you had opened the volume at page 307 and read this instead:

> The world is too much with us; late and soon,
> Getting and spending, we lay waste our powers;
> Little we see in Nature that is ours;
> We have given our hearts away, a sordid boon!
> This sea that bares her bosom to the moon;
> The winds that will be howling at all hours,
> And are up-gathered now like sleeping flowers;
> For this, for everything, we are out of tune;
> It moves us not. Great God! I'd rather be
> A pagan suckled in a creed outworn;
> So might I, standing on this pleasant lea,
> Have glimpses that would make me less forlorn;
> Have sight of Proteus rising from the sea;
> Or hear old Triton blow his wreath'd horn.

Could you then have walked away? Better still, perhaps you started reading *The Prelude*, Wordsworth's autobiographical poem, an entirely absorbing picture of the growth of a poet's mind. Wordsworth wrote some fairly appalling poetry – don't we all? – but he also wrote some of the most marvellous this country has ever seen.

Wyatt, Sir Thomas (1503–42)

I quoted a sonnet by Wyatt in the entry on the **sonnet**, but, because Wyatt is not very well known these days, I felt that he deserved an entry of his own. After all, this poem that I now quote does have a compelling power:

> They flee from me that sometime did me seek
>   With naked foot, stalking in my chamber.
> I have seen them gentle, tame, and meek,
>   That now are wild and do not once remember
>   That sometime they put themself in danger
>   To take bread at my hand; and now they range,
>   Busily seeking with a continual change.
>
> Thanked be fortune, it hath been otherwise
>   Twenty times better; but once, in special,
> In thin array, after a pleasant guise,
>   When her loose gown from her shoulders did fall,
>   And she me caught in her arms long and small;
>   And therewithall sweetly did me kiss
>   And softly said, 'Dear heart, how like you this?'
>
> It was no dream: I lay broad waking.
>   But all is turned, thorough my gentleness,
> Into a strange fashion of forsaking;
>   And I have leave to go, of her goodness,
>   And she also, to use newfangleness.
>   But since that I unkindly so am served,
>   I would fain know what she hath deserved.

Since Wyatt was imprisoned on suspicion of being one of Anne Boleyn's lovers, perhaps he knew exactly what he was talking about in the above poem.

Wycherley, William (1640–1716)

One of the **Restoration dramatists**, Wycherley is not terribly well known, largely because his two best plays, *The Country Wife* (1675) and *The Plain Dealer* (1676), are so sexually explicit that they have rarely been allowed on the stage.

Y

yahoo

In the last book of *Gulliver's Travels*, Gulliver finds himself on an island where creatures resembling human beings are called Yahoos. They are a selfish, violent, uncivilised group, and represent **Swift**'s most desolating picture of mankind.

Yeats, William Butler (1865–1939)

Being born in Ireland, Yeats was almost inevitably involved in Ireland's struggle to break free of English control, and much of his poetry reflects this struggle. But Yeats could also write personal poems that are unbearably touching, like this *Prayer for My Daughter*:

> Once more the storm is howling, and half hid
> Under this cradle-hood and coverlid
> My child sleeps on. There is no obstacle
> But Gregory's wood and one bare hill
> Whereby the haystack- and roof-levelling wind,
> Bred on the Atlantic, can be stayed;
> And for an hour I have walked and prayed
> Because of the great gloom that is in my mind.
> I have walked and prayed for this young child an hour
> And heard the sea-wind scream upon the tower,
> And under the arches of the bridge, and scream
> In the elms above the flooded stream;
> Imagining in excited reverie
> That the future years had come,
> Dancing to a frenzied drum,
> Out of the murderous innocence of the sea.
> May she be granted beauty and yet not
> Beauty to make a stranger's eye distraught,
> Or hers before a looking-glass; for such,
> Being made beautiful overmuch,
> Consider beauty a sufficient end,
> Lose natural kindness and maybe

The heart-revealing intimacy
That chooses right, and never find a friend.
Helen being chosen found life flat and dull
And later had much trouble from a fool,
While that great Queen, that rose out of the spray,
Being fatherless could have her way
Yet chose a bandy-legged smith for man.
It's certain that fine women eat
A crazy salad with their meat
Whereby the horn of plenty is undone.
In courtesy I'd have her chiefly learned;
Hearts are not had as a gift but hearts are earned
By those that are not entirely beautiful;
Yet many, that have played the fool
For beauty's very self, has charm made wise.
And many a poor man that has roved,
Loved and thought himself beloved,
From a glad kindness cannot take his eyes.
May she become a flourishing hidden tree
That all her thoughts may like the linnet be,
And have no business but dispensing round
Their magnanimities of sound,
Nor but in merriment begin a chase,
Nor but in merriment a quarrel.
Oh may she live like some green laurel
Rooted in one dear perpetual place.
My mind, because the minds that I have loved,
The sort of beauty that I have approved,
Prosper but little, has dried up of late,
Yet knows that to be choked with hate
May well be of all evil chances chief.
If there's no hatred in a mind
Assault and battery of the wind
Can never tear the linnet from the leaf.
An intellectual hatred is the worst,
So let her think opinions are accursed.
Have I not seen the loveliest woman born
Out of the mouth of plenty's horn,

Because of her opinionated mind
Barter that horn and every good
By quiet natures understood
For an old bellows full of angry wind?
Considering that, all hatred driven hence,
The soul recovers radical innocence
And learns at last that it is self-delighting,
Self-appeasing, self-affrighting,
And that its own sweet will is Heaven's will;
She can, though every face should scowl
And every windy quarter howl
Or every bellows burst, be happy still.
And may her bridegroom bring her to a house
Where all's accustomed, ceremonious;
For arrogance and hatred are the wares
Peddled in the thoroughfares.
How but in custom and in ceremony
Are innocence and beauty born?
Ceremony's a name for the rich horn,
And custom for the spreading laurel tree.

It is grossly misleading not to quote at least one of Yeats's political poems, but after the beauty of *A Prayer for My Daughter*, I no longer have the urge.